AF595831

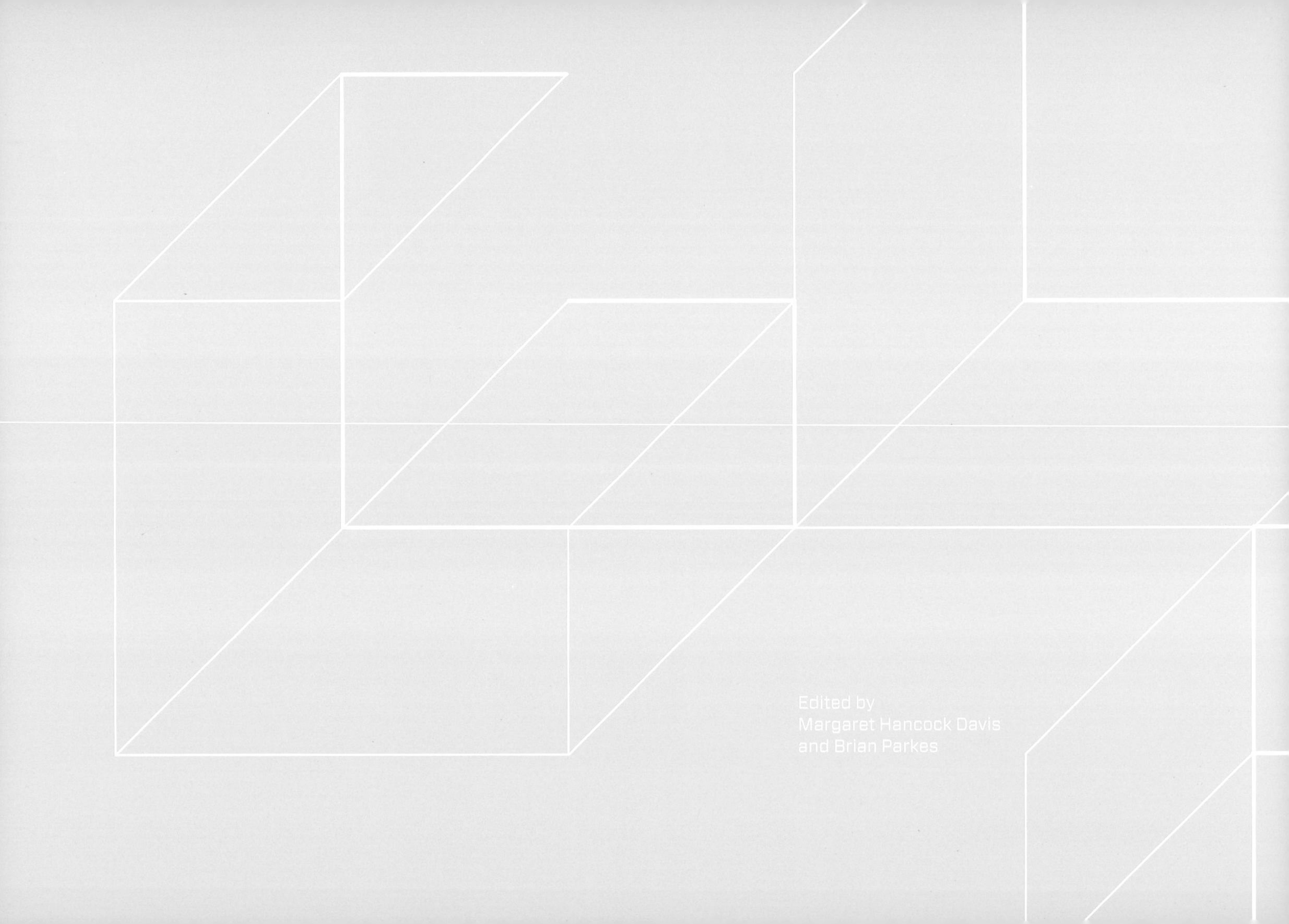
Edited by
Margaret Hancock Davis
and Brian Parkes

Jam Factory

First Published in Adelaide, Australia in 2015

Published to coincide with the exhibition *GLASS: art design architecture*, shown at JamFactory, Adelaide from 13 February to 24 April 2015 before touring nationally.

Published by JamFactory
19 Morphett Street
Adelaide SA 5000

www.jamfactory.com.au

ISBN 978-0-9807910-6-8

Co-curators:
Margaret Hancock Davis and Brian Parkes

Curatorial Assistant:
Adele Sliuzas

Catalogue Editors:
Margaret Hancock Davis and Brian Parkes

Copy Editor:
Theresa Willsteed

Art Direction and Design:
Stephen Goddard, Project Two

Printed in China for Imago

All measurements have been given height before width before depth in millimetres.

This exhibition has been assisted by the Australian Government through the Australia Council for the Arts, its arts funding and advisory body.

JamFactory acknowledges the support of the South Australian Government through Arts SA and the assistance of the Visual Arts and Crafts Strategy, an initiative of the Australian, State and Territory Governments. JamFactory's Exhibitions Program is also assisted by the Australian Government through the Australia Council.

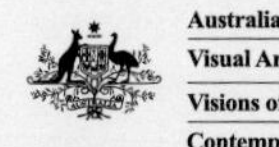

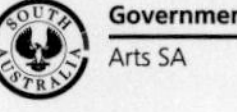

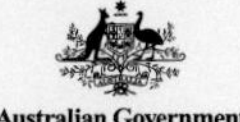

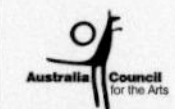

DESIGN SPONSOR

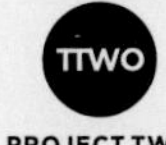

Contents

Foreword
Brian Parkes 6

Introduction
Margaret Hancock Davis and Brian Parkes 10

Softenings:
From subjects to objects
Robert Cook 14

Presence and absence —
glass in architecture, interiors, design
Penny Craswell 24

Adelaide Botanic Garden's
three centuries of glass
Stephen Forbes 38

Looking through glass,
or the visibility of invisibility
Thomas Mical 44

Artists, designers & architects 50

Contributors 242

Acknowledgements 246

Artists, designers & architects
Andrew Simpson / Vert Design 50
Architectus 58
Blanche Tilden 66
Charles Wright Architects 76
Clare Belfrage 84
Deb Jones 92
Elliat Rich 100
illumini 108
Janet Laurence 116
Jess Dare 126
Jessica Loughlin 134
KeepCup 144
Mark Douglass 152
Max Pritchard Architect 160
Mel Douglas 168
Nicholas Folland 176
Richard Whiteley 184
Ruth Allen 192
Tom Moore 200
Tonkin Zulaikha Greer /
Taylor Cullity Lethlean / Aurecon 208
Wendy Fairclough 216
Woods Bagot 224
Yhonnie Scarce 232

Foreword

Brian Parkes

***GLASS: art design architecture* explores innovative and outstanding ways that glass is being used by artists, designers and architects in Australia in the 21st century. The exhibition builds on the highly successful format of *WOOD: art design architecture* — a collaboration between JamFactory and the Adelaide Botanic Gardens — which launched in Adelaide in February 2013 and toured to eight venues across Australia. We are delighted that the GLASS exhibition will be shown in 15 venues nationally over almost three years.**

JamFactory is a unique not-for-profit organisation located in the Adelaide city centre. It supports and promotes outstanding design and craftsmanship through its studios, galleries and shops, and is recognised nationally and internationally as a centre for excellence.

Glass has been an important medium within the history of the JamFactory since it was established in 1973. JamFactory's Glass Studio is the longest-running hot glass studio in Australia and has provided an important hub for artists and designers working with hot glass. JamFactory's intensive two-year, post-tertiary Associate training program is considered one of the pre-eminent places for training in hot glass in the world. Entry into the program is on a competitive basis, and in recent years Associates have come to us from the United States, Canada, Mexico, Japan, New Zealand and the United Kingdom as well as various parts of Australia.

JamFactory's Glass Studio is also a busy production facility that designs and produces successful products for retail and wholesale markets, along with a broad range of bespoke commissioned work including awards, trophies, glassware, lighting installations and public art projects. The studio is regularly engaged by artists, designers and architects to prototype and produce products or components for new projects. Each new job that comes into the studio provides fascinating training opportunities and experiences for our Associates.

I would like to take this opportunity to thank the 23 exhibitors in *GLASS: art design architecture* for their willingness to participate and for allowing us to present their works. These influential artists, designers and architects, drawn from six of the eight Australian states and territories, were selected over two solid research periods in 2013 and 2014. The diversity of their work and stories is what makes this project so rich.

I would like to particularly acknowledge the exhibition's Co-curator and project manager Margaret Hancock Davis for her tireless work in realising the ambition of this significant project — including securing initial funding, liaising with all of the exhibitors and

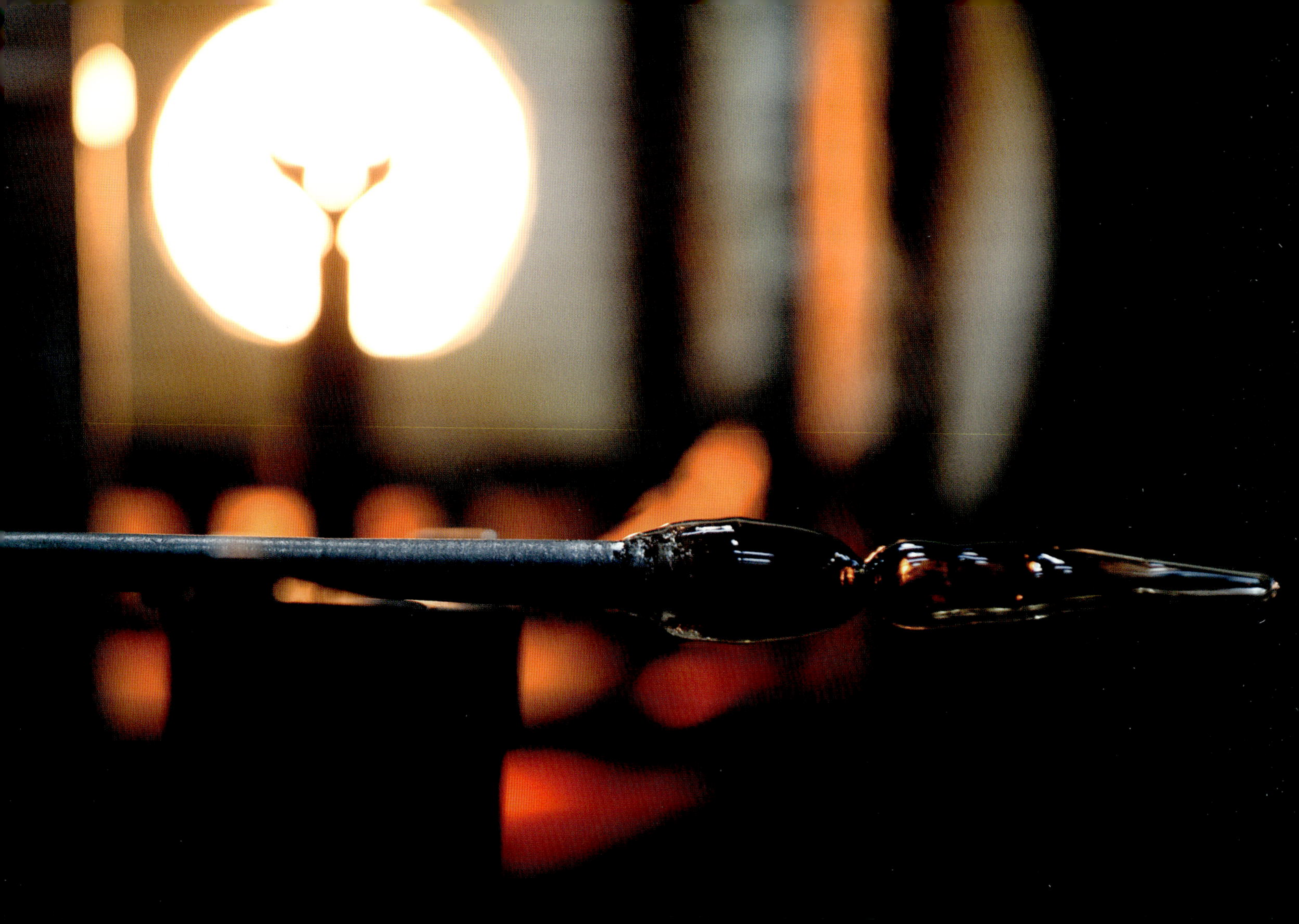

◂

Yhonnie Scarce working at JamFactory's glass studio producing her blown glass bush bananas.
Photo: James Grose

stakeholders, and managing the complex logistics for such a major tour. Margaret has been ably assisted by JamFactory's Assistant Curator Adele Sliuzas, who also deserves special thanks.

A key feature of this exhibition has been the design and fabrication of the display furniture and related elements, based once again on the model developed for *WOOD: art design architecture*. The exhibition design has been led by independent Sydney-based designer Stephen Goddard, in conjunction with the Creative Director of JamFactory's Metal Design Studio Christian Hall and a group of Associates from the Metal and Furniture Studios.

Stephen Goddard has also designed this wonderful catalogue and we thank him for his significant personal contribution to both this and the previous *WOOD* project, which together stand as evidence of an outstanding collaborative relationship that we hope to build on into the future. I must also thank copy editor Theresa Willsteed, as well as all of the contributing writers and the many photographers whose work has helped to create such a beautiful publication.

An exhibition of this scale requires much support, and I would like to acknowledge the principal funding that JamFactory receives from the South Australian Government through Arts SA, and from the Commonwealth Government through the Australia Council for the Arts. The development of the exhibition and its extensive national tour has been greatly assisted by additional Commonwealth funding through Visions of Australia, and I thank the Australia Council and the Minister for the Arts, Senator the Hon George Brandis QC, for this crucial support.

We hope that this exhibition will inspire audiences around Australia to consider the social, cultural, economic and creative possibilities of glass, to think about our relationship to it, and to consider its capacity to be a defining material of the 21st century.

Brian Parkes
Chief Executive Officer
JamFactory

Introduction

Margaret Hancock Davis and Brian Parkes

Glass has been an important medium in the history of civilisation. Archaeologists have found that early man used obsidian (volcanic glass) to make spear tips, while evidence shows that man-made glass was produced as a form of glaze from 3500 BC in Mesopotamia. Rudimentary forms of hollow glass container have been made using sand-casting processes since 1500 BC and glass blowing, as we know it today, emerged in the 1st century BC. The first glass windows were produced in Alexandria in around 100 AD. Since these earliest times we have used this deeply seductive material in increasingly sophisticated ways, and today we see glass as an important structural material in building, and at the cutting edge of technology, being used in sensors, fibre optics, interactive touch-screens and flexible glass.

Glass is a shape-shifting, liquid material. Its transparency often renders it invisible: how conscious are we of the actual glass substance in the mirror we look into in the morning; the windscreen we stare through on our way to work; the watch-face we check as we arrive; the screen we stare at or the window we look out for respite; not to mention the bottle and glass we might reach for on our return home?

Of course glass can also inspire and delight, and it is a material that has been favoured by artists, designers and architects over the centuries for both its formal and conceptual qualities. The history of art, design and architecture is peppered with extraordinary achievements of human endeavour, ingenuity and audacity in which glass has been a central feature.

In developing this exhibition, we found ourselves reflecting on the power and influence of many of these. They range from the 176 narrative and symbolic stained-glass windows that create a medieval cinema in the 13th-century Chartres Cathedral, to the inventive engineering feat of Joseph Paxton's cast plate-glass Crystal Palace, built for the Great Exhibition of 1851. At a smaller scale, they also include the unprecedented meticulousness of the Harvard Museum of Natural History's collection of more than 3000 hyper-realistic glass botanical specimens created in Germany by Leopold and Rudolf Blaschka between 1887 and 1936.

As unapologetic modernists, we also considered some of the enduring symbols of modernism across art, design and architecture, such as Marcel Duchamp's *The bride stripped bare by her bachelors, even (The large glass)*, 1915–23; the iconic *Savoy vase* designed by Alvar and Aino Aalto in 1936 (and still being produced by iittala today); Philip Johnson's 1949 Glass House in Connecticut and Ludwig Mies van der Rohe's towering 1958 steel and glass Seagram Building in Manhattan.

Closer to home, we were reminded of the earliest production of glass artefacts in Australia by Aboriginal artisans of the Kimberley region. From the 18th century, they fashioned beautiful glass spearheads and cutting tools from glass bottles discarded by Macassan fishermen (who regularly visited Australian shores in search of trepang to export to China). The faceted edges of these objects echo the same formal qualities found in the chunky hammered and chiselled shards and blocks of cast-coloured glass used by Leonard French in his stained-glass works, such as the remarkable ceiling of the Great Hall, 1965–70, at the National Gallery of Victoria (one of the largest stained-glass ceilings in the world), or the 16 large windows at the National Library in Canberra, 1967, each three and a half metres high.

In this exhibition we have brought together products, projects and works of art that reflect many of the current preoccupations with glass within contemporary art, design and architecture in Australia. The exhibitors represent an expansive range of approaches to working with glass and many have a strong personal association with the material.

The range of work in the exhibition is extreme — from fine, hand-crafted jewellery to a high-tech glass skyscraper — and hopefully encourages audiences to think expansively about the human connections to glass, and to look at familiar things through a new lens. We hope viewers might consider the architectural qualities of a glass necklace or the jewel-like detailing of a glass office tower.

We have deliberately drawn attention to the technologies and craft processes of working with glass in the studio and within industry. The skills of glaziers, glass blowers, cutters, engravers and kiln-formers are on display within the various projects — sometimes as heroic protagonists and sometimes as quiet collaborators. Glass is a complex material requiring specialist knowledge at each stage of production.

Formal concerns such as transparency and translucency, reflection and refraction or light and luminosity are evident in many of the featured works. In others we see spatial concerns such as the way glass frames and contains a subject or substance (actually and metaphorically), as well as references to the fields of botany, chemistry and alchemy or the rich histories and traditions of working with glass itself. There are also concerns relating to sustainability, with investigations of heat retention for passive climate control and the opportunities for the re-use and recycling of glass.

This exhibition combines the genres of art, design and architecture to provide a full-circle view of glass in contemporary visual culture. The varied nature of the work of the 23 featured exhibitors and the supporting texts in this publication offer a fresh and unfurling perspective of the importance of glass in our daily lives, and its value in the expression of who we are.

Margaret Hancock Davis and Brian Parkes

Softenings: From subjects to objects

Robert Cook

Just as materials are not infinitely malleable, neither are they infinitely poetic. Their cultural and psychological resonances take shapes determined, limited and opened up by their uniquely trippy molecular jungles. When we work with a substance, therefore, we work at the complicated juncture of reference and physical resistance. Of course, these junctures are multiple, but again not infinite. As such, they tend to coalesce into specific forms, as the fields we know by media distinctions (glass, ceramics, painting, for example) reflect certain structures of thought and process that guide, if not absolutely determine, their activities.

In order to gain a slightly better angle on the thing called 'Australian glass' — or even 'Australian art that uses glass' — we might, then, be well served by stepping out and back from it as a field, and considering the ways that glass has been employed in its more conceptual modes over the 20th and early 21st centuries in art (and the places where art meets architecture).[1] Seen alongside these artistic examples Australian glass can, I think, be understood as a continual softening of the overtly conceptual and harrowingly existential in favour of the felt and the romantically expressive; in doing so it can equally (and symptomatically) be seen as refracting the more hard-nosed avant-garde machinations by turning them into retro-modern poetics, out of time and place. And, as we come at this, it is quite evident that the decisive difference between Australian glass and how it has functioned in modern and contemporary art is that in the latter, glass is about subjectivity, and in the former, glass is about the object. Both, I think, have elements of radicality, but only if we open our minds to such possibilities. I hope this essay is the start of that process. But it is, just that: only a start.

And as this is little more than a sketch, I'll stick to the big names: Marcel Duchamp, Ludwig Mies van der Rohe and Philip Johnson, Dan Graham and Josiah McElheny. Together, they have set the agenda for the conceptual use of glass at its most challenging and exacting, and as being most tightly aligned with the agendas of modern and contemporary art in its critically explorative guises. Accordingly, their practices are the ultimate foils for the field of Australian glass and craft, which operates on altogether different lines and through altogether different fields of dispersal.

Okay, Duchamp. As is well known, Duchamp pitched — by way of purposefully lodging everyday objects in art spaces — that art can be anything at all. In doing so, art is foregrounded as a mental and cultural (including economic) category of experience and production.

It's a move that sets in motion the thing he called 'non-retinal art', now known broadly as conceptualism. It is this, I feel, that glass signifies perfectly. For now, though, let's turn, almost too obviously, to *The bride stripped bare by her bachelors, even (The large glass)*, 1915–23. Images and descriptions of it abound online so I'll cut to the chase here and posit that the work, at its most basic level, exists like a glacial open wound — a sharp, continual, nagging, unsettling problem. Duchamp messed around with it for eight or so years and its meaning (its meanings) was and remain practically unsolvable.

I mean, what the hell is this thing about? Perched somewhere between a dressmaker's pattern and a mechanical clothesline, a partition and a window, *The large glass* is elusive and frustrating. Which may well be the point, especially given the title — it activates frustration as nothing is released by the work. It is an exercise in holding things, energies, back. These moves connect the sexual with intellectual forms of frustration. Indeed, the bachelors wait to marry (even though they already have a bride), and as they do, they remain bachelors and, as such, the bride is not really a bride at all: she is an entity in two states, a before and after, simultaneously. This looping, doubling and deferral make sense when we think of its seemingly endless construction and reconstruction, combined with Duchamp's own opaque commentary on it and that of others. It is as much a game as anything else. And in this game, what we might see is that glass signifies teasingly non-committal non-expressiveness. Duchamp himself described its knot thusly:

> Use 'delay' instead of picture or painting ... It's merely a way of succeeding in no longer thinking that the thing in question is a picture — to make a delay of it in the most general way possible, not so much in the different meanings in which delay can be taken, but rather in their indecisive reunion.[2]

Now, while Duchamp implicitly posited that art can be anything, his materials did signify in a metaphorical fashion. Let's take *In advance of a broken arm/(from) Marcel Duchamp*, 1915. It is a snow shovel originally (an editioned object) sourced from a hardware store in New York. It hangs from the ceiling of a gallery, and 'says' — because we have allowed it to — that anything can be art. The work also 'allows' us to marvel at its prosaic beauty and the lo-fi elegance of its purposeful design; at its functional potential; and at its original purpose, which is to prevent someone falling over and breaking their arm during a snow fall (yes, two types of falling!). Like the urinal *Fountain*, 1917, therefore, Duchamp's objects have (at least) several 'functions': poetic, practical and provocative.

From this, and in relation to *The large glass*, the brittle, fractured quality of it, its tetchy transparency must also be read in terms of the difficulty of finding meaning when things are ostensibly 'see-through'. The meaning is right there under our noses! This is; we see it; but our not-seeing-it-even-after-seeing-it is the point. Here, Duchamp uses glass to tease our hermeneutic impulse to find more, and to propel his game of non-retinal art. The work is fundamentally ambivalent, therefore, and as such it speaks of a certain separation of viewer from work and viewer from meaning (in addition to separating male and female). The transparency of glass doesn't unite. It separates. It slices us in two.

As an icon of the inability/unwillingness to express — to be expressive generally, lewdly taken — Duchamp's work coincides with the material embrace *and* critique of the modern, of which glass was so often a key component. After all, as Peter Conrad has pointed out, Walter Benjamin once said that the apogee of modern civilisation was to live in a glass house.[3] Here's how Benjamin put it himself:

> To live in a glass house is a revolutionary virtue par excellence. It is also an intoxication, a moral exhibitionism that we badly need. Discretion concerning one's own existence, once an aristocratic virtue, has become more an affair of the petit-bourgeois existence.[4]

Additionally, the architecture of Le Corbusier, one of the period's most iconic designers, often tended 'towards a universally transparent exteriority'.[5] The radically open order that these modes of living would presume come from a deep commitment — at least in Le Corbusier's thinking, Benjamin's is more fluid — to modern, purist rationalism, in which the transparency of the self and its projects has seamlessly become part of its machines of living. Conrad rightly calls such ideals into question, saying that we humans seem never to live up to them.[6] Perhaps it is the case that the modernism in our minds is always disappointed in us. We fail the machines and regimes of our secular transcendent aspirations as full visibility pushes us inwards into an introjected panoptical nightmare.

Key structural symbols of this are, obviously, Johnson's Glass House, 1949, and Mies's Farnsworth House, 1945–51, (the model of which inspired Johnson's house). Both are rectangles inserted into manicured, yet richly picturesque, natural settings. The proposition seems clear: humans might best be inserted into nature and opened out to it. Yet, as ever, glass is a veil of separation, not a point of

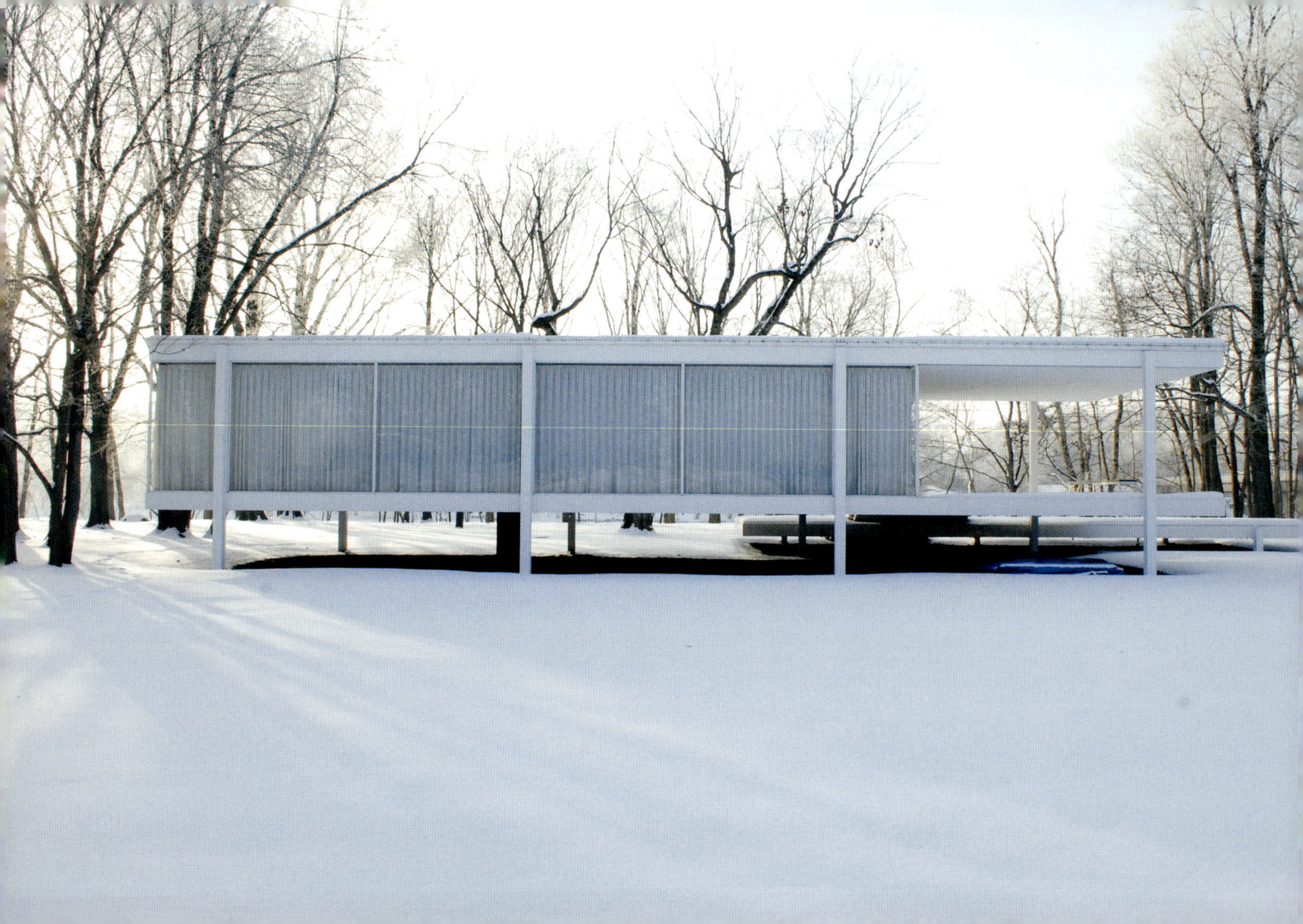

◂
Ludwig Mies van der Rohe
Farnsworth House, 1945–51
Plano, Illinois, USA
Photo: Jonathan Rieke
(creative commons)
https://www.flickr.com/photos/jonathanrieke/5334924554/

connectivity. It freezes the scene as a scene — as landscape (codified not encountered, interpreted not experienced). I imagine the little man (why a man, why little?) living there, wandering, puttering about, gazing at the sculpture, and becoming kinetic sculpture himself as he is framed by these glass sheets, a little fish guy in his art aquarium. The subject of rational ocular modernism, as it seeks to re-establish ties with the natural world it actually intends to transcend, is set 'free' from his tasks and left to float, around and around. The elimination of labour implied here creates pure brain, the human as captive, a zoo thing, a thing without purpose. The house amplifies this, turning rest, and living itself, into spectacle. The transparent medium of modernism does this. Visibility holds one to task, all the time, always subject to the modern super ego, always apparent to natural and cultural predators.

Interestingly, between 2006 and 2009 the American experimental photographer James Welling went to Connecticut numerous times to shoot the Glass House. His resulting images were made from layers of coloured plastic held over the lens of his camera to amplify his take on the place. As he said, 'this big glass box, plunked down in the Connecticut landscape, seems like a conceptual sculpture, a gigantic lens in the landscape'.[7] Under Welling's layerings, this lens becomes a brilliant, psychedelic bleed-out experience, fragmented and made drunk from washes of colour. In doing so, its Spartan aspect shifts and radically recomposes itself — like a kind of drug trip, the experience becomes the connected one that undercuts the modern division of tasks and its incipient alienation.

Instead of changing aesthetic (and therefore ideological) tones as Welling does, fellow American artist Dan Graham took the ideas inherent in the glass houses (and, very importantly, Mies's Barcelona Pavilion, 1929) and pushed them as far as they'd go in existential, subjective terms. For instance, a piece from 1978 called *Alteration* to a suburban house (never made except as a potent model) saw him replace a back wall in a suburban house with a mirror. The effect was a mirroring of the interior activity as well as that of the street in the house. Beatriz Colomina describes it as ensuring that 'passers-by are exposed, swallowed up by the house, incorporated into the interior as part of the decoration, a kind of wallpaper'.[8] Instead of the personal separation that defines suburbia, every gaze is brought, awfully, together — the person outside is caught by the gaze of the house and vice versa. It is a kind of horror of visibility. Though in this and other works there is a coolness at play as well, an establishing of possibility and the shrill heat is all my (and Colomina's) reading. Mostly Graham was, in his own words, concerned with the 'the subjectivity of the spectator'.[9] As such, Graham's works morphed into pavilion forms based on what he called existing 'public pavilions', such as bus stops. These spaces act as incisions that make us aware of ourselves as subjects of the world and, as always, public entities. As we 'turn fractal' in and outside of their spaces we stage a loss of interiority that essentially acts out the end game of the modern. Indeed, as Birgit Pelzer puts it, 'Graham's paradigm touches on dialectical operations of coming together and alienation, intersection and separation'.[10] It seems he is for and against Mies and Johnson, and with Duchamp on the undecidability of meaning.

The younger artist Josiah McElheny extends this restless, ambivalent criticality into infinity. McElheny is treated as a material-conceptual artist whose works are not 'expressions' but 'engagements with' materiality. A highly skilled glass maker, he has employed glass in various capacities, mostly to investigate the histories and sub-histories of modernism. His work *Buckminster Fuller's proposal for Isamu Noguchi for the new abstraction of total reflection*, 2003, for example, was based on Noguchi's forms, which were in turn responses to polishing Brancusi's bronze sculpture *Leda*, 1926, when Noguchi worked as Brancusi's assistant and discovered in *Leda* a work and a world with no shadows.[11]

McElheny went on to make numerous other works featuring glass objects on mirrored tables as he explored modernity as an endless 'act of self-examination'. His *Island universe*, 2008, took this further still. A physical articulation of the Big Bang, each point has a glass end in which the viewer sees themselves mirrored, becoming part of the beginning of the universe. His works are deep engagements with the intricacies of modernism and its most radical scientific inquiries, as well as its unthought histories and styles. As Tom McDonough puts it:

> his works remind us that modernity's beliefs in the power of illumination and the promise of seeing as a transcendental experience (as embodied in glass, 'pure, clear and invisible, empty of symbols') were subtended by the dispelling of shadow as imperfection, unevenness, as a 'hole in light'.[12]

As with Graham, these are not sculptures as such, but things that engage with the larger field of sculpture as it moves, post Brancusi, from the plinth and into the world, and acts on the subject him— or herself.

Okay, I think that's enough of the players who have said what is definitive about the medium of glass outside its craft and commercial heritage. Connected to the movements of modernism, the heat is on the interleaved ideas and experiences of separation, alienation, functionality, machinism and the infinity of the non-expressive. Glass is fundamentally extra-sculptural in these instances, and fundamentally architectural and fundamentally conceptual. It is also fundamentally *analytical*. All are about subjectivity at its most challengingly existential — they are definitely not about being objects of contemplation. Or when they are about contemplation, they double and triple and quadruple this looking so that one gets lost within it.

In relation to this, there is no doubt at all that, as I said at the start, Australian glass is a series of softenings that function in the way Conrad thought we all challenge the strictures of the modern. (On a related note, this has got to be why mirrors are always breaking in horror movies: they cannot contain the tension of the human as pure image. The unconscious strikes back, as it always does).

Australian glass is not overtly, strategically critical of the use of glass in the ways outlined above, and it is not engaged in any meta-ness. Instead, it introduces a poetics and atmospherics that is the repressed (or at least the flipside) of the conceptual glass arena. So, while Australian glass 'employs concepts', obviously there is no artist who is truly conceptual. Glass has no Ian Burn. Our tradition is totally antithetical to that. Its works add value to life as it is lived and do not critique its foundation of being. They offer screens into the landscape as it blissfully envelops us, as we sink into it as we would a warm rockpool. It is sensual and evocative. When it evokes high modern, such as in Richard Whiteley's works, it is as a small-scale James Turrell mapping the world that we sit in and outside of by virtue of our relative height. Equally, Jason Sims contains the fluoro-tube colour bursts of Dan Flavin, keeping them tight to the object even when the light spills out. And when glass is political it is so in a narrative, representational sense. Similarly, Jessica Loughlin's works pull us into the world, but do not push us to infinite oblivions. I could go on, but the point is the same: the critique of subjectivity is not so, not ever, apparent. Australian glass deals with objects not subjects.

Read in these comparative terms, it might appear as if such softening in Australian glass is a turning away from seriousness. In most cases that's how it would be read — the dominance of critically circulated international art trumps all. Yet, let's take a different look at it. One of Australia's most successful art exports, Ricky Swallow, offers a way we might do so. It's not his own work — though that, in fact, speaks volumes on this subject also — that does so, but a show he curated for David Kordansky Gallery in

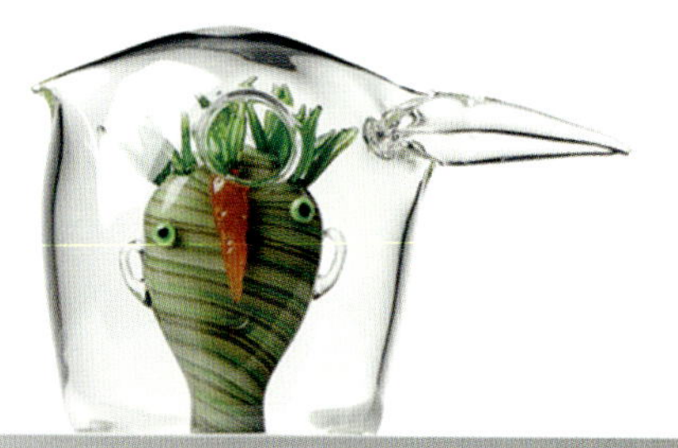

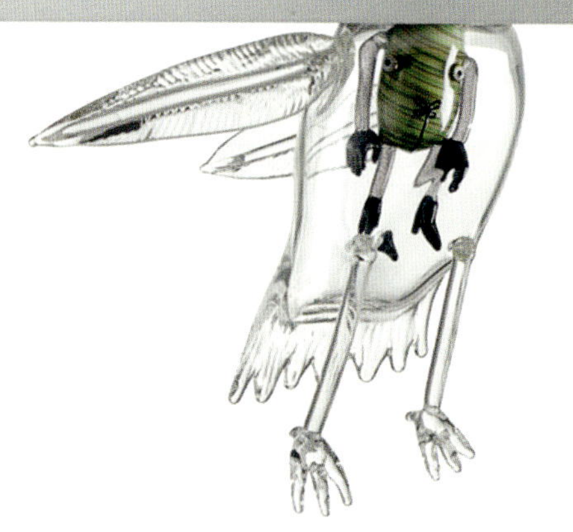

2013, called *Grapevine*, which featured the works of five American ceramic artists. I remember seeing the install shots on the web. It was perfectly laid out! Swallow allowed each work to speak of its own idiosyncratic approach to modernism, resonating on its own terms outside the blandishments of progressive histories. As he did (and he wrote lovingly about this as well) these works were seen as being quite radical explorations of where strands of the modern might go if we abandoned straight history as a dominant paradigm and embraced the fracturing rhizome. This is another kind of modernism — a kind that continues to expand and fold over itself, to create new forms and formations, new pulses and ranges and tones of thinking and making. We just have to make spaces to really get them on these terms.

And it strikes me that this rhizome is where Australian glass is. It feeds against the conceptual by way of the social (makers coming together), and the handmade as a thing to revere, and the expressive (even when it is cool and design focused), and finds new paths to new waterfalls. The works that make up Australian glass are maps to them in fact, and some of them are pretty far from the beaten track! See Tom Moore's amazing output for instance. In all, though, there is a softening of the challenge to our being. It is, again, a field that accepts the world as it is and brings us closer

◂
Tom Moore
Self Portrait with Radically Amphibious Armour, 2012
hot joined blown and solid glass, metal fastenings, shelf
440 x 680 x 180
Photo: Grant Hancock

to it. It asks questions, sure, it pitches ideas, but it generally doesn't shake us. Instead, it welcomes.

Its objects, though, allow our subjecthood to remain respectfully intact and allow us to find ways to make the intellectual spaces we need to make, like Ricky Swallow, and to appreciate its possibilities. From these spaces they start unpicking things. And what happens from that point is a whole other story. It is the story of Australian glass proper, seen in its most richly resonant particularity that shapes a hundred other stories about the modern and post-modern, vectors that are continually up for reinvention. I think it would be one that looked at the way the 'object's objectness' functions as a set of propositions that move towards articulating the personal artistic styles outside and beyond the aesthetic. It would be a big story, but probably quite necessary if we are to truly understand the unique contributions of our incredible makers in this country.

1. So ... take this word 'conceptual'. I have used it in a very non-technical way throughout this essay. I think people get it: it focuses on the mind and not the sensual — but yes, they are aligned, and my use is super generalised. And, an artist like Dan Graham, I think, would not consider his work conceptual at all — I recall reading some place about how he positioned his work against artists such as Kosuth. Anyway, though I know readers will understand its use, I point it out because it is also symptomatic of a range of generalisations I've made in this essay, and some highly subjective interpretations.
2. Marcel Duchamp in Calvin Tomkins, *Duchamp: A biography*, Chatto & Windus, London, 1997, p 1.
3. Peter Conrad, *Modern times, modern places: Life and art in the 20th century*, Thames & Hudson: London, 1998, p 293.
4. Anthony Vidler, 'Fantasy, the uncanny and surrealist theories of architecture, Centre for the Studies of Surrealism and its Legacies, UK, 2003, p 4, viewed 27 August 2014, http://www.surrealismcentre.ac.uk/papersofsurrealism/journal1/acrobat_files/Vidler.pdf.
5. ibid., p 5.
6. Peter Conrad, op. cit.
7. James Welling in the exhibition press release for *Glass House*, David Zwirner, New York, 2010, viewed 26 August 2014, http://www.davidzwirner.com/exhibition/glass-house/
8. Beatriz Colomina, 'Double exposure: Alteration to a suburban house, 1978', in Birgit Pelzer, Mark Francis and Beatriz Colomina, *Dan Graham*, Phaidon, London, 2001, pp 82–83.
9. Dan Graham, in *pressPLAY: Contemporary artists in conversation*, Phaidon, London, 2005, p 248.
10. Birgit Pelzer, 'Double intersections: the optics of Dan Graham', in Birgit Pelzer, Mark Francis and Beatriz Colomina, op. cit., p 75.
11. Tom McDonough, 'Shadow play', in *Parkett no 86: John Baldessari, Carol Bove, Josiah McElheny, Philippe Parreno*, Parkett Editions, Zurich, 2009, p 111.
12. ibid.

Presence and absence — glass in architecture, interiors, design

Penny Craswell

The increasing availability, affordability and technical performance of glass over the past 100 years has radically changed our buildings inside and out. The development of the curtain wall in the early 20th century, which allowed the external skin of a building to be non-load bearing, was a major catalyst in the use of glass for facades, with modernist masters such as Walter Gropius and Ludwig Mies van der Rohe creating new kinds of buildings with a focus on transparency, free flow of space and blurring of inside and out.

The continuing innovation in glass, which is now a structural and load-bearing material, has resulted in more transparent buildings, with glass used as a way of creating a structure that highlights other elements of the building or landscape — glass as a kind of absence. On the other hand, glass is also used as a hero in its own right, to create sculptural buildings and shapes that are symbolic of modernism or progress — here, glass is very much a statement of presence. So these two qualities — presence and absence — inform much of the symbolic and practical use of glass in architecture, interiors and design.

Transparency, light and shopping

In 1909 in Kansas City, USA, the Boley Clothing Company opened its new store, a building designed by Louis Singleton Curtiss. It was among the first glass curtain-walled buildings in the world. Architecture scholar Keith Eggener explains in an article in *Design Observer* that the purpose here was twofold. The first was to create an opportunity for window shopping. Society was changing from being production-oriented to being consumer-oriented, so the focus had to be on the product. The emergence of window shopping was one of the vehicles used for this purpose. Secondly, the glass facade brought light into the interiors, which had the effect of implying a kind of moral virtue. At the time, consumerism in the more religious parts of the United States was often equated with sin, so by bringing light into the space, Boley was allaying fears that shopping was sinful. After all, to be transparent means to be truthful. If you are communicating well, you are being crystal clear. Because of the abundance of natural light, these retail environments in the USA became known as 'daylight stores'.[1]

Skip forward 100 odd years and another seminal moment in the technological advancement of glass in architecture also occurred in a retail environment. Architecture firm Bohlin Cywinski Jackson worked with glass engineer James O'Callaghan and Apple's Steve Jobs on an innovative glass staircase that has become an Apple store trademark. The first Apple glass staircase was built for Apple's SoHo store in New York and a number of other stairs were designed and constructed throughout North America, Europe

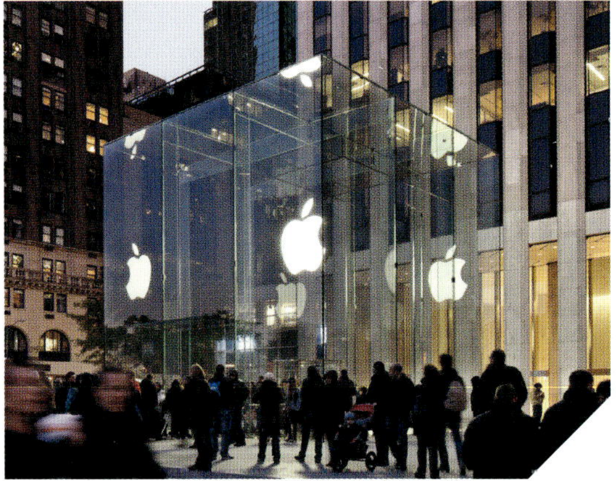

▸ Bohin Cywinski Jackson Architects
Apple Store Fifth Avenue,
2004–06
Fifth Avenue, New York City, USA
Photo: Peter Aaron/Esto

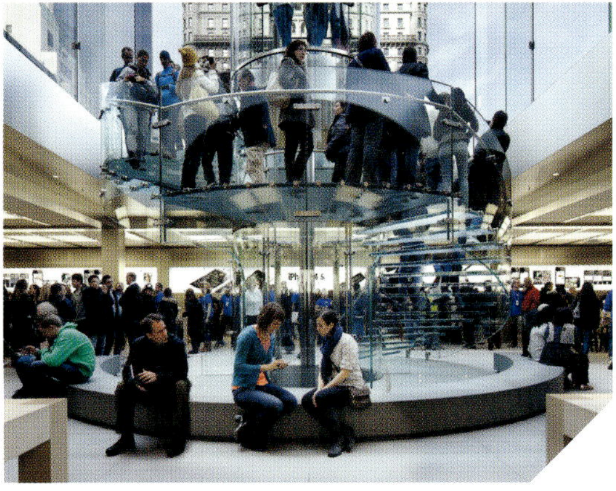

▾ Glass staircase,
Apple Store Fifth Avenue
Photo: Peter Aaron/Esto

and Asia, including glass stairs with free-standing and wall-mounted angle turns and spiral designs. Elements of the stairs were originally patented by Steve Jobs in 2002, with subsequent patents covering a number of innovations in structure and hardware, such as laminated glass production and a panel construction that is point-supported.[2]

The innovation of the glass stairs at various stores went hand in hand with the increased use of glass in the stores and especially the facade, utilising advances in the properties of glass in order to make panels larger, and using glass as a structural element. The culmination of the design was in another New York store, this time in 5th Avenue in 2006. From street level, the store presents as a large transparent glass cube with an Apple logo shining in white above a doorway. The doorway opens to a spiral glass staircase that leads the customer to the Apple store below. According to architects Bohlin Cywinski Jackson, this is the world's first self-supporting glass spiral staircase and cylindrical glass elevator.

Just like Boley, Apple is playing on light and transparency as metaphors for its brands, implying that they are trustworthy and open. Interestingly, the retail redesign that resulted in the increased use of glass in Apple stores also led to the Genius Bar. This service gives Apple customers the ability to speak directly to Apple staff on issues of maintenance, as well as education on Apple products. Modelled on a hotel concierge, the values of light and truthfulness again are paramount, and once again marry architectural transparency with symbolic transparency.

The transparent workplace

In workplace design, the use of glass to create visual transparency has also been used as a metaphor for company values. Transparency has been increasingly cited as a central value in modern business (and government), with Paul Finch, Editorial Director of *The Architects' Journal*, writing that the term 'transparency' is a buzzword that has become a cult in business and government, and has spread to architecture and design. While Finch is doubtful that transparent buildings such as the Swiss Re building, 2004, (the 'Gherkin' in London) are actually transparent in the sense of being completely open to scrutiny, he does point to the symbolic link between the two.[3]

Glass is an ubiquitous material in the modern office tower, with a glass facade standard on many tall buildings since the 1950s and 1960s, when architects such as Mies and Skidmore Owings & Merrill used skeletal steel frames and glass curtain walls to design the first glass skyscrapers. Glass served to let light in and create views for those office workers who had been promoted, with the 'corner office' the ultimate marker of prestige. More junior staff were meanwhile relegated to the dark core of the building. It wasn't until much later that glass was used in workplace interiors, breaking down the old hierarchies by creating visual connection and bringing light further into the core of the space. In the contemporary designs, communal areas are more often placed near the perimeter, with closed offices and cubicles replaced with glass offices or open-plan workspaces. Even in the most open-plan workplaces when walls are removed entirely, glazing is still widely used to separate meeting rooms and as balustrades for stairs, allowing light to penetrate as deeply as possible into large floor plates.

At Lloyds in London, completed in 1986, architect Richard Rogers effectively turned the building inside out, placing services around the exterior of the tower and allowing the centre of the building to exist as a magnificent glass atrium topped with a barrel-vaulted glass roof. The purpose here is twofold: to allow light through the roof and down into the interiors; and to achieve transparency, allowing the insurance traders who work at Lloyds to make visible the inner workings of the firm. Rogers says: 'Because Lloyd's is fundamentally a marketplace, they had to be able to see each other working — they needed great transparency.'[4]

Woods Bagot
National Australia Bank, 2013
Docklands, 700 Bourke Street,
Melbourne
Photo: Trevor Mein

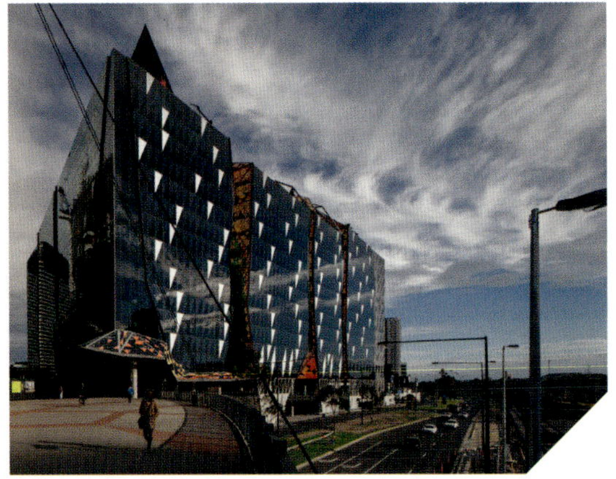

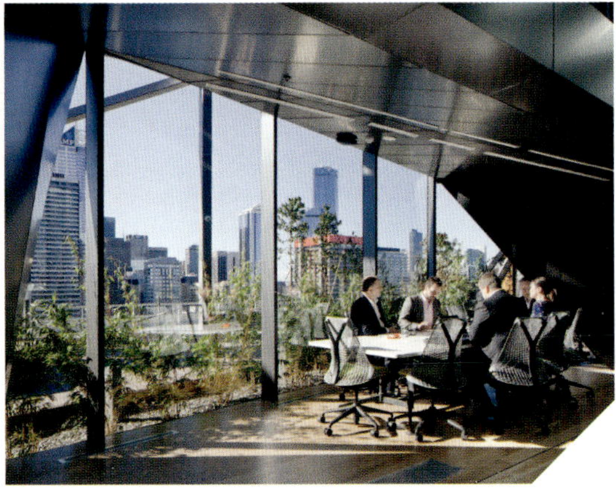

Replacing the cubicle with glass was one of the major workplace innovations in the Googleplex, Google's Silicon Valley headquarters designed by LA-based workplace designer Clive Wilkinson in 1998. Wilkinson called cubicles in a recent Dezeen interview 'humiliating, disenfranchising and isolating' and described how he convinced Google to replace these with glass meeting rooms.[5] Wilkinson also worked closely with Woods Bagot on the interiors of One Shelley Street, Sydney, 2011, collaborating with base building architects Fitzpatrick & Partners and workplace consultants Veldhoen + Company to create a workplace using the principle of activity-based working, creating diversity of choice for workers. As part of this shift, a significant aspect of the open-plan design is a series of glass meeting pods that jut out into the atrium.

At the National Australia Bank's new workplace at 700 Bourke Street in Melbourne, 2013, Woods Bagot again used glass as a major factor in the creation of a workplace focused on flexibility and the power of teamwork. The triangular building features large floor plates, with glazed vertical fissures in the facade cutting into the internal space, providing an integrated division of space for the hubs, while allowing light into the internal spaces. With flexibility the defining concept for workplace design of the future, glass will continue to be used, but less as a simple replacement for the cubicle. New workplaces that provide a variety of spaces for different kinds of work will continue to use glass to allow for collaboration and for acoustic separation without the loss of visual transparency.

Glass as absence in residential architecture

While the lofty ambitions of a transparent business or government body provide a handy metaphor for transparent buildings and interiors, in residential design, where privacy is important, glass is used for different reasons. Philip Johnson's Glass House and Mies's Farnsworth House are two leading modernist houses of the mid 20th century that used glass and steel to create clear, modern lines with an emphasis on the horizontal. Both were designed and built in the USA during the same period — the Glass House between 1945 and 1949 in New Canaan, Connecticut, and the Farnsworth House between 1945 and 1951 in Plano, Illinois. These houses created an open plan for living, a concept that was radical at the time. They both responded to their environment, with Johnson's Glass House grounded and Mies's Farnsworth House seeming to float above the ground. However, the essential reason for the use of glass in both houses is the same: uninterrupted views of the surrounding landscape and the blurring of inside and outside.

Architects designing houses, especially those in remote areas, have been using the same principles ever since. The use of glazing creates a connection with nature that is ultimately appealing. In addition, recent advances in the environmental and safety properties of glass such as thermal insulation, noise reduction, shatterproof qualities and fire protection, makes it more practical as a material choice. It can be seen in many houses in Australia and New Zealand that make the most of bush, beach or mountain views.

Glass has been used in residential design in even more radical ways, including Sou Fujimoto's House NA, 2010,which features 21 separate floor plates stepped at various heights and sizes, allowing for separation and connection for the residents in a completely transparent residence.[6] An experimental (unbuilt) house designed by Milanese architects Santambrogio Milano features three storeys of pale-blue tinted glass living, in which walls, floors (apart from the ground floor in timber), roof and furniture (including the bed) are all glass.[7]

While these radical experiments in the use of glass in houses raise questions of privacy in the abstract, the increasing use of large expanses of glass in apartments and houses in built-up areas is having a very real impact on privacy for city-dwellers. Glass is often used to let in more light, make small rooms

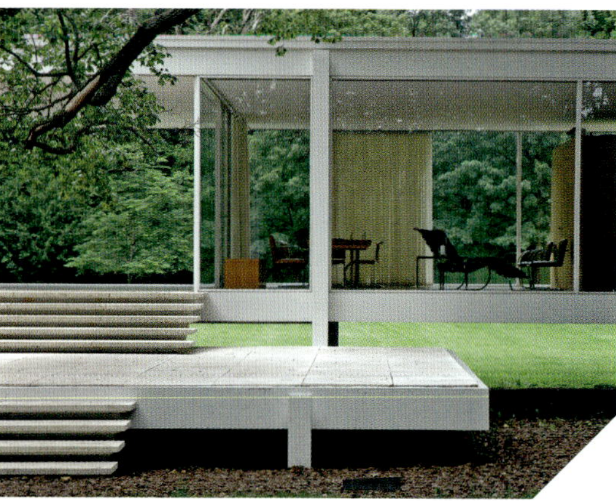

▸ Ludwig Mies van der Rohe
Farnsworth House, 1945–51
Plano, Illinois, USA,
Photo: James Vaughan
(creative commons)
https://www.flickr.com/photos/xray_delta_one/4294005857

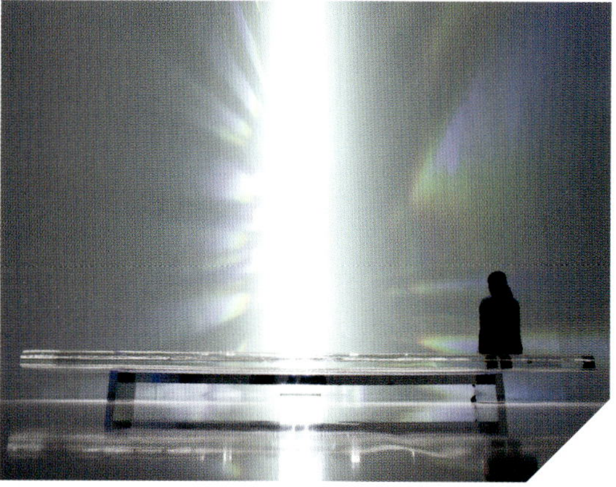

▾ Tokujin Yoshioka
Waterfall, 2005–06
optical glass
400 x 4400 x 700
Photo: Tokujin Yoshioka Inc.

seem larger, and create views out, which has the subconscious effect of making you feel like you are in a larger space and connected to the outside. While these are significant positives, some have begun to question the increasingly extensive use of glass in residential architecture, and its effect on our personal privacy at home. In an article for *Design Observer*, Steven Heller asks: 'Why would anyone want their intimate life exposed to any peeping Tom, Dick or Harry? In other words, what were the architects thinking?'[8] This example clearly shows that transparency is not always a positive, particularly for residential design.

Blurring inside and out — the glasshouse

Glass used in residential architecture allows views out onto the landscape, blending interior and exterior, and creating the sensation of being outside in the greenery while enjoying the comforts of a protected environment. The glasshouse is an extension of this — a protected space for plant life that gains the benefits of the sun while being protected from pests and extreme weather conditions such as frost and scorching sun. The greenhouse at Grüningen Botanical Garden in Switzerland, 2012, by Buehrer Wuest Architekten provides a beautiful example of a recent glasshouse. Its glass is supported by steel beams designed with a geometry inspired by cell division, to create a natural, organic form.[9]

The greenhouse theme has been used in other architectural typologies as well, in buildings such as Jean Nouvel's Fondation Cartier in Paris[10], 1994, where the glass facade is extended to the perimeter of the site, allowing a view from the street through to the greenery beyond. Nouvel's more recent building, One Central Park, 2013, in Sydney, features the largest vertical garden in the world. In this case, glass plays a secondary, yet vital role as a material used in balconies and other structural elements, allowing the plant life to be the most visible design feature.

Glass furniture design — material challenges

While the use of glass in architecture allows transparency, or a sense of absence, the same is true of furniture design. However, because the material is cold and hard, furniture designers who use glass often face the challenge of how to make the material more soft and inviting for use in interiors. Most designers who use the material are interested in its transparent nature. Japanese designer Tokujin Yoshioka has used glass often in his practice, along with plastics and other colourless, clear materials, exploring transparency and reflectivity. His *Waterfall*, 2005–06, and *Chair that disappears in the rain*, 2002–03, are solid slabs of glass that play with distortion and optical illusion, such as ripples that evoke the animated surface of water.[11]

The *Diapositive* furniture series, 2014, designed by French designers Ronan and Erwan Bouroullec for Glas Italia, represents a technological innovation thanks to its use of thermo-welded glass. The only additional materials used in the two desks, bench and shelf are wood and felt, used to protect and soften hard corners and surfaces. These, in combination with the use of coloured glass, create a series of geometric forms that are predominantly glass, offering transparency and a play on light, yet have warmth to them.

While other designers such as Naoto Fukasawa, Nendo, Karim Rashid, and Konstantin Grcic have created furniture pieces in glass to explore transparency in recent years, these themes are also able to be explored in the use of transparent plastics, such as the *Ghost*, 2002, chair by Philippe Starck, which creates the same effect with a lightweight, flexible and more comfortable material.

Glass as presence and form

Glass has been used as a vital tool in the creation of transparency, whether for symbolic purposes or to provide access to landscape or light. However, glass is not always used as absence, to highlight something else. It is often also used as a material that is determinedly present, in solid or sculptural form. In particular, glass has been used as a symbol for progress and modernism.

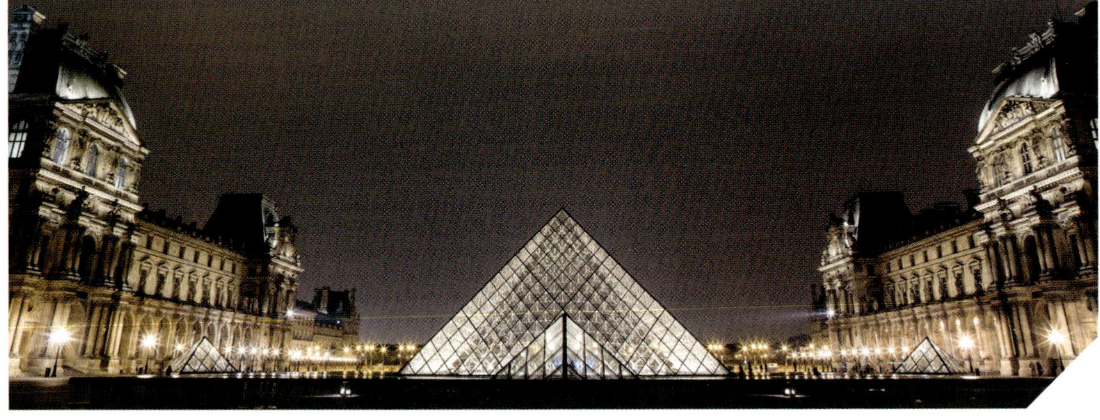

I M Pei
Pyramide du Louvre, 1989
Cour Napoleon, Palais Louvre, Paris, France
Photo: Adrien Sifre (creative commons)
https://www.flickr.com/photos/adriensifre/8614860569/

Perhaps the earliest example of this is the Crystal Palace, designed by Joseph Paxton in 1851 for the Great Exhibition of the Works of Industry of All Nations. The building wowed six million people in Hyde Park, London in the six months it was open. At the time, it was a marvel to see a building made of glass, and it became a symbol of Britain's industrial and technological progress, as well as modernity. Jumping forward more than 130 years, another example of a glass structure as modernist symbol is the Pyramide du Louvre, 1989, by Chinese-born American architect IM Pei. These glass and steel sculptural forms completed in 1989 are a stark contrast to the French Renaissance architecture of the Louvre Palace, creating a modernist statement that, while receiving a negative reaction from some Parisians at the time, has become widely accepted as a symbol of contemporary Paris.

Completed in 2008, the TKTS ticket booth is a solid glass building that makes a sculptural statement in the centre of bustling Times Square, New York. The booth uses glass in a way that is both conceptually and technically impressive. With concept design by Australian architects Choi Ropiha and design development by Perkins Eastman, the structure acts as a booth for buying tickets on one side, while the other features a long wide staircase lit in red that acts as a viewing platform and a meeting point. The entire structure is made of glass, including internal glass beams that transfer weight to all-glass bearing walls, made with structural glass laminate, developed in collaboration with structural glass innovator Dewhurst Macfarlane.[12] A striking object, the booth uses glass not for the effect of transparency, but to create a memorable and distinctive presence in the centre of New York.

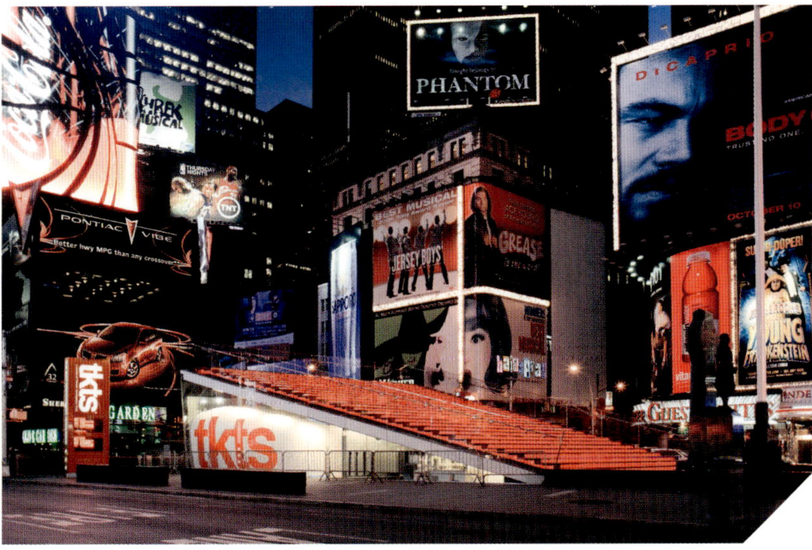

John Choi & Tai Ropiha (CHROFI)
TKTS Tickets Booth, 2008
Times Square,
New York City, USA
Photo: Emily Wamsteker

Glass and light — absence and presence

Glass can be used to create absence or presence, but one category allows it to do both. The combination of glass and light, particularly in the case of chandeliers and their contemporary reinterpretation, allows glass to be absent, as transparency is fundamental and light becomes the hero; *and* present, as the entire repeating structure provides an illuminating display.

Glass objects strung together and illuminated as a collection have become a major trend in glass lighting, along with other reinterpretations of the chandelier that use new materials or shapes to reinvent the form. One of the most impressive examples is by British designer Thomas Heatherwick, whose 1994 installation for the Wellcome Trust atrium in London features 142,000 glass spheres (or 15 tonnes of glass) suspended on nearly a million metres of wire.[13] This monumental work has provided inspiration for a number of similar installations and ideas in which glass is suspended and illuminated.

Swarovski's Crystal Palace, which ran each year at the Milan Furniture Fair from 2006 to 2010, commissioned well-known designers and architects to create lighting installations and chandeliers, with highlights including Arne Quinze's *Dream saver*, 2007, a tunnel-like installation filled with suspended crystals. Another

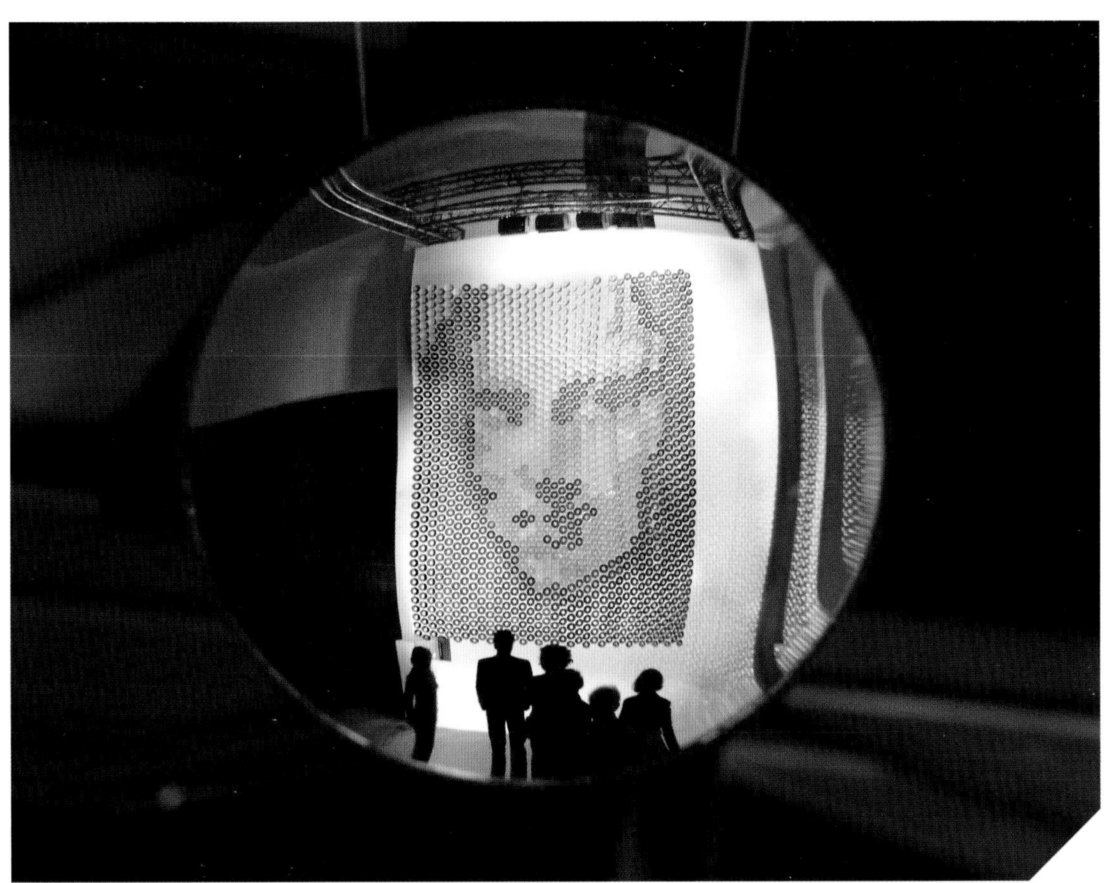

Paul Cocksedge
Veil, 2008
Swarovski crystals
3940 x 2970
Installation view,
Swarovski Crystal Palace,
Salone del Mobile,
©Salone del Mobile
Photo: Leo Torri

conceptual piece, *Veil*, 2008, by UK designer Paul Cocksedge, featured a four-metre-high curtain made of 1,440 crystals, with a pattern in the curtain that can only be seen in a mirror, when the face of the Mona Lisa appears as if by magic in the crystals.[14]

At the Milan Furniture Fair in 2014, Czech brand Lasvit held a similar exhibition of new installations and chandeliers that play with glass in new ways, including *Magnetic*, 2014, by Libor Sostak, which features a series of glass objects hung from wire. In this case, the height of the objects slowly shifts, creating a wave that undulates through space. Other reinterpretations of the chandelier in the exhibition include the *Frozen light*, 2014, by Czech designer (and art director of Lasvit) Maxim Velčovský, which looks like ice; and *Crystal rock*, 2014, by Arik Levy, in which the pieces are formed to imitate precious rocks.[15]

Glass — always modern

Glass has undergone a number of technical and performance innovations, enabling it to be used in increasingly novel ways in architecture and design. Starting with the glass curtain wall, the developments have continued over the past 100 years: thermal and environmental glass, shatter-proof glass, load-bearing and structural glass, thermo-welded glass, photovoltaic cells that transform light, and iGlass, which changes from clear to opaque at the flick of a switch. The latest thing? Transparent solar panels, recently announced by researchers at Michigan State University[16] (though they are yet to be sold commercially). Further innovations will no doubt follow: Ulrich Knaack, Head of the Facade Research Group in Delft, envisages a future in which glass will be folded or moulded in situ.[17]

Endlessly flexible, glass is an increasingly versatile material for use in architecture, interiors and design. However, its strength as a material also comes from its capacity to signify and symbolise. In his 1938 inaugural address as Director of Architecture at Armour Institute of Technology, Mies said: 'We must remember that everything depends on how we use a material, not on the material itself.'[18] Through glass, architects and designers can imply trustworthiness, create a flow for living, or bring the outdoors in. They can also signify modernism, highlight the beauty of landscape, or dazzle the senses in a crystalline display of light.

Jean Nouvel
Bâtiment de la Fondation Cartier pour l'art contemporain, 1994
Boulevard Raspail, Paris, France
Photo: Luc Boegly

1. Keith Eggener, 'The uses of daylight', designobserver.com, 14 May 2012, viewed 23 September 2014, places.designobserver.com/feature/louis-curtiss-boley-building/32938/
2. Gary Allen, 'Apple store glass staircases', ifoapplestore.com, nd, viewed 23 September 2014, www.ifoapplestore.com/apple-store-glass-staircases/
3. Paul Finch, 'Crystal balls', newstatesman.com, 24 June 2002, viewed 23 September 2014, www.newstatesman.com/node/143264
4. '60 seconds with Richard Rogers', lloyds.com, 22 July 2013, viewed 23 September 2014, www.lloyds.com/news-and-insight/news-and-features/interviews/interviews-2013/60-seconds-with-richard-rogers
5. Claire Thomas, 'Google was cubicleland when we started designing offices for them', dezeen.com, 17 March 2014, viewed 23 September 2014, www.dezeen.com/2014/03/17/office-design-google-clive-wilkinson-interview/
6. 'House NA/Sou Fujimoto Architects, archdaily.com, 30 April 2012, viewed 23 September 2014, www.archdaily.com/230533/house-na-sou-fujimoto-architects/
7. Danny Hudson, 'Santambrogiomilano: glass house series', designboom.com, 12 January 2013, viewed 23 September 2014, www.designboom.com/architecture/carlosantambrogio-glass-house-series/
8. Stephen Heller, 'People in glass apartments', designobserver.com, 1 October 2009, viewed 23 September 2014, designobserver.com/feature/people-in-glass-apartments/11167
9. 'Greenhouse at Grüningen Botanical Garden by Buehrer Wuest Architekten', dezeen.com, 3 September 2012, viewed 23 September 2014, www.dezeen.com/2012/09/03/greenhouse-at-gruningen-botanical-garden-by-buehrer-wuest-architekten/
10. Megan Sveiven, 'AD classics: Fondation Cartier/Jean Nouvel', archdaily.com, 26 October 2010, viewed 23 September 2014, www.archdaily.com/84666/ad-classics-fondation-cartier-jean-nouvel/
11. Blaine Brownell, 'Manipulating the material mode: the transformation of material meaning in contemporary Japanese design' in Elvin Karana, Owain Pedgley and Valentina Rognoli (eds), *Materials experience: Fundamentals of materials and design*, Elsevier, Oxford, 2014.
12. 'DuPont™SentryGlas® case study, TKTS booth in Times Square advances use of structural laminated glass', dupont.com, nd, viewed 23 September 2014, www2.dupont.com/SafetyGlass/en_US/assets/pdfs/tkts-structural-glass.pdf
13. 'Bleigiessen, Wellcome Trust, London, UK', heatherwick.com, nd, viewed 23 September 2014, www.heatherwick.com/bleigiessen/
14. *Veil*, 2008, Paul Cocksedge, swarovskicrystalpalace.com, nd, viewed 23 September 2014, www.swarovskicrystalpalace.com/swarovskicrystalpalace/collections/custom/veil
15. Ben Hobson, 'Lasvit's new lighting collections "combine craftsmanship with advanced technology"', dezeen.com, 11 April 2014, viewed 23 September 2014, www.dezeen.com/2014/04/11/lasvit-emotions-glass-lighting-show-milan-2014-maarten-baas-arik-levy-maxim-velcovsky/
16. 'Solar energy that doesn't block the view', msutoday.msu.edu, 19 August 2014, viewed 23 September 2014, msutoday.msu.edu/news/2014/solar-energy-that-doesnt-block-the-view/
17. Ulrich Knaack, Tillmann Klein and Marcel Bilow (eds), *Imagine 01 facades*, 010 Publishers, Rotterdam, 2008.
18. Ludwig Mies van der Rohe, 'Inaugural address as Director of Architecture at Armour Institute of Technology,' 1938, reprinted from *Philip Johnson, Mies van der Rohe*, 3rd edn, Museum of Modern Art, New York, 1978, pp 196–200.

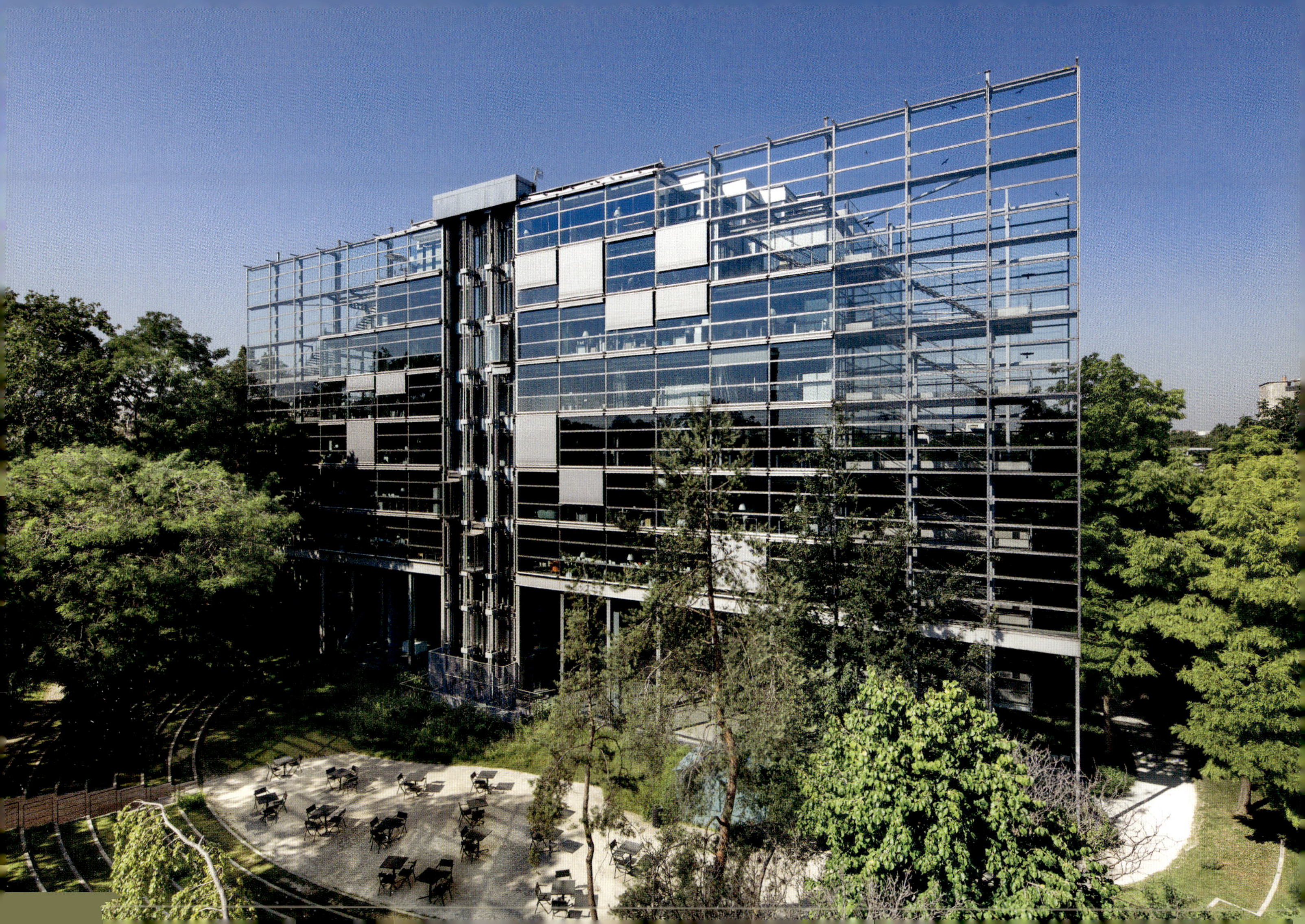

Adelaide Botanic Garden's three centuries of glass

Stephen Forbes

Botanists, and perhaps plants, treat glass with some suspicion. The idea of placing a physical barrier between a plant and the Sun, while still expecting an environment suitable for photosynthesis, seems poorly conceived. The transformation of light into life through photosynthesis is the basis of life on Earth. While a glass 'house' might facilitate control of heating, humidity and watering, an Edenic environment for a plant begins with photosynthesis, which is dependent on light wavelengths largely within the visible range and particularly at the blue and red ends of the visible spectrum. Miraculously, glass does transmit photosynthetically-active light, although that ability depends, sometimes inversely, on other qualities of the particular glass. These other qualities include heat insulation, light diffusion, surface treatments (for instance, reflective or self-cleaning coatings), colour and tensile strength. The audacity of placing a physical barrier between a plant and the Sun through the construction of glass houses has seen some remarkable successes.

The story of glass houses, as displayed in Adelaide Botanic Garden, is a powerful one spanning three centuries, but rarely read in a coherent way. Botanical historian, Frans Stafleu, suggests the narrative might begin with Luca Ghini at Pisa botanic garden in 1547. Ghini utilised south-facing windows for the successful cultivation and overwintering of southern and south-eastern European species of *Nerium*, *Citrus* and *Laurus* in tubs — the so-called cubicula tepida. But Pisa's claim as the originator of botanic gardens, herbaria and glass houses might be extravagant — the story might well have begun in ancient Rome.

Cubicula tepida (or warm rooms) with south-facing windows expanded to grand orangeries. However, the use of masonry to support glass is limiting — such constructions are well suited for orangeries into which plants might simply be moved over winter. The limitations on both the area and quality of glass (especially on ceilings) present a challenging and often hopeless situation for photosynthesis. Wood, of course, is a fine alternative to masonry for a purpose-built glass house, and provides a light, strong and malleable fabric to support glass. The choice of timber is critical. At Cambridge, the 1888 pine glass houses managed 40 years before being replaced with teak in the 1930s; and the teak lasted nearly 75 years prior to a full pane-by-pane restoration in 2005. Sadly Adelaide's timber 1868 Victoria House succumbed to the elements long ago, although the masonry plinth and pond survived a range of iterations.

The Industrial Revolution presented new opportunities for plant collection across the globe, while new horticultural technologies, such as the Wardian case,

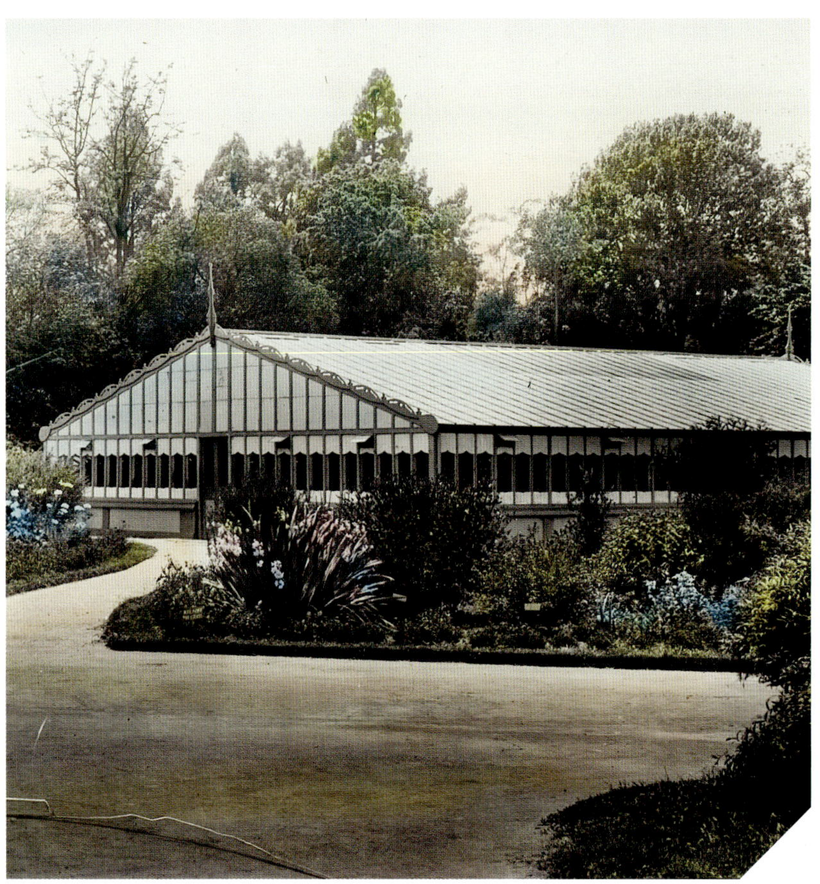

allowed for the successful shipment of new plant discoveries. The first test of Dr Nathaniel Ward's glazed cases saw the successful shipping of tender plants from London to Sydney in 1833. The arrival of a primrose in full bloom was a 'sensation ... so great, that it was necessary to keep the case under constant strict surveillance'.[1] Of course, the Industrial Revolution also allowed the glass house to blossom.

Adelaide's botanic garden begins on Light's 1837 Plan of Adelaide. However, a series of unfortunate events saw the Adelaide Botanic Garden only reach its current site in 1855. George Francis, the Garden's first director, built a fine domed conservatory in 1859, which disappeared a century later under the Royal Adelaide Hospital's extension into the Garden.

Francis's successor, Richard Schomburgk, oversaw construction of the 1868 timber-framed Victoria House to show off the giant Amazon waterlily (*Victoria amazonica*) he discovered with his brother, Sir Robert Schomburgk, in British Guiana (now Guyana). Their specimens allowed London botanist John Lindley to describe the waterlily for science in 1837 and dedicate the waterlily to Queen Victoria as *Victoria regia*. The waterlily is, astonishingly, intimately involved in glass-house design and construction, providing the blueprint for its own cultivation.

The repeal of the *Glass Act* in 1845, together with advances in the working of iron, allowed Joseph Paxton to envisage, design and build a conservatory based on the architecture of the waterlily's leaf at Chatsworth House (the Duke of Devonshire's estate in Derbyshire). Paxton's conservatory was the first to allow sufficient light to penetrate the structure, to allow flowering and saw the first waterlily flower in cultivation in 1849. This success, and the charismatic nature of the waterlily, led to the establishment of so-called 'Victoria houses' in botanic gardens in Adelaide and around the world. Further, Paxton's successful adoption of the lily leaf as a model for the Chatsworth House conservatory ultimately resulted in the acceptance of his proposal, still based on the waterlily leaf, for the Crystal Palace — the home of the 1851 Great Exhibition in Hyde Park. The Crystal Palace, relocated to Sydenham, was later home to the Sydenham School of the Arts, where glass designer René Lalique was likely influenced by Paxton's audacious biomimicry. The Crystal Palace remains feted in architecture as the progenitor of the glass-and-steel skyscrapers that provide the fabric of modern cities. The rapid development of glass-and-iron technology, and new approaches to design, saw a proliferation of grand conservatories internationally.

In Adelaide the fine Palm House, 1877, signifies the Industrial Revolution's technology and remains a rare

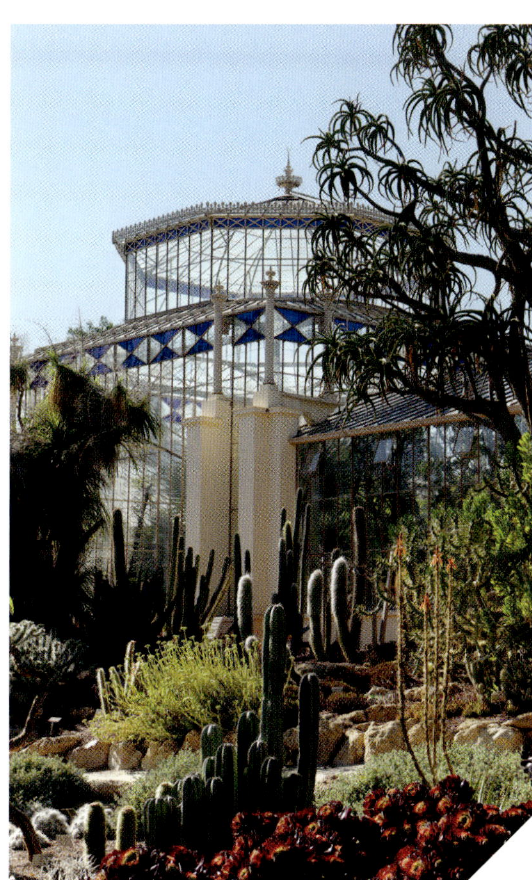

◂◂

Victoria House, 1868
Adelaide Botanic Garden,
North Terrace, Adelaide
Photo: Botanic Gardens Archives

◂

Gustav Runge
Palm House, 1877
Adelaide Botanic Garden,
North Terrace, Adelaide
Photo: Grant Hancock

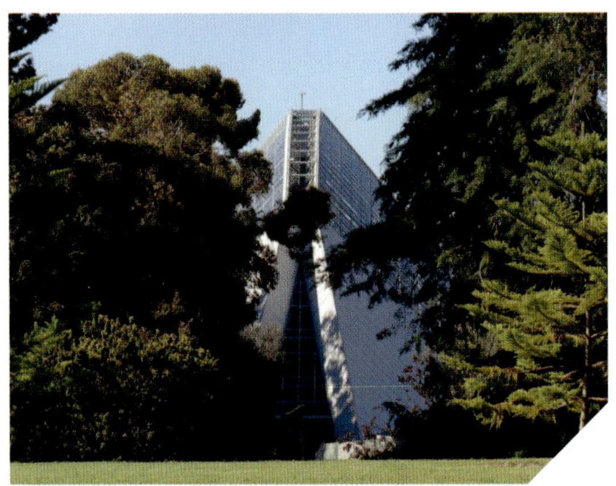

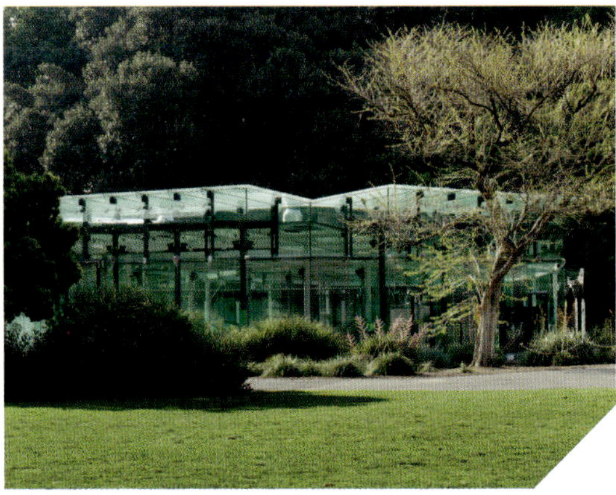

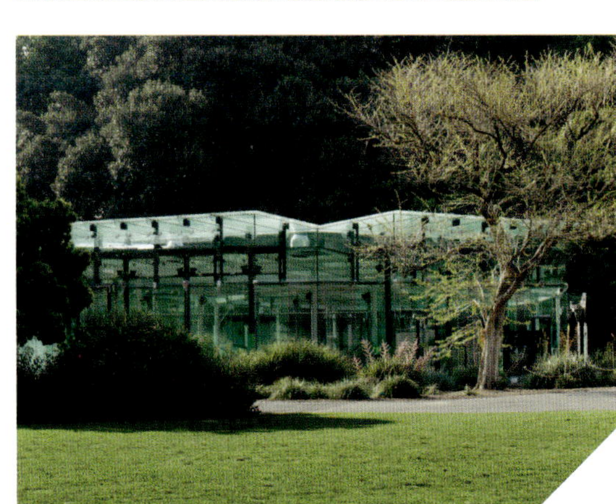

◂

Guy Maron
Bicentennial Conservatory, 1989
Adelaide Botanic Garden,
North Terrace, Adelaide
Photo: Grant Hancock

▾

Flightpath Architects
Amazon Waterlily Pavilion, 2007
Adelaide Botanic Garden,
North Terrace, Adelaide
Photo: Grant Hancock

jewel. Prefabricated from wrought and cast iron, and likely flat-packed from J Hoper of Bremen in Germany under supervising architect Gustav Runge, this 100-foot (30.5 metre) long and 30-foot (9.1 metre) wide structure reached Adelaide in 1875 and opened in 1877. The Palm House was beautifully restored under Brian Morley's directorship and re-opened in 1995. Last year Jess Hood's *Equinox* photography exhibition in the Santos Museum of Economic Botany explored the Garden's archive and the relationship between glass, light and life.

The Gardens waited another century for the largest single-span conservatory in the world: 100 metres long, 47 metres wide and 27 metres high. Architect Guy Maron's steel-framed construction incorporates 2434 m^2 of toughened glass panels, and is clad with insulated aluminium panels at its base. The curved segmental and conical form evolved from the need to standardise and prefabricate glazing and framing prior to it being lifted into position. The prefabricated aluminium-framed glass panels comprise a series of 28-metre long and 2.4-metre wide assemblies, supported by 28 trusses. Guy's groundbreaking design and execution won the RAIA Sir Zelman Cowan Award for Public Buildings in 1989 and, after 25 years, was recently recognised with the RAIA SA Enduring Architecture Award and provisionally listed as South Australia's youngest heritage building.

The remnants of the 1868 Victoria House provided the brief for the new Amazon Waterlily Pavilion, completed in 2007 to coincide with the sesquicentenary of the Adelaide Botanic Garden opening to visitors on its current site. The new millennium allowed the construction of the temple-like glass house, utilising 80 per cent structural glass elements including roofs, support beams, transfer wall beams and load-bearing columns, with only a small amount of steel providing some internal support. Here, the glass performs the work ordinarily done by concrete and steel, again necessitating groundbreaking design solutions and wholly customised fittings, including triple-laminated glass columns with a load-bearing of 2.5 tonnes. An Australian first, the completed glass house won the Australian Engineering Excellence Award for Connell Wagner in 2008.

So, the story of three centuries of glass-house design is well told here. The first timber-framed Victoria House opened in 1868; the cast and wrought-iron Palm House characterising the Industrial Revolution opened in 1877; the landmark aluminium-framed Bicentennial Conservatory opened in 1989; and the load-bearing structural glass Amazon Waterlily Pavilion opened in 2007. These exemplars of 19th-, 20th- and 21st-century glass-house technology illustrate major advances in maximising light penetration and allowing plant life, minimising energy and other resource requirements and managing the continuing challenges of growing plants and maintaining both the physical and growing environment. Together, with the presence of the 1868 Victoria House still evident in the original pond, Adelaide Botanic Gardens' presentation of the history of glass houses is likely unrivalled internationally.

1. Stephen H Ward, *On Wardian cases for plants, and their applications*, John van Voorst, London, 1854, p 17.

Looking through glass,
or the visibility of invisibility

Thomas Mical

Transparency in glass is never quite as it first appears. Transparency today has been naturalised — it is often the default position of surfaces, rarely a spectacular exception. The medium of glass is often imagined as an absence, but to our everyday sensory experience the glass surfaces of the hypermodern world are never purely empty, never purely neutral. Architectural glass today retains a very slight resistance, something like an ultrathin gauze-like filter between our perception and our cognition of the 'see-through' world. In the past, handcrafted looking glasses, anatomical models and other functional devices in glass calibrated and clarified sets of relations, at multiple levels simultaneously.

In the origin myths of architectural transparency stretching back to the birth of the industrial production of glass, glass was the vehicle for equating seeing with knowing. Nineteenth-century innovations leading to 20th-century float glass and other processes marked the turning point, in that manufactured lenses (later screens) were also the origin of mechanised seeing and new techniques of increasingly precise and invasive industrial vision and representation, from photography to X-rays.

The modernist fetishisation of transparency (as concept) in glass (as matter) naturalises this origin myth, while using these new media formations as sources for recall. From the visionary projection of Ludwig Mies van der Rohe's 1919 Glass Skyscraper competition design, to the clever rhetoric of László Moholy-Nagy's 1938 *The new vision*, the Bauhaus agenda of abstraction serving industrialisation filtered into and redefined the dominant modernist optic, one that was relearned and repeated compulsively over the interwar period (and after). This use of glass is performative in production and in daily use, and there is a passive exhibitionism sustained within today's omni-transparency. The allure of the architectural image of glass as signifier of modernity was just as obsessively pursued as the desire for transparency. And it is a curious condition that today, still, in most people's imaginations, these two conditions — concept < > matter — are equated, again and again. We can also recognise that in glass, the differences between concepts and materiality of transparency can also be mapped onto the two divergent meanings of sense (as common sensical and rational, but also as sensual and experiential), and in this way the sense of transparency is a complex of relations, not a singular ideal.

The cool utopias of the 20th century operated as large-scale diagrams of social relations operating with transparent optical-spatial conduits of indoor-outdoor abstract environments. At the small scale, we can recognise the tendency of individual glass surfaces of 20th-century modern architecture as indexical, as signalling the proximity of this utopianism and ideal optics. Thus the utopian and indexical come to support a pervasive myth of omni-transparency to support our clear and distinct visual perception of the differential surfaces of the spaces of modernity. Glass surfaces in their near invisibility point to other contexts, and so are always indexical (borrowing from Rosalind Krauss and Charles Sanders Pierce before her) — the mere presence of sometimes see-through and sometimes reflective glass surfaces recall other situations of transparency, such as in glasses or mirrors. Glass itself, when industrialised in production, is indexical also of its origins in manufactured modernity, which then points to other traits of modernity (such as repetition, efficiency or extensivity). The rise of the useful glass surface in modern architecture works beyond functional determinism to operate also as a recurring imaginary condition of transparency, a deliberate fantasy, a looking-glass condition, perhaps even as the mirror-stage of self-recognition or self-reflection of the modern architect's ambitions for clarity and certainty.

The pulsation of the differential spatial layering of modern architecture, intertwined with the material facts of construction, was used to diminish difference and support an active subscription to a universal space. The functional space of extension and subdivision, which requires first a model of spatial extensibility, postulated on a model of uniform optical transparency. This universal space of modernity — the smooth free-flowing plazas, the efficient empty lobbies and other unencumbered minimalist interiorities — supports this homogenous visual field of smooth space.

Certainly there were exceptions to this convergence of universal space and glass technology, such as Bruce Goff's recycling of glass ashtrays into diffracting residential glass walls, or Samuel Mockbee's recycling of discarded auto windshields into a glass canopy, but in most cases mechanisation took command. Consider the edge of a piece of glass: it reveals the process of making, the depth of the material and compounds the optical performance with an eccentric condition of edge-being. In modern architecture usually the edge reveals the dominant and recessive ideas driving the process of making, but with glass surfaces the edge is (ideally) banished or concealed from the force effect of planarity. Aligned sheets and surfaces of glass are preconceived as smoothed, following the spatial logic of endless continuity that they reflect. The telltale edges are hidden or displaced outside the realm of perception, ideally exiled, while their performance criteria and indexical qualities are revealed. This appears as a new form of glass construction, organised as a smooth space of an expansive omni-transparency, but still assembled from contiguous and identical pieces. Glass is the foundational skin condition of expansive spatial presence, one that offers the promise of exposing the mysteries of interiority while reflecting the image of the self back to the self.

The dissociation of the materiality of glass seeing through the invisible has long been productively and provocatively glossed over in the practice of architecture. Glass and seeing-through are often equivocated, made the same, in many of the monuments and documents of modern architecture. Like the empty cell or blank sign, glass is an empty medium, a null data set supporting an architecture that appears to be without intrinsic content. The negative, empty, or blank signifier presumed in transparency-in-glass doesn't ever fully exist — it is always troubled by the hint of reflections, the mechanics of emergent illusions and subtly distorted desires to see into the sense of the world.

There needs to be some accounting of these distortions within the glass world. The potentially haunting effects of a pure omni-transparency, produced in the haunting slight reflections and outlines of ourselves mirrored, and these reflections merged into the outlines of elements within the shallow spaces behind the glass, may be a flatland realm of after-images, of apparitions and optical traces whose purpose is to recall the slight divergence of glass and transparency. The particular optical tension of seeing the space behind collapsed with the space before is now commonplace in glass lobbies and passageways. It is a tension that can work as a generator of optical delight from the nearly see-through spaces of late modernity. The experiential gestural and visceral experience of glass blowing, leaving traces of the muscle memory and prior molten states have been translated into the objectified industrial production of glass, created with advanced performance specifications. This can be seen as a demystification or displacement, like the processes leading from alchemy to chemistry. Displaced into industry and media, the fanciful alchemical traces barely linger within our current a priori expectations of transparency as immediacy.

Cognitive reflection upon the optical reflections of modern architecture leads us to question the purity of transparency and the indexical glass surfaces of modern architecture. Seeing through transparency operates under specific contextual conditions, and the belief in their permanance and uniformity are thus culturally determined and an acquired manner of understanding seeing. From stories of people running from cinematic trains to people walking into glass doors, seeing and knowing are more accurately processes of acculturation and accumulation, not givens. To see complete transparency, or at a higher level of skill, to see actual invisibility, requires hypersensitive attention, and experience within the paradigm of mechanised seeing, as well as familiarity with the habits of a type of seeing in the ceramics of glass, which seems to exist as a default position. There are actually a great many ways to represent transparency, and simultaneously many materials to accomplish transparency beyond glass technics, and to this end the architectural search will have to become one of 'what comes after transparency?'.

Indeed, there is such a modern sensitivity to the multiple modes of understanding seeing, which appears when glass surfaces appear. This was an ambition supported by those early avant-garde writings of Mies and Maholy-Nagy. Mies certainly showed the dislocation of glass and its indexical qualities in his 1929 Barcelona Pavilion, where the reflectivity of the mullioned green glass walls is mirrored in the hollow granite walls, also highly polished but cut wafer-thin to create translucency. Both materials thus framed reveal their original molten state and their cultural performative expectations at the edge of normative transparency-in-glass. In response to this project, in the late 20th century Japanese architect Toyo Ito theorised a range of new Miesian transparencies, including aquatic transparency, erotic transparency, and opaque transparency.[1] His work, and that of the diagram architects of that era such as SANAA, seeks to minimise the differences and delays between sharp lines and open voids within spatial planning diagrams and their translation into the ultra-thin abstraction of material formal surfaces on the construction site. Today the engineered transparency of architectural glass continues to be a recurring source of questioning the normative universal spaces, which can deliver possible advances, as there are now structural glass columns and glass stairs available.[2] The glass surface has become not only the apparent phenomenological skin of the world, but now also points to emerging invisible structures within.

Glass is a type of seeing originating in the craft process of ceramics, but it also operates as an object that potentially proposes a new type of glass culture. The early 20th-century Russian artist Vladimir Tatlin claimed that art and architecture would operate within a revolutionary 'culture of materials', which today would be tending towards a culture of invisibility. Imagine taking a real-time survey today of a spatial situation (e.g. a waiting room, classroom, grocery store) by tracking the location and placement of all the glass elements simultaneously. These would be a minority of the physical materiality of the environment, but would draw a majority of our attention to their uses (touchscreens, glasses, thermos linings etc). Such a conjectural mapping of operational glass culture, when interlaced with acts of glass (as art, as disruptor, as transformer), points towards an emerging new model of glass culture and glass environments in which the false equivalence of looking and knowing could be dissociated, giving rise to a greater variety of new optics, strange encounters and unknown pleasures. Transparency today is now something more pervasive, less aligned with seeing and moving closer to tropes of transmission. Transparency can be liberated from glass, and invisibility is a closely related ideal dependent on prior models of transparency, and has emerged as a multi-disciplinary endeavor in its own right. The persistence of the glass surface, crafted or manufactured, is still a material fact and aesthetic opportunity. But it seems as if every generation must come to understand its own mode of transparency.

1. See Ulrich Schneider's *Toyo Ito: Blurring architecture 1971–2005*, Charta, Milan, 1999.
2. See Michael Bell and Jeannie Kim (eds), *Engineered transparency*, Princeton Architectural Press, New York, 2009.

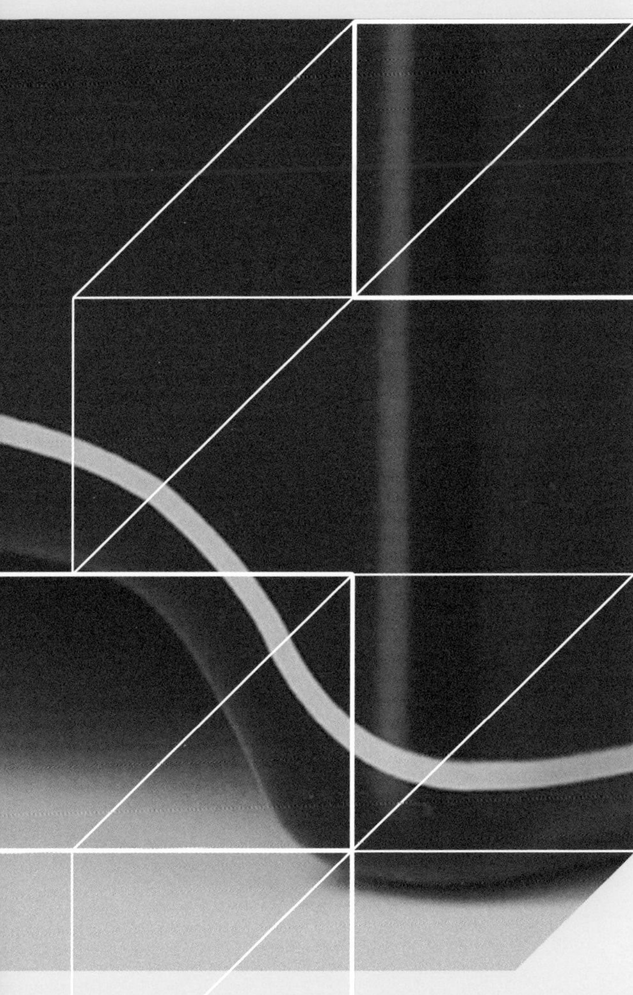

Andrew Simpson / Vert Design

born 1982, Darwin, Northern Territory
lives Sydney, New South Wales
Vert Design, established 2005,
Sydney, New South Wales

Andrew Simpson is an accomplished industrial designer and product engineer, and he is the principal of Vert Design, a design house and studio practice based in Redfern, Sydney. As an industrial designer, his practice is human focused — the end user's needs guide the way he develops products. Rather than starting with a selected material, Simpson works with the material most appropriate for the function, and following this decision, he decides on the method of production.

When he was at university Simpson worked as an assistant glass blower and cold worker, finishing and polishing works for Robert Wynne of Denizen Glass. He found that this grounding in 'real world' design gave him a unique set of skills that he has been able to utilise throughout his career. For Simpson, glass studios are very much still modelled on the traditions of the 19th-century factory floor: work was developed and pricing set within fixed costs for material and labour, and items were produced within a specific time, whilst also allowing for failure rates due to the handmade process. While working with Wynne, Simpson seized any spare time to produce his own cost-efficient production range.

Since graduating with an Honours degree in Industrial Design from the University of Technology, Sydney, Simpson has become the 'go to' designer for other leading Australian designers wishing to work in glass, and in 2005 he founded Vert Design, to provide innovation to glass blowing in Australia.

Designing with glass is always about compromise and astute knowledge. Simpson's knowledge has led to him brokering the design and manufacture process for a number of designs including Trent Jansen's *Long neck*, 2007, made from recycled bottles; Adam Goodrum's *Boab*, 2007, and *Revolution vase*, 2007; and the award-winning *Stilla* carafe, 2009, designed in partnership with Sydney-based silversmith Oliver Smith.

Working with accomplished glass blowers such as Ben Edols to prototype the *Stilla* carafe, Simpson drew upon Vert Design's experience in developing deep-drawing techniques for Adam Goodrum's *Boab*, which helped them in refining *Stilla*'s exacting geometry. While searching for an off-shore producer for *Stilla*, manufacturers told Simpson that it couldn't be made in glass; however because he had prototyped the work, he was able to show his glass sample, stating 'yes it can and this is how'.

This drive to challenge preconceived ideas about glass production has led Simpson to investigate new forms of mould making. Traditionally, glass-shaping moulds are made using turned wood moulds in the hot shop, but Simpson contested this and, drawing on his industrial design skills, he successfully created CAD (Computer Aided Design) moulds in aluminium for a range of small-run production jobs.

From this glass-focused beginning, Vert Design has expanded its range of services from concept development through to detailed design, including CAD modelling and prototyping, as well as engineering and production management for clients ranging from boutique brands to multinational organisations. Vert also produces a small range of production items.

Working within the virtual and with glass, Vert has carved a niche designing bottles and packaging for a number of companies, including Blackmores, as well as working with bio-medical companies in the production of single-dose applicators.

Margaret Hancock Davis

Previous page
Detail of the decorative punt on the *Alaskan Rock Bottle*, 2013
glass
200 x 150 x 100
Photo: Andy Lewis

▸

The *Incalmo* series are made from recycled solar panels.
Incalmo, 2010
soda lime glass
vase 300 x 100 dia.
Photo: Andy Lewis

▸▸

Simpson developed deep drawing on CAD for designer Adam Goodrum enabling the production and manufacture of *Boab*, 2007.
Boab, 2007
sodalime glass
800 x 400 dia. (large)
Photo: Andy Lewis

▸▸▸

Experience gained from *Boab* enables Simpson to work out the exacting geometry of *Stilla Carafe*, 2009, designed in partnership with Oliver Smith.
Stilla Carafe, 2009
blown glass
180 dia.
Photo: Courtesy the artist

◂

Vert Design's high quality renders of glass have seen them work with a number of companies to design bottles clients have included Blackmores.
Blackmores bottle cad render, 2014
Photo: Vert Design

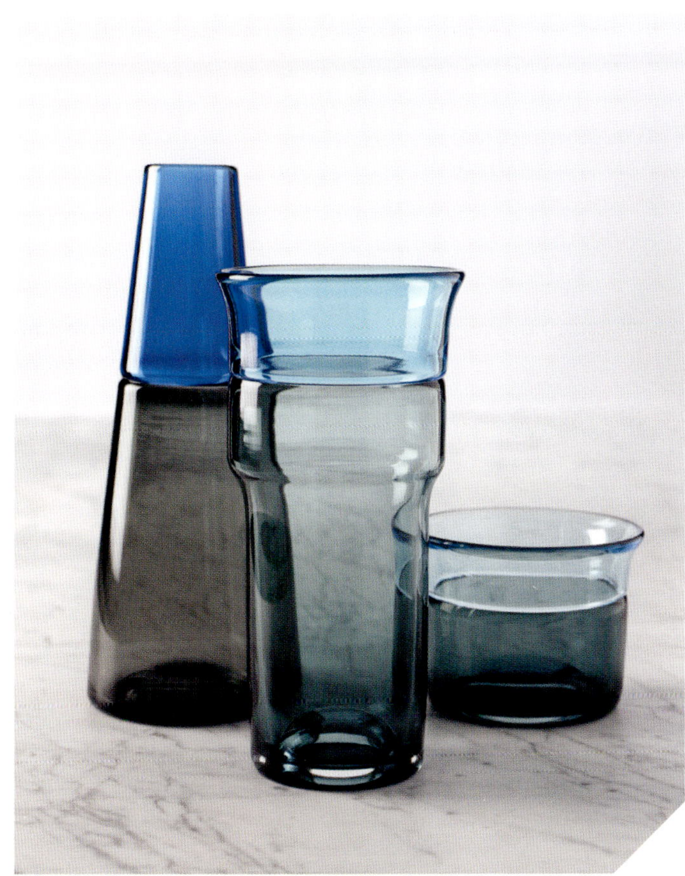

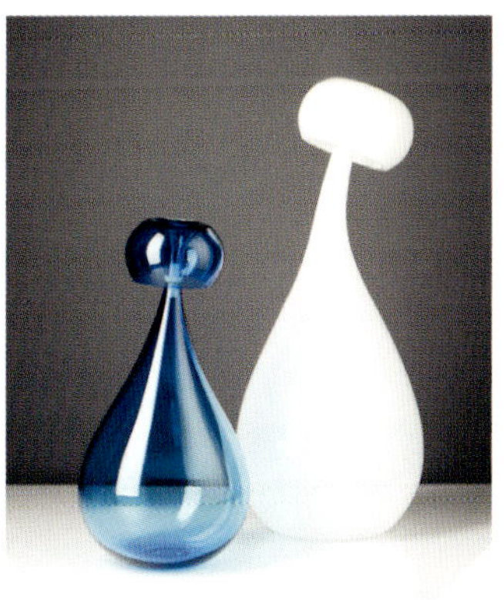

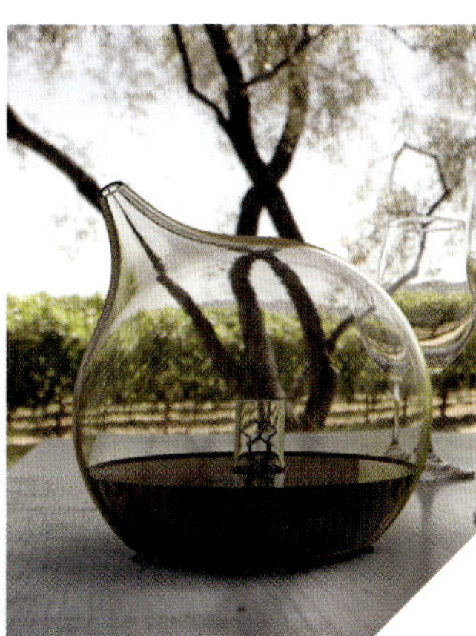

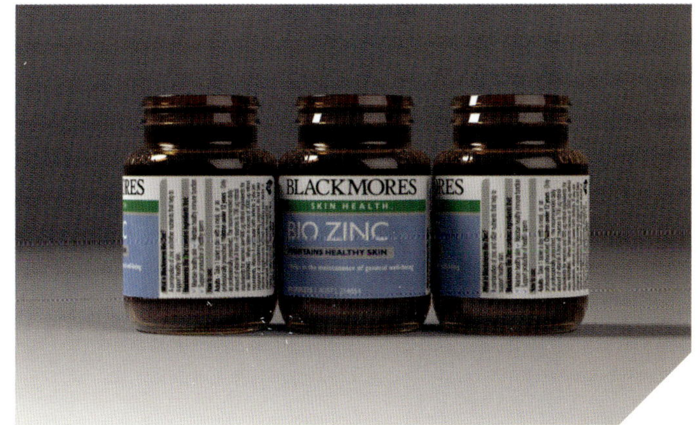
BLACKMORES
SKIN HEALTH
BIO ZINC

Alaskan Rock

Alaskan Rock is a small-batch, artisanal vodka made in Australia with packaging and branding by Vert Design. The brief was to create a design that would have a masculine edge and reflect the brand's strong and distinctive spirit.

The bottle design is made from black hand-finished Mexican glass, with white, raised lettering and a distinctive sculptural punt. Punts, the indentation in the base of a bottle, are a legacy of the glass-blowing process, which were made redundant by industrial glass-making techniques — they now exist purely as an aesthetic detail. Vert's team decided to exaggerate the punt's formal qualities, creating a bottle with a sculptural form denoting an Alaskan mountain range.

The prototype was blown by a team of glass blowers at Canberra Glassworks, and the finished design produced in Mexico.

Alaskan Rock, 2013, was the winner of London's D&AD Packaging Design Award, 2013 and in the Best New Pack category in the PKN Shelf Shout Awards, 2013.

cad render steel mould, 2009
300 x 200 x 150
Photo: Vert Design

Wishing to push glass blowing techniques Simpson and vert design produces glass blowing moulds in a range of materials. These cad render images are of the production mould for the *Alaskan Rock* bottles currently produced by master glassblowers in Mexico.
Alaskan Rock steel mould, 2009
bottle 300 x 200 x 200
Photo: Vert Design

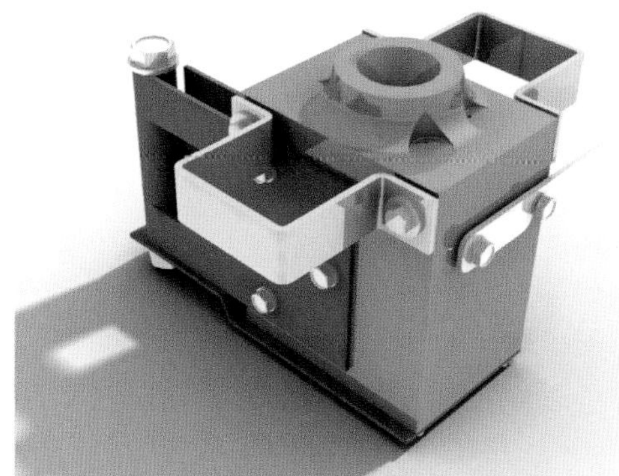

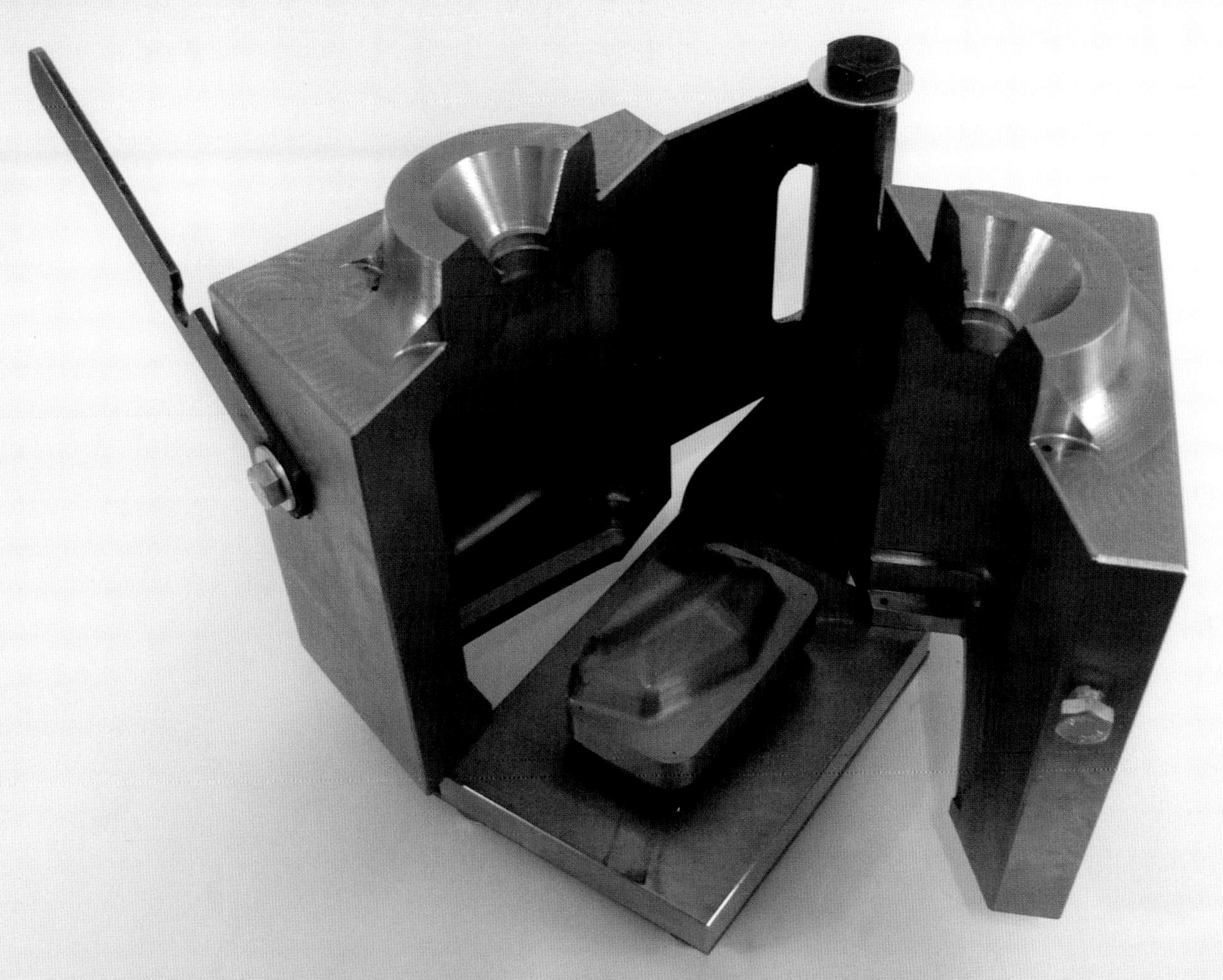

▸
Prototypes of the *Alaskan Rock* bottles were produced by a team of glassblowers at the Canberra Glassworks.
Photo: Vert Design

▸▸
Alaskan Rock Bottle, 2013
glass
200 x 150 x 100
Photo: Andy Lewis

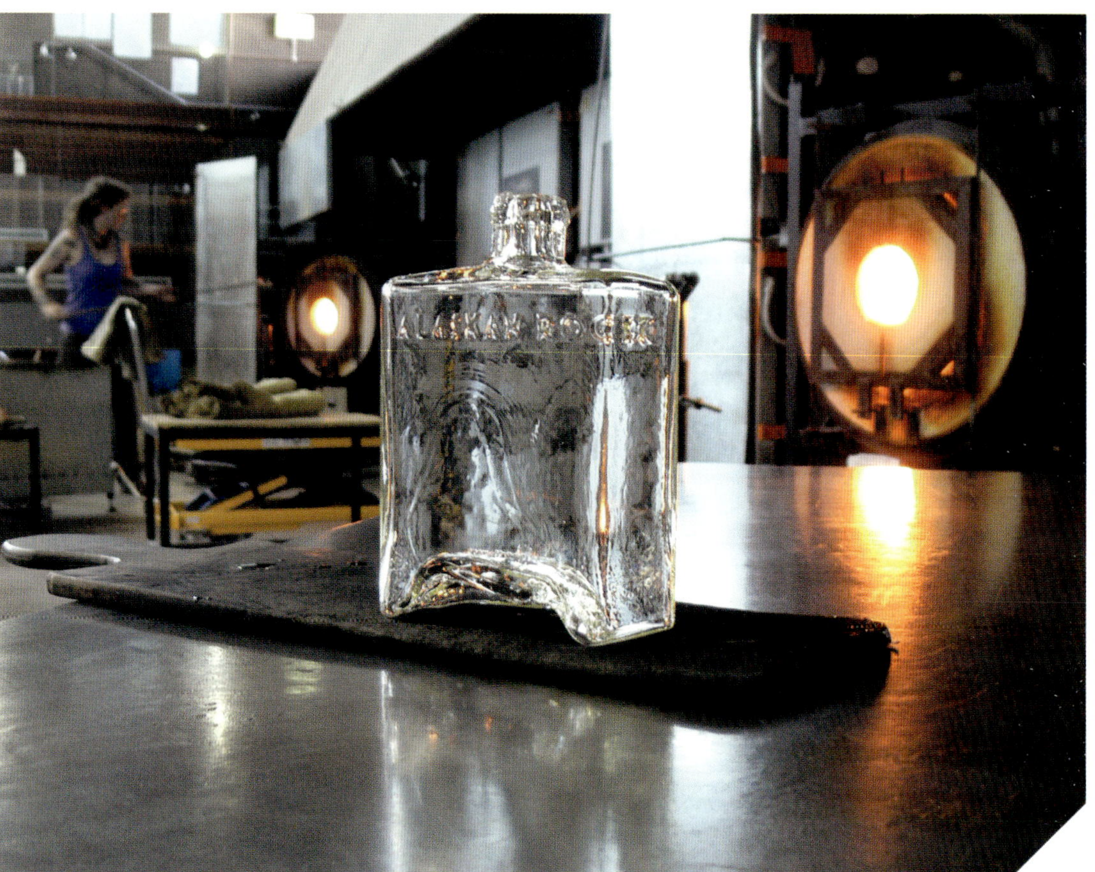

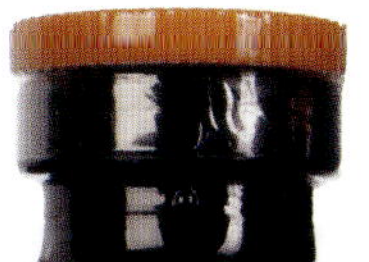

ALASKAN ROCK

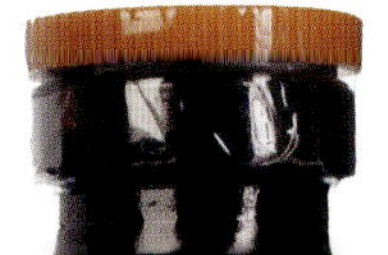

ALASKAN ROCK®
VODKA
Alaskan Rock is a small-batch artisanal vodka made in Australia from malted barley. It is double distilled in copper pot stills for a smooth finish and crisp flavour. You can enjoy Alaskan Rock vodka neat, straight up, on ice or mixed with whatever takes your fancy. We like it neat and freezer cold.
Our vodka is named after a cocktail incident involving happy Italian restaurateurs in Melbourne, Australia, during the 1970s (long story) and is presented in blackest-of-black hand-finished Mexican glass (even longer story). It's a nice vodka in a nice bottle. Res ipsa loquitor, people.
750 ml
Approx. 24 Standard Drinks
VODKA 40% ABV
(80 Proof)
Please drink Alaskan Rock® vodka responsibly.
Batch
1
Bottle
29
Produced & Bottled
8/2012
PRODUCT OF AUSTRALIA
This bottle is hand-finished. Each is unique and quite heavy. Best from the freezer. Pour with care.
AR
www.alaskanrock.com
Alaskan Rock Pty Ltd,
Sydney, NSW, Australia.

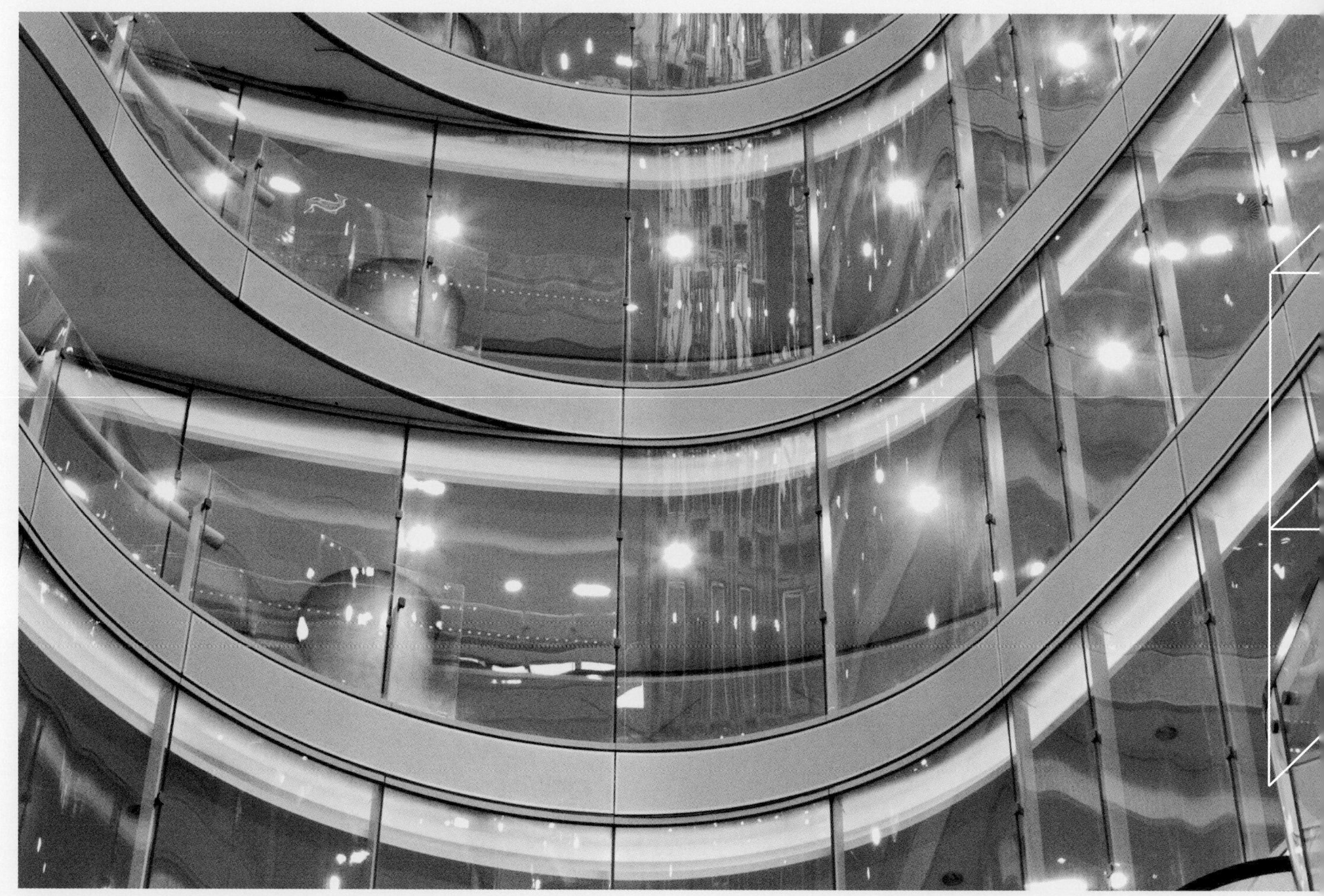

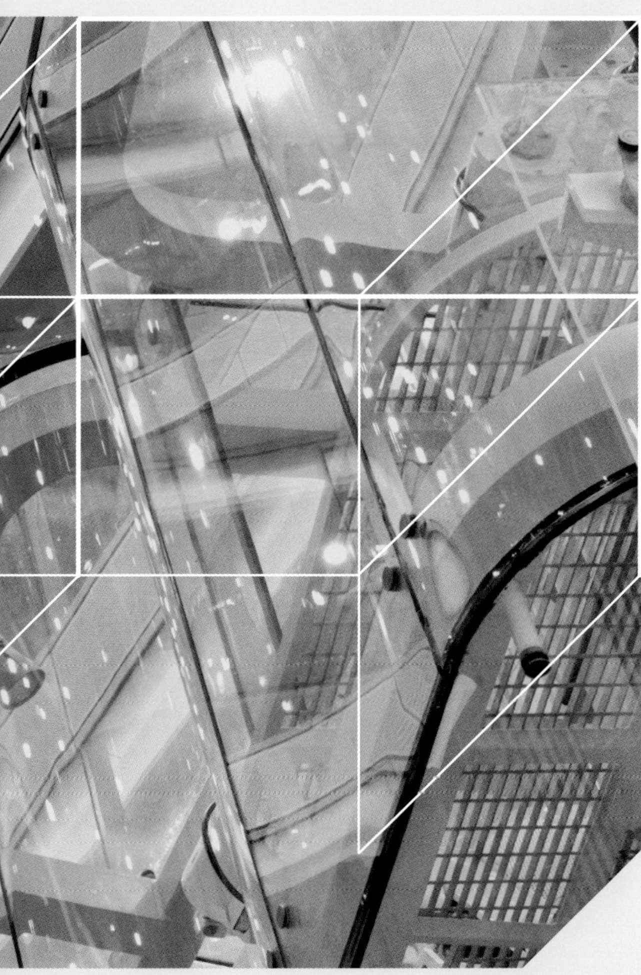

Architectus

Established 1980's, Sydney, New South Wales

Architectus brings together the experience of more than 200 leading architects, designers and planners, with offices in Auckland, Brisbane, Christchurch, Melbourne, Shanghai and Sydney. With a strong track record in the core areas of architecture, interiors, urban design and planning, Architectus has specialist expertise in education, public buildings, commercial, industrial, residential, aviation and transport, sustainable design, retail and hotels.

Working closely in association with Ingenhoven Architects (Germany), Architectus's 1 Bligh Street, Sydney, 2009–11, is a highly sustainable office tower, achieving a 6 Star Green rating from the Green Building Council of Australia. It is a compelling 29-storey conversation about the potential of architecture to merge technical, material and natural solutions to deliver super-efficient spaces attuned to people and the environment.

Within this project, the architects have fully embraced the technical and functional qualities of glass as a major contributor to the aesthetic and ecological performance of the building, and its success as a social environment — hundreds of people work there each day amid ample natural light and with stunning views of the adjacent harbour.

Creating public space in an undercroft, and carving airspace between surrounding buildings, 1 Bligh Street rotates against the grid. Freeing itself from the surrounding box corners, it turns strategically towards the harbour, offering the workers inside an unobstructed view of the water and the world outside. The building's elliptical geometry intelligently resolves the urban constraints of the site, offering unexpected value for the developer, occupier and broader public.

Wrapping the building in a dynamic transparent lens, the design of its double-skin facade evolved from Christoph Ingenhoven's RWE Headquarters building in Essen, and comprises an inner layer of double-glazing and a semi-permeable outer skin of very clear 'low iron' glass. A one-metre-wide cavity houses computer-controlled louvre blinds that react to the sun's movements to keep the building interior shaded throughout the day.

A fundamental aspect of the design, the curved skin of glass plays out a double life of concealment and revelation. Setting back the elements from the building to create an epidermis over the ventilated cavity, the glazing and louvres shroud and protect the occupier.

Internally, the building is organised around a full-height glazed atrium, which acts as the lungs of the building. This heart-shaped void rises between two cores. High-speed glass-clad lifts surge up and down, delivering people to naturally ventilated breakout spaces and offices. At the apex of the atrium, the glass lid of the building has been lifted to create a generous rooftop terrace with mature banksias.

Within this building a radical abundance of glass invites natural daylight to reach deep into every part of the interior. The glazed atrium roof invites reflections of clouds deep into the heart. It is surprising how rare this really is.

German architect Christoph Ingenhoven, who led the project, describes the building as a 'supergreen' office tower:

> We see sustainability as an important, self-evident and noticeable part of corporate identity. Green building design is our [Ingenhoven's] core competence. We have realised buildings all over the world according to the highest certification standards. But we aim for a holistic commitment that reaches far beyond. The challenge is to top the minimal standards required. That is what we call 'supergreen'.

As the sun retreats, the transparency of the facade offers unparalleled clarity. Views stretch across the

Previous page
Architectus + Ingenhoven
1 Bligh Street, Sydney, 2009–11
Building owned by Dexus Property Group and Cbus Property.
The ultimate transparency. The carefully detailed atrium glass façade also incorporates the glass lift motor rooms.
Photo H.G.Esch

▸

The naturally ventilated glass atrium runs the full height of the building (130 metres) enhancing connectivity and access to natural light and fresh air for all occupants.
Architectus + Ingenhoven
1 Bligh Street, Sydney, 2009–11
Building owned by Dexus Property Group and Cbus Property
Photo: H.G. Esch

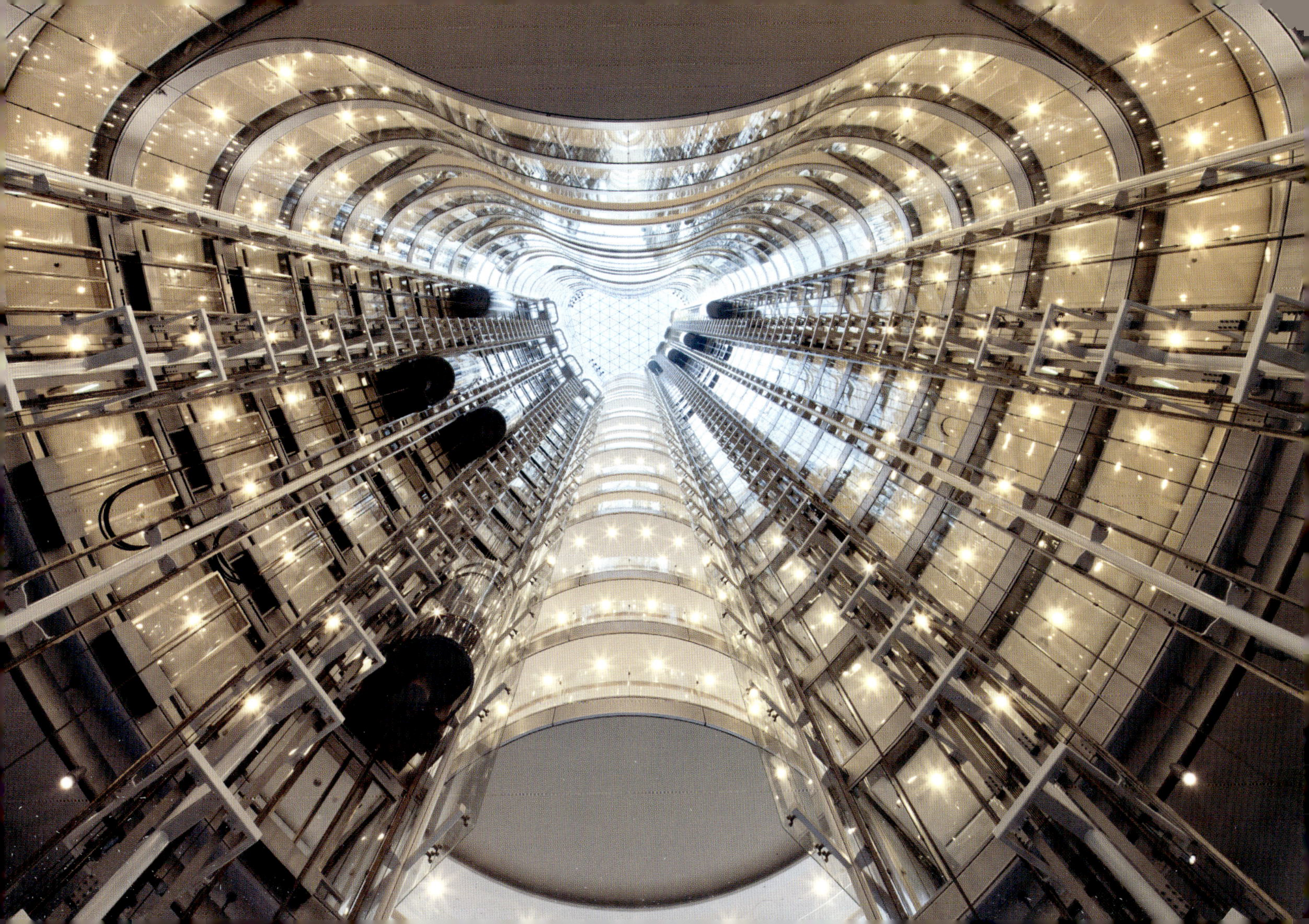

city to the harbour and beyond. Yet this is not a one-way transaction — this level of transparency also works in reverse. Workers in adjacent buildings and passing pedestrians gaze deep into the building, accessing the mercantile theatre of the day. The architecture becomes part of the spectacle of the city, breaking the dominant convention of the curtain wall to reflect in machine silence.

Ewan McEoin

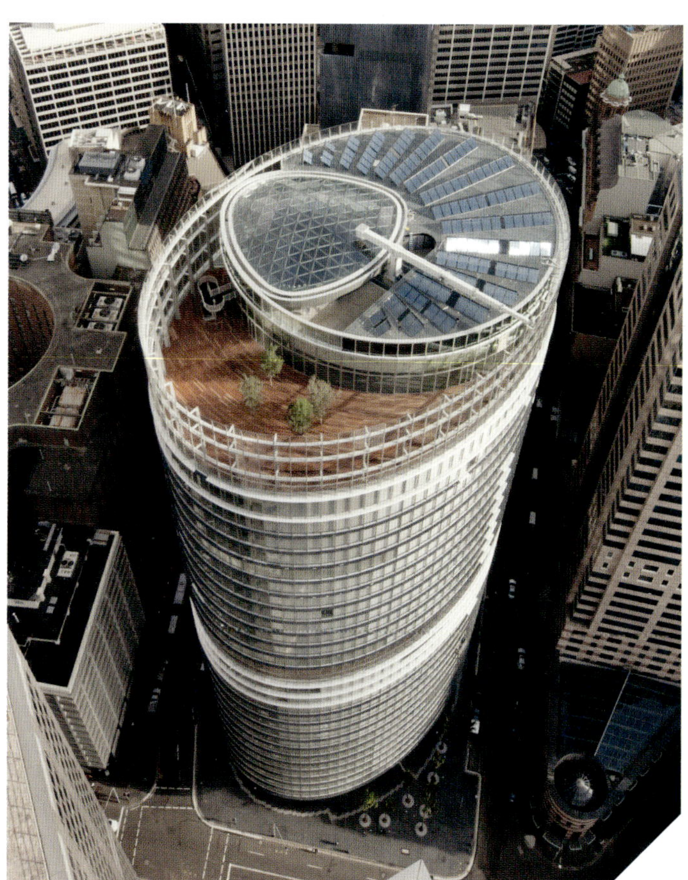

▸

The fifth façade comprising a protected green roof-scape, atrium and solar panels. Photo: H.G. Esch

▸▸

Ultimate transparency day and night via the double skin façade. Photo: H.G. Esch

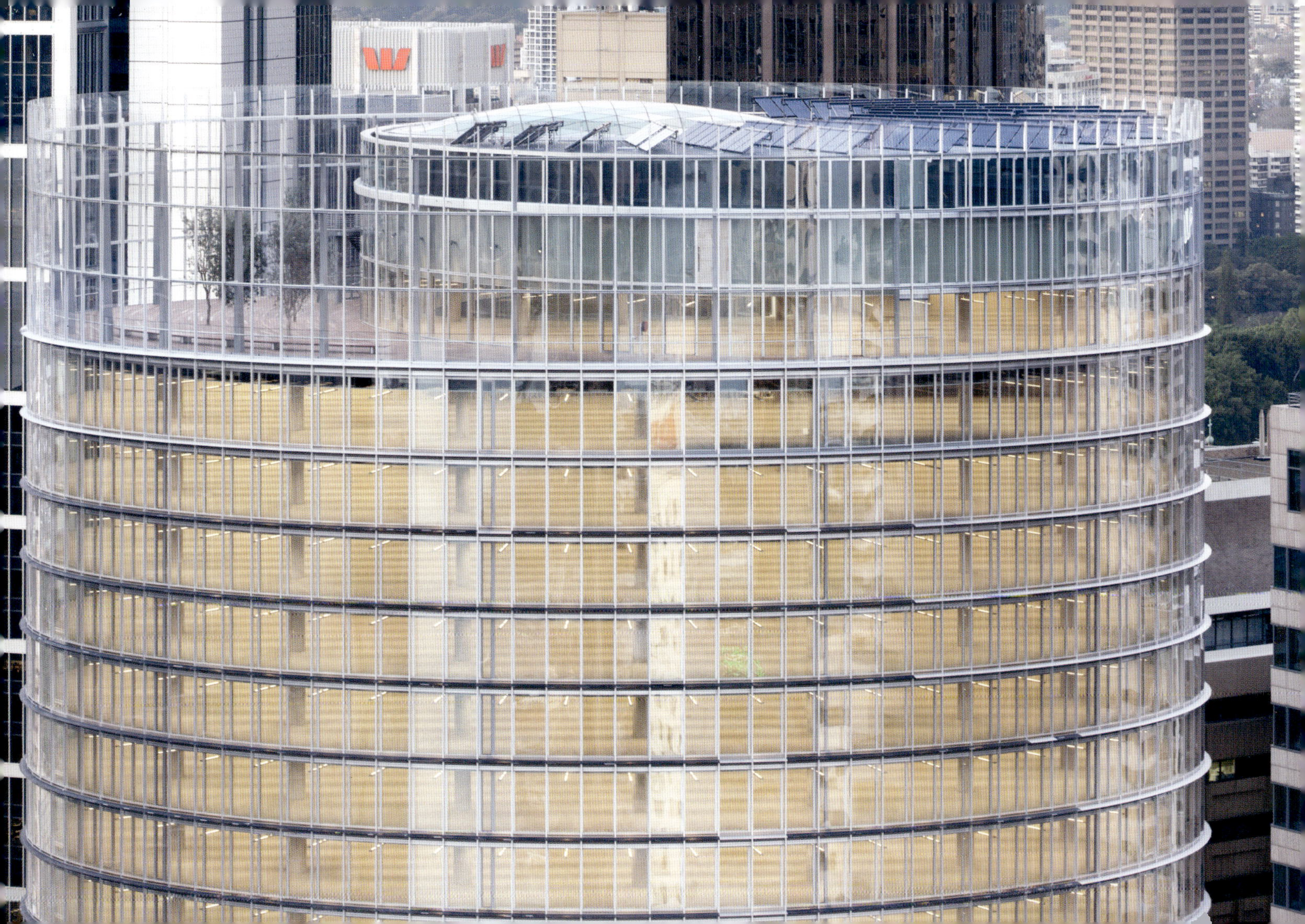

1 Bligh Street, Sydney

At 1 Bligh Street, Sydney, 2009–11, the architects embrace the technical and functional qualities of glass as a major contributor to the aesthetic and ecological performance of the building and its success as a social environment. A fundamental aspect of the design, the double-layered glass skin plays two key roles of concealment and revelation. Depending on the time of the day, it shrouds and protects the occupier from the harsh sun, or invites natural light deep into the heart of the building, revealing unparalleled views to the harbour. The transparency also invites those outside to gaze deep into the building, accessing the mercantile theatre of the day.

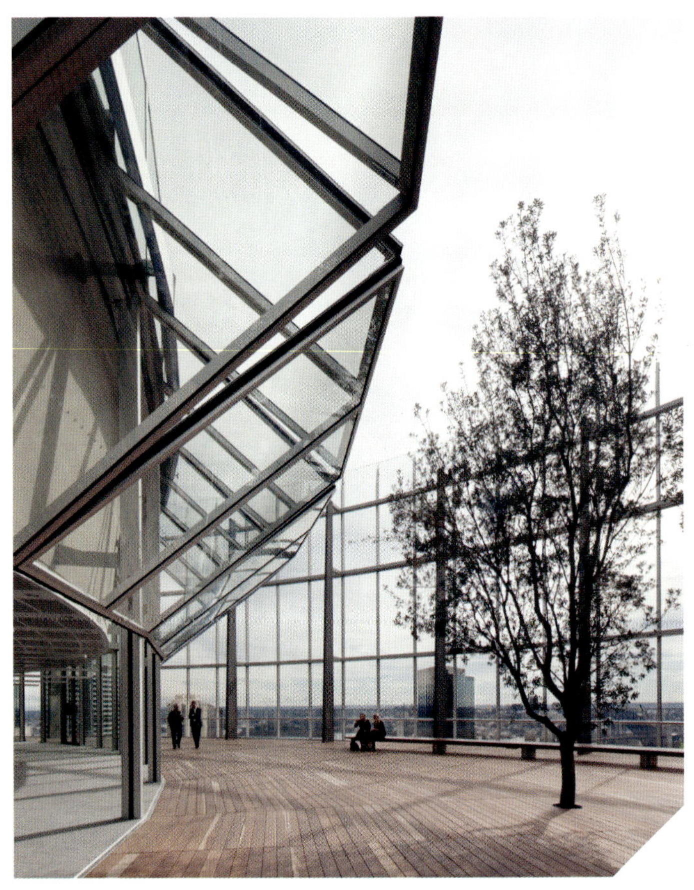

▸

6 metre high operable glass uplift doors provide connectivity to the external rooftop terrace. Photo: H.G. Esch

▸▸

View of 1 Bligh Street from Sydney Harbour. Photo: H.G. Esch

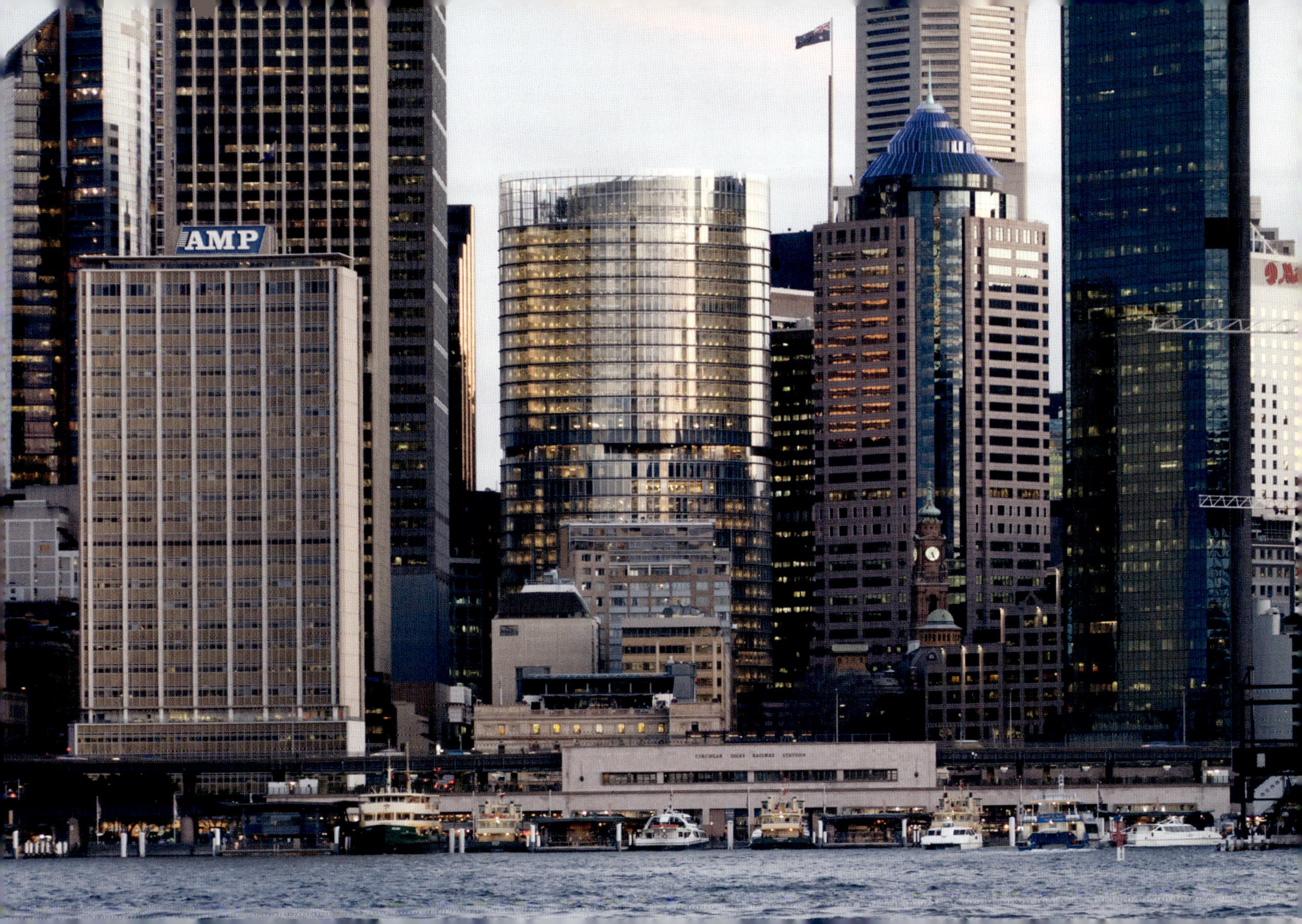
AMP

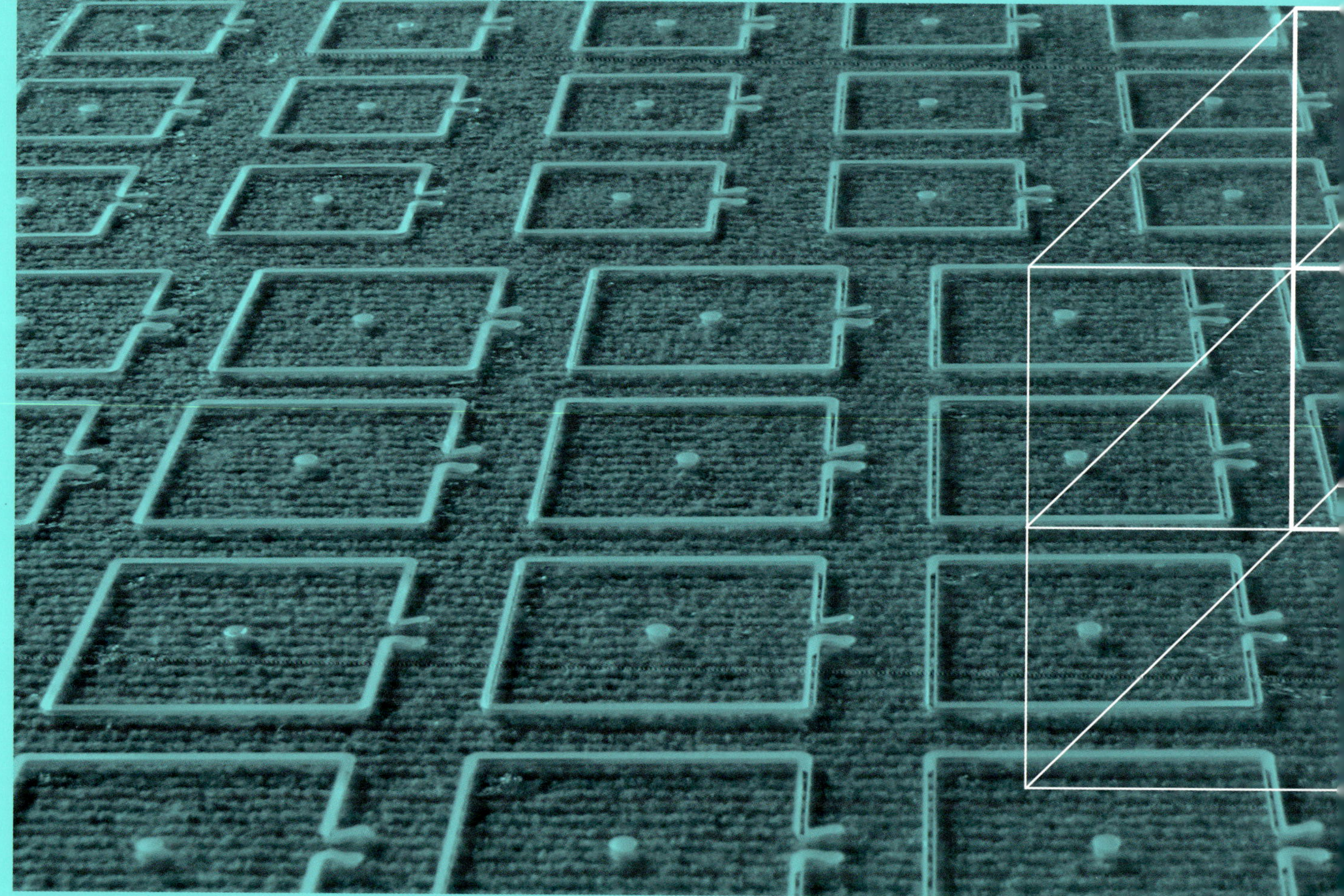

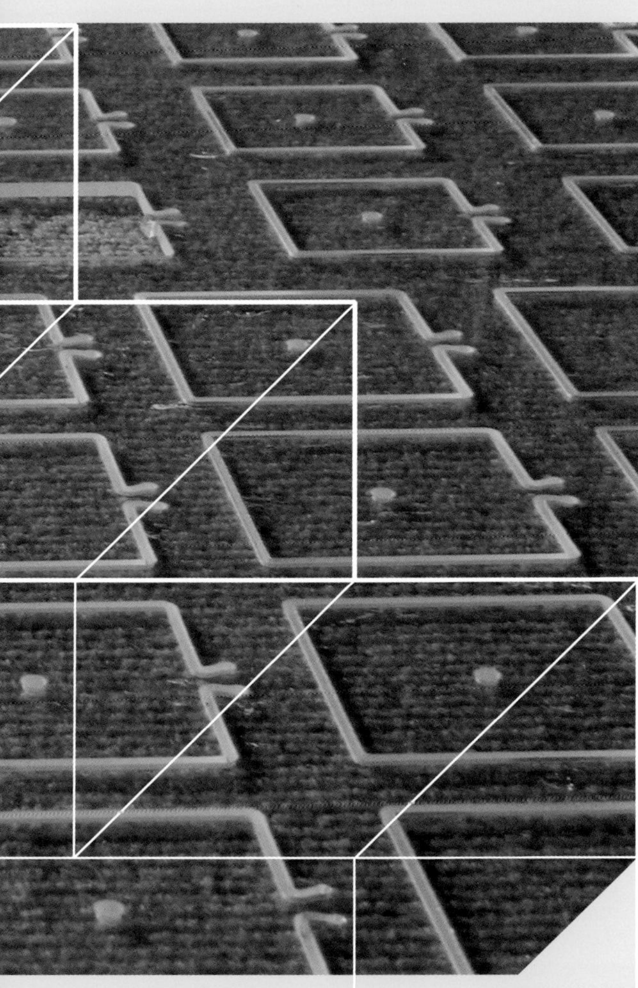

Blanche Tilden

Born 1968, Kiama, New South Wales
Lives Melbourne, Victoria

Intricately combining glass and metal, leading Australian jeweller Blanche Tilden produces innovative and technically beguiling works that explore the tensions between the fragility and rigidity of her chosen materials.

Tilden's fascination for glass was piqued at an early age. The granddaughter and daughter of BHP Port Kembla steel workers, Tilden fondly remembers the humorous family expression 'your father is a steel maker not a glass maker', used to move any family member who stood in front of the television for too long. For the young Tilden, this saying posed a question: 'How is glass made?'

Completing school, Tilden made her way to Sydney College of the Arts to pursue glass blowing; however as she progressed in her studies, she became more rapt with the art of jewellery making. Jewellery provided her with the chance to combine an array of materials in innovative ways. Combining her dual passions, she moved to Canberra to study at the Canberra School of Art, Australian National University, where, in 1992, she graduated with a Bachelor of Visual Arts (Glass) and in 1995 with a Graduate Diploma in Gold and Silversmithing.

Tilden's desire to understand how things work and her interest in the interface between the handmade and the machine-made have always been driving forces in her practice. Her recent body of work has looked to architecture for inspiration, in particular the great exhibition buildings of the 19th century. Superbly utilising glass in their design, these buildings emphasised German architect Bruno Taut's statement that glass was the quintessential material for the modern world, due to its capacity to hold and disperse light.

The Crystal Palace is considered to be one of the first modernist buildings. It was designed by architect Joseph Paxton and built in Hyde Park, London, in 1851, to highlight Britain's Imperial power and the wonders of the colonies. It utilised prefabricated cast iron and cast sheet glass, a material that had only recently been perfected by James Hartley, in 1848. This building grew in scale as modules were added, a construction mechanism Tilden exploits in the making and design of her neckpieces.

The Palais des Machines is the other great example of this style of architecture that Tilden references. Built for the 1889 French Exposition Universelle, by architect Ferdinand Dutert and engineer Victor Contamin, it showcased the pinnacle of the Industrial Revolution, at a time when the machine was king. Providing an uninterrupted span of 115 metres, this building was made possible by exploiting the structural innovation of the three-pin hinged or portal arch. Although used previously in bridge construction, this was the first application of the arch on such a large scale. The machine was not only celebrated in the exhibits, visitors were also transported around this building in lifts and moving bridges, further celebrating the mechanical wonders of the age.

Unfortunately neither building exists today — the Palais des Machines was demolished in 1910, and the Crystal Palace was destroyed by fire in 1936. Tilden's knowledge of these buildings is therefore derived from the rich photographic records, plans and drawings of the time. These black and white images emphasise the graphic qualities of the buildings, and Tilden responds to these repeated visual elements by making the rectangle and line the building blocks for her neckpieces.

Buildings as a source of inspiration may seem unusual for a jeweller, but Tilden's work reminds us that all buildings are made to human scale. Buildings exist to house people — they are where we go to work, live,

Previous page
Glass components for Tilden's necklaces being water-jet cut using CAD.
Photo: Les Pinkerton

▸

Tilden's jewellery references the great exhibitions buildings of the 19th century including Ferdinand Dutert, *Palais des Machines*, built for the 1889 Paris Universal Exhibition, Grenelle, Paris, France.
Photo: Courtesy the artist

▸▸

Blanche Tilden lampworking in her studio.
Photo: Rhiannon Slatter

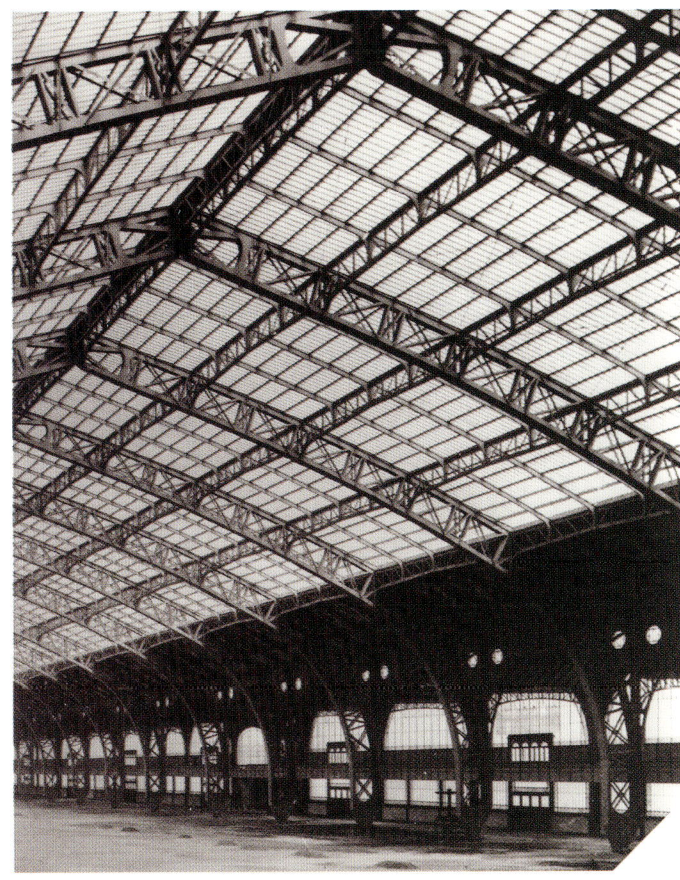

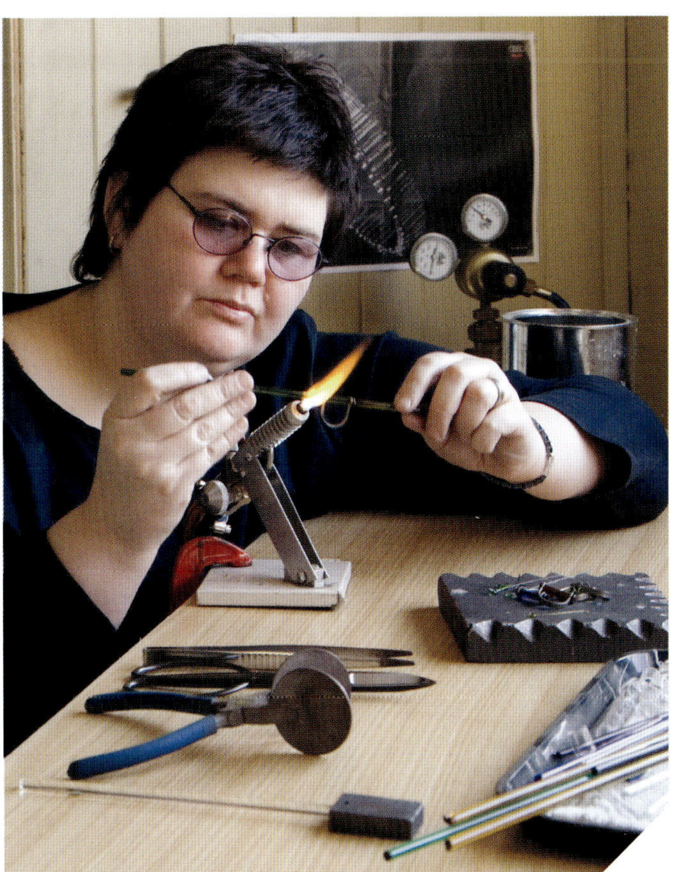

learn and engage with ideas. Domestic architecture is often on a modest scale, built closer to human size, while buildings constructed to memorialise or celebrate man's achievements are often larger scale. The relationship to human scale and the human body are integral to a jeweller. To be successful, jewellery needs to fit on the body and move with it. Tilden's clever articulated chains have the fluidity and grace in their machinations to allow this movement in glass, a material not readily seen to have such capabilities.

Margaret Hancock Davis

▸
Ann Jakle wearing *Parallel*, 2010 necklace.
Photo: Marcus Scholz

▸▸
Petit Palais necklace, 2012
waterjetcut, cold worked and lampworked borosilicate glass, 925 silver
20 x 170 dia.
Photo: Jeremy Dillon

▸▸▸
Dutert necklace, 2010
waterjetcut, cold worked and lampworked borosilicate glass, oxidised 925 silver
8 x 280 dia.
Photo: Jeremy Dillon

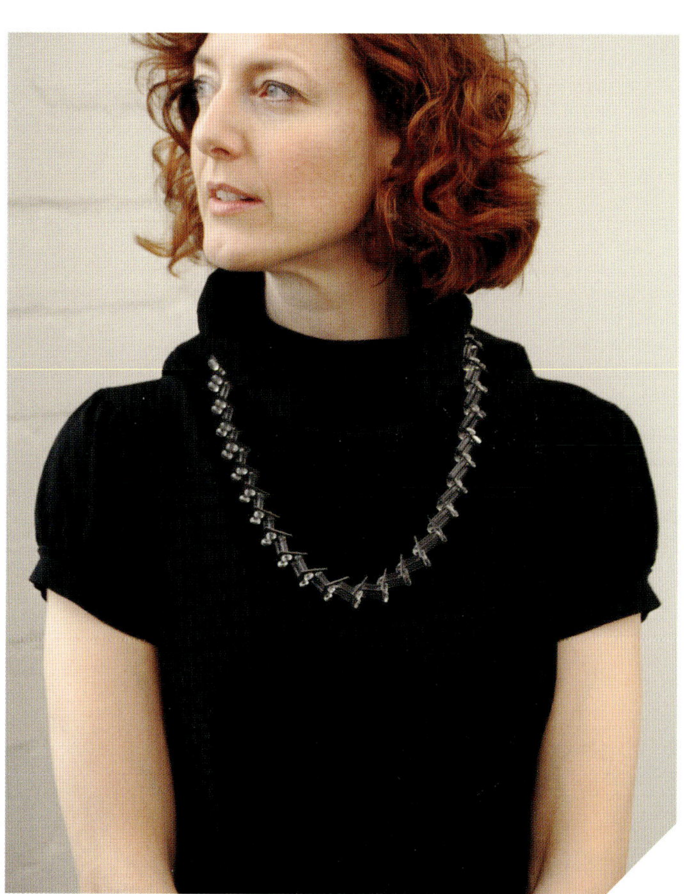

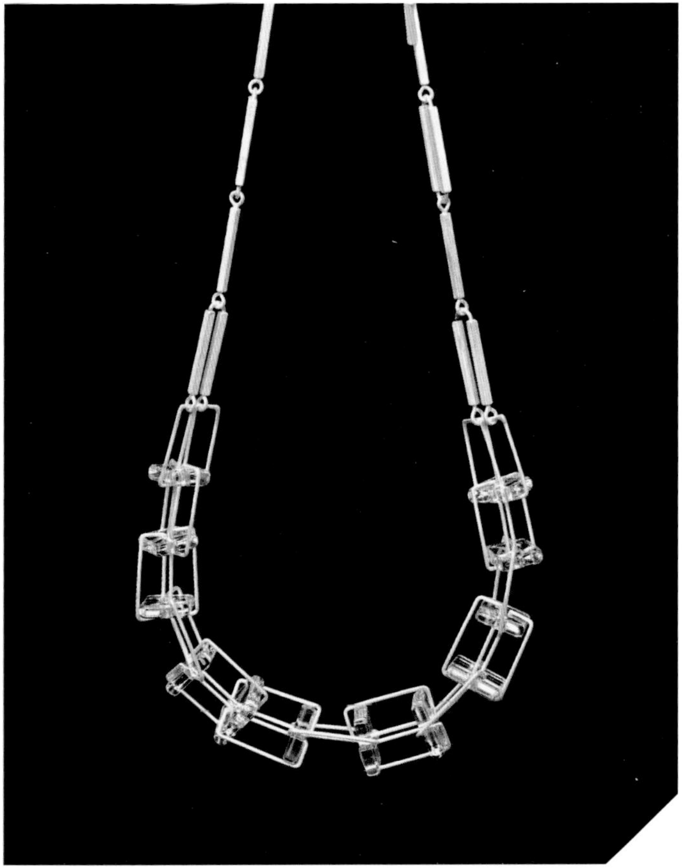

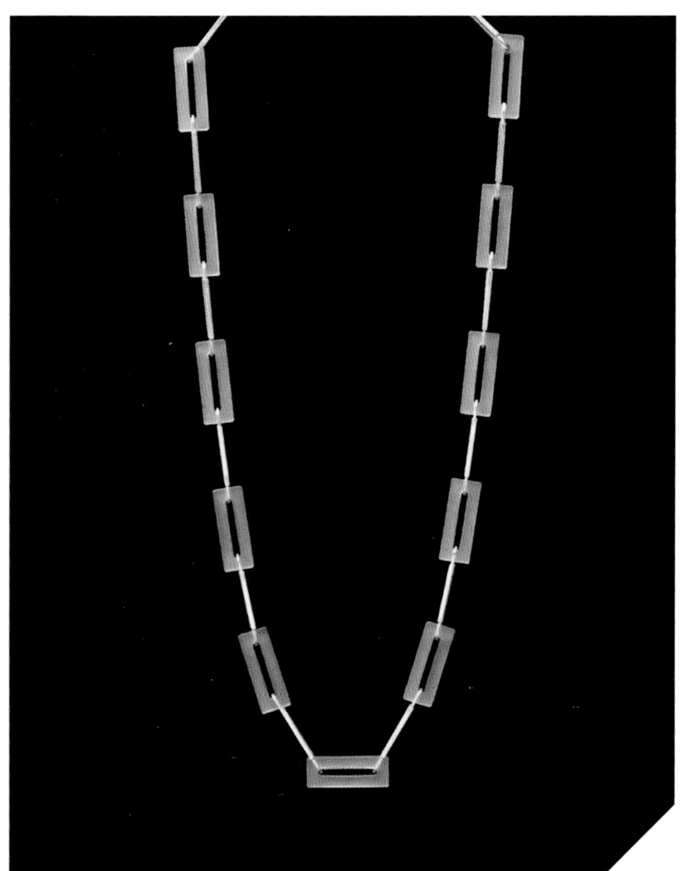

Grand Palais Necklace

Working with clear borosilicate glass, Tilden has the components of her necklaces water-jet cut by Glasslite, a precision engineering company in Coffs Harbour, NSW, which specialises in manufacturing glass components for lighting applications.

Tilden has worked closely with the company to create these smaller components, a skill Glasslite developed from cutting glass components for architectural lighting. Once cut, Tilden must meticulously hand finish and flame-work each unit, before constructing her necklaces with silver wire linkages. The silver links arc oxidised, referencing the black cast-iron elements of the Crystal Palace and the Palais des Machines.

The *Grand Palais Necklace*, 2014, draws upon the jewellery convention of grading strung necklace components from large at the front to small at the back — a traditional example of this gradation is a strand of pearls — while also referencing the glass and metal construction of the Palais des Machines. Tilden was drawn to a particular photograph of the Palais de Machines when making this work. In the photograph, the scale of the building illustrated the effect of diminishing perspective, leading each repeated element of the building to proportionally recede — that is, the glass panels of the building echo the traditional jewellery form.

Grand Palais necklace, 2014
water-jet cut, cold worked and lampworked borosilicate glass, oxidised 925 silver
40 x 380 dia.
Photo: Grant Hancock

Overleaf
Grand Palais necklace (detail), 2014
Photo: Grant Hancock

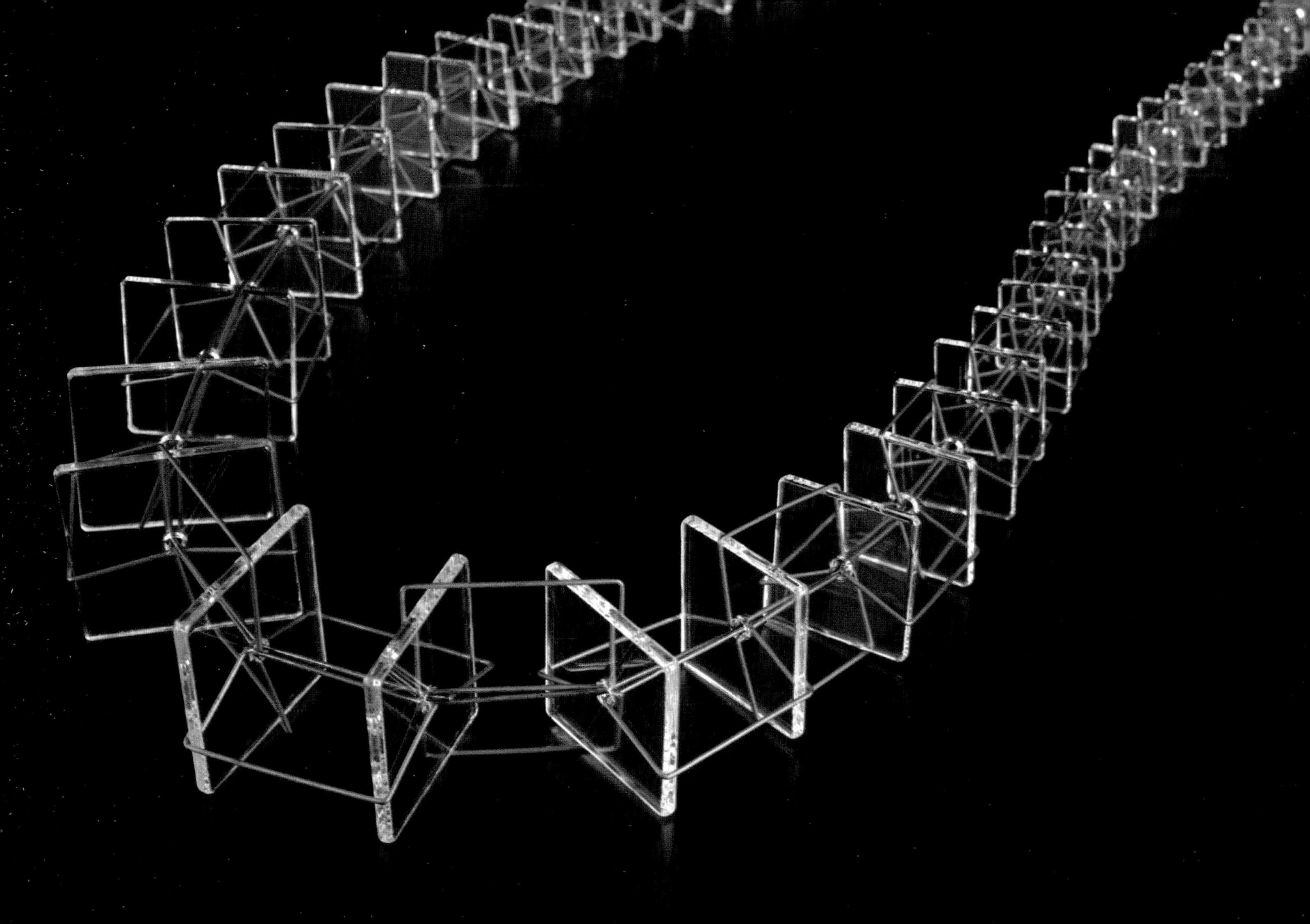

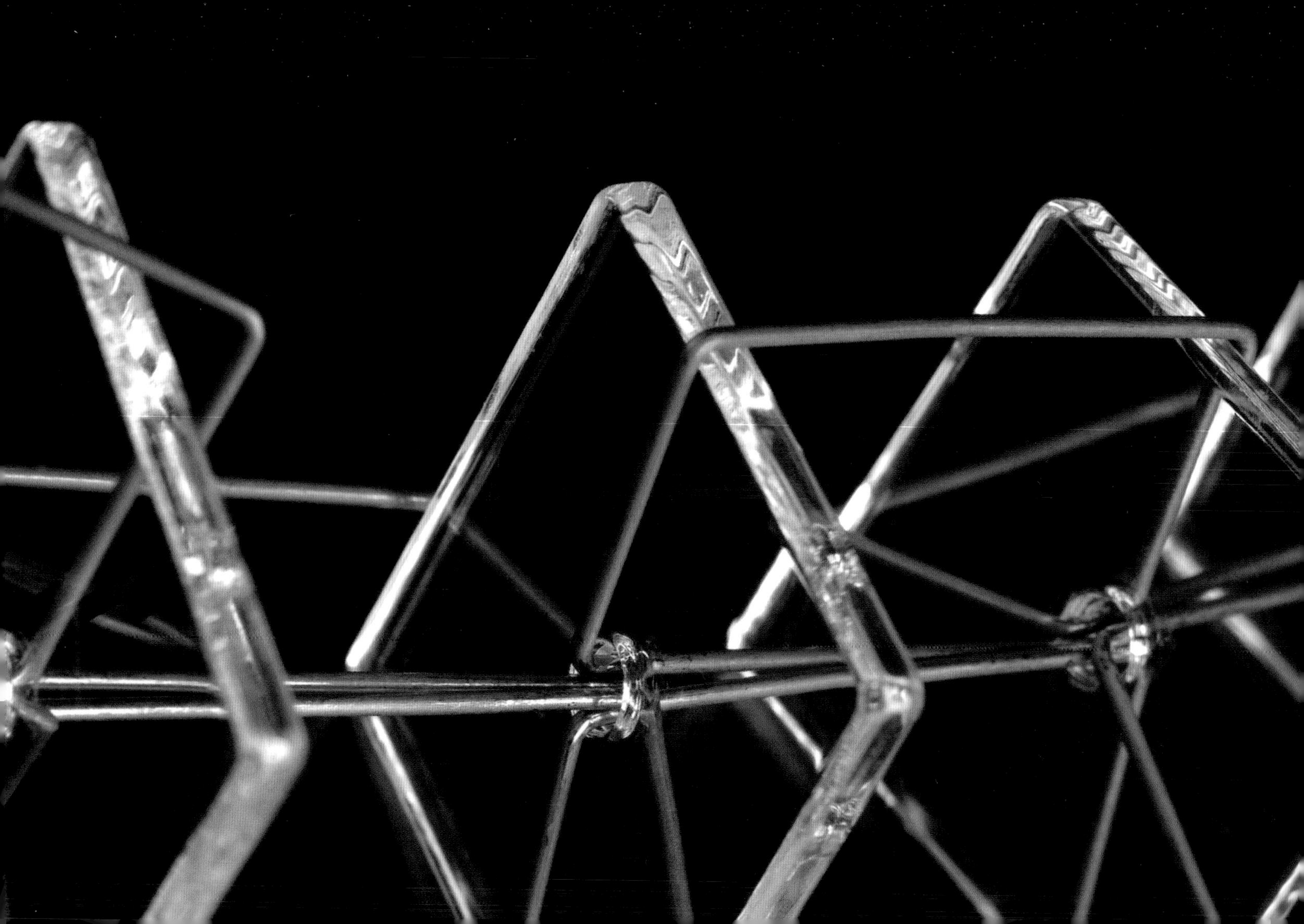

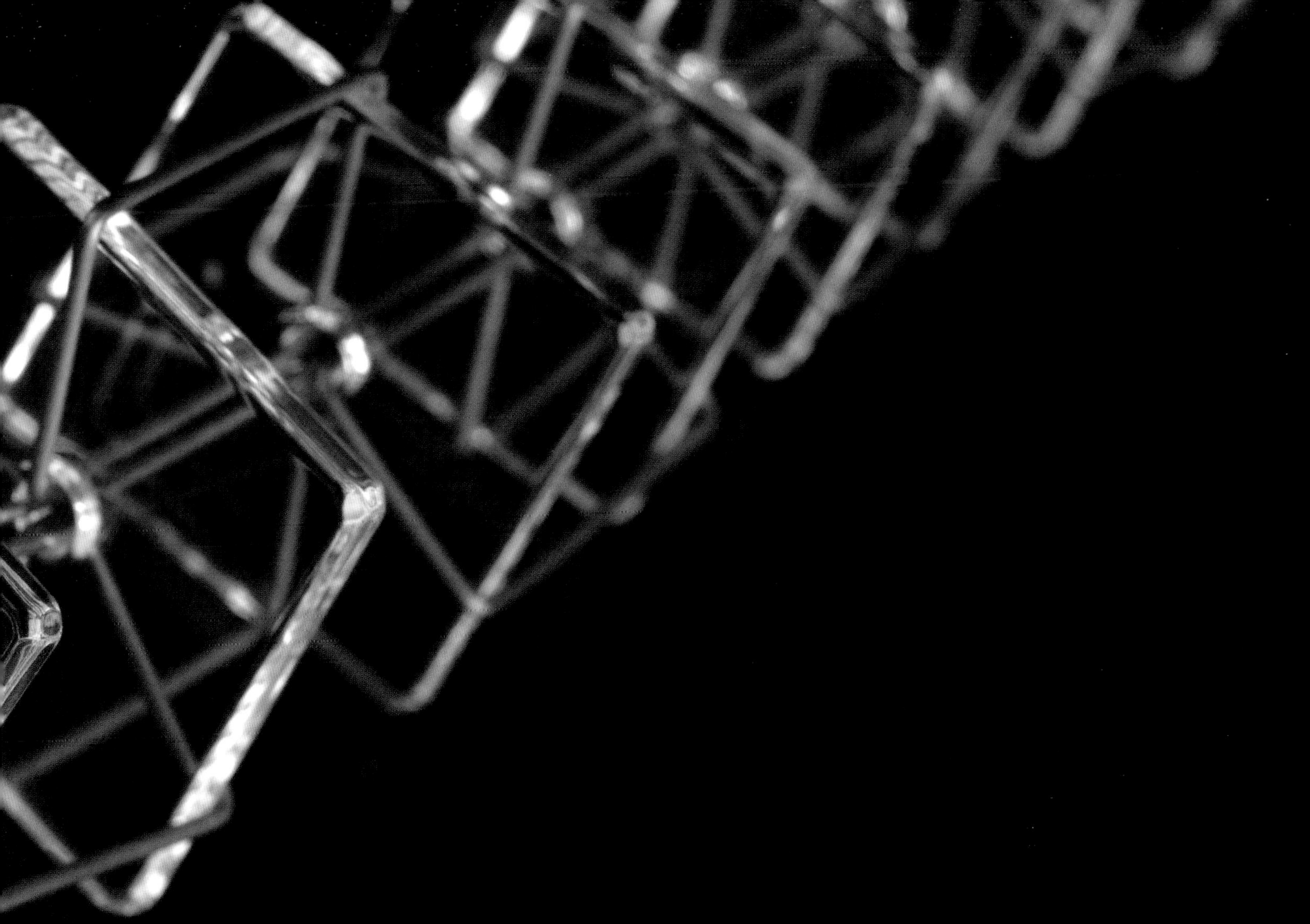

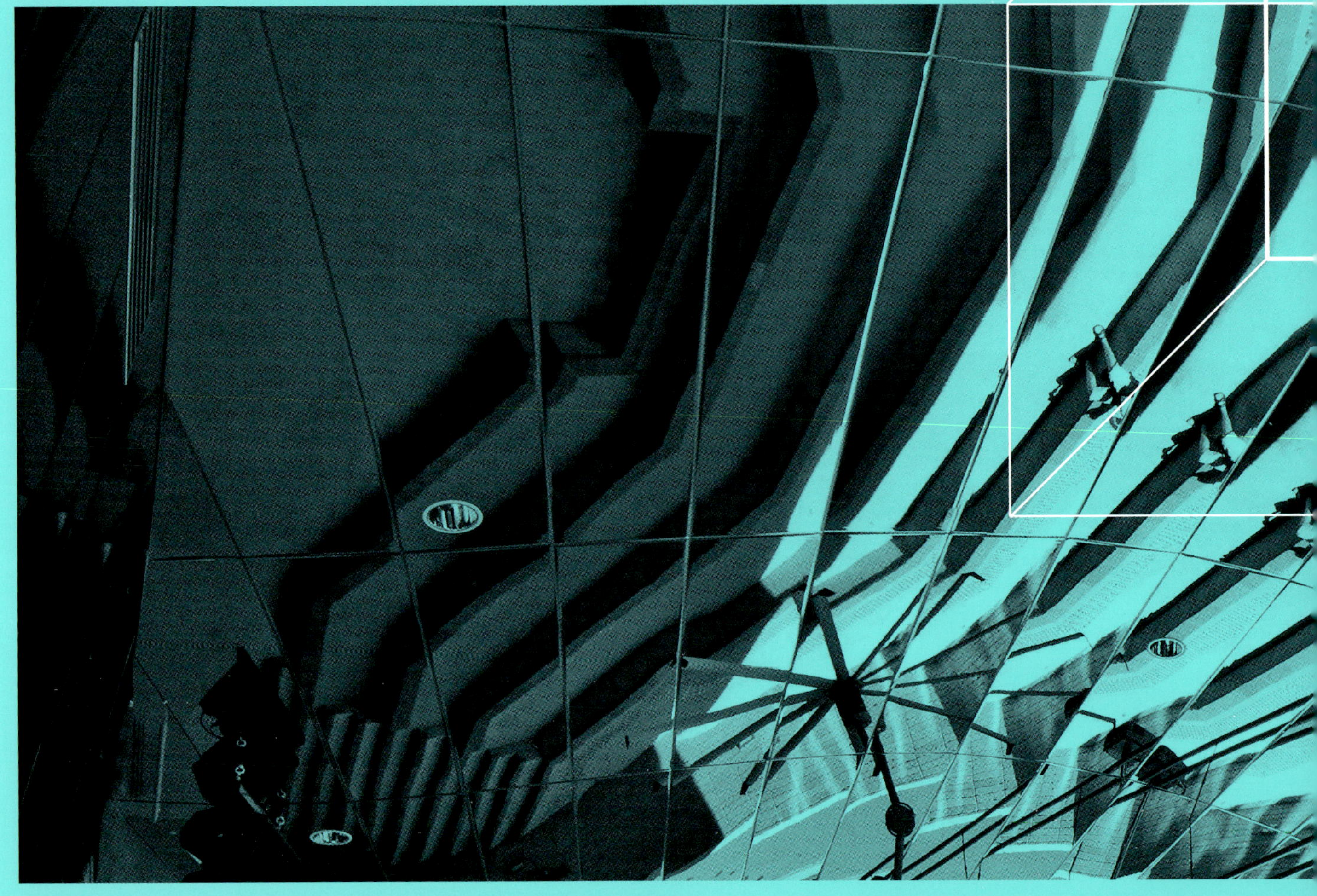

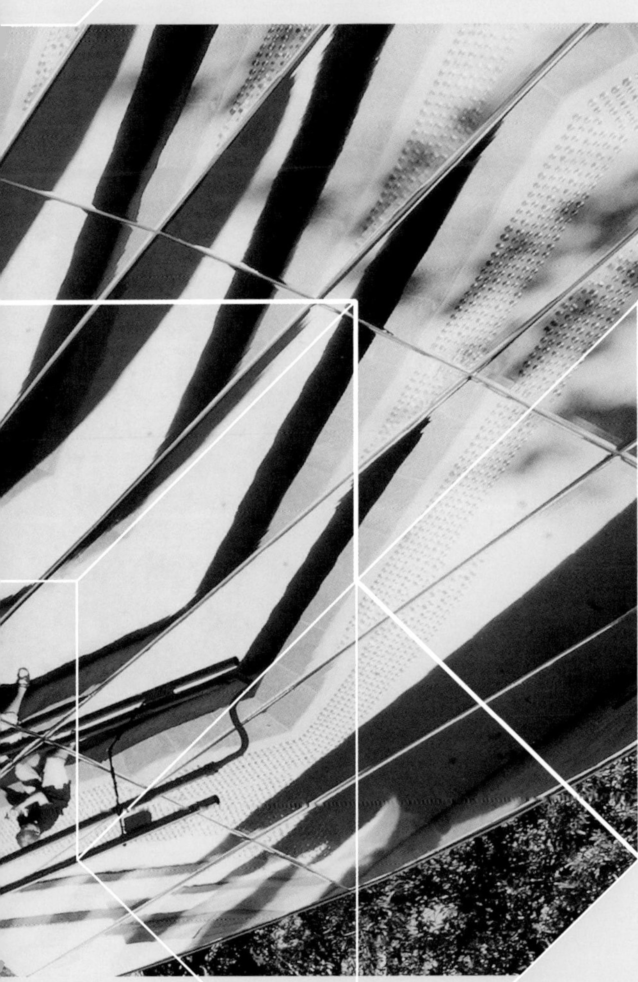

Charles Wright Architects

Established 2004, Port Douglas, Queensland

Glass is a substance designed to capture the gaze. Its ability to transmit light, to reflect and refract, makes it an attractive material with multiple applications. In architecture, glass is most often a component for looking through — transparency is the key to the function of windows, doors and room dividers. However, for the Cairns Botanic Gardens Visitors Centre, 2012, reflection is the key element. Designed by Charles Wright Architects, the building is a dramatic example of tropical architecture. Clad in a mirrored surface, the entire building is a reflection of the dappled rainforest canopy within the Cairns Botanic Gardens.

Charles Wright Architects was established by Director Charles Wright in 2004. As a north Queensland-based firm, it is interested in creating innovative buildings that are sympathetic to the region and ecologically sustainable — it is working to develop a new vernacular for tropical architecture. The firm represents a shift towards innovation, research and experimentation within tropical architecture, with a strong emphasis on open design processes with the client. The Cairns Botanic Gardens Visitors Centre is a perfect example of this, combining environmental design with innovative materials and technology.

Given a brief that the building should blend seamlessly with the environment, Charles Wright Architect's design takes on a chameleon-like camouflage. Using a mirrored surface, the building reflects the tropical green foliage of the surrounding botanical gardens. The result is stunning — the building is transformed by the reflection into a moving, living image. The facade reflects changes in the environment, responding to the weather, season and time of day. The mirrored surface combines with the organic, curving walls of the building to create optical effects. The multiple angles of the mirrored panes flow along the arc of the building, transforming it into a 'hall of mirrors'. The amphitheatre that runs underneath takes on a performative element, as visitors' reflections bounce between surfaces.

Through the development of the project, Charles Wright Architects was faced with the problem that an exoskeleton of glass mirrors would be unreasonably heavy. The solution was to find a material that maintained the reflective qualities of glass, but was much lighter. The reflective cladding that was selected has never been used in Australia before, and is made from a very thin stainless-steel composite. This material was combined with one-way mirrors to allow the building's office workers a stunning view of the botanic gardens. So, while much of the building is in fact not glass, it imitates the qualities of mirrored glass, blending seamlessly between cladding and one-way mirror.

A final component of the building was a collaboration with environmental and public artist Jill Chism. Her meditative glass artworks have been installed along the glazed promenade facades of the building. Chism's digital images are sandwiched between two layers of glass, providing an immersive experience that connects with the outside environment, and can be viewed from inside and out.

Adele Sliuzas

Previous page
Cairns Botanic Gardens Visitors Centre, 2012
Collins Avenue, Edge Hill, Queensland
Photo: Patrick Bingham-Hall

▸

The mirrored smart fix façade reflects the surrounding garden. The northern block contains the café terrace and opens to the major interpretation display and information space, whilst the southern block is an office building for council staff.
Photo: Patrick Bingham-Hall

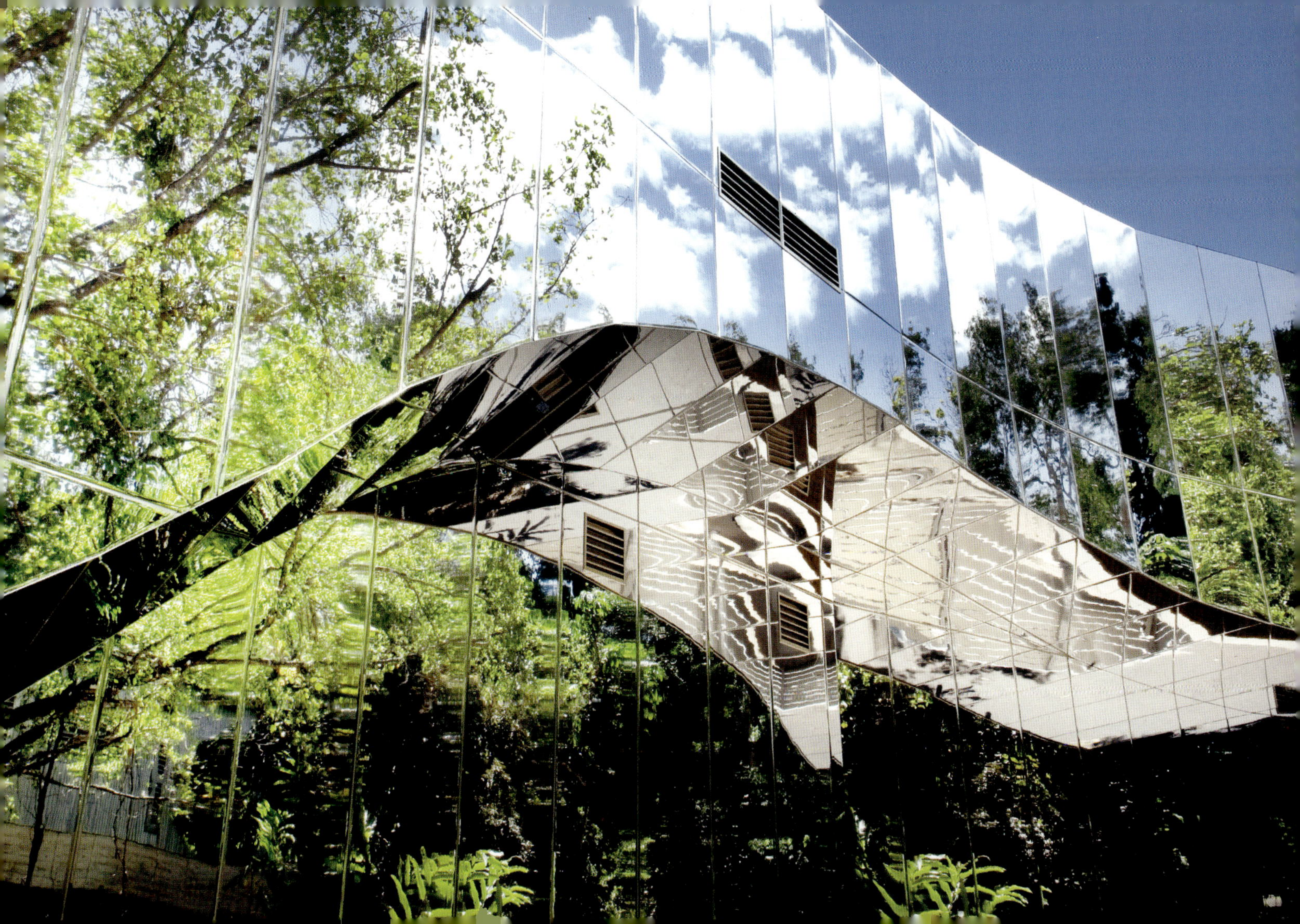

The Cairns Botanic Gardens Visitors Centre

Sitting within the contours of the landscape, the Cairns Botanic Gardens Visitors Centre, 2012, is a gateway to both the botanic gardens and the Tanks Arts Centre. Comprised of two buildings connected by a central promenade, the building is host to a range of activities, from cafe to council offices, information centre and public space. Charles Wright Architects developed the space to make the most of the climate, creating an amphitheatre that sits underneath the promenade and eaves of the building. This area of deep shade provides respite from the elements, and creates a space for people to congregate in wet weather.

▸

View from outdoor covered Amphitheatre, area is lit by the reflections on the ground.
Photo: Patrick Bingham-Hall

▸▸

Undercover corridor separating the northern and southern blocks acts as a social space.
Photo: Patrick Bingham-Hall

▸▸▸

Jill Chism's artworks are installed along the naturally ventilated corridor. This corridor serves a linear sequence of cellular office spaces that all open out to the shared staff terrace on the south.
Photo: Patrick Bingham-Hall

Overleaf
Plentiful shade provided by the roof overhangs which offers respite from the tropical heat.
Photo: Patrick Bingham-Hall

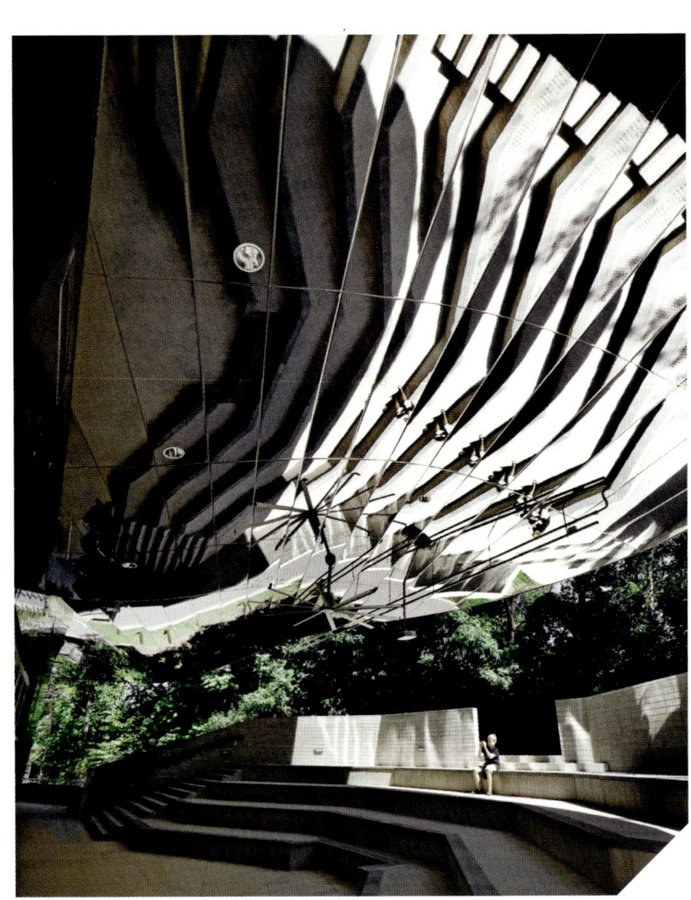

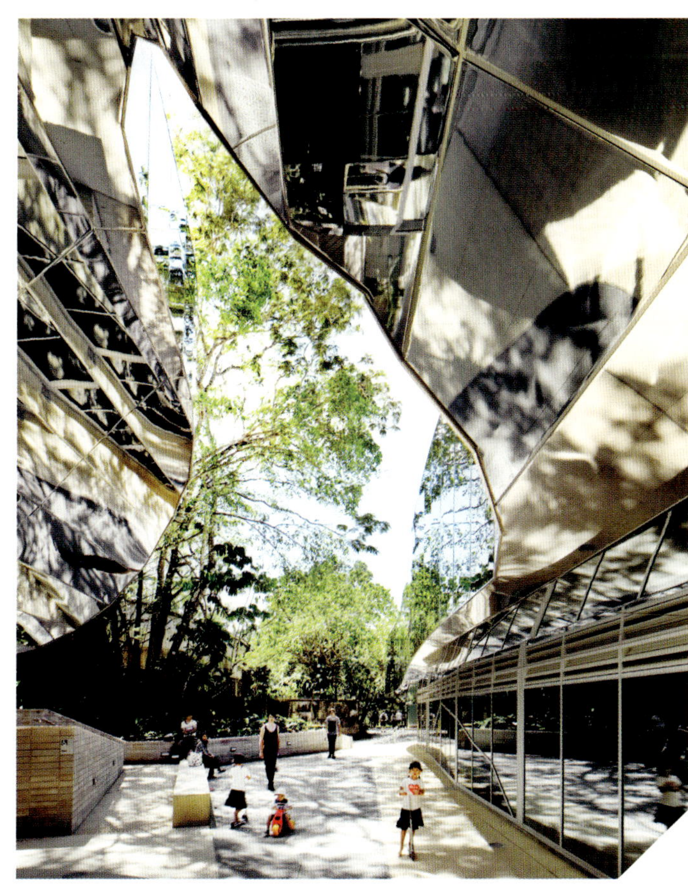

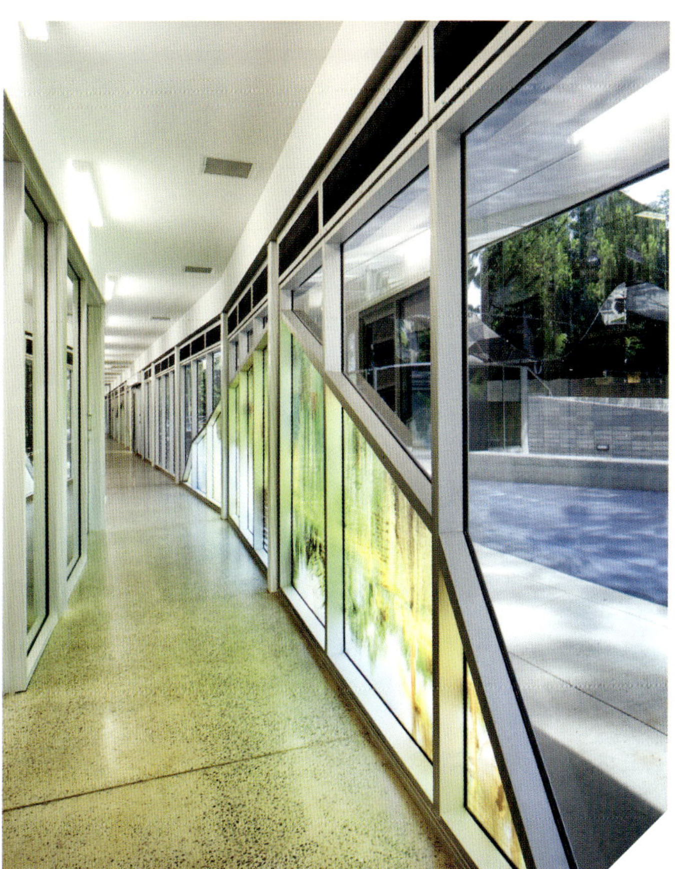

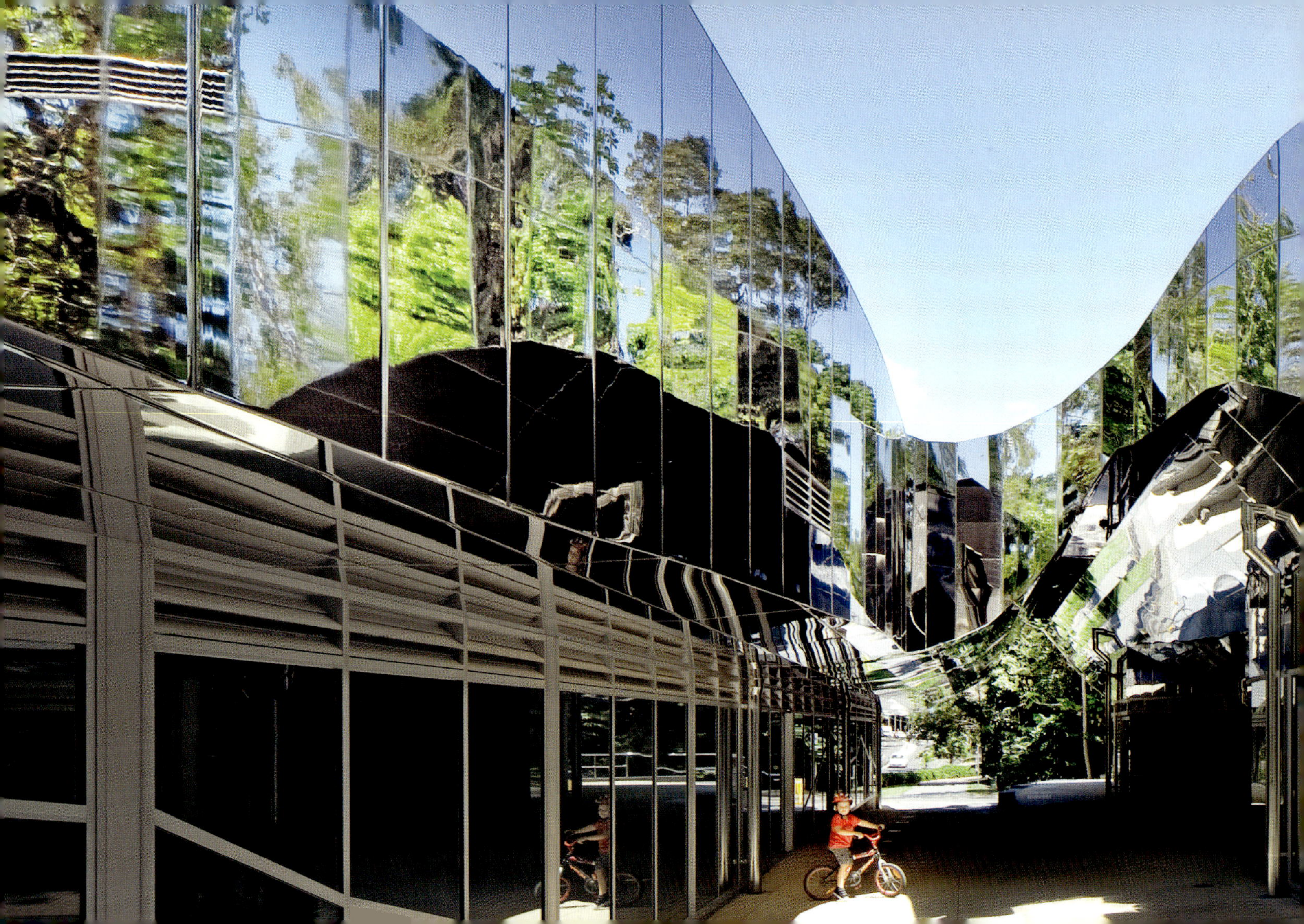

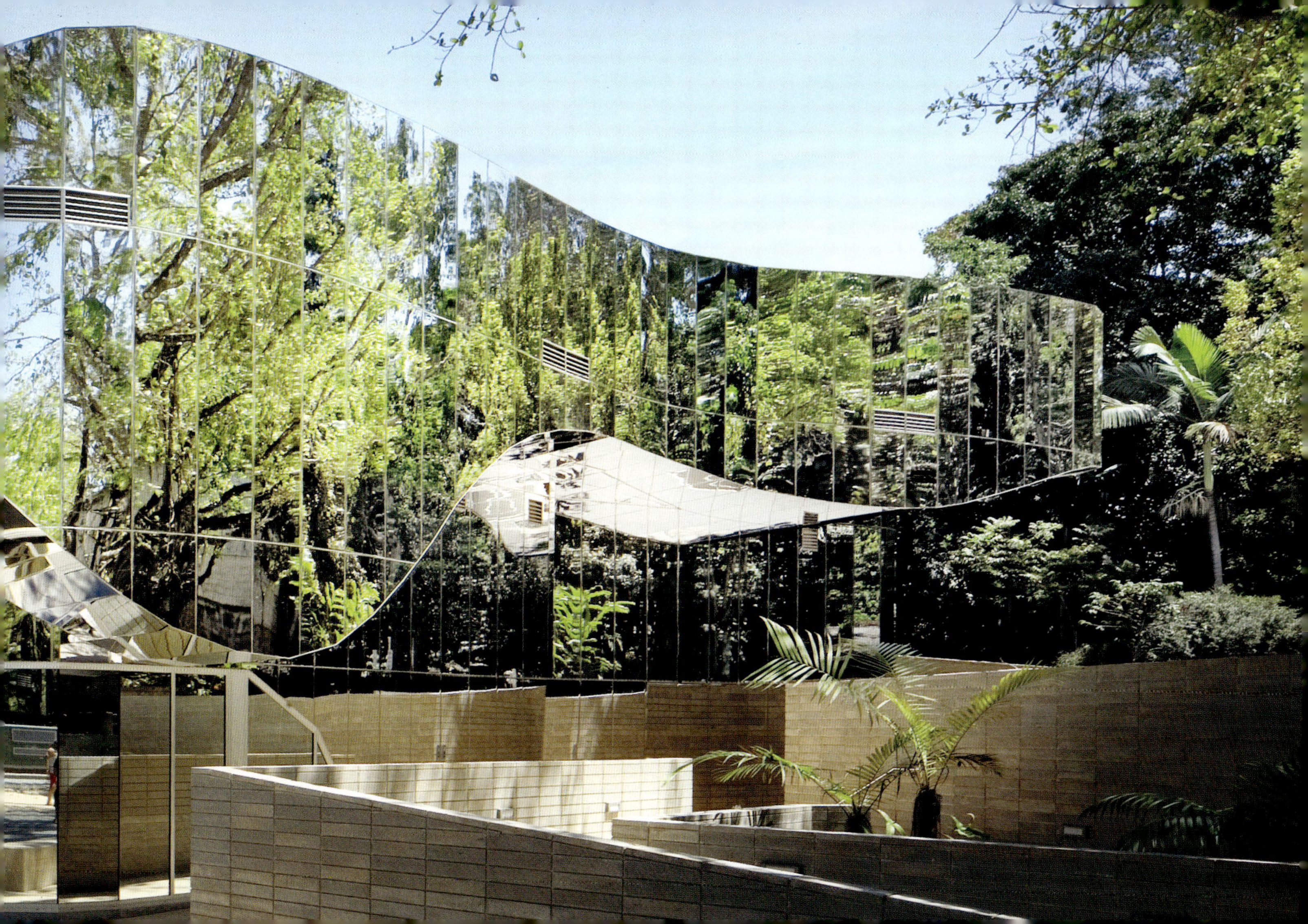

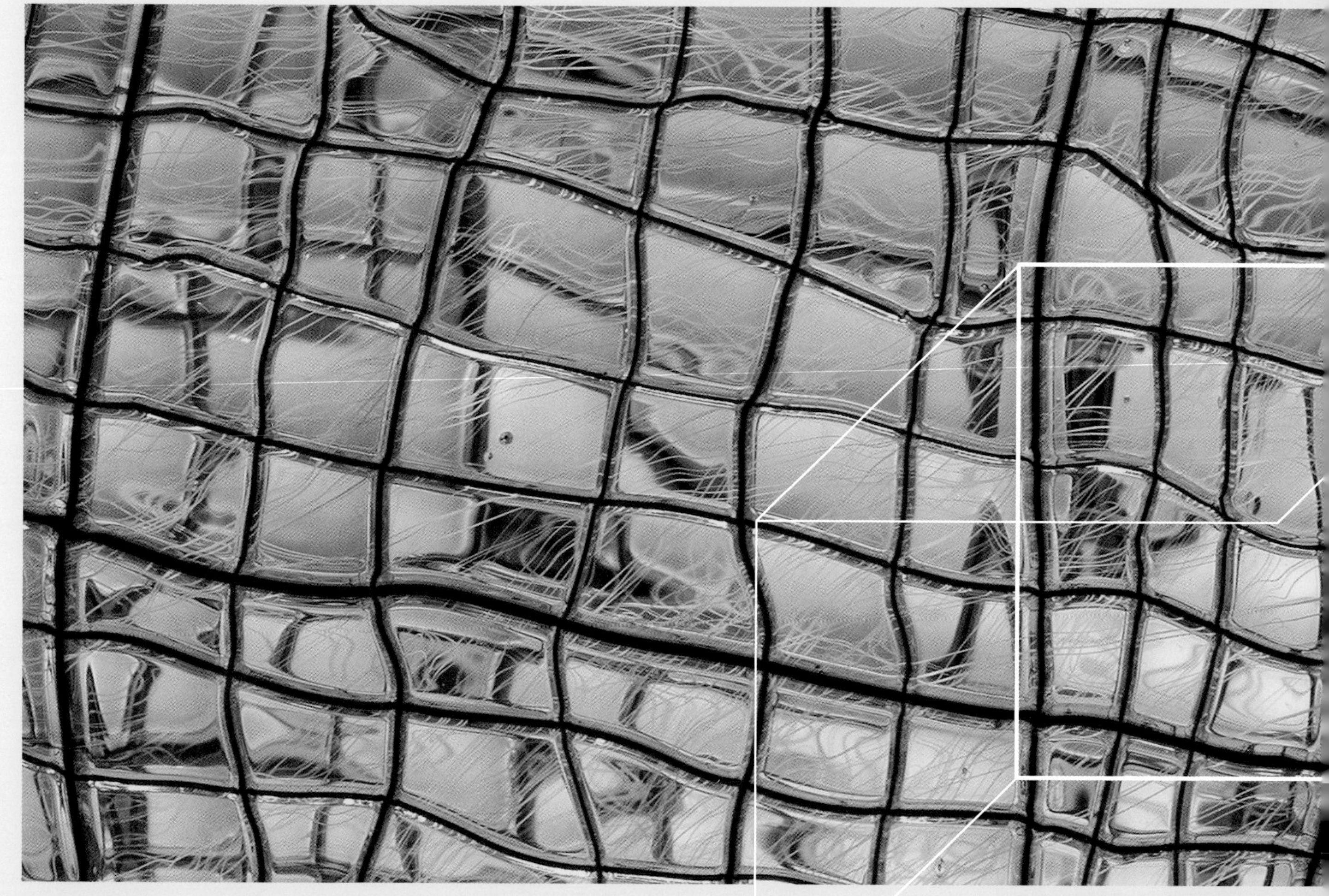

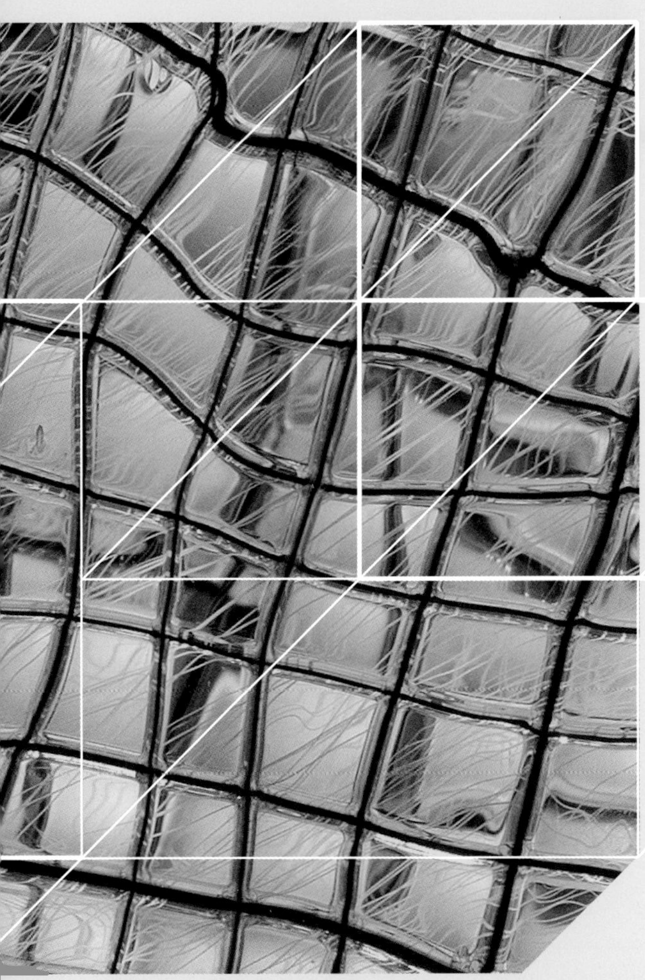

Clare Belfrage

Born 1966, Melbourne, Victoria
Lives Adelaide, South Australia

As with most glass blowers, Clare Belfrage was initially drawn to the extraordinary alchemical properties of molten glass. As a material, glass provides infinite possibilities. From the most prosaic of everyday forms like the glass tumbler, it can be pushed and corralled, creating innovative conceptual artworks and everything in between. Belfrage acknowledges that this first allure is only part of what has sustained her keen interest, in a career spanning more than 25 years.

For Belfrage, glass is the perfect medium. Not immediately obvious, glass production combines aspects of Belfrage's three main passions: music, sport and art. Like a lot of music, glass is often produced in a team environment — when the team is working well, it is like a virtuoso performance where everything comes together flawlessly and, conversely, if one of the team is not working well the results are less than desired. As in sport, glass making is physically demanding — one needs to be fit to spend hours in front of the furnace and glory-hole heat. You must also be strong to handle the work at the end of a blow pipe. These attributes, along with glass's suitability for expressing ideas, drive Belfrage.

Graduating from Monash University in 1988, Belfrage spent the next two years working for Michael Hook[1] at Resolution Glass Works in North Melbourne as a production glass blower producing mould-formed goblets and perfume bottles. It was an exciting time in Melbourne for glass blowers, with the newly-opened Meat Market hot shop providing an open-access hot-glass studio for hire. Belfrage fondly remembers the sense of community at the time, when she and other 'glassies' seemed to eat, sleep and dream glass.

This keen sense of community of glass blowers has seen Belfrage work in a number of group studios. She currently works from the JamFactory's studio, having first joined the JamFactory as an Associate in 1991, and later becoming the studio production manager in 1996. In 1997 she was a founding member of Blue Pony — an influential studio she shared with other glass artists such as Tom Moore, Gabriella Bisetto, Tim Edwards and Jessica Loughlin — and in 2009 she was offered the position of Creative Director of the newly established Canberra Glassworks. She developed and oversaw the programming of exhibitions, the professional artist-in-residence program and artists' access, and education programs for artists and the public.

Belfrage developed a number of thought-provoking projects during this time, including the *Ten Squared* exhibition, part of the Centenary of Canberra's focus on history and heritage.

Belfrage's involvement in glass education began in 1994, when she was employed to introduce glass studies at Curtin University, Perth. She remembers clearly the very rudimentary facilities there then. Since then, she has lectured in the glass programs at the University of South Australia, and Ohio State University, USA. She has also taught numerous workshops throughout Australia, and in New Zealand, Japan and the United States.

Margaret Hancock Davis

1. Hook had trained at Nick Mount's production studio, Budgeree Glass, in East Gippsland, and during this time had met US-based glass blowers such as Dick Marquis and Dante Marioni. Marioni subsequently spent time at Resolution Glass Works while Belfrage was working there.

Previous page
Open Weave, #3112 (detail), 2013
blown glass with cane drawing
470 x 300 x 80
Photo: Rob Little

▸

Leaf Circuitry Group, 2008
blown glass with cane drawing, acid etched
495 x 600 x 210
Photo: Grant Hancock

▸▸

Clare Belfrage applying glass stringers at the Tacoma Museum of Glass, Seattle, USA, 2009.
Photo: Ken Emly

▾

Clare Belfrage speaking at the opening of *Under my Skin*, Kirstie Rea solo exhibition and launch of Canberra Glassworks Centenary of Canberra Artistic Programs, 2013.
Photo: Courtesy of artist

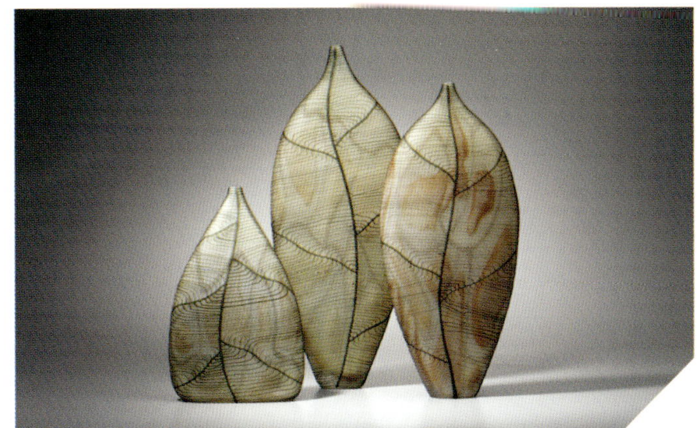

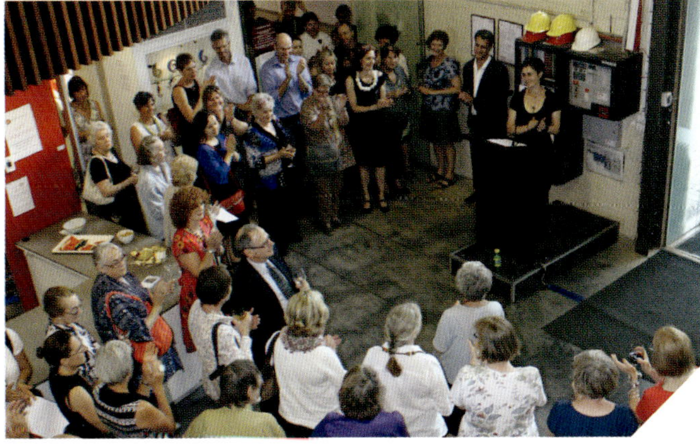

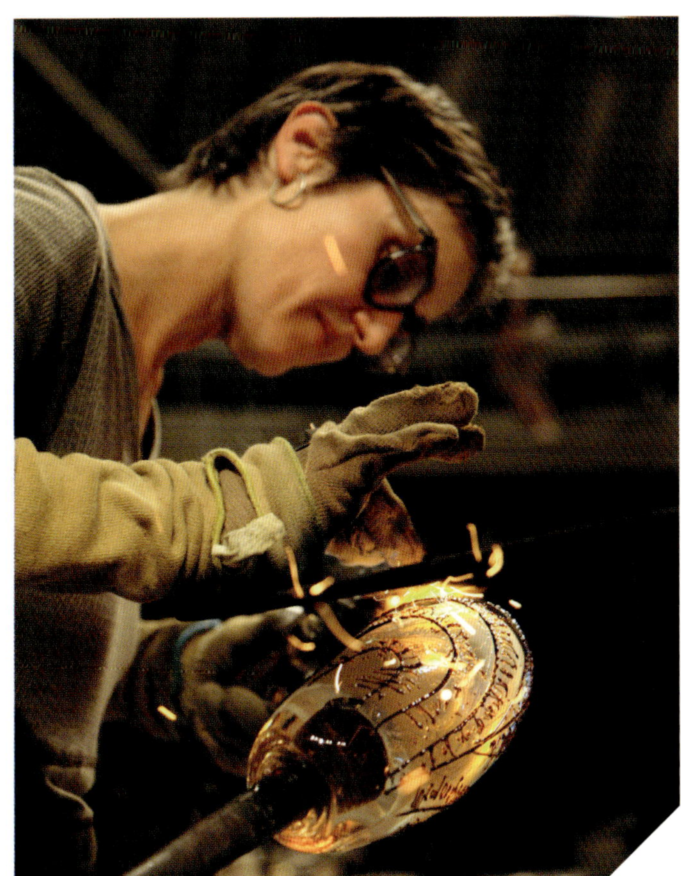

Russet and Brown Collection

Belfrage is known for her distinctive works in which complex patterns of fine glass lines trace her forms. Line work is common in glass production, however the line work in Belfrage's glass is not produced through traditional cane making. Rather, Belfrage 'draws' upon her forms with fine glass rods known as stringers. The process is time consuming, as each line is fused to the surface in the hot shop.

Inspired by patterns in nature, Belfrage originally applied the stringers to the surface of a blown form, creating a rich textural surface referencing rocks, mosses and plants such as Xanthorrhoea. In recent works she has applied the stringers at a much earlier stage of production, producing a more fluid line. She then meticulously cold works them, creating a soft, smooth surface reminiscent of wave-action-weathered glass fragments found on the shore.

Russet and Brown Collection, 2014, suggests growth resulting from the laying-down of matter, whether rocks forming over time, or textiles being produced as someone knits or weaves.

▸
Russet and Brown Collection, 2014
blown glass with cane drawing, hand sanded and polished
420 x 600 x 280
Photo: Pippy Mount

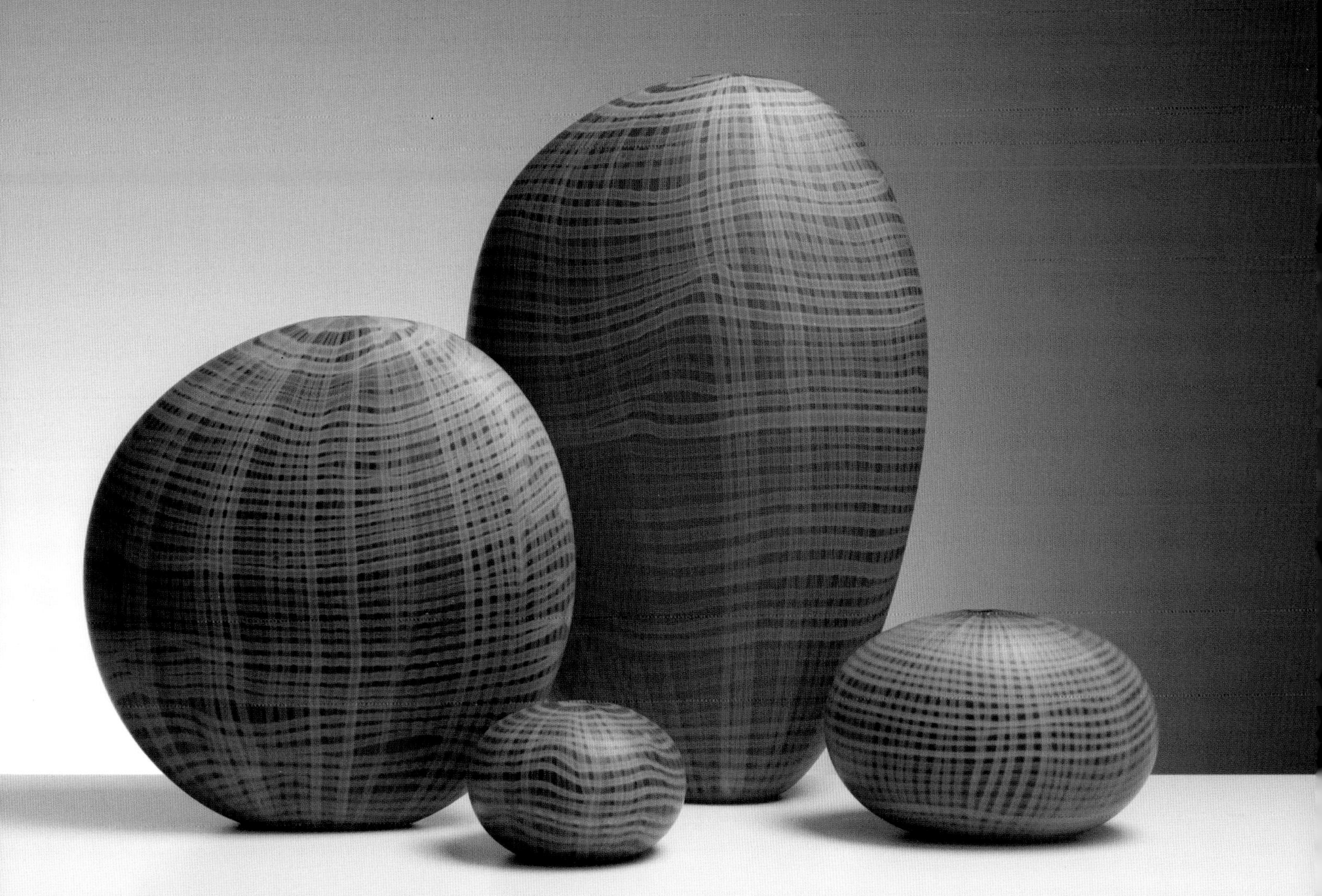

Awash in black

The sea's power is captured in *Awash in black*, 2014 — the lines swell and move in across the surface in ghostly form, referencing the majestic power of the ocean with its ever-shifting sands and currents of water.

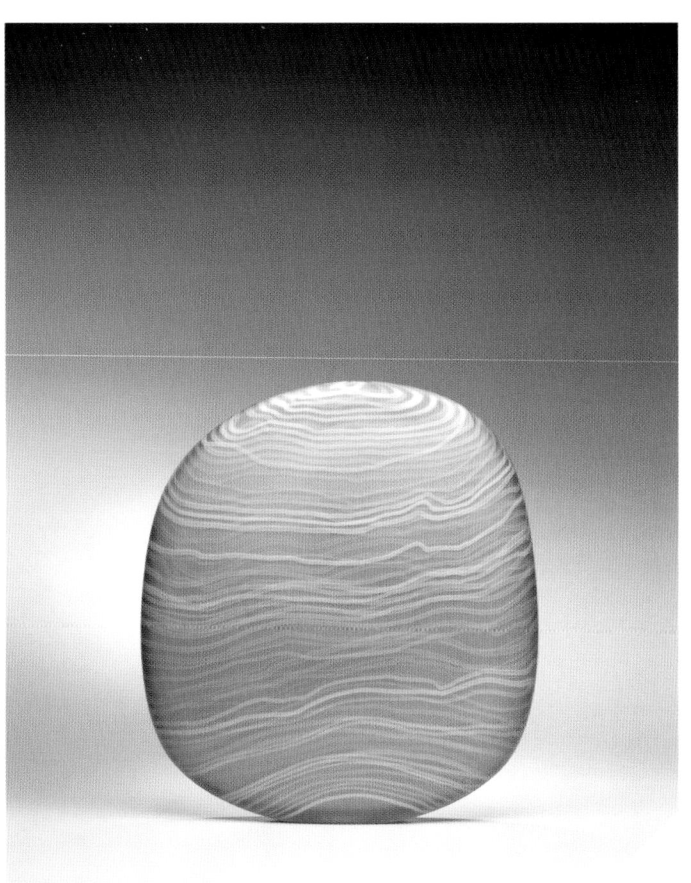

▸
Awash, #010414, 2014
blown glass with cane drawing,
hand sanded and polished
520 x 450 x 70
Photo: Grant Hancock

▸▸
Awash in black, 2014
blown glass with cane drawing,
hand sanded and polished
460 x 470 x 60
Photo: Pippy Mount

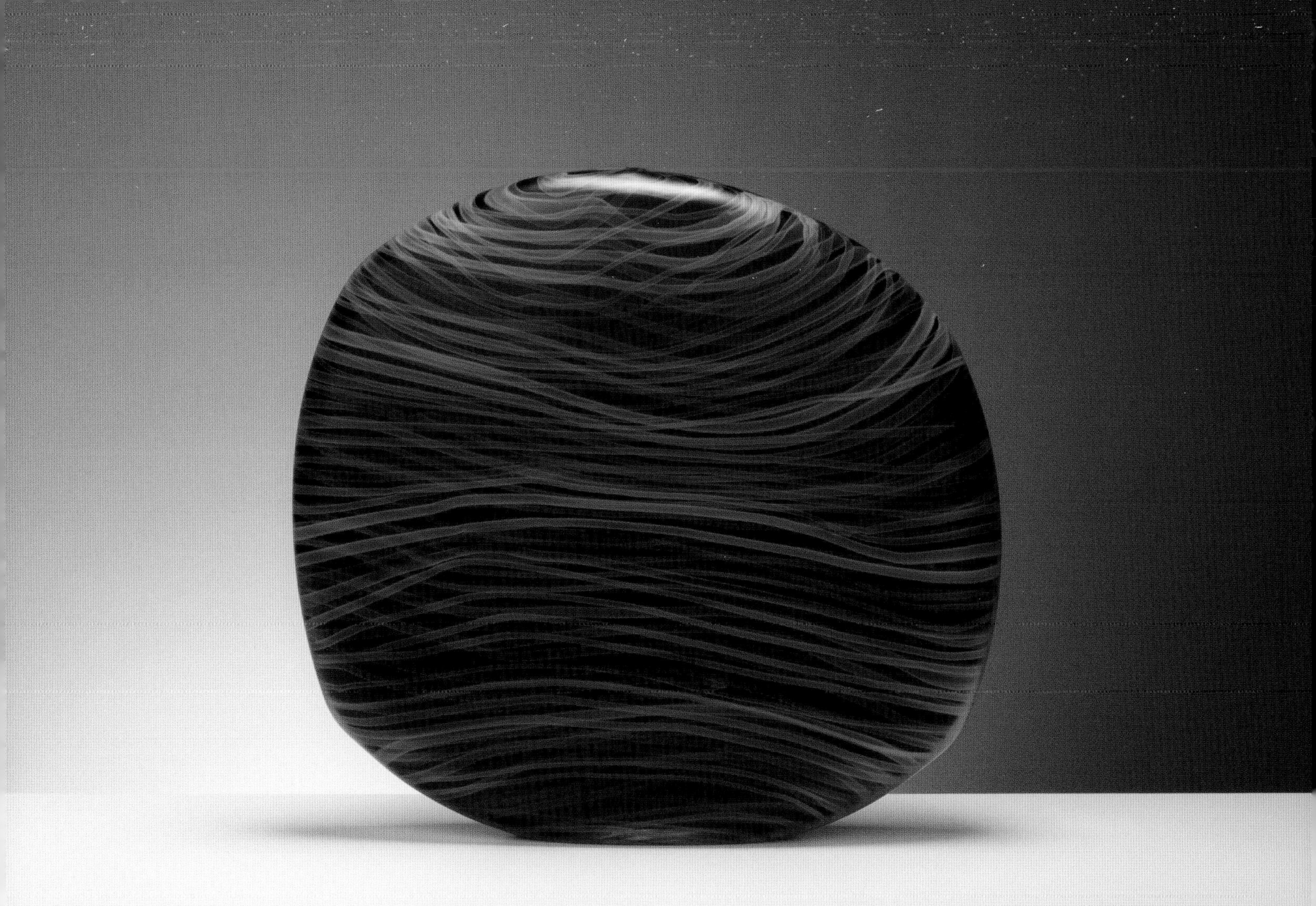

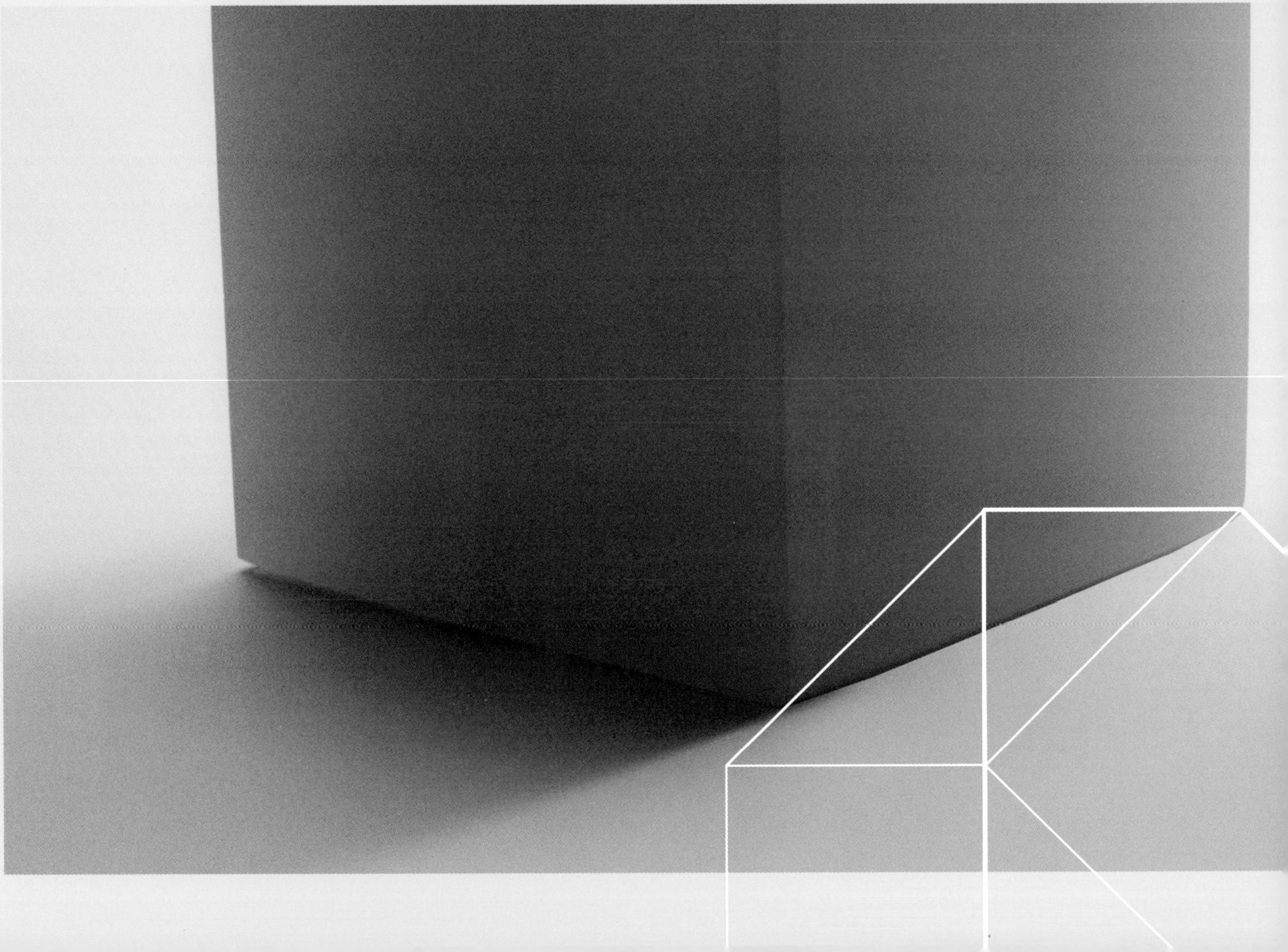

Deb Jones

Born 1963, Parkes, New South Wales
Lives in Adelaide, South Australia

Deb Jones has been exploring ideas through glass for more than two decades. Her hands-on conceptual approach to the physical and metaphoric properties of glass along with her broad interest across art, design and architecture have resulted in a creative output which includes public art, product design, architectural interventions and outstanding sculptural works — all unified by restraint and a highly refined, minimal aesthetic.

Jones initially studied Graphic Investigation and Sculpture at the Canberra School of Art, Australian National University, completing a Visual Arts degree in 1989. Her subsequent desire to explore an idea that could only be realised in glass, led her to enroll in a Graduate Diploma in the glass studio at the same school — under the mentorship of influential artist and educator Klaus Moje.

In 1993 Jones relocated to Adelaide — as many graduates of the Canberra School of Art have — to undertake the two-year traineeship in the JamFactory Glass Studio. During her traineeship

Maquettes of internal thoughts

'They are the ideas that just won't go away.

… Ideas such as
Water to solid, not quite solid, empty
Defined space, contained and preferably transparent
Swimming pools and empty rooms
The transferring from two dimensions to three dimensions
Building materials such as paper and cardboard
And of course humans
Not perfect ones
The folds and dints of human intervention
And the potential that still exists in the unfinished.

It all seems to return to a lean pallet of ideas and colour.'

Deb Jones

Maquettes of internal thoughts, 2014
mixed materials, dimensions variable, height approx 150mm
Photo: Grant Hancock

Overleaf
Maquettes of internal thoughts, 2014

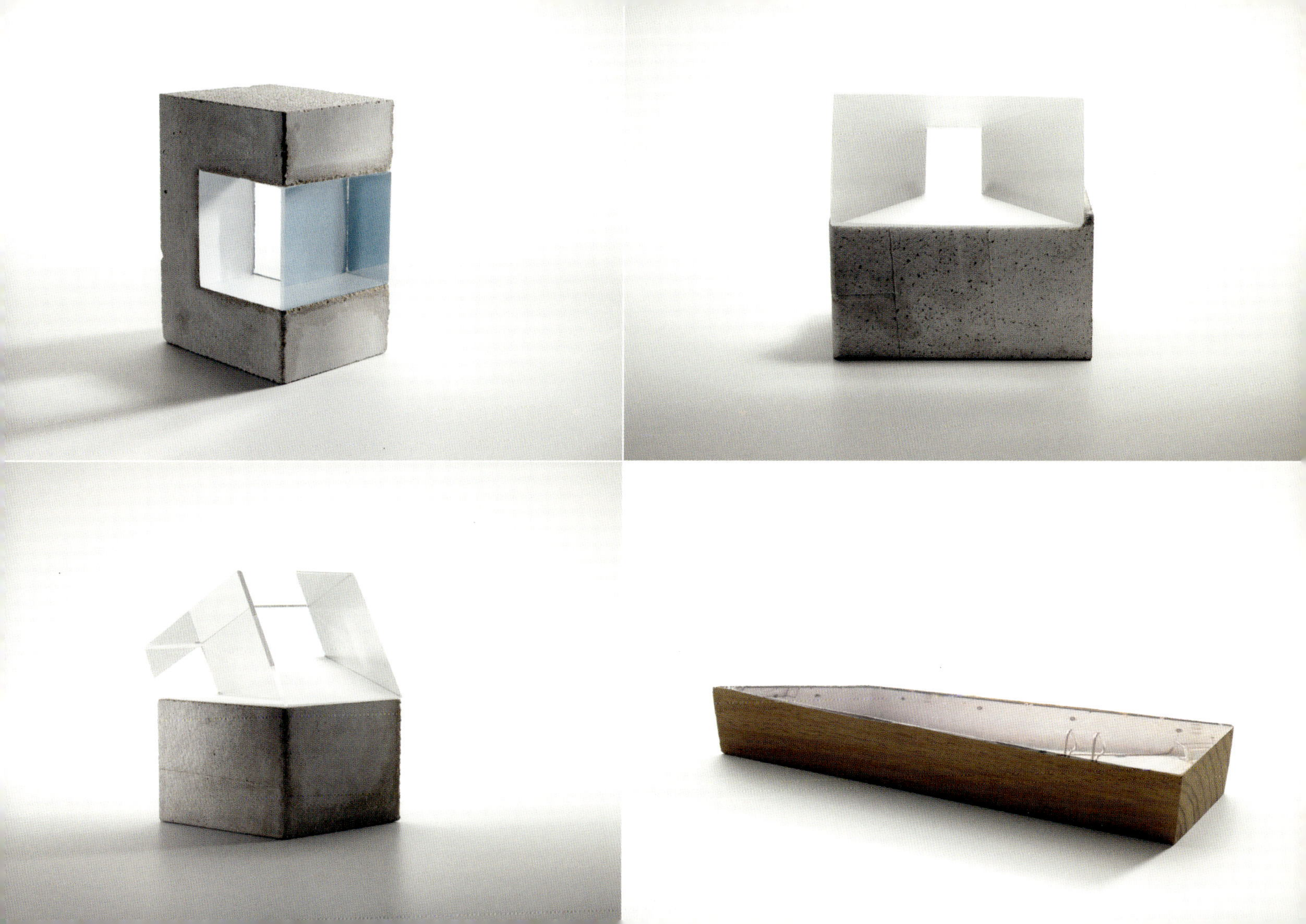

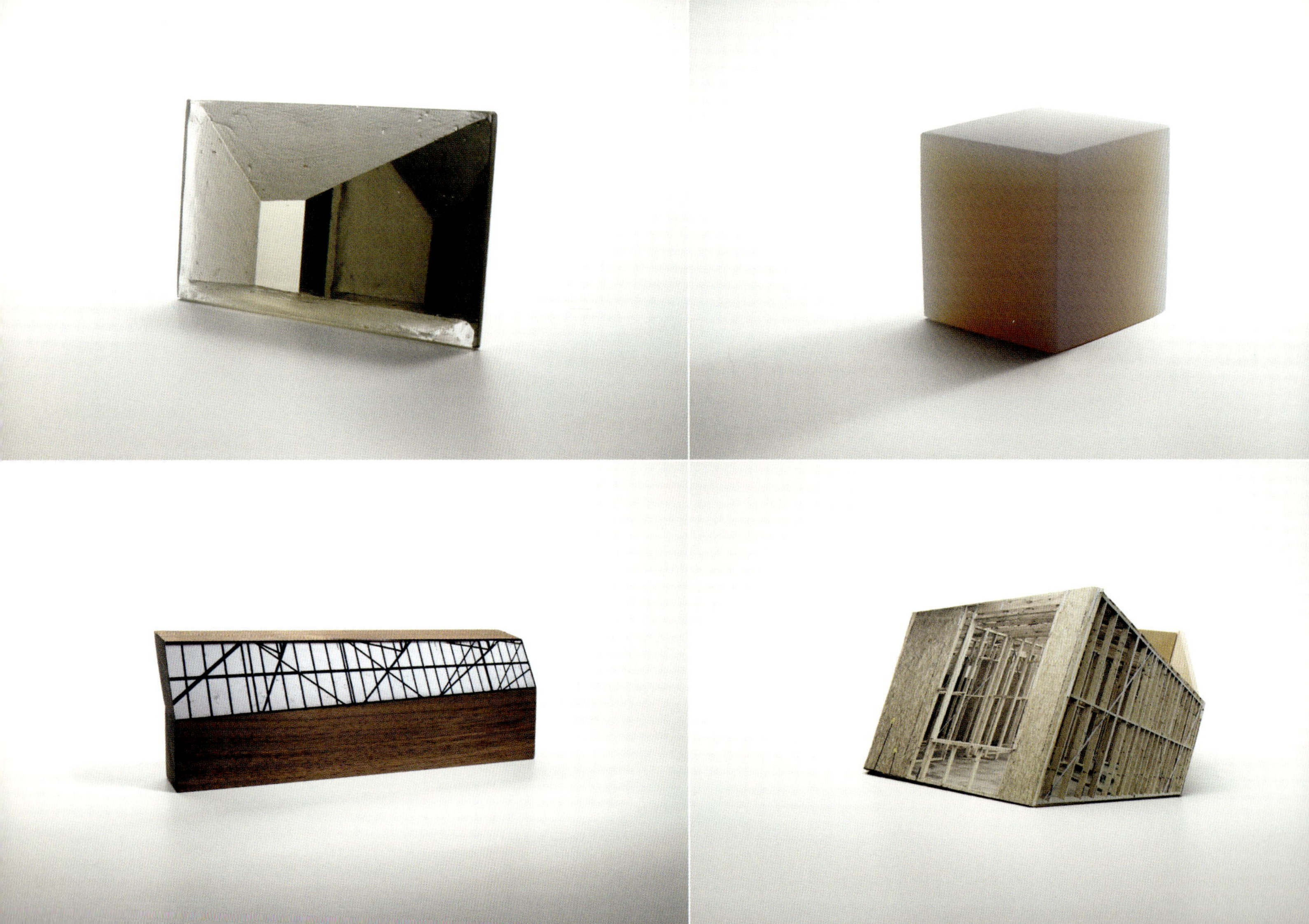

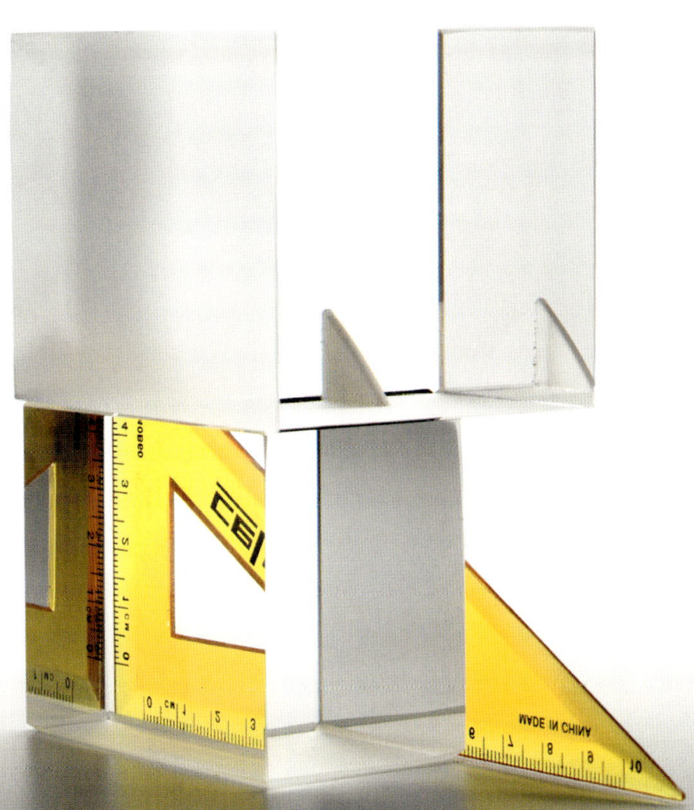
MADE IN CHINA

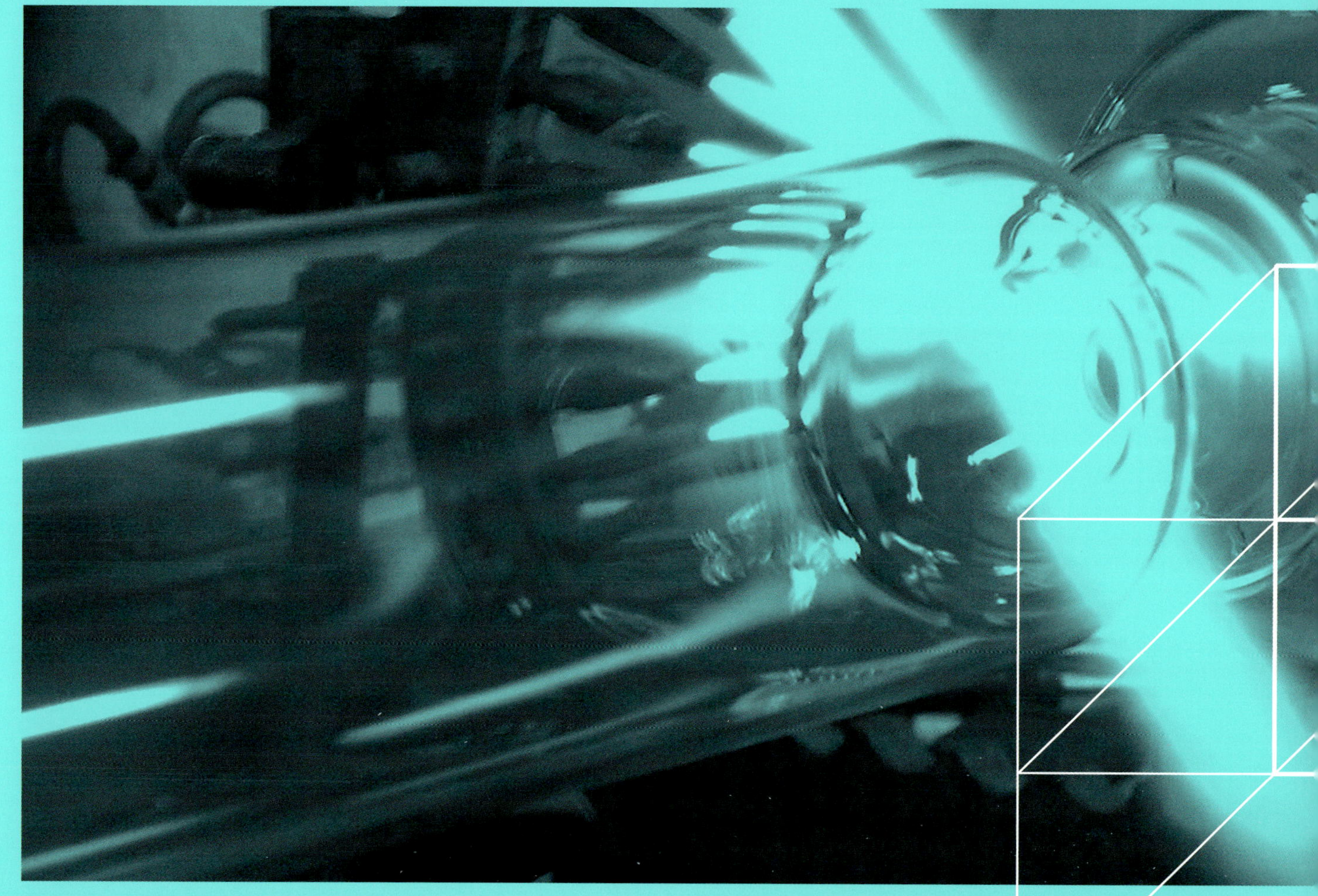

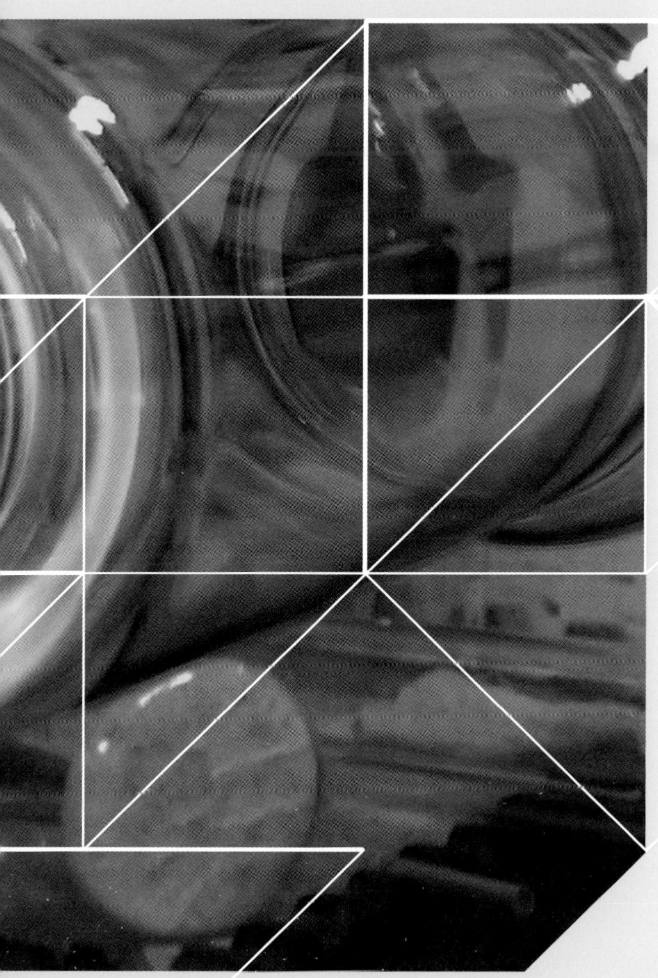

Elliat Rich

Born 1978, Paris, France
Lives Alice Springs, Northern Territory

When someone asks you do you want a cup of tea, is this all they are asking? Alice Springs-based designer Elliat Rich does not think so. With a design practice encompassing public art, jewellery, object design, the development of cross-cultural resources and other client-directed work, Rich employs design as a means to facilitate an experience, and enhance personal engagement and connection to each other and to place.

Rather than relying solely on the conventions of material choices and longevity of materials to create sustainability in her design, Rich reflects upon and questions our relationship to objects and the importance (or otherwise) they play in our lives. Interrogating everyday rituals in a process she describes as 'slow-motion seeing', Rich creates highly thoughtful objects that enrich, re-imagine and add meaning.

So what does having a cup of tea with someone really mean? This is not only a question about the consumption of a hot beverage; the request implies the desire to take time, to slow down and connect with someone. Looking at the apparatus that supports the ritual of a cup of tea, Rich was drawn to the impact the traditional camp-fire billy had on people, as opposed to the electric kettle. An iconic example of simple utilitarian design, the camp-fire billy creates a space for contemplation. Taking time to boil a billy gives people the chance to unwind, relax and connect, whereas the electric kettle, though providing expediency, stripped away people's ability to bond and be responsive to the process of making tea. Wanting to make the camp-fire billy portable and able to be experienced in any place, Rich designed *The Urban Billy*, 2013.

The Urban Billy went through many design and prototyping iterations before Rich settled on the final design. The design provides two drinking cups, highlighting that this activity is something to be shared and, with the billy taking about 30 minutes to boil, it provides the desired time. The transparent borosilicate glass enables one to watch the entire process of tea preparation. The movement of the water as it heats, the changing size, form and sound of the bubbles as the water comes to the boil, and the change in colour and leaves as they infuse, all enhance the experience.

After graduating with a Bachelor of Design from the College of Fine Arts, University of New South Wales in 2003, Rich undertook a six-month internship at the Centre for Appropriate Technology in Alice Springs, and continued working with Indigenous communities there for three years. In 2005, she returned to university to undertake her Honours degree, during which time the first iterations of *The Urban Billy* were developed. In 2007 her *Mycelium Pendant*, 2006 (a jewel made from growing mould), *The Lichen*, 2003 (a durable three-in-one piece of canvas that can be transformed into a swag/sleeping sack, tarpaulin or jacket) and *The Urban Billy* were all finalists in the Bombay Sapphire Design Discovery Award. *The Urban Billy* subsequently won the People's Choice award.

In 2008 Rich was awarded the Northern Territory Research and Innovation Award, and in the same year she won an episode of the new inventors for *The Lichen*. In the following years she branched into public art projects, and exhibited new work internationally with *The Other Hemisphere*. In 2012 she moved to Adelaide, working at JamFactory, where she co-curated the first in this series of exhibitions, *WOOD: art design architecture*. She has since returned to Alice Springs, setting up Elbowrkshp with her shoe-making partner James B Young.

Margaret Hancock Davis

Previous page
Rich worked with scientific glass blower Kent Carruthers in the production of *The Urban Billy*.
Photo: Elliat Rich

▸ ▸▸
Kent Carruthers in studio producing *The Urban Billy*.
Photo: Elliat Rich

▸
Oscar Prieckhaerts turning the sleeve and lid components for *The Urban Billy*.
Photo: Elliat Rich

▸▸
Each component of *The Urban Billy* was calibrated to precise measurements ensuring it held the right amount of water, or white spirit for its function.
Photo: Elliat Rich

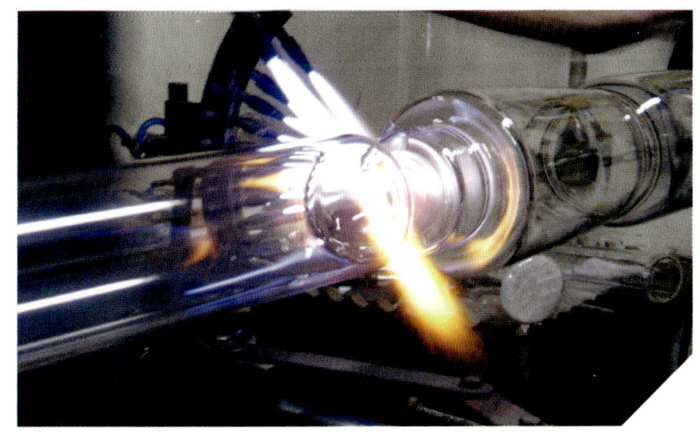

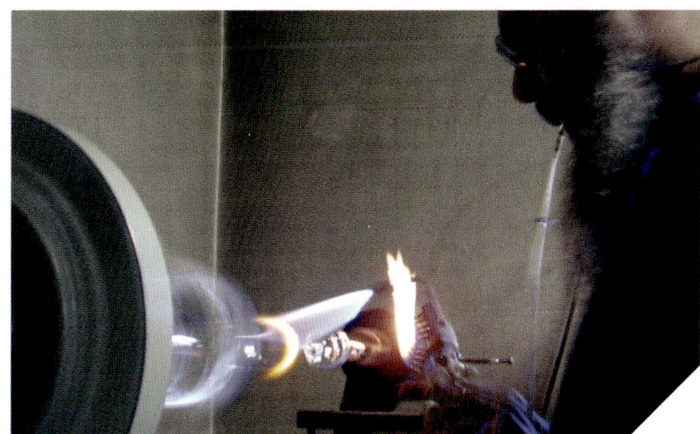

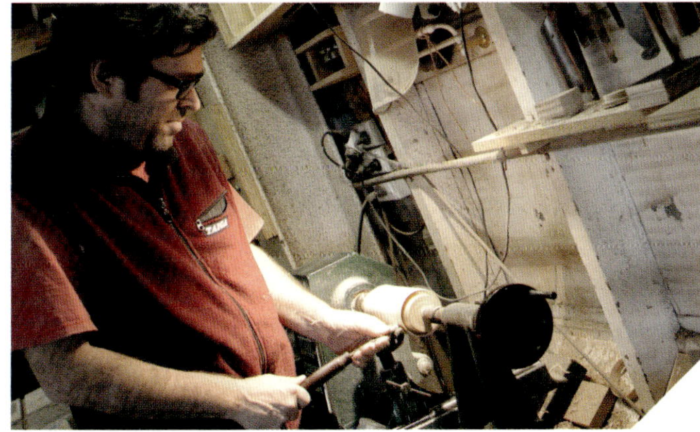

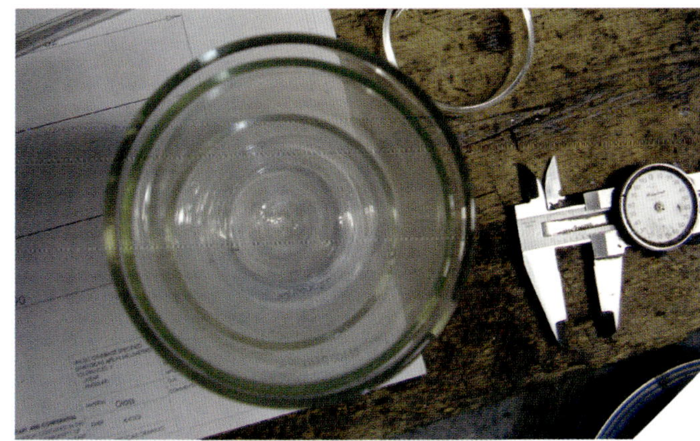

The Urban Billy

The Urban Billy, 2013, consists of five glass components: two drinking glasses with timber sleeves; a white-spirit burner; water chamber with timber lids; and a windbreak that doubles as a stand for the water chamber when in use. Its pared-back simplicity belies the precision and accuracy of each unit. During prototyping, Rich worked closely with scientific glass blower Kent Carruthers to ensure that each component of the billy not only fitted within each other for the pack up, but also that its scale was suitable for its role — for example, the methylated spirits reservoir holds just the right amount of white spirit to boil water for the two cups provided. The mountain ash sleeves and lids are individually formed and turned by Oscar Prieckhaerts to match each glass component. The sleeves provide both insulation for the hand when drinking, and absorb movement when packed up.

▸

The Urban Billy, 2013
hand-formed borosilicate glass, mountain ash
225 x 90 x 90
Photo: Grant Hancock

▾

The Urban Billy takes 30 minutes to boil facilitating time for two people to catch up and talk.
Photo: Grant Hancock

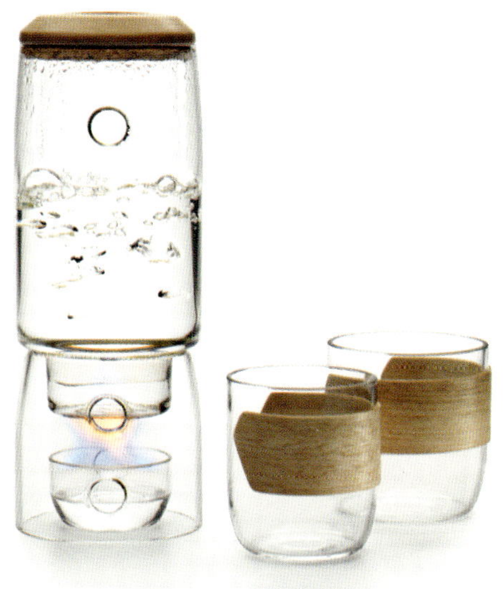

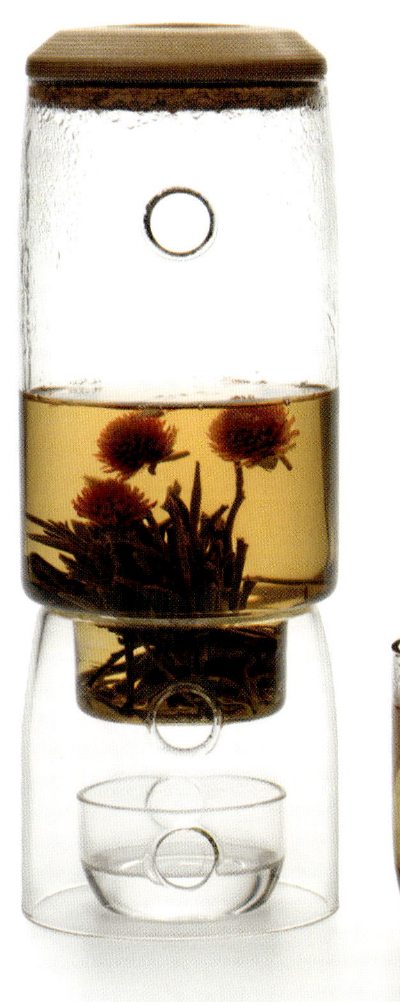
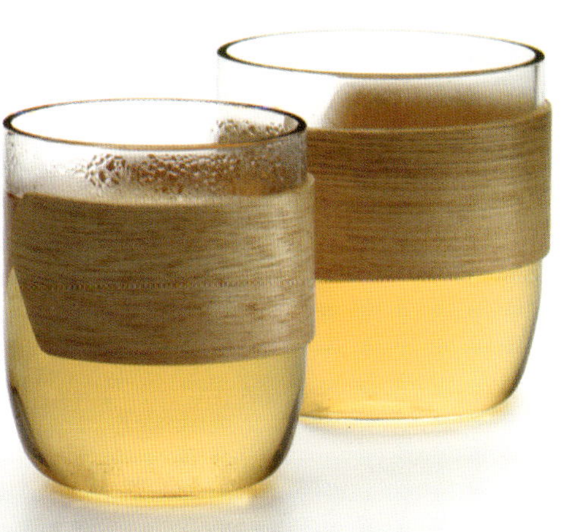

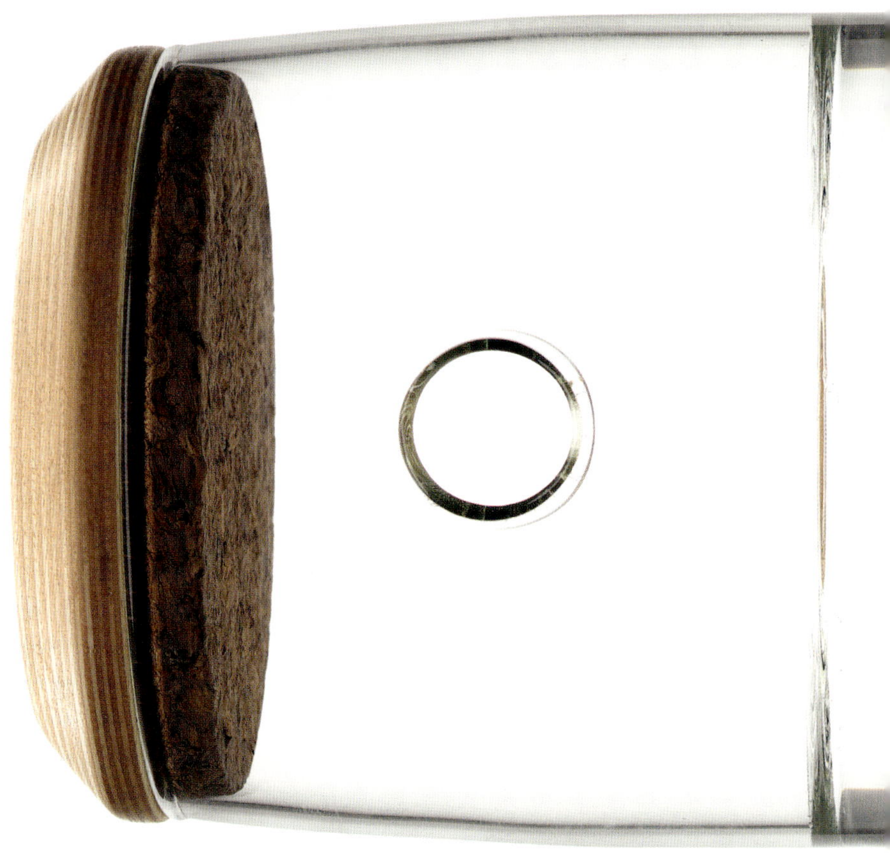

The Urban Billy packed.
Photo: Grant Hancock

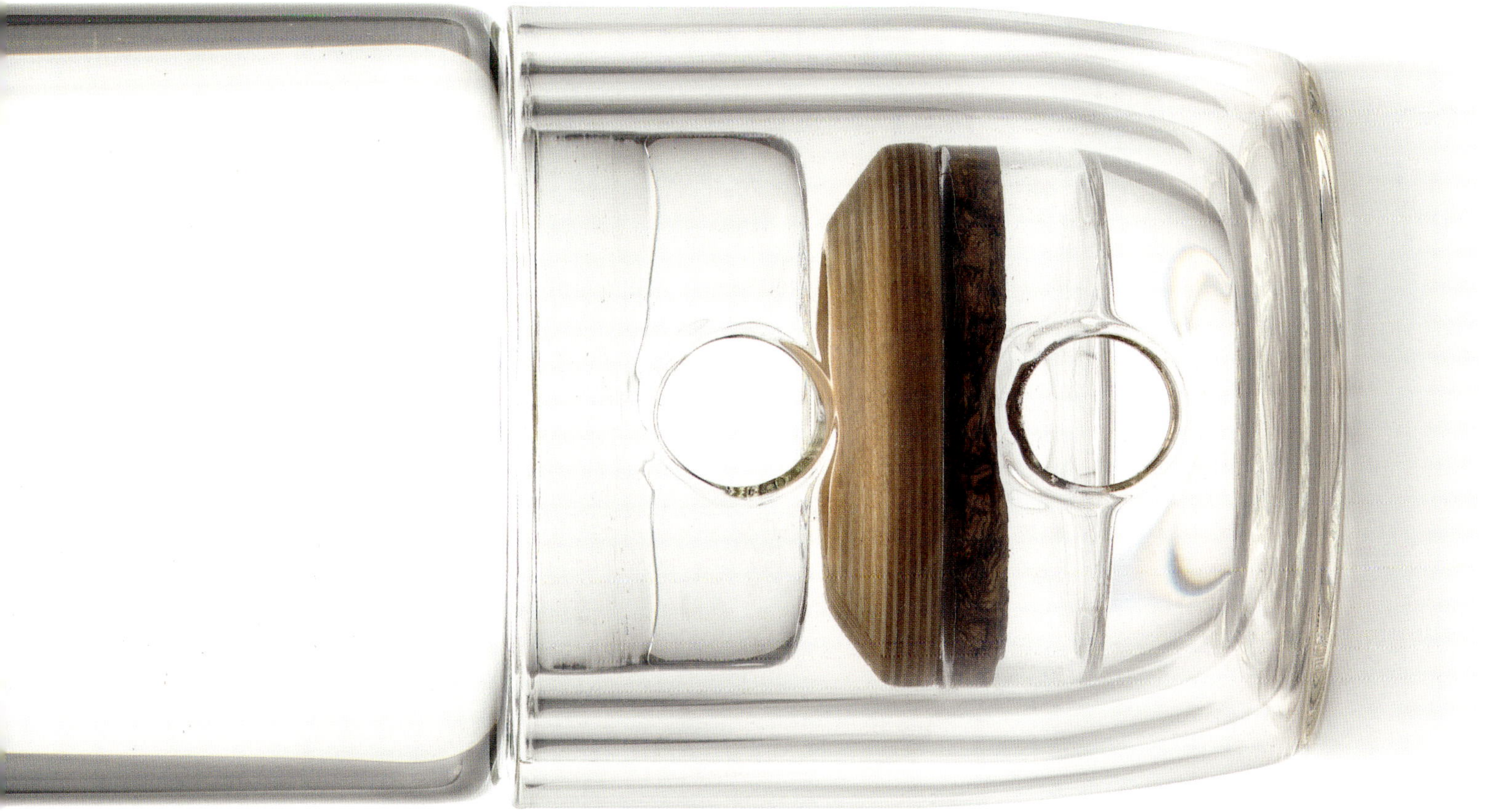

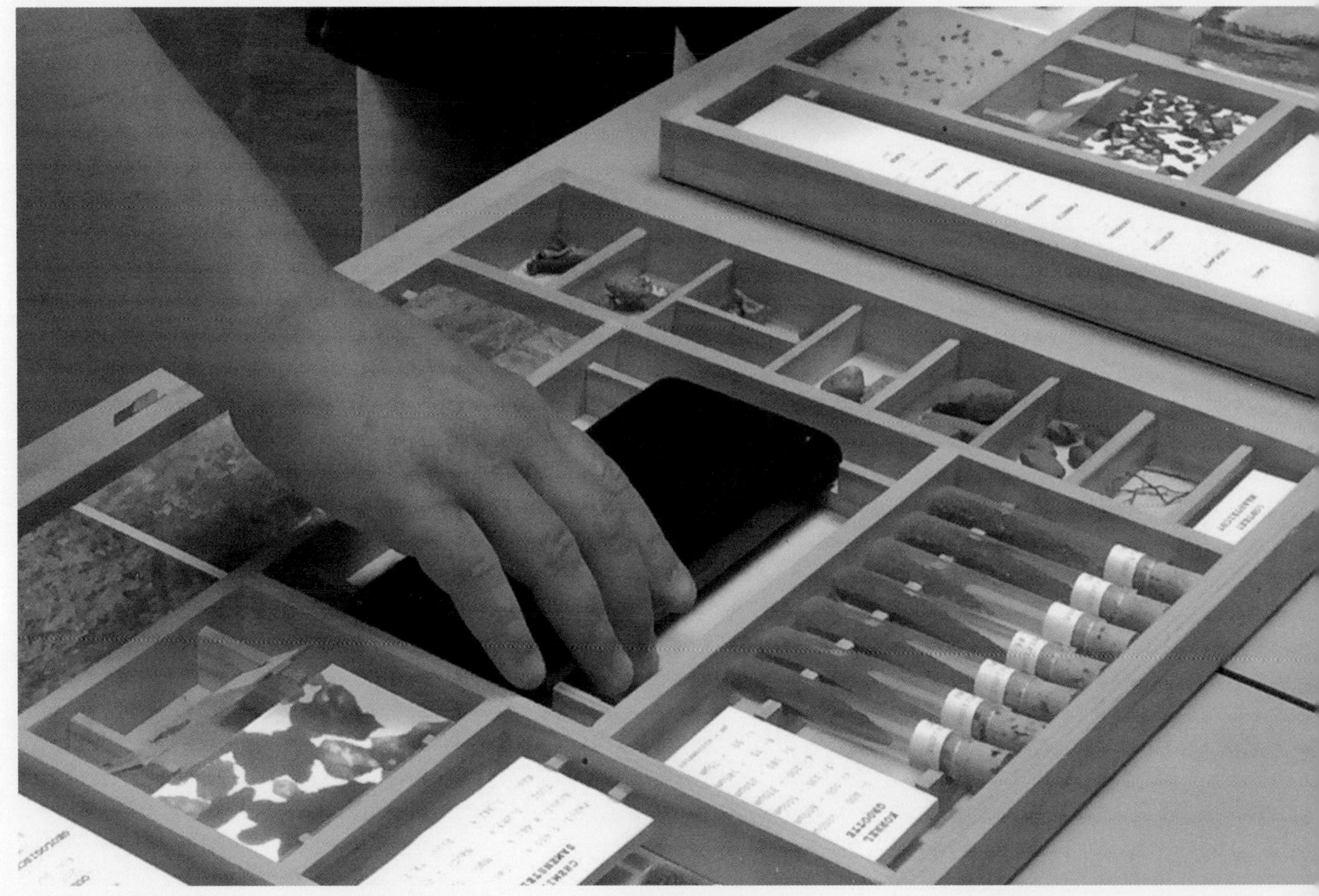

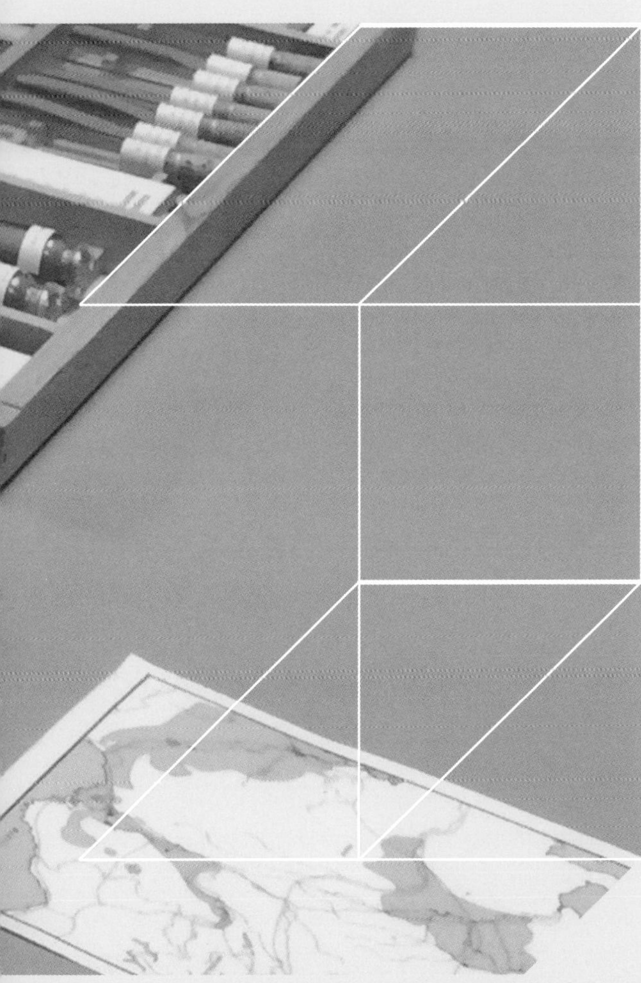

illumini

Established 2010, Adelaide, South Australia
Karen Cunningham
born 1978, Adelaide, South Australia
Mandi King
born 1982, Columbus, Ohio, USA
Both live in Adelaide, South Australia

Karen Cunningham and Mandi King formed the design and business partnership, illumini, in 2010. Both experienced glass artists, they completed an Associateship at JamFactory concurrently in 2006–07, after which they shared a studio together for a number of years at JamFactory and Blue Pony Studios. Originally from the United States, King studied at New York State College of Ceramics and Pilchuck Glass School, where she later became a teaching assistant. Cunningham trained as a glass artist at the University of South Australia, and travelled to Pilchuck as part of her Associateship at JamFactory. In 2012 Cunningham was appointed Creative Director of the Glass Studio at JamFactory. For *GLASS: art design architecture* they have designed and manufactured an artisan greenhouse. The project investigates architectural elements on a domestic scale, and re-examines the greenhouse through the lens of a glass artist.

The illumini business model is centred on craft, design, sustainability, experimentation and community. Creating artisan products, Cunningham and King are seeking to carve out a market in which clients value the knowledge and skills of a craftsperson. The illumini design process begins with looking at the materiality of glass, including qualities of transparency, the ability to transmit heat and light, and its malleability when hot. Each of their products is designed to highlight one of these qualities. The *illumini Decanter*, 2009, investigates the ability for glass to re-join when hot. The decanter features a central connection point, where the hot glass has been tacked together. The shape acts as a handle and also aids in the aeration of wine. The *Holey light*, 2012, looks at the transparency of glass and its ability to diffuse light. In this product, they combine handcrafted elements with a water-jet glass cutting technique, which enables them to produce shapes that would not be achievable by hand.

Each illumini project looks at sustainability, and ways that energy can be reduced or materials can be recycled. For the *illumini Greenhouse*, 2014, Cunningham and King began by considering how sheet-glass offcuts could be recycled to form glass panels. This idea follows on from the process used for the *Holey light*, which incorporated timber offcuts from the Otto timber mill and other wood studios. Spending time at Canberra Glassworks as an artist in residence, King experimented with waste sheet glass from the studio. This workshopping allowed them to test and trial techniques for reclaiming glass. Although these techniques are not being incorporated into the current greenhouse design, they are now part of the illumini repertoire, and may find their way into future projects. Sustainability is taken a step further with a focus on sustainable culture and community. With each product, illumini aims to utilise and develop the skill sets of a community of glass blowers and craftspeople. The production of the objects acts to enhance and preserve the skills of craftspeople, while at the same time providing them with interesting and challenging work.

Research and development are key aspects of the illumini design process. On a recent Australia Council Helsinki Studio Residency, Cunningham and King met with artists, designers and architects whose practices parallel their own design language. Making connections with makers, they admire Scandinavian designers for their sensitivity to material, their concern for environmental and cultural sustainability, and for creating a strong philosophy of design.

Adele Sliuzas

Previous page
Karen Cunningham in the Atelier NL Studio, Eidenhoven, Netherlands, 2012
Photo: Mandi King

▸

Mandi King
Bubbleboxes, 2009
blown glass
dimensions variable
Photo : Tom Roschi

▸▸

Karen Cunningham
Dishee Stacking Bowls, 2009
blown glass
300 x 220 dia.
Photo: Michael Haines

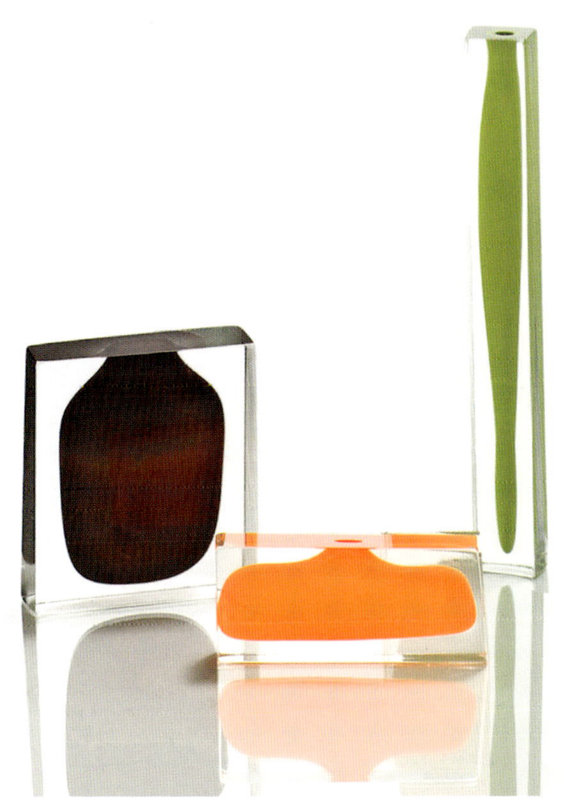

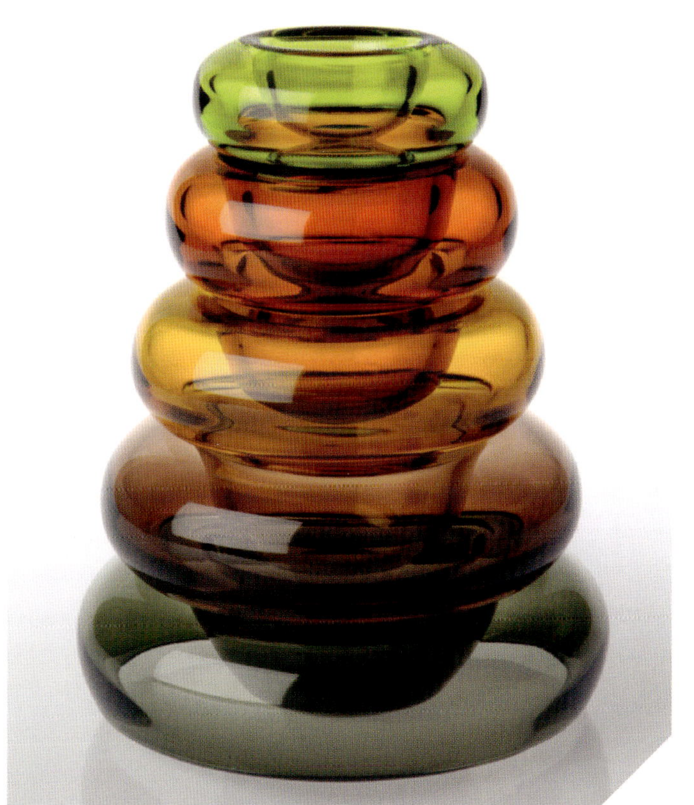

▸

illumini Decanter, 2009
blown glass
300 x 130 dia.
Photo: Ashley Page

▸▸

Holey Light 1 and 2, 2012
laminated plywood, float glass,
light fitting
160 x 240 x 80
360 x 360 x 80
Photo: Grant Hancock

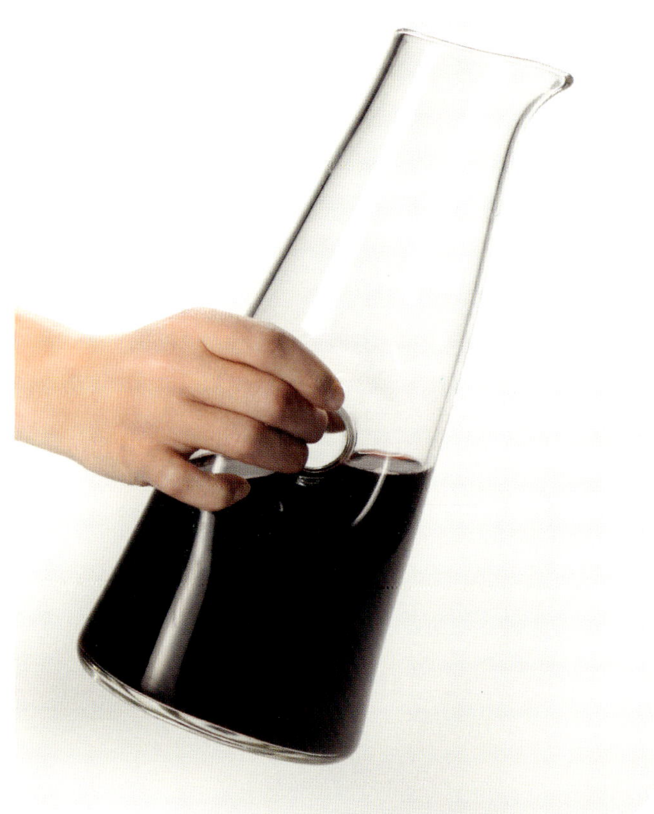

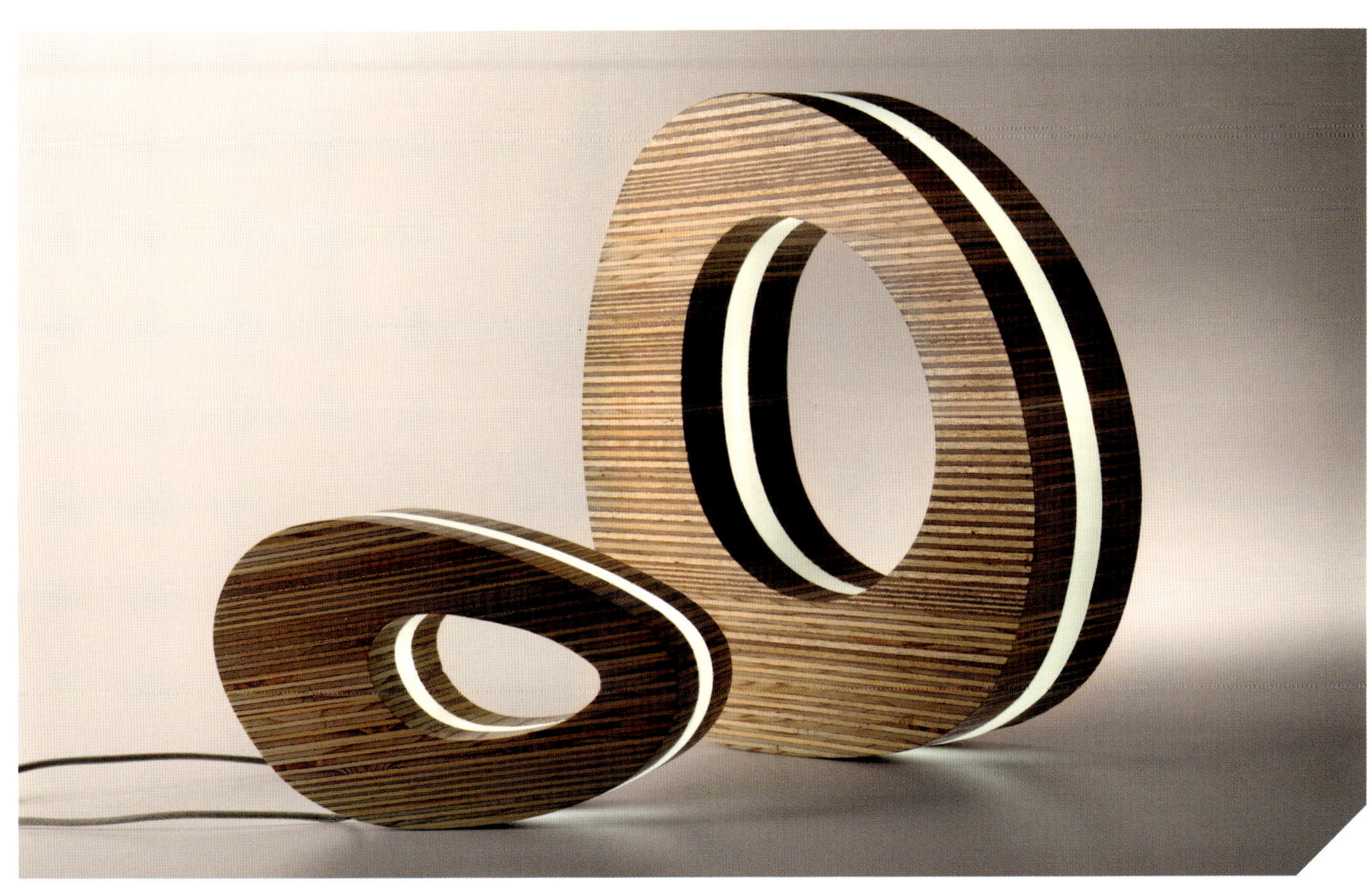

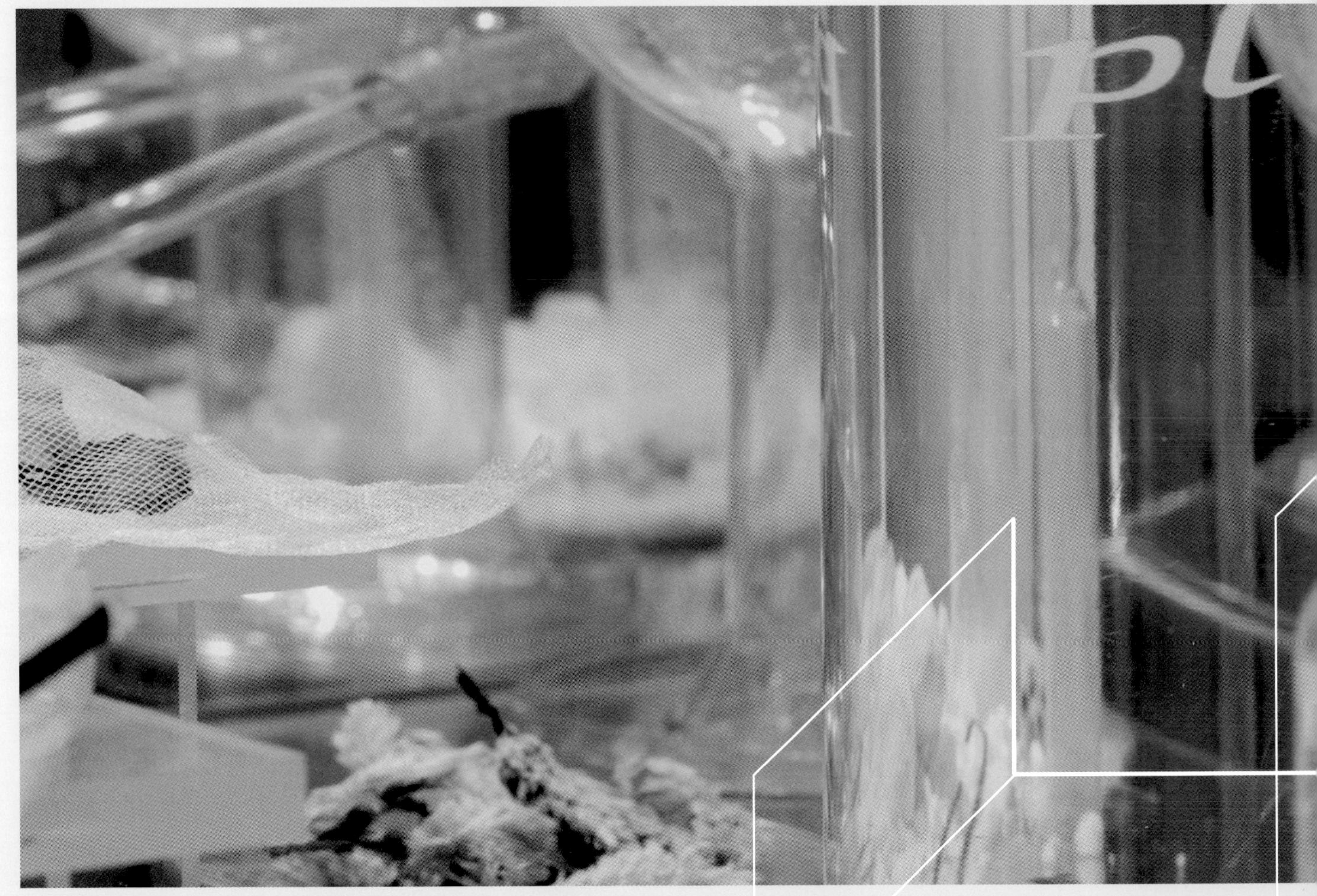

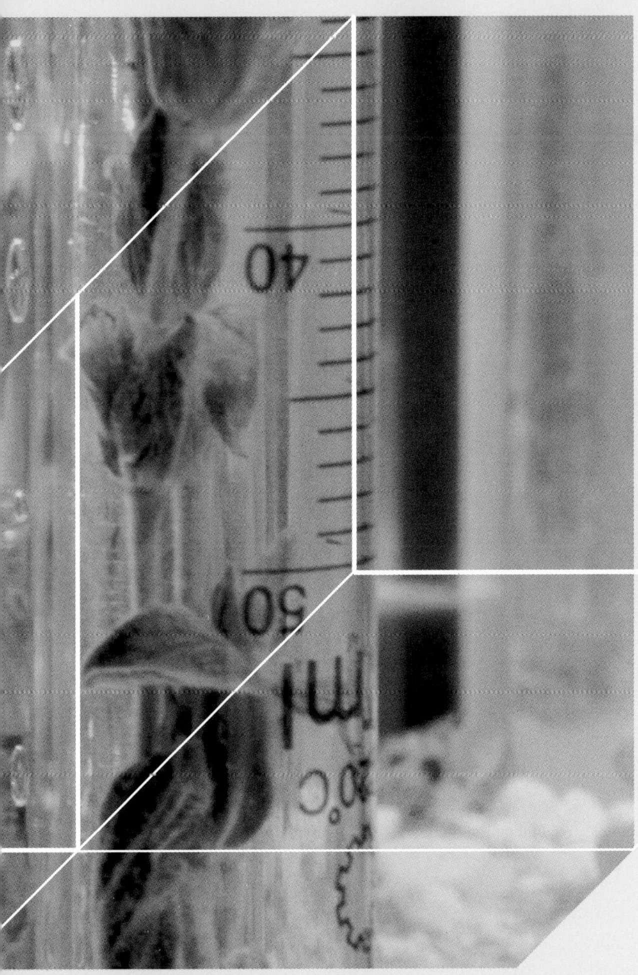

Janet Laurence

Born 1949, Sydney, New South Wales
Lives Sydney, New South Wales

One of Australia's most celebrated visual artists, Janet Laurence has established a poetic practice that engages with the concerns of our denuded and fragile planet. Her evocatively layered works can be found in the public realm, private domestic spaces and the white cube of the gallery.

Working at the nexus of art and science, Laurence sees art as a means to reveal the wonder and mysteries of the natural world, while also asking her audiences to consider the difficult and often fraught relationship we have with it. Long before climate change and environmental degradation became the focus of mainstream discussion, Laurence looked to the environment for inspiration, and drew upon its deep interconnectedness with all of life in her work. She puts to the forefront of our minds something so obvious, but so often overlooked and forgotten in our busy, pre-packaged world: we are completely dependent on plants, as they provide us with nutrition, the ability to see, and the oxygen we breathe.

Not wishing to be didactic in her approach, it has only been in recent works that Laurence has consciously included a layer of activism. A growing sense of urgency in the planet's plight has led to this activism. Her considered installation, *Waiting: a medicinal garden for plants,* 2010, which combined living, ailing and dead plants in a 'plant hospital' at the Royal Botanical Gardens for the 17th Biennale of Sydney, and the immersive environment of *After Eden*, 2012, commissioned by Sherman Contemporary Art Foundation and featuring endangered animals, use empathy as the best weapon against our inactivity.

Throughout her work Laurence juxtaposes the real with the man-made. She combines an unconventional palette of art materials — ash, moss, wax, minerals, oxides, dried and living plants, taxidermied birds and animals, laboratory glass and scientific apparatus — with haunting photographic images that include pristine landscapes and empty ghost-like glass houses printed on glass and Perspex.

Laurence regularly uses glass in her sculptural installations. Its appeal is multilayered and includes its mineral lineage and alchemical capabilities; its translucency and transparencies, which can be used to reveal and veil; its facility to transform or transmit light; and its capacity to reflect, project and distort.

Glass is a multifaceted material. Through it, the inner workings of life reveal themselves when viewed through the glass lens of the microscope. Life is categorised, preserved and displayed in a museum's glass vitrines, and personal collections are presented behind glass in *wunderkammers* or cabinets of curiosities. Historically, grand structures of glass and cast iron were built to celebrate the spoils of colonisation and our industrialised world, while botanic scholarship and experimentation occurs in vaulted glass houses. In her work, Laurence employs all these glass tropes for revealing, preserving and remembering.

Laurence studied in Italy, the USA and Australia, receiving a Masters of Fine Art in 1993 from the University of New South Wales. In 1986 and 1992 she was awarded Australia Council Fellowships. She is the recipient of both a Rockefeller and Churchill Fellowship. Laurence was a Trustee of the Art Gallery of NSW (1996–2005). She is currently a Visiting Fellow with the University New South Wales Art & Design. Her works have been presented in leading exhibitions — including the 9th and 17th Biennales of Sydney (1992 and 2010), Echigo-Tsumari Art Triennale (2003, 2006) and the Australian Perspecta (1985, 1991, 1997) — and are found in major collections both nationally and internationally.

Margaret Hancock Davis

Previous page
In Memory of Nature (detail), 2010
acrylic, scientific glass, dried plants, seeds, sulphur, salt, amethyst, owl specimens, shellac, tulle, wood, burnt bones, hand-blown glass, oil paint, mirrors
dimensions variable
Installation view, BREENSPACE, Sydney, 2010 Photo: Jamie North

▸ ▸▸

Waiting – A Medicinal Garden for Ailing Plants, 2010
transparent mesh, mirror, oil, acrylic, scientific glass vessels, plants (living and dried), tulle, blown glass, silicon tubing, minerals, crystals, seeds, water
3000 x 5000 x 3000
Installation view, *The Beauty of Distance: Songs of Survival in a Precarious Age*: 17th Biennale of Sydney, Royal Botanic Gardens, Sydney, 2010
Photo: Jamie North

▾

Ghost glasshouse, 2003
seraphic-fired screenprinted glass, stainless steel, texts of extinct botanical species
4000 x 5000 x 1500
Installation view, private garden
Photo: Courtesy of the artist

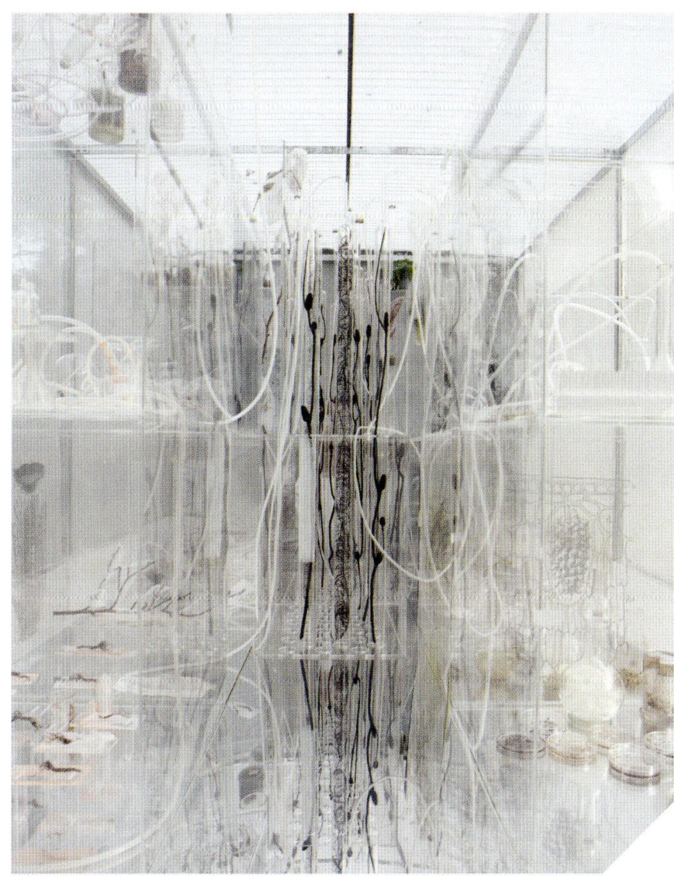

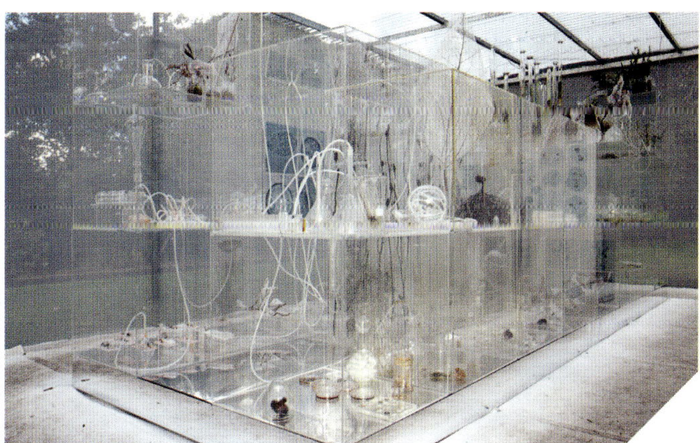

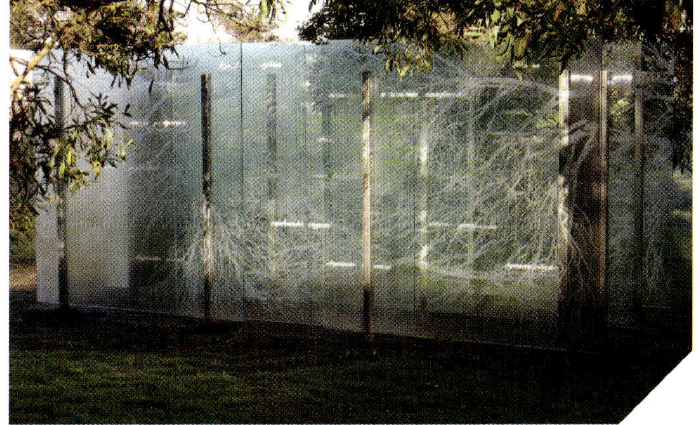

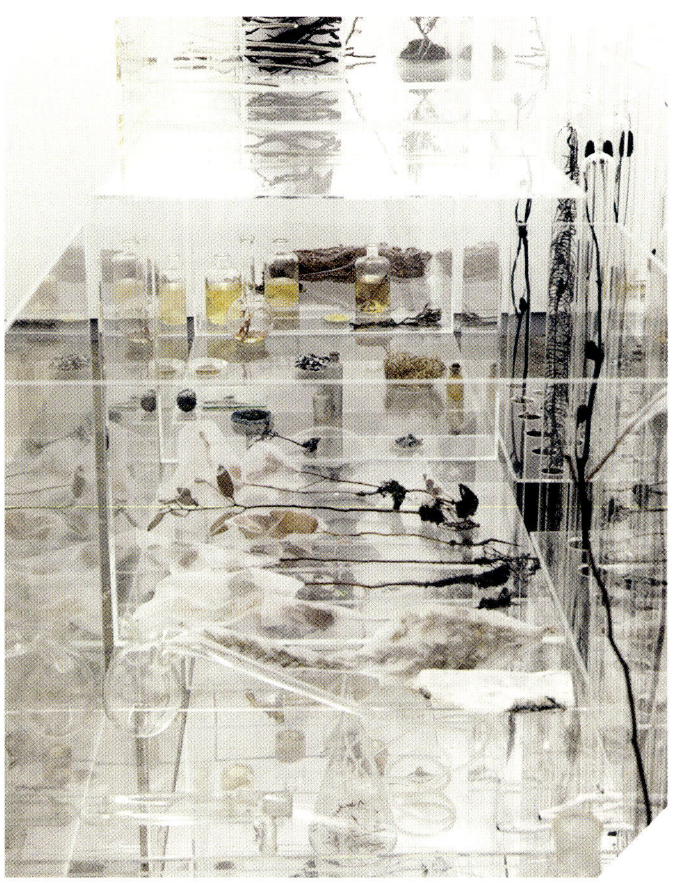

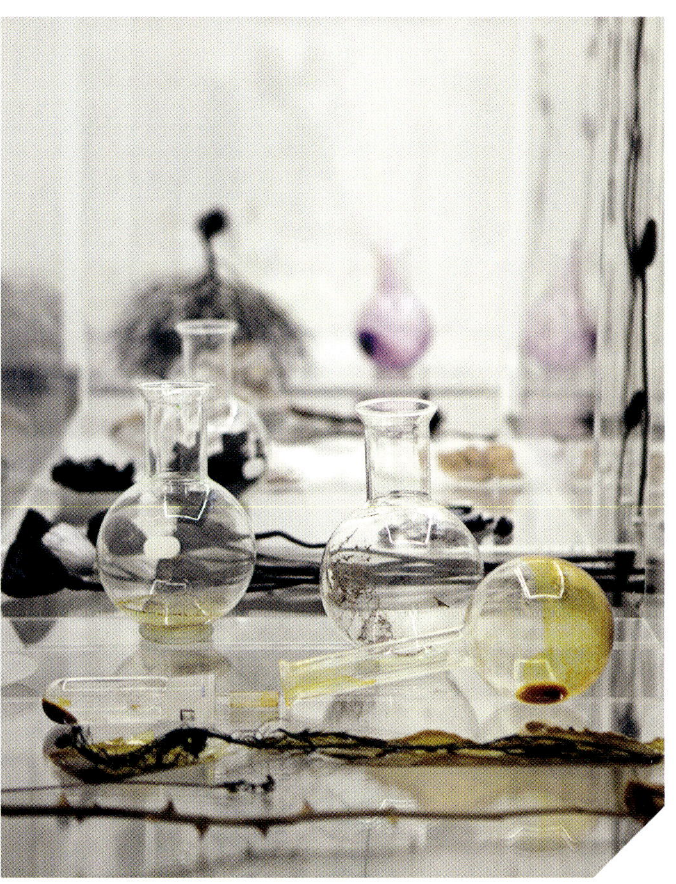

◂ ◂◂

In Memory of Nature (detail), 2010
Photo: Jamie North

▸

Janet Laurence
photographed with her work
Waiting – A Medicinal Garden for Ailing Plants, 2010
Photo: Jamie North

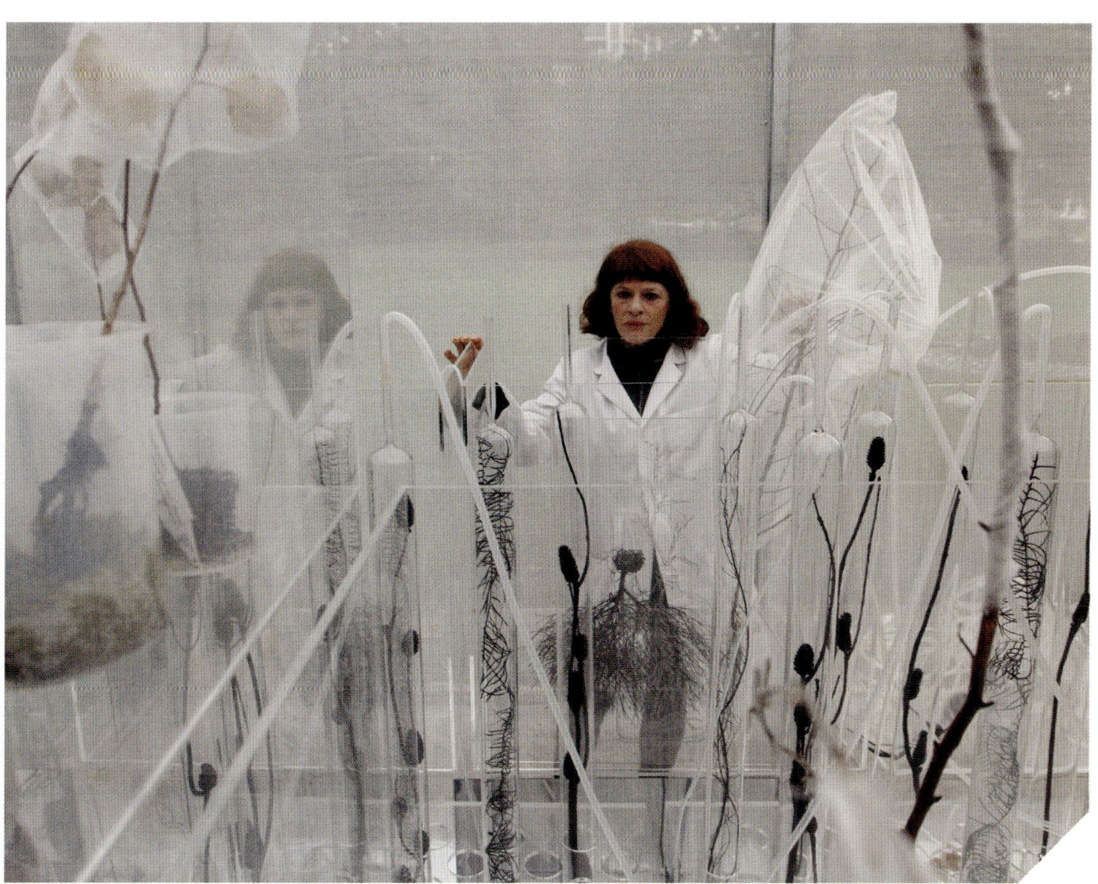

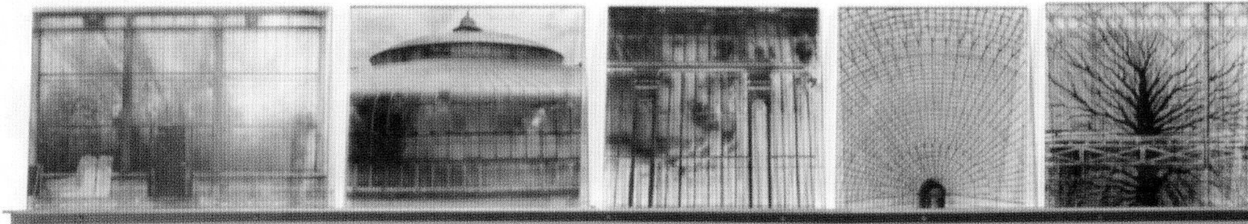

Botanical Residues (after the Great Glasshouse), 2005
duraclear, photographs on acrylic
dimensions variable
Photo: Courtesy of
Arc One Gallery

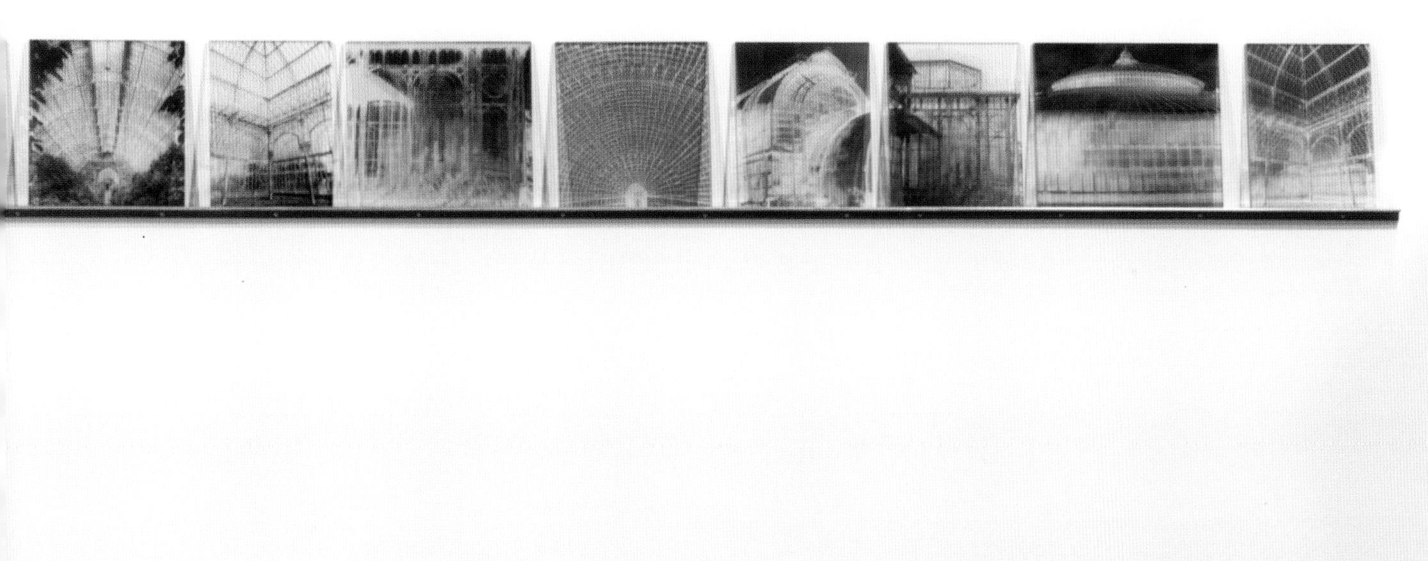

Natural History

Part of the *Landscape and Residue* series, *Natural History*, 2008, presents a scorched lab-like table pierced through with large scientific glass vials. Each vial contains burnt plant forms, delicately threaded through by Laurence to create a vertical carbonated forest. This work refers to two of Laurence's earlier bodies of work. The first — *Cellular Gardens (where breathing begins)*, 2005 — was created as an artistic response to the revival and healing of native forests after bushfires. In this work Laurence placed glass vials feeding and nurturing the scorched landscape as it regenerated. These vials mimicked the green fresh shoots that take hold after such devastation. The second — *Carbon Futures*, 2008 — was produced with glass artist Gabriella Bisetto. Laurence worked with Bisetto to create glass eggs that contained the ashes of plant material. Freshly cut plants were introduced during the glass-blowing process, and when the heat ignited the specimens, the resultant ash and blackened plants and seeds were captured and preserved in the glass forms.

▸
Natural History (Landscape and Residues Series), 2008
glass vials, botanical specimens, wood, steel, polished aluminium mirror
1500 x 2000 x 500
Photo: Courtesy of Arc One Gallery

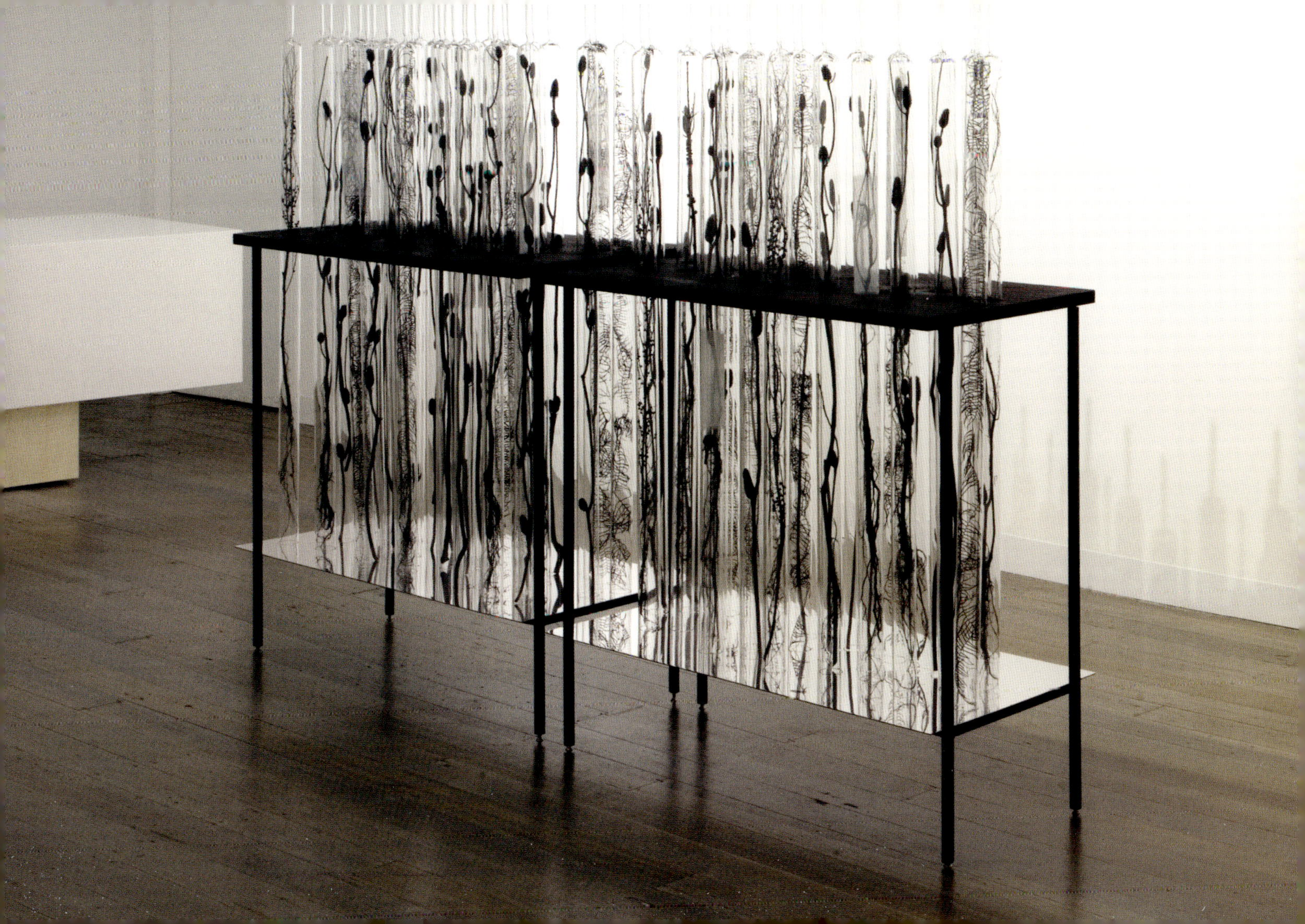

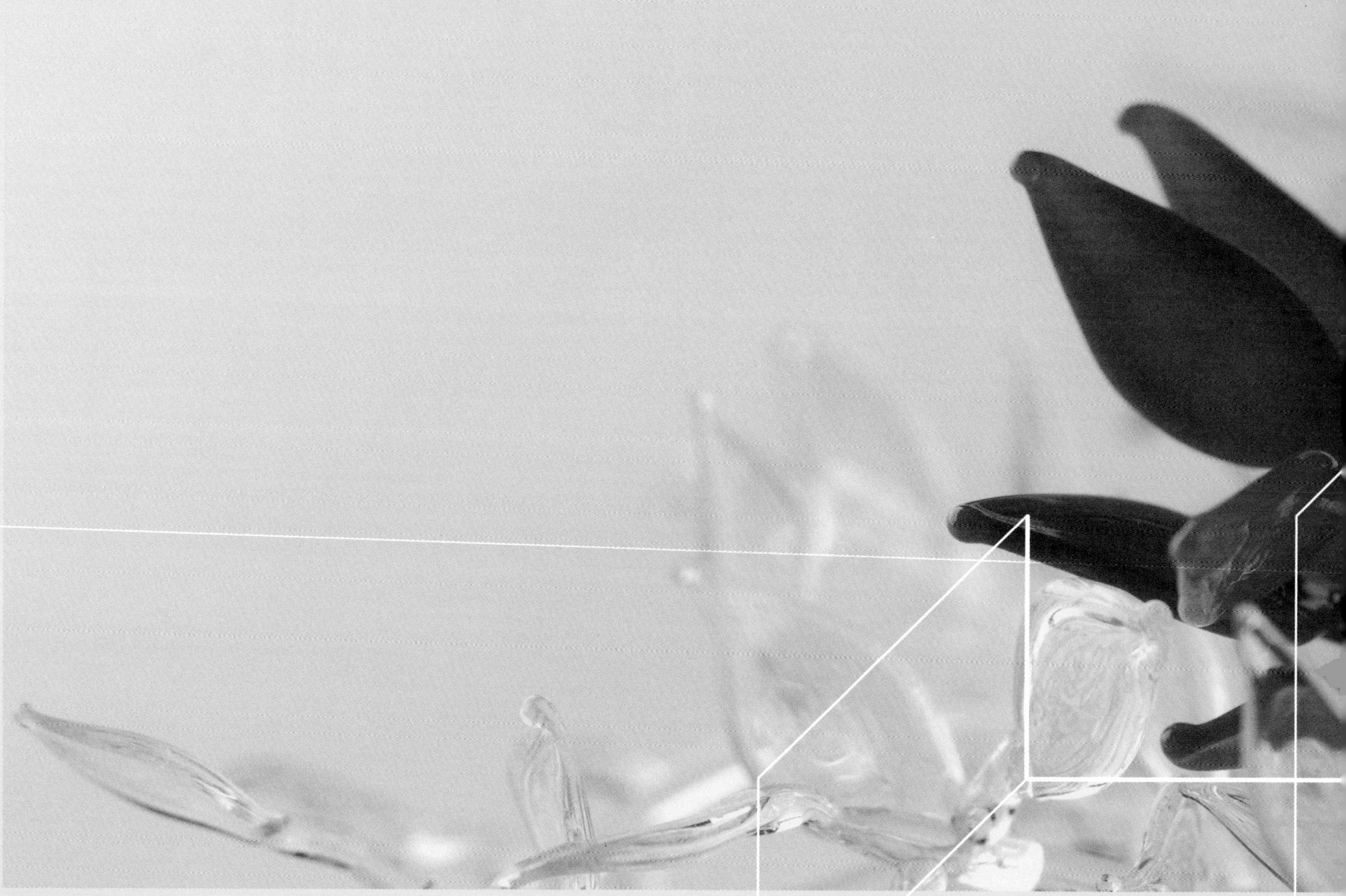

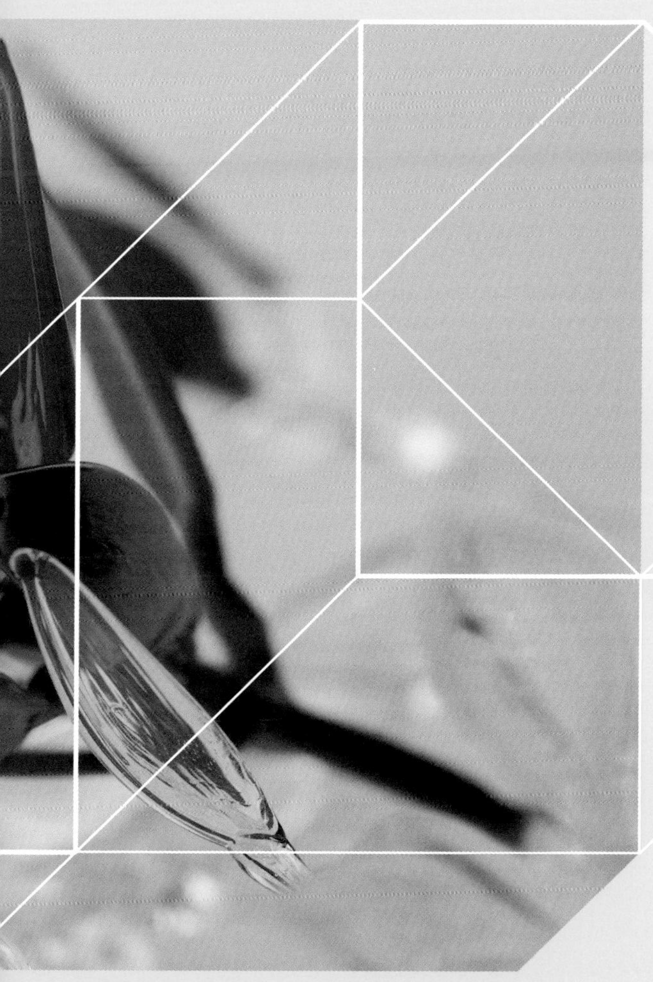

Jess Dare

Born 1982, Adelaide, South Australia
Lives Adelaide, South Australia

'I'm a lampworker, a jeweller, a glass maker, a gardener, a collector and a designer.'

Jess Dare, 2013

Some of us are lucky to experience a classic 'ah ha' moment, when we just know what we should pursue in life. This happened for jeweller Jess Dare while travelling through Europe. On this fateful trip she visited the island of Murano in Venice. Famed for its centuries-old glass-making tradition, Murano provided the key to her future. Transfixed by the lamp workers creating their work, Dare wanted to know more.

Lamp-worked glass is created when coloured glass rods, heated over a flame, are twisted and pulled into shape using various tools. Its meticulous nature complements the jewellery skills Dare developed as part of her Bachelor of Visual Arts degree at the Adelaide College of the Arts TAFE SA. To expand her skills, she has also undertaken workshops with leading national and international lamp-work practitioners, including Loren Stump.

After completing her degree in 2007, Dare became an access tenant at the internationally-renowned Gray Street Workshop. This workshop provides a supportive studio environment of valuable exchange between emerging, mid-career and established practitioners. In April 2010, Dare became a partner in the workshop, joining co-founders Catherine Truman and Sue Lorraine in continuing its legacy and shaping its future, including establishing the workshop's gallery space.

In her work, Dare draws inspiration from the powerful works of Leopold Blaschka (1822–95) and his son Rudolf (1857–1929). Their virtuosity in lamp-worked glass saw them produce botanical specimens of a calibre that has never been reproduced. Throughout the late 19th century, the Blaschka sea creatures were sought-after internationally by natural history museums and aquaria, because they allowed the study of the natural brilliant colours of soft-body creatures that would otherwise fade when preserved. In 1887 the Blaschkas were contracted to create the Ware Collection of over 3000 flowering plants for Harvard University, which soon became their most famous collection. In 2012, Dare undertook a residency at SquarePeg Studios in Sydney — a studio set up following the Gray Street model — and it was during this time that she was able to explore the wonders of the Sydney Royal Botanic Gardens and treasures of the Australian Museum. The greatest trove she discovered was the museum's collection of Blaschka sea anemones.

Dare was given rare access to the collection. To her disappointment, due to their age and very fragile nature, a number of the pieces have now broken. But this damage gave Dare the opportunity to look more closely at their structures and to contemplate how they were made, informing her own making practice.

Family, nurturing and the drive to preserve memories are important to Dare. The sense of slow fostering and persistence required to tend to a beautiful garden is a process she enjoys and has acquired through an intergenerational conversation. Her grandfather is cited as a considered influence. An accountant by day and avid gardener at home, he tended the ground with the same meticulous detail found in Dare's work. He kept detailed listings of his gardens plants, which were way in excess of 400; he noted when they were bought, how much he had paid for them and where in the garden he planted them; and in the back of these journals, his daily rainfall and temperature lists provide a glimpse into the transitory nature of time. The loss of her grandfather in 2011 prompted Dare to develop her *Conceptual flowering plant series*, 2013–14.

Margaret Hancock Davis

Previous page
Conceptual flowering plant series, 2013–14
lamp-work glass
dimensions variable
Photo: Grant Hancock

▸
Jess Dare working in her studio.
Photo: Courtesy of the artist

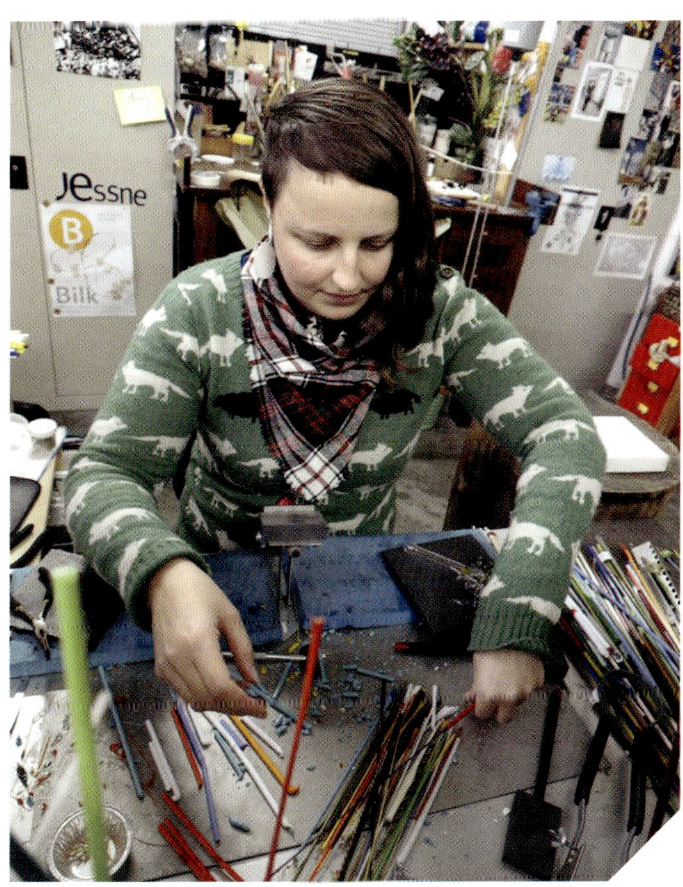
Jessne
B
Bilk

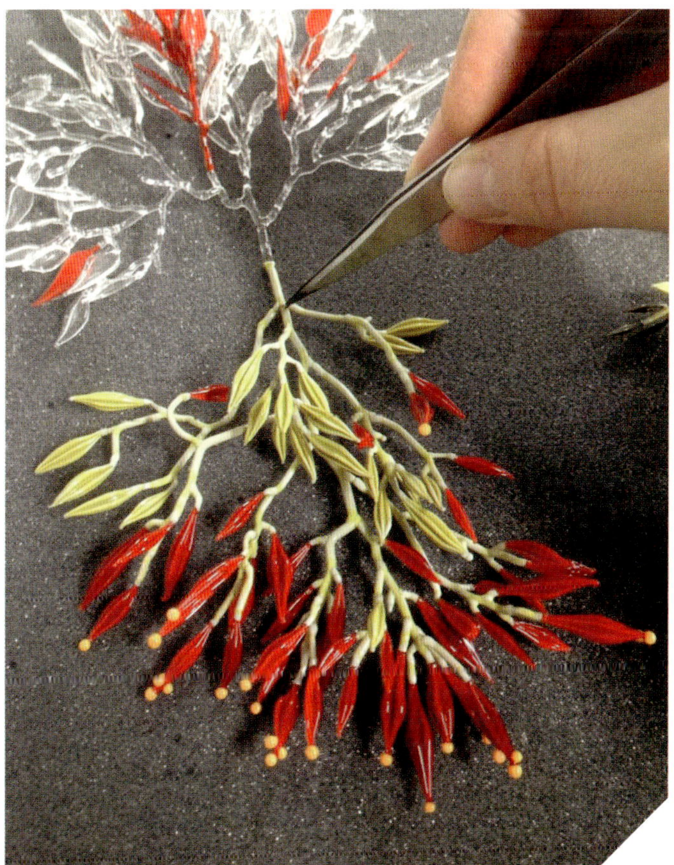

Conceptual flowering plant series

The marking of time and the fleeting nature of memory are at the heart of the *Conceptual flowering plant series*, 2013–14. Not aiming to create true replicas of nature, Dare brings together the delicate structural elements of plants, leaves, stems, buds, flowers and shoots, which by their own nature seem fragile and ready to break. Within the works, the rich vibrant colours often lose their saturation, fading to clear — a metaphor for the transience of memory.

The series title is named after Pierre Jean Francois Turpin's conceptual flowering plant of 1837, which was a teaching aid popular in the 19th century. It depicts an imaginary plant that incorporates the characteristics of many diverse flowering plants, with various kinds of stamens, leaves, stems, bulbs, tubers and even leaf galls.

▸
Conceptual flowering plant series, 2013–14
lampwork glass
dimensions variable
Photo: Grant Hancock

Overleaf
Conceptual flowering plant series, 2013
Photo: Grant Hancock

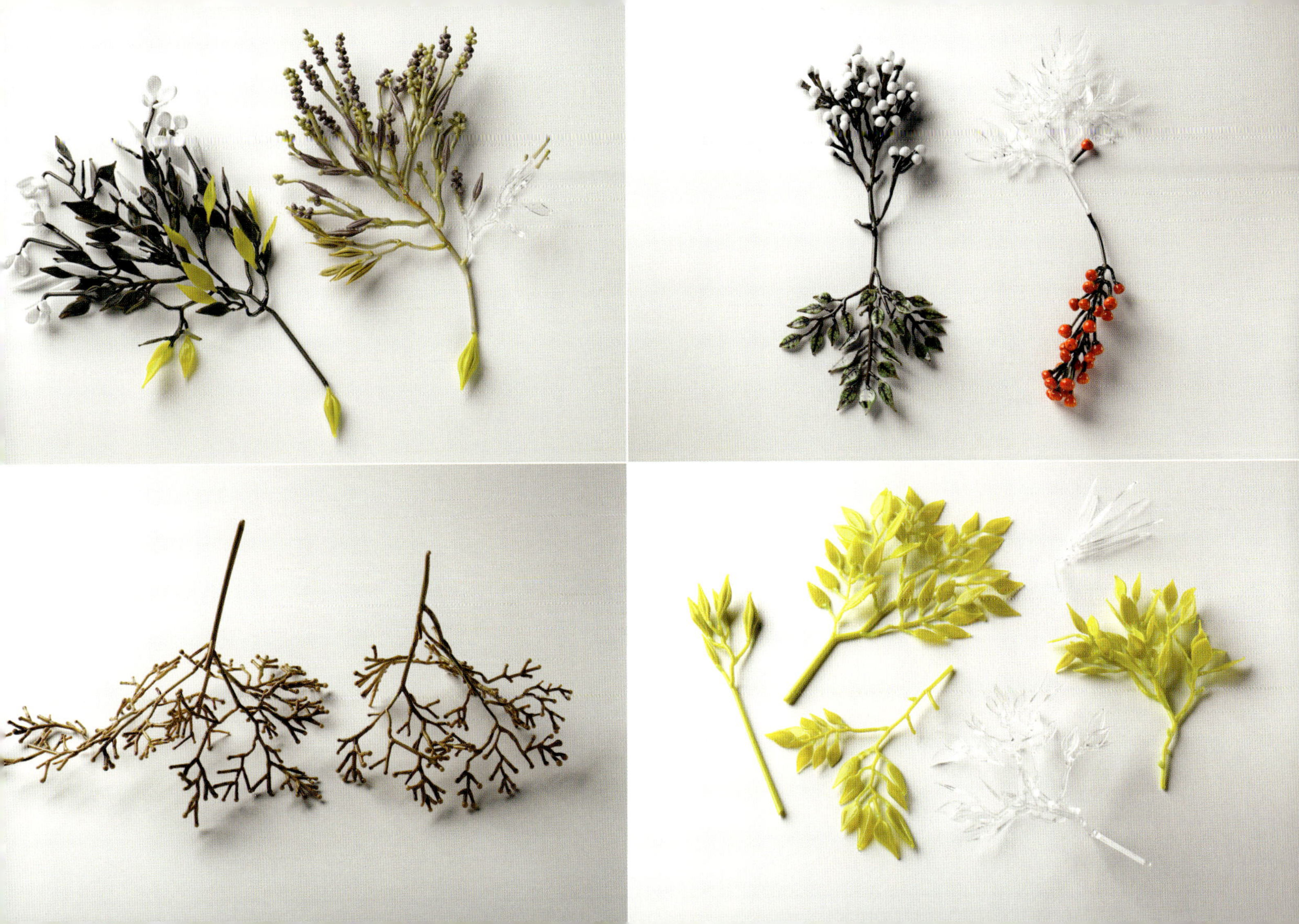

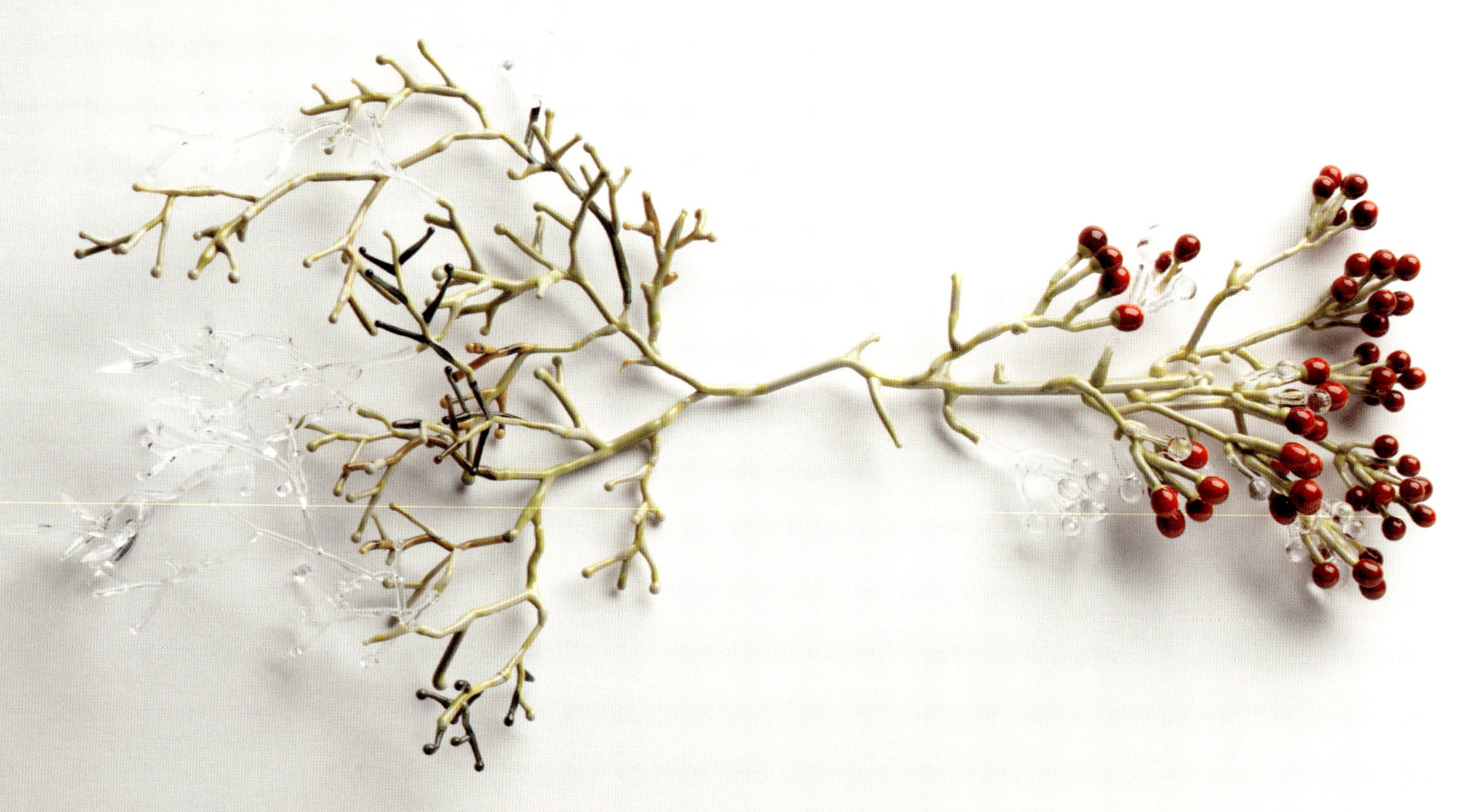

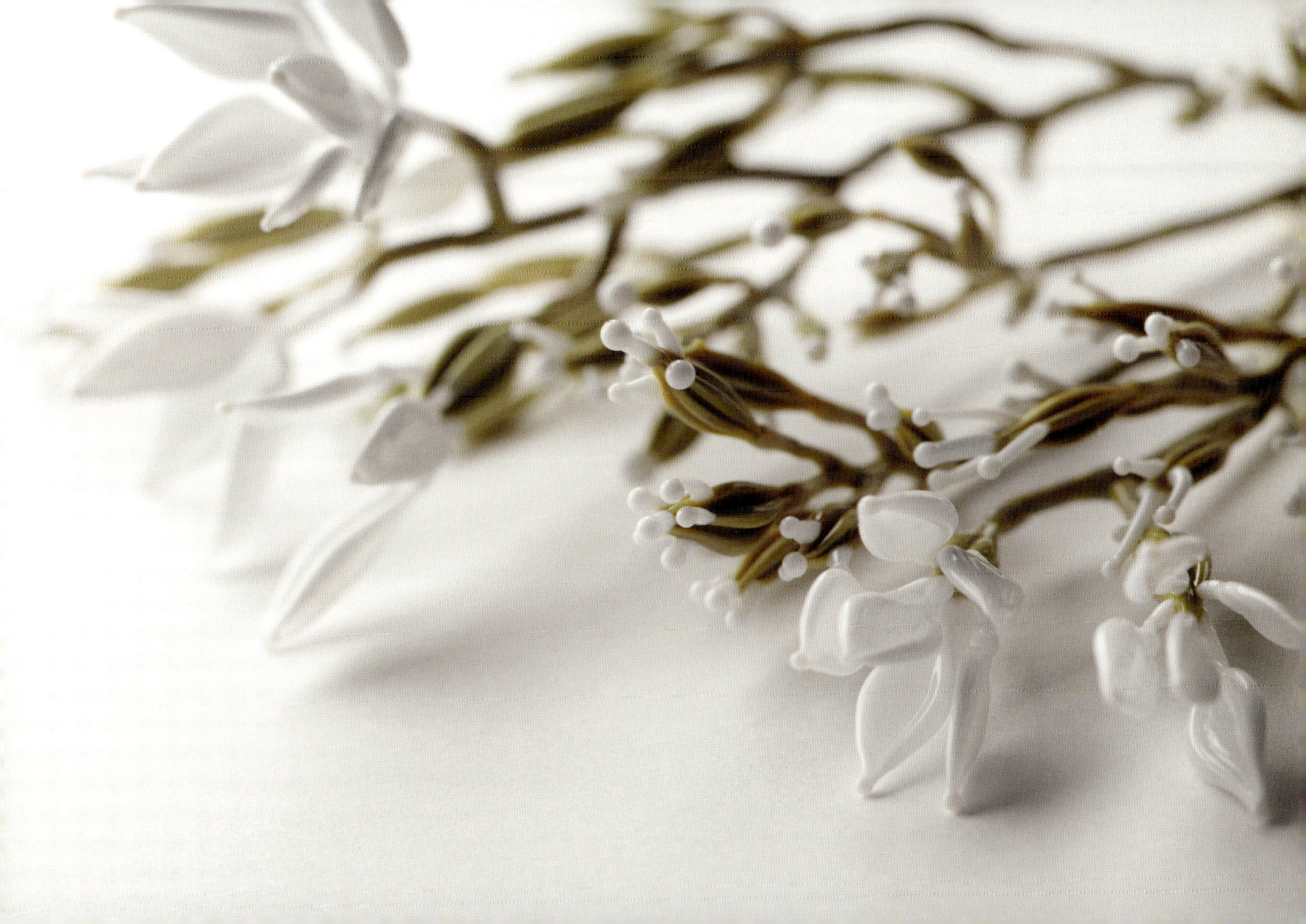

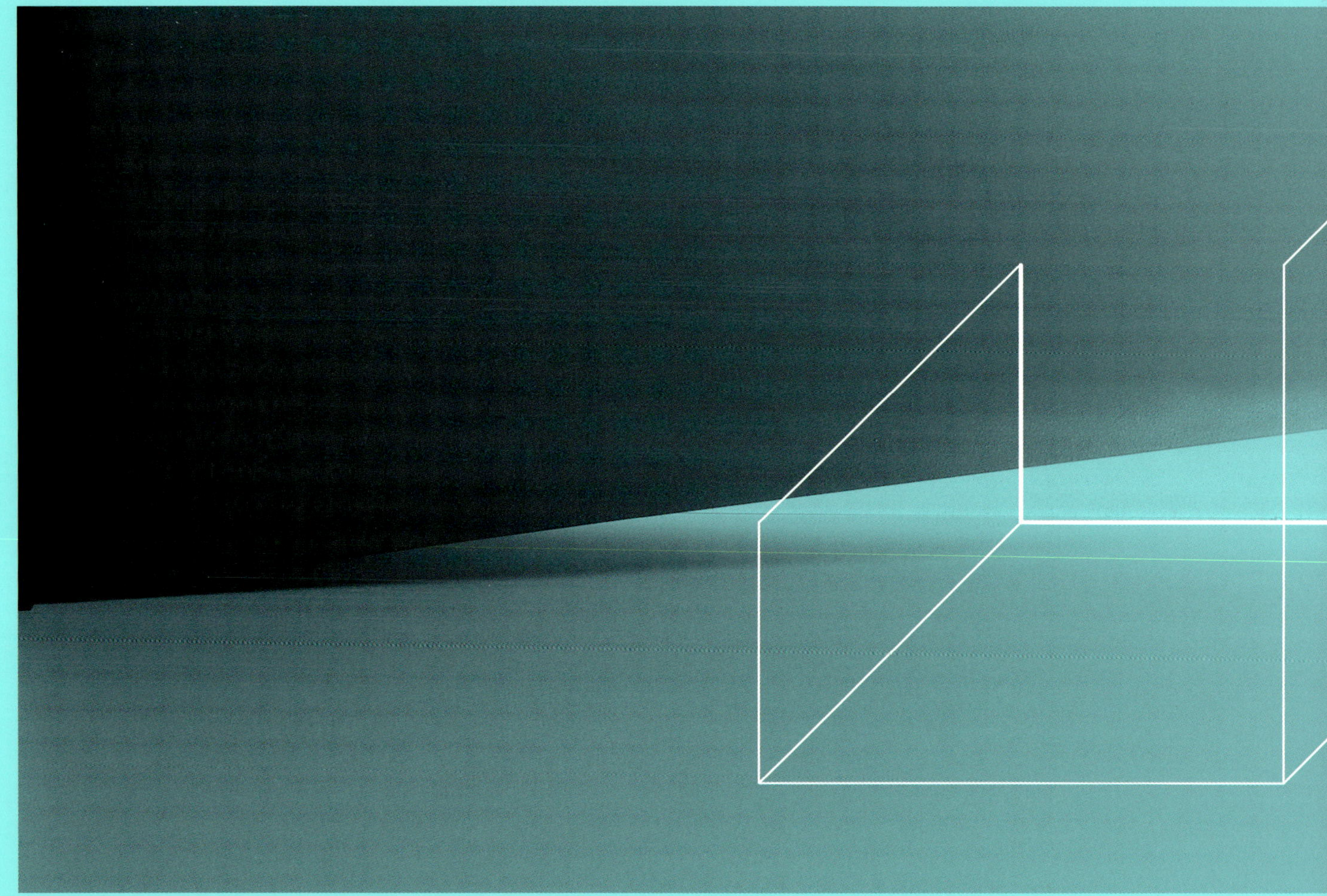

Jessica Loughlin

Born 1975, Melbourne, Victoria
Lives Adelaide, South Australia

'The intensity of this pure white landscape allows us to walk through the colour of air.'

Jessica Loughlin, 2014

Australian artists are often drawn to respond to the wide open spaces of our landscape. Its gouged surface, eroded by water through millennia, creates vast flat horizons that provide a rich reflective space where time can slow. Only very few artists are able to capture this sublime stillness in their work. Jessica Loughlin's enigmatic and cerebral glass sculptures and wall panels afford us this rare presence, allowing us to be in the now, and to enter a meditative state where all thought is concentrated.

The far north of South Australia is a landscape formed by the memory of water. It is a stripped-back, parched landscape where water works its way through river channels spanning thousands of kilometres, to slowly fill the expansive salt lakes, Kati thanda (Lake Eyre), Lake Frome and Lake Torrens. The water's progress through this extensive draining system is forced south by flooding rains in Far North Queensland.

On its arrival, these lakes team with life — pelicans, black swans and whistling ducks appear in their tens of thousands to breed. But it is not this rare cacophony that draws Loughlin to these landscapes; rather it is the mesmerising light, and the simmering haze of distance, a space unknown — the space between.

Loughlin is most preoccupied with this unreachable distance. As we move closer, this space moves further away, creating a continual play between what is real and what is imagined. Using the ability of glass to hold and transmute light, Loughlin's sculptural forms — *into the blue*, 2012 and *Through distance #2*, 2006 — are technically complex. Employing multiple layers of fused glass, these works graduate levels of opacity and density in the glass surface to create an indefinable space. It is as if Loughlin was sculpting with pure light.

The rigours of Loughlin's constrained palette of tonal greys can be traced to the exacting training she received as a child from Richard Liddicut in suibokuga, Japanese ink brush painting. It is hard to imagine many children having the patience to grind their solid ink block for long periods and to work within such a limited colour range; however, this focus of intent and clarity of thought resonates in Loughlin's glass works.

Loughlin's very individual approach to the medium has resulted in her reductive monochromatic works being recognised nationally and internationally. She is a leader in her process of kiln-formed glass, and is known for both her technically precise works and innovative methods of production. A graduate of the Canberra School of Art, Australian National University, Loughlin's formative years as an artist were influenced by Stephen Procter. His rigour encouraged Loughlin's deep understanding of the materiality of glass, and gave her the sense of its lyrical nature.

Loughlin has been the recipient of Australia's leading glass awards: the Tom Malone Prize in 2004 and 2007, and the Ranamok Glass Prize in 1997. In 2001 she was awarded the international Urban Glass Award, New York, and she has undertaken numerous residencies. Her work can be found in the permanent collections of the Corning Museum of Glass, New York, the National Gallery of Australia, Canberra, the Victoria and Albert Museum, London, and the Musée de Design et d'Arts Appliqués Contemporains in Lausanne, Switzerland.

Margaret Hancock Davis

Previous page
Outside In (detail), 2006
kiln formed cut
and constructed glass
600 x 650 x 145
Photo: Grant Hancock

▸

Through distance #2, 2006
kiln formed, cast, and cut glass
370 x 570 x 50
Photo: Grant Hancock

Overleaf left
into the blue, 2012
kiln formed, cast, cut,
and constructed glass
420 x 580 x 140
Photo: Grant Hancock

Overleaf centre
quietening 4, 2004
kiln formed and cut glass
500 x 500 x 30
Photo: Grant Hancock

Overleaf right
the interior, 2010
kiln formed and cut glass
470 x 450 x 90
Photo: Grant Hancock

open space 20, 2005
kiln formed and
cold worked glass
730 x 680 x 30
Photo: Grant Hancock

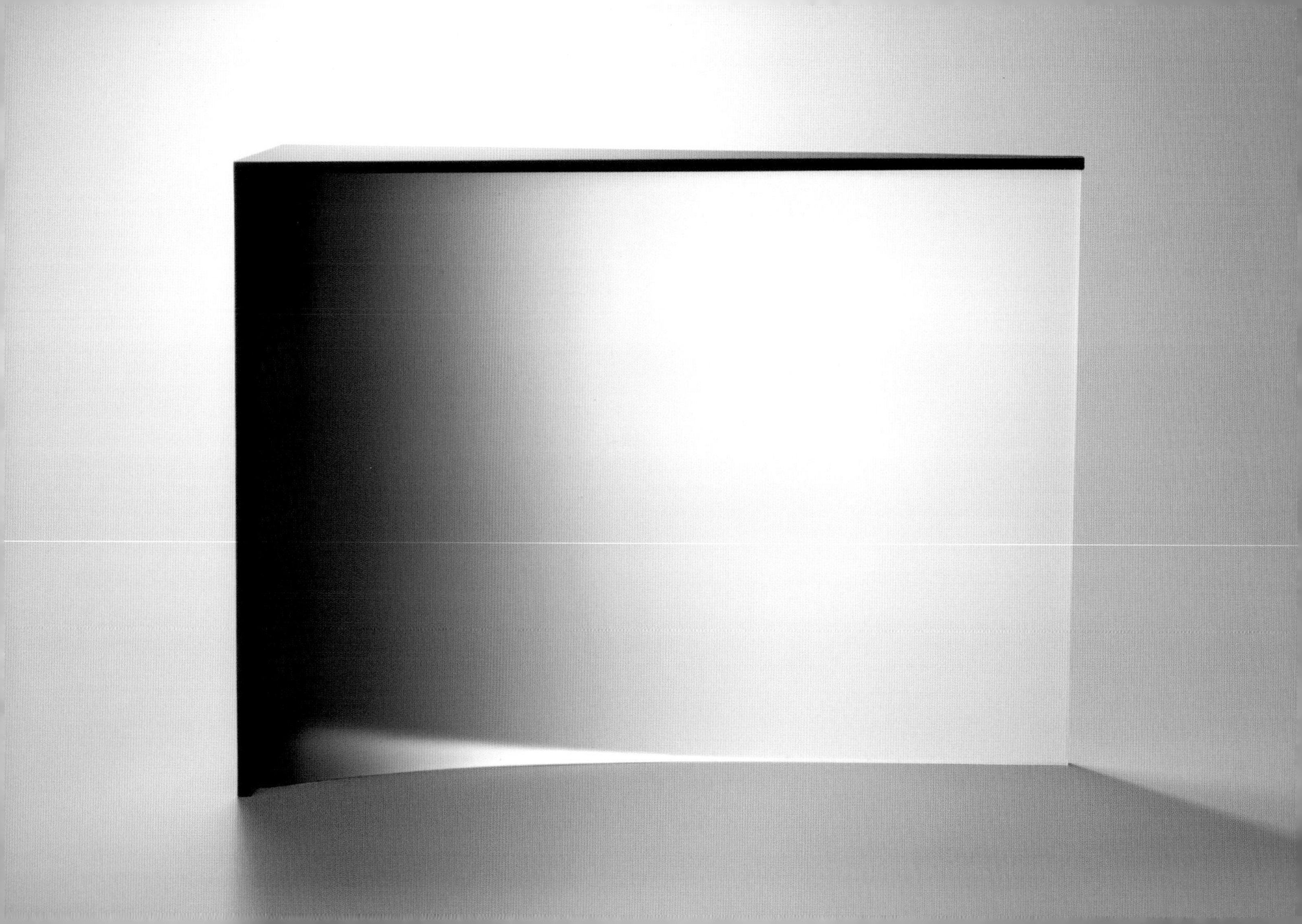

continuum

In *continuum*, 2014, Loughlin responds to the ever-shifting presence and nature of water in the barren Australian landscape. The cycle of evaporation, leaching of salts, condensation and rain, is explored not only in the imagery created, but also in the means of production. The painterly effect Loughlin achieves in these wall panels emerges from grinding glass to a powder, and then suspending the powder in water to create a milky slurry that she gently guides across the surface. The liquid powdered glass is then left to evaporate, leaving traces on the glass — a memory on the surface where water has once been.

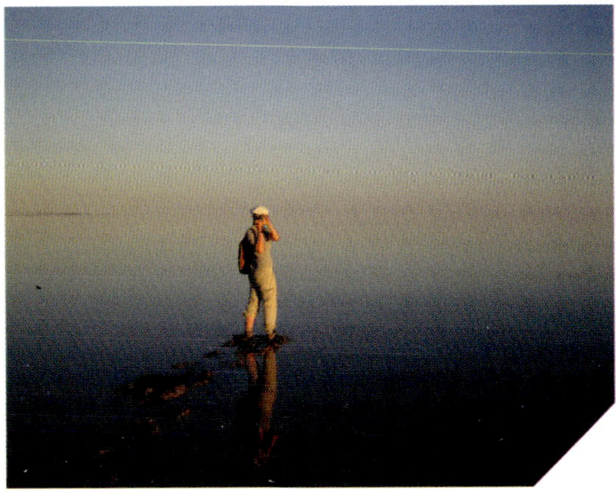

◂
Jessica Loughlin
at Kati Thanda (Lake Eyre)
Photo: David Gartelmann

▸
Jessica Loughlin
Installing *an ever changing constant xiv*, 2012
Photo: Rachel Harris

Overleaf
continuum, 2014
kiln formed glass
330 x 3400 x 25
Photo: Grant Hancock

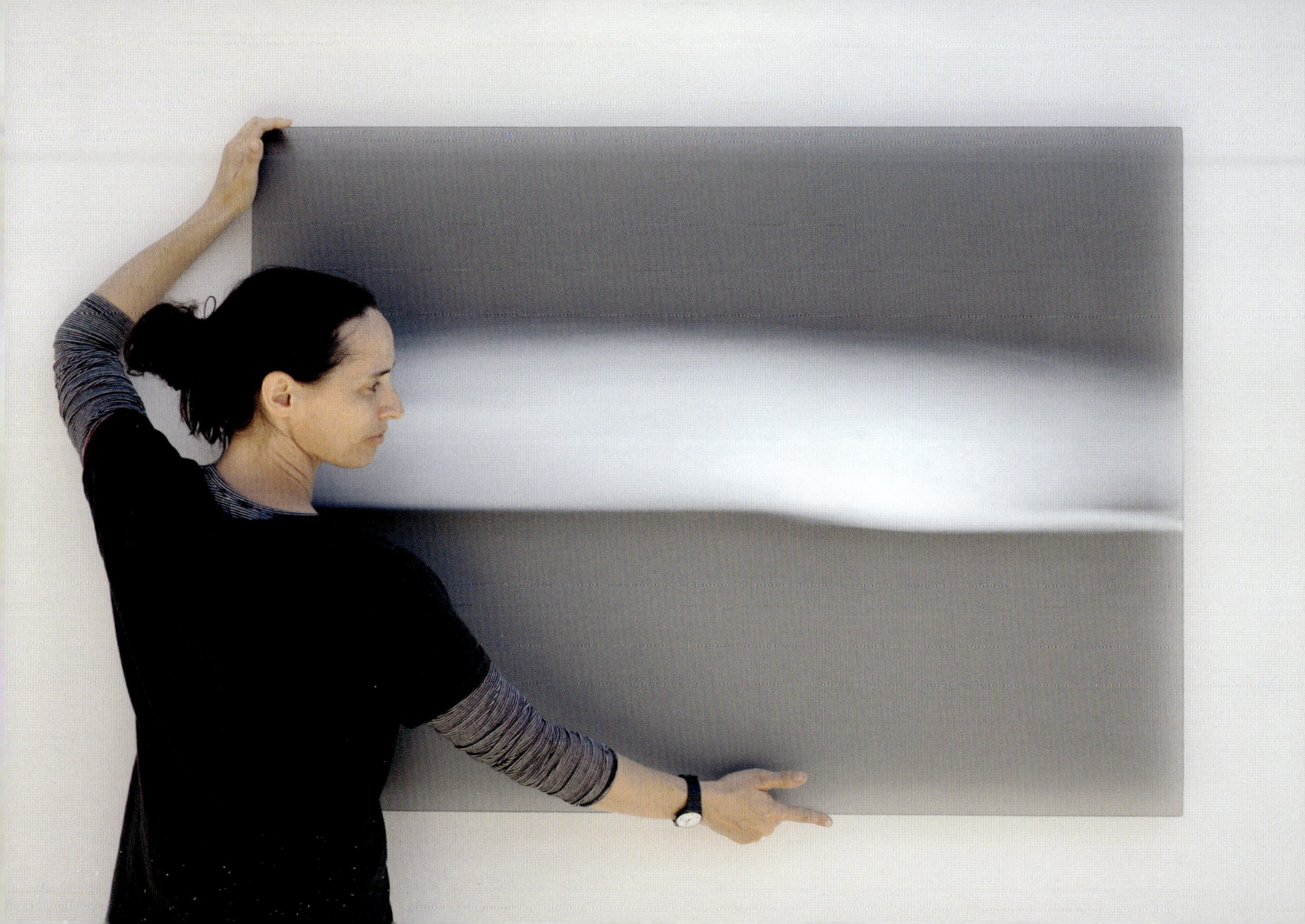

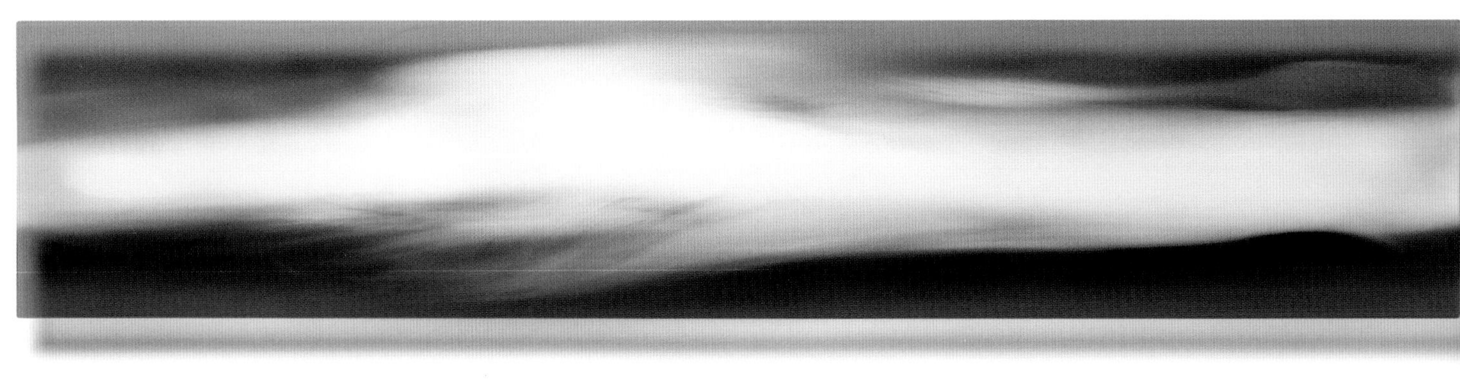

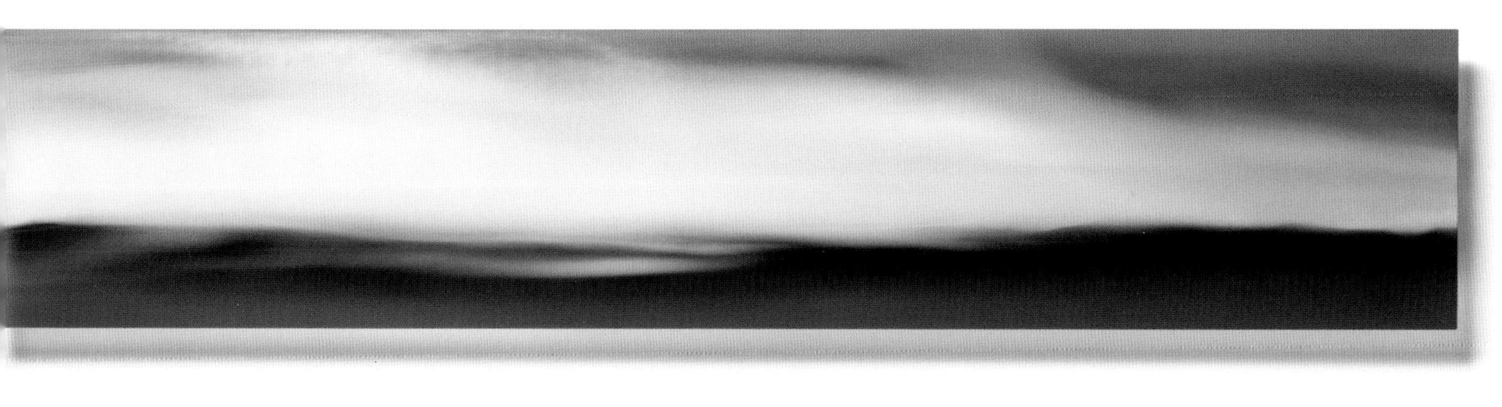

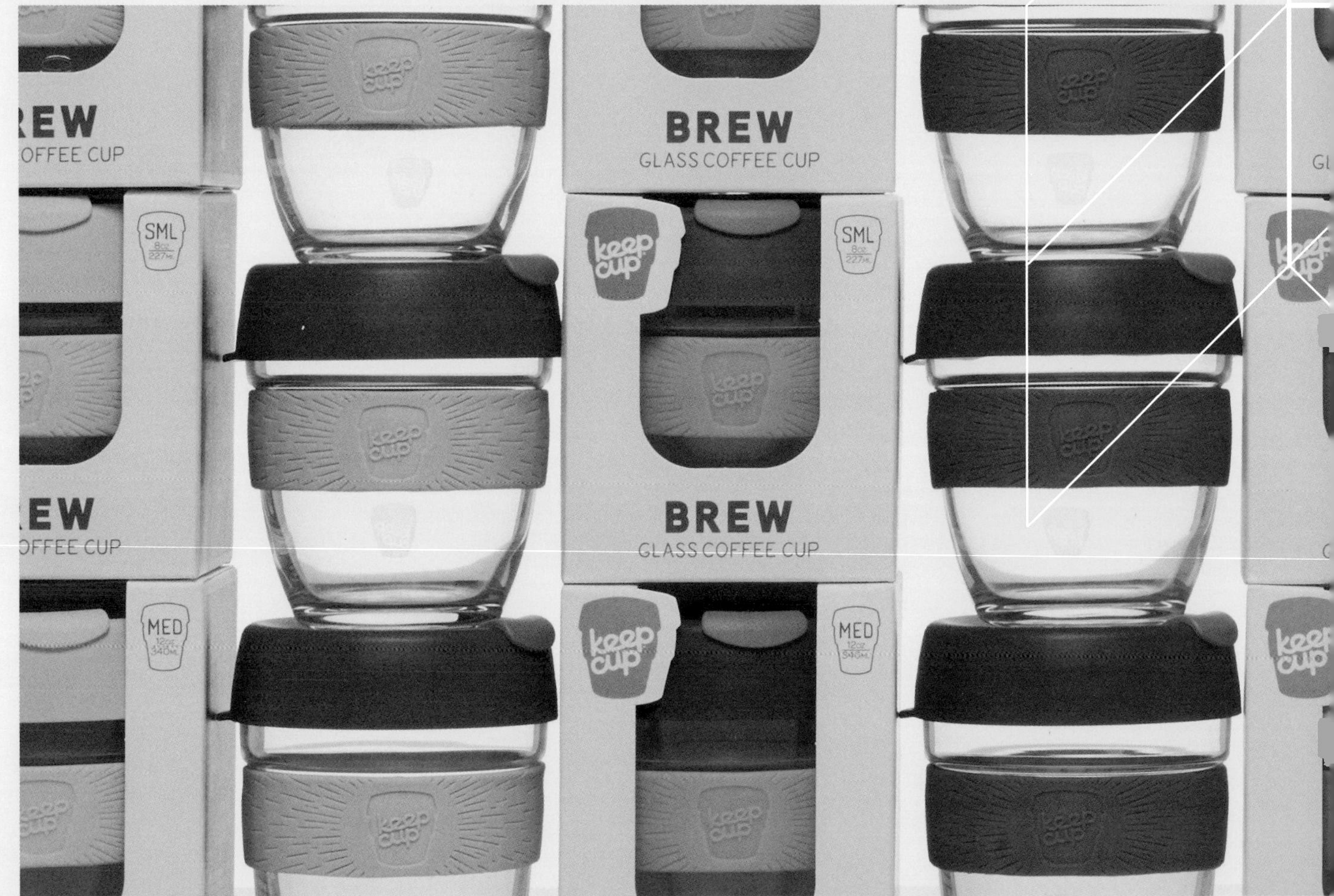
BREW
GLASS COFFEE CUP
SML
8oz
227ML
keep cup
MED
12oz
340ML

KeepCup

Established 2009, Melbourne, Victoria

Abigail Forsyth

Born 1971, Glasgow, Scotland

Jamie Forsyth

Born 1972, Glasgow, Scotland

Both live in Melbourne, Victoria

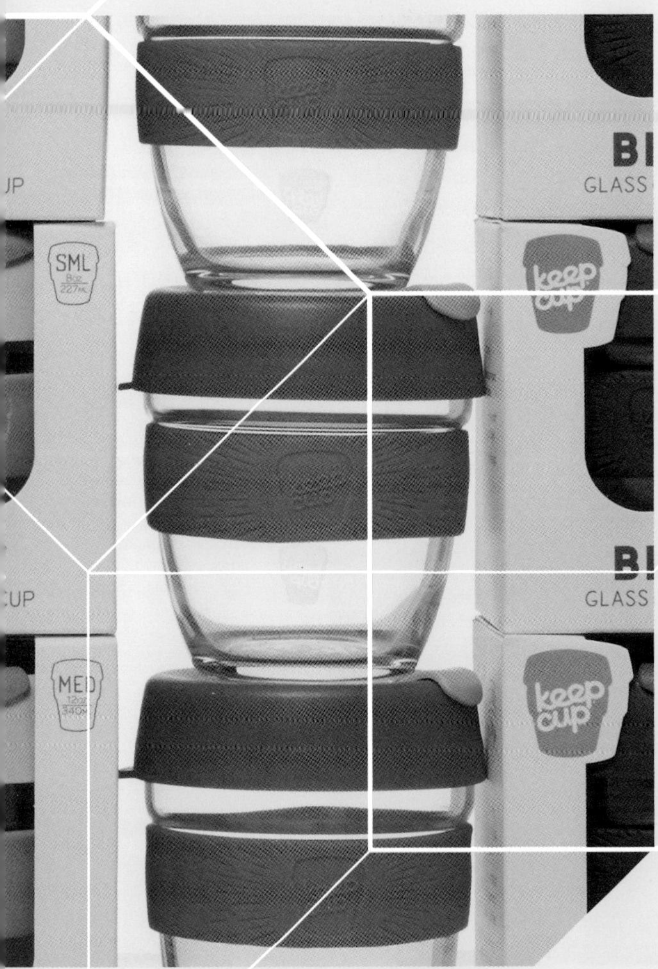

Melbourne-based entrepreneurs Jamie and Abigail Forsyth are the brother-and-sister team behind KeepCup. Born from a desire to change the way that coffee drinkers use disposable cups, the brand is about sustainability and re-usability. A design solution to an environmental problem, the *KeepCup*, 2009, is a barista-standard re-usable cup manufactured in Australia and sold all over the world. Five years after the launch of the original *KeepCup* at a Federation Square design market, they have released a new design in glass: the *KeepCup Brew*, 2014.

The Forsyths come from a coffee background — they run a string of cafes throughout Melbourne. Designing the re-usable cup to fit within Australian cafe culture has been key to their success, and is part of the reasoning behind expanding the brand. Their insider industry knowledge influenced their design process — they realised that the cup needed to be easy for both customer and barista to use. The *Brew* range is an extension of this philosophy, combining the usability of the original with a level of material sophistication.

KeepCup Brew
and Limited Edition KeepCup Brew Cork

The *KeepCup Brew*, 2014, pays respect to the multi-sensory aspects of drinking coffee, not just the caffeine fix. As well as incorporating a glass vessel, the lid has been developed to allow the drinker to better experience the aroma and texture of the coffee, while the transparency means that the barista's handiwork is on display. In terms of sustainability, after just ten washes the *Brew* breaks even in terms of energy and resources used to make it. So, it not only saves waste, it also saves natural resources and energy.

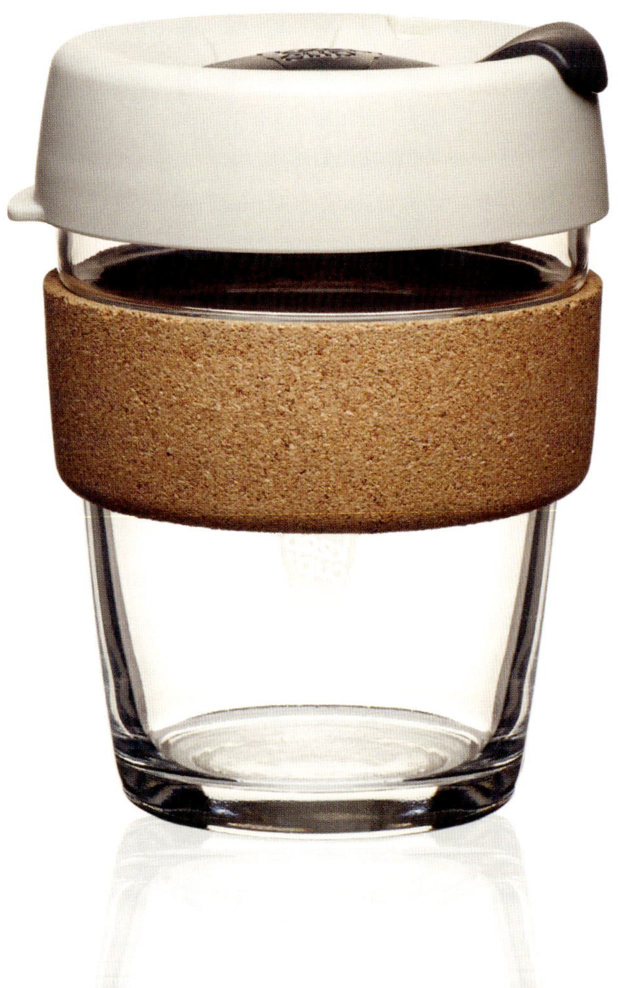

▸

KeepCup Brew,
Special Edition Cork, 2014
soda lime glass, polypropylene, polyethylene polymer (TPU), silicone
120 x 85 dia.
Photo: Cameron Murray

Overleaf
KeepCup Brew in the new Alchemy range of colours.
Photo: Cameron Murray

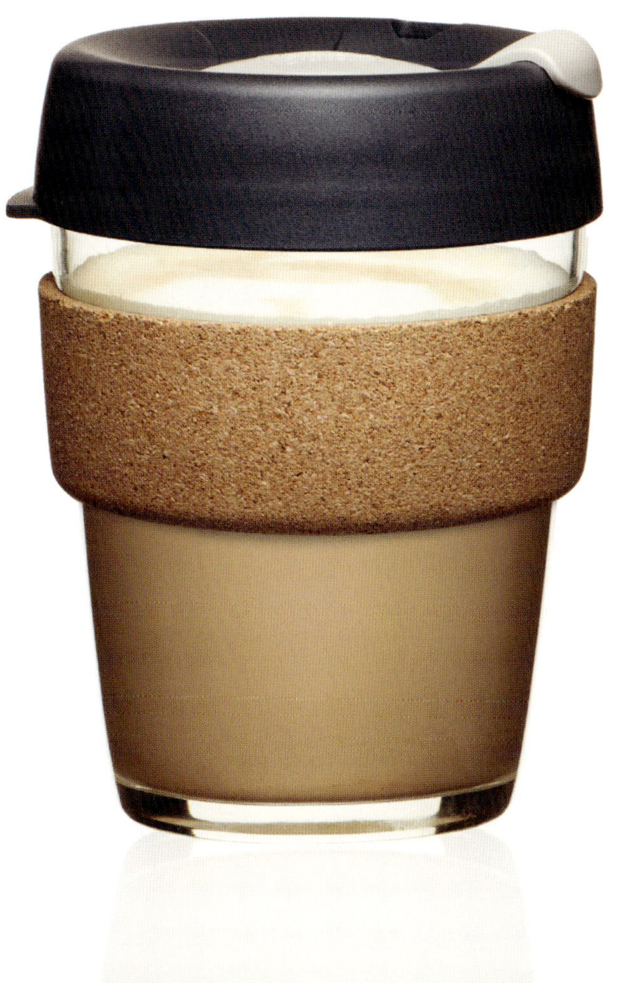

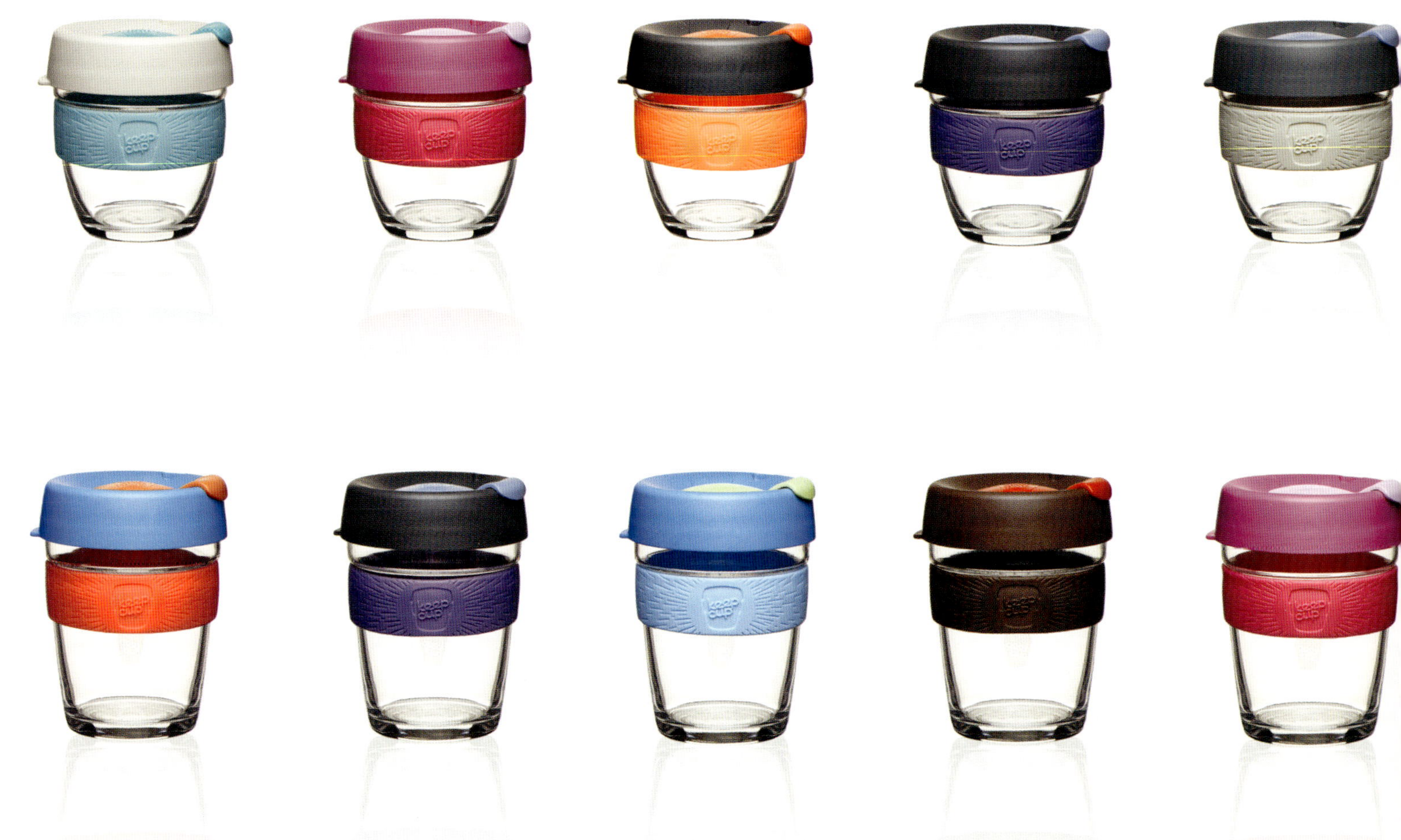

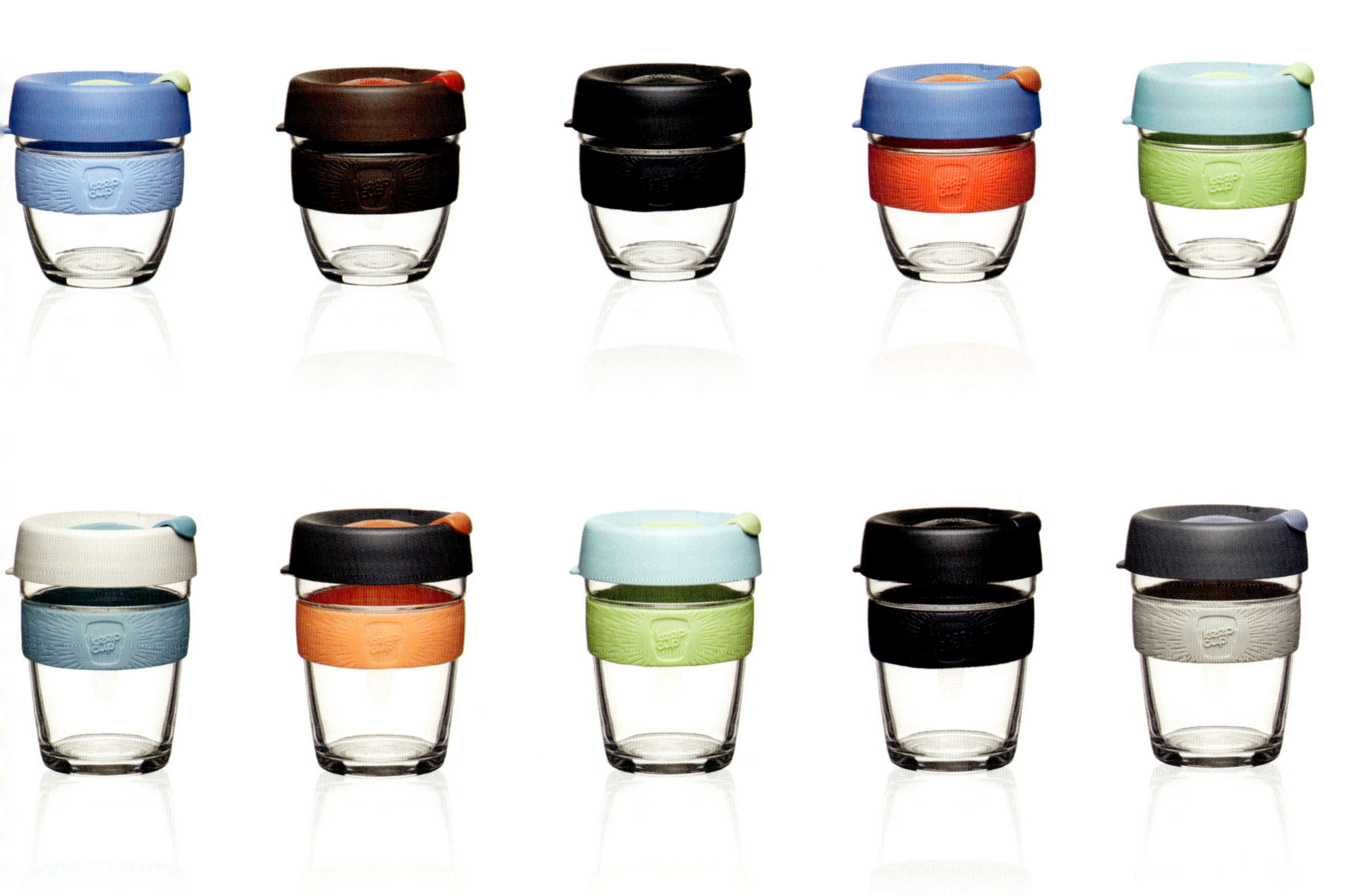

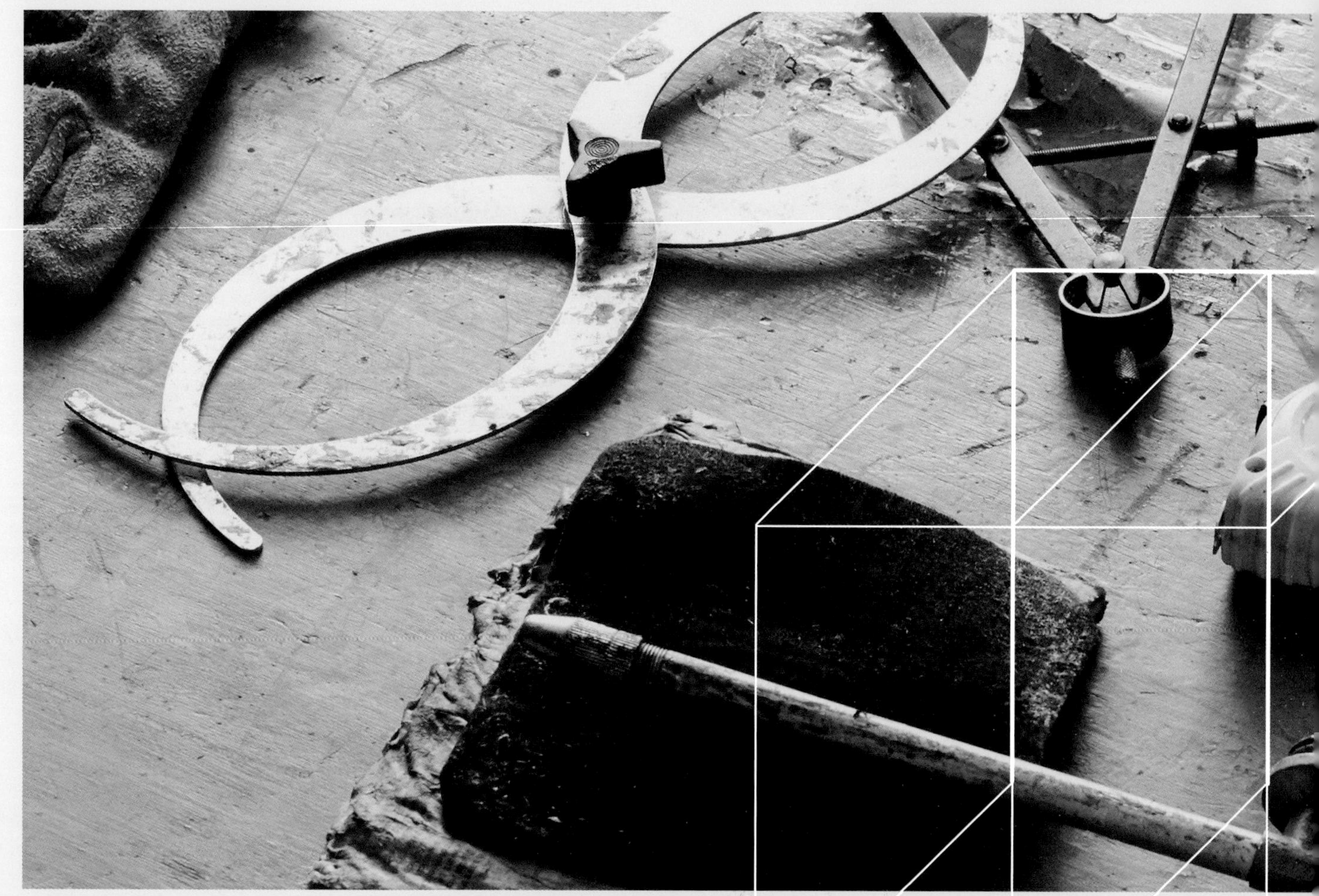

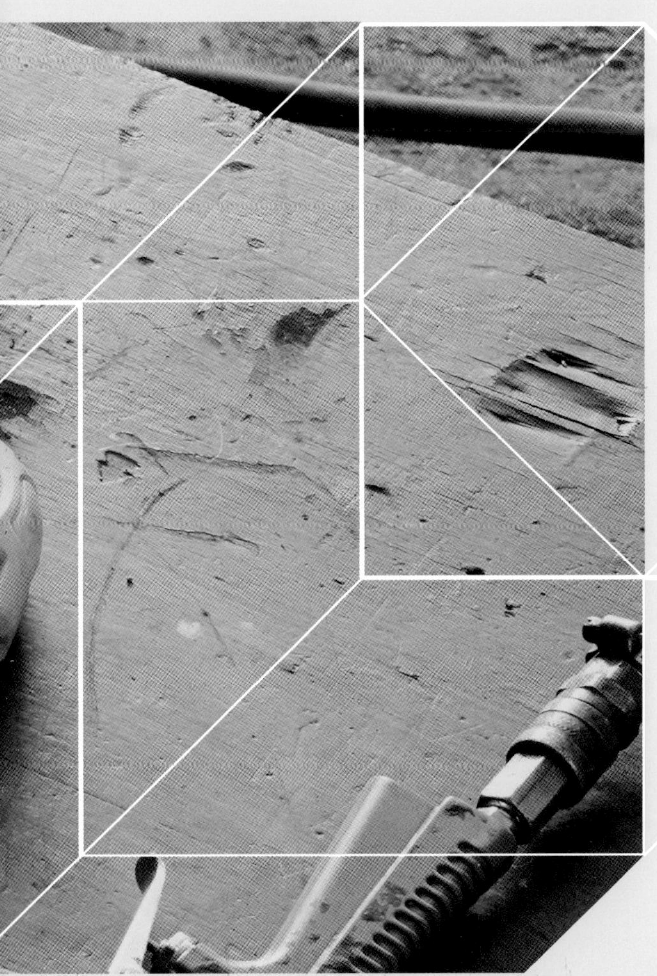

Mark Douglass

Born 1964, Ballarat, Victoria
Lives in Melbourne, Victoria

Mark Douglass is a well-known and respected glass artist and all-round creative entrepreneur, with a reputation for collaboration and a diverse practice spanning art glass, commercial lighting, bespoke commissions and retail.

Anchored around the medium of glass for more than 20 years, Douglass is adept at navigating the vagaries of Australian creative practice.

Building upon his foundation in glass art, he has gradually diversified and broadened the commercial focus of his studio, finding a resilient business model through a broad array of outputs. With this diversity comes the capacity to manage in-house product development and the manufacture of standardised products that sit alongside one-offs and commissions.

It seems Douglass is never far from a batch of molten silicate, nor does he shy away from a new business idea. He has developed a unique capability to stretch his chosen medium and methodology of production accordingly.

Douglass is a well-established and respected art-glass practitioner represented by commercial galleries both in Australia and internationally. His commercial 'Design Range' of lighting and interior work is produced under his eponymous brand, and sold both commercially and by retail at his Richmond studio. His work regularly brightens the interior of Melbourne residences and notable restaurants.

His studio and production facility doubles as a commercial gallery, with an in-house team spanning interior, industrial and graphic design. As with many small creative practices, the studio is a hub for events, collaborative projects and mentorship.

Extending the medium and the output of the studio, Douglass accepts occasional commissions for residential and commercial interior projects — from lighting constellations, art commissions and building facades, to smaller-scale works for the hospitality industry.

Through the intricate process of heating, blowing, shaping and cooling, Douglass crafts robust sculptures, vases, lights and bowls that embrace vibrant block colours and forms that defy classification. Some are minimalist, while others reveal a taste for embellishment and theatricality.

While glass-blowing techniques date back thousands of years, high-tech heat-resistant paints give Douglass's work distinct colour clarity, and enable him to explore pattern and intricate line work.

Both sides of his practice — the art and the design — enhance one another, ensuring that his art glass demonstrates a sense of interiority, informed by many years working intimately with the creation of spaces. Conversely, his lighting pieces and homewares offer products embedded with high-quality production values, refined form and a deep knowledge of material.

Douglass claims to 'design with the whole environment in mind'. He follows his instincts, allowing the properties of his chosen material to come to the foreground and enabling his broad array of outputs to be united.

Ewan McEoin

Previous page
Mark Douglass's studio detail.
Photo: Eve Wilson

▸

Mark Douglass in his Mordialloc glass studio.
Photo: Eve Wilson

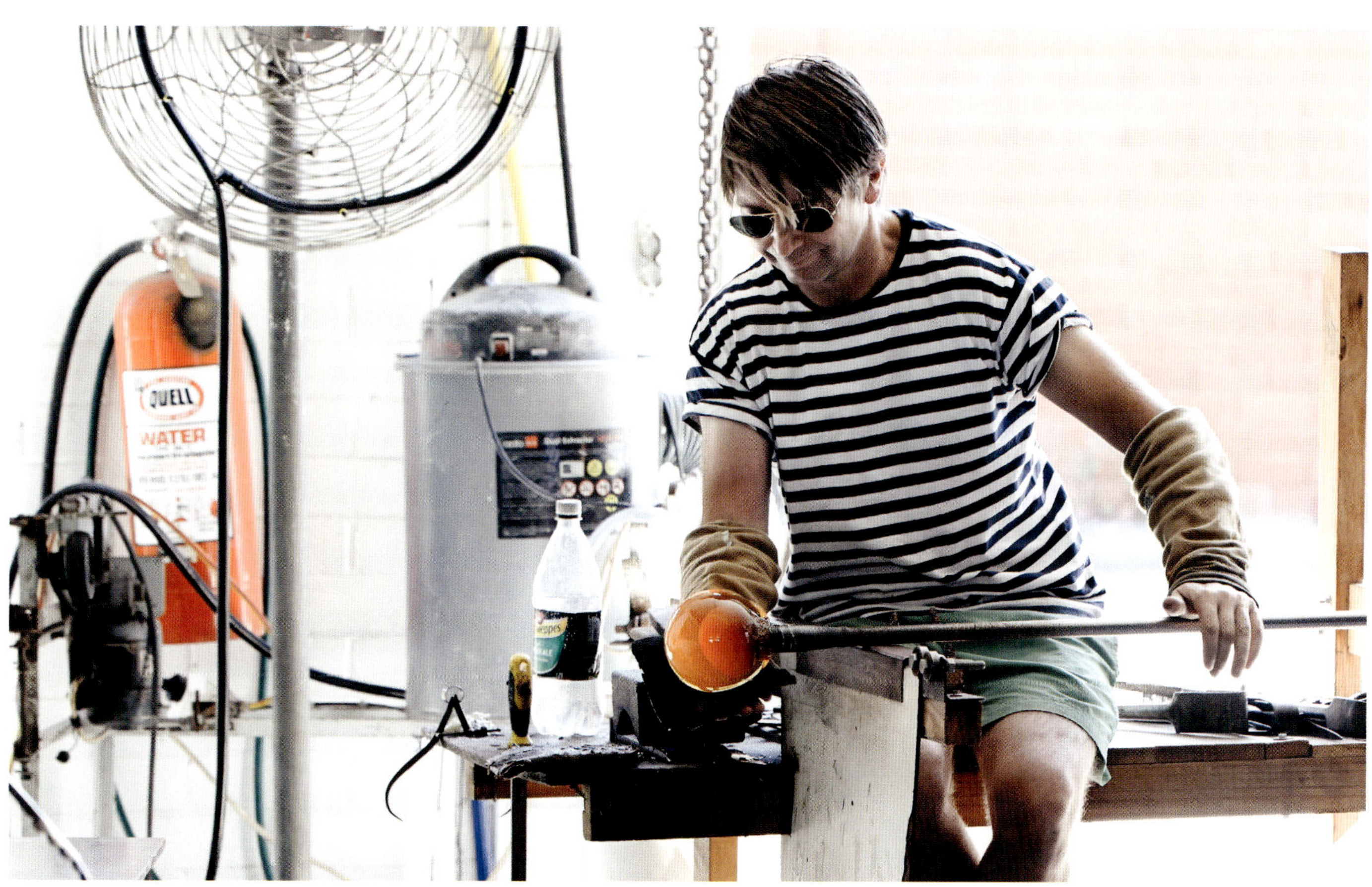
QUELL
WATER

▸

The Richmond showroom of Mark Douglass.
Photo: Eve Wilson

▸▸

Silver Bloom, 2009
blown silvered glass and steel
350 x 1200 dia.
Photo: Courtesy of the artist

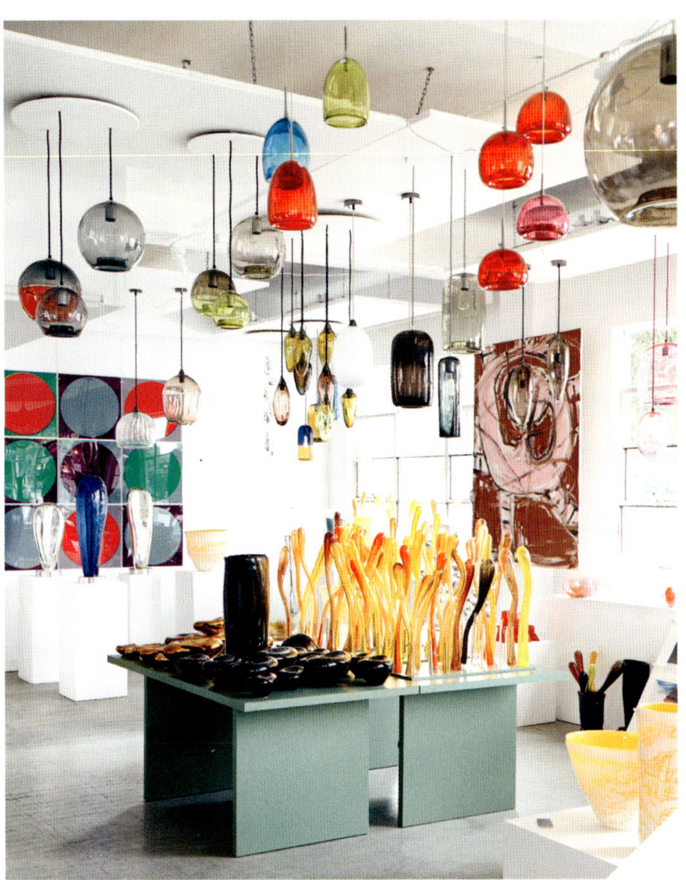

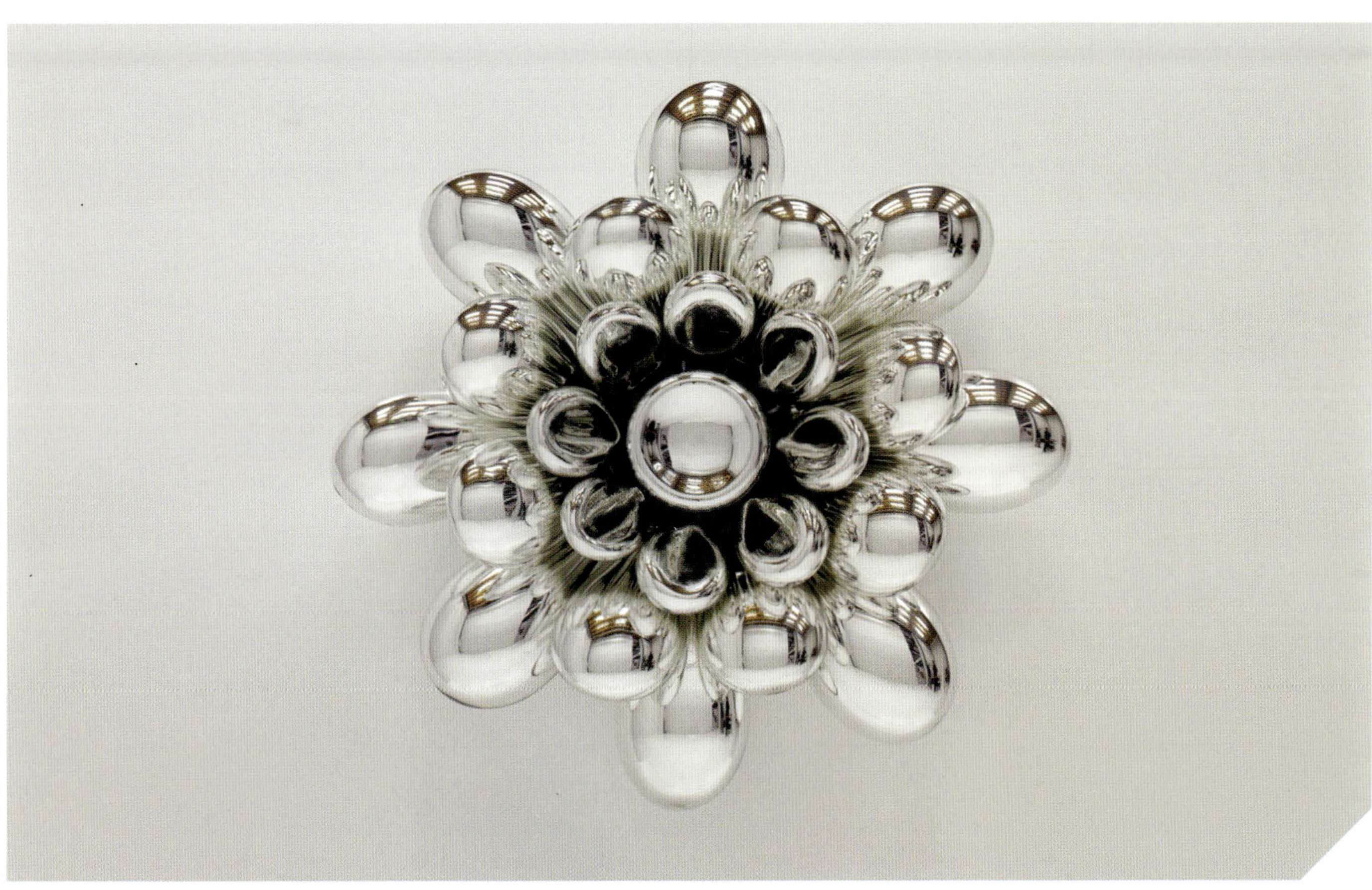

Cleo, Orb, Modernist and Ivy

Mark Douglass is a well-known and respected glass artist and all-round creative entrepreneur, with a reputation for diverse practice. Anchored around the medium of glass for more than 20 years, Douglass has the capability to stretch his chosen medium and methodology of production. His commercial 'Design Range' of lighting — represented here by *Cleo, Orb, Float, Modernist* and *Ivy*, 2014 — are created at his studio with heating, blowing, shaping and cooling glass. This robust yet elegant commercial lighting merges the ancient art of glass blowing with an inherent understanding of interiority and commercial relevance. The works embrace the materiality of glass in vibrant block colours and uncomplicated forms. Douglass follows his instincts and allows the properties of his chosen material to come to the foreground.

▸

Designer Range, 2014
blown glass pendant lights
Basic orb – 210 dia.
Optical float – 350 x 300 dia.
Custom optical orb – 270 dia.
Cleo – 350 x 110 dia.
Ivy – 220 x 200 dia.
Photo: Courtesy of the artist

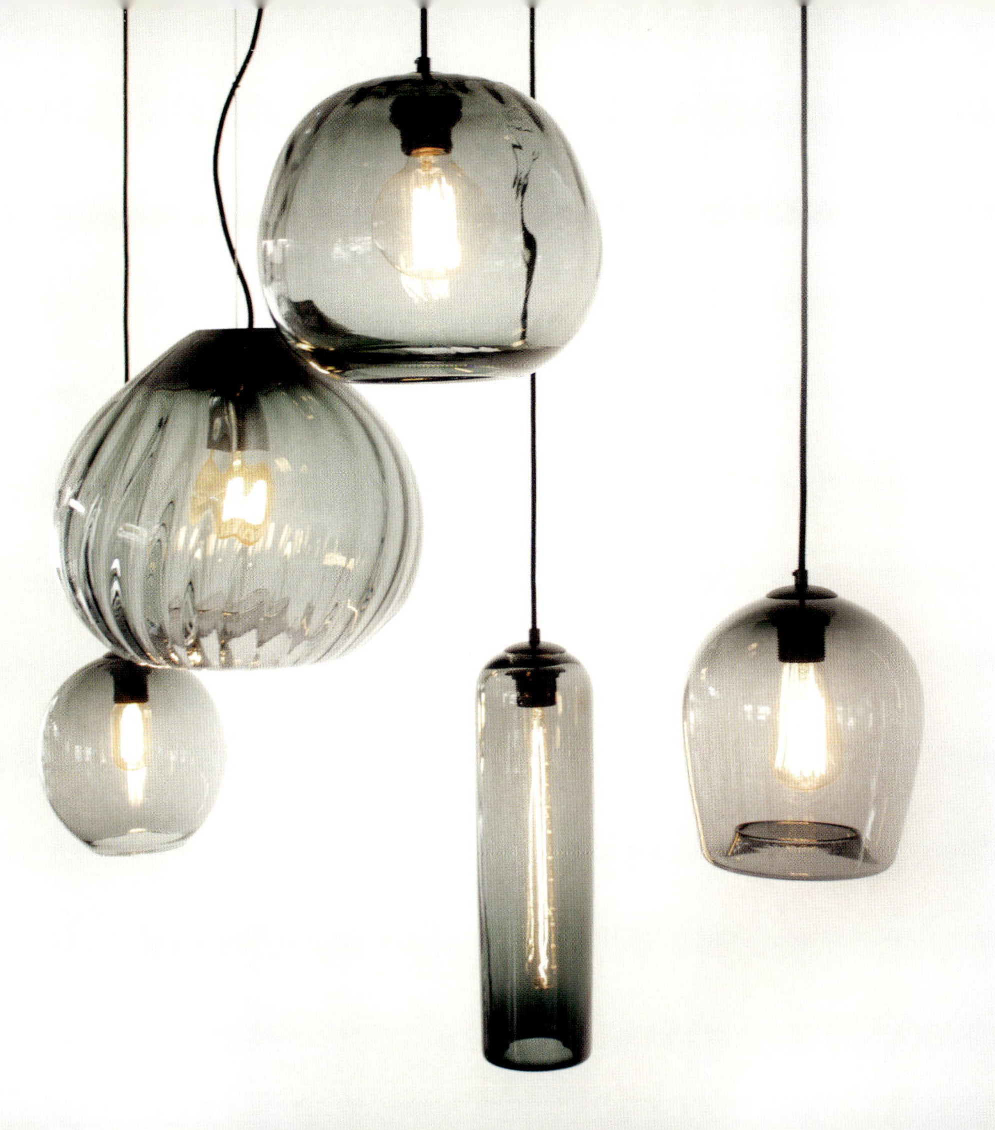

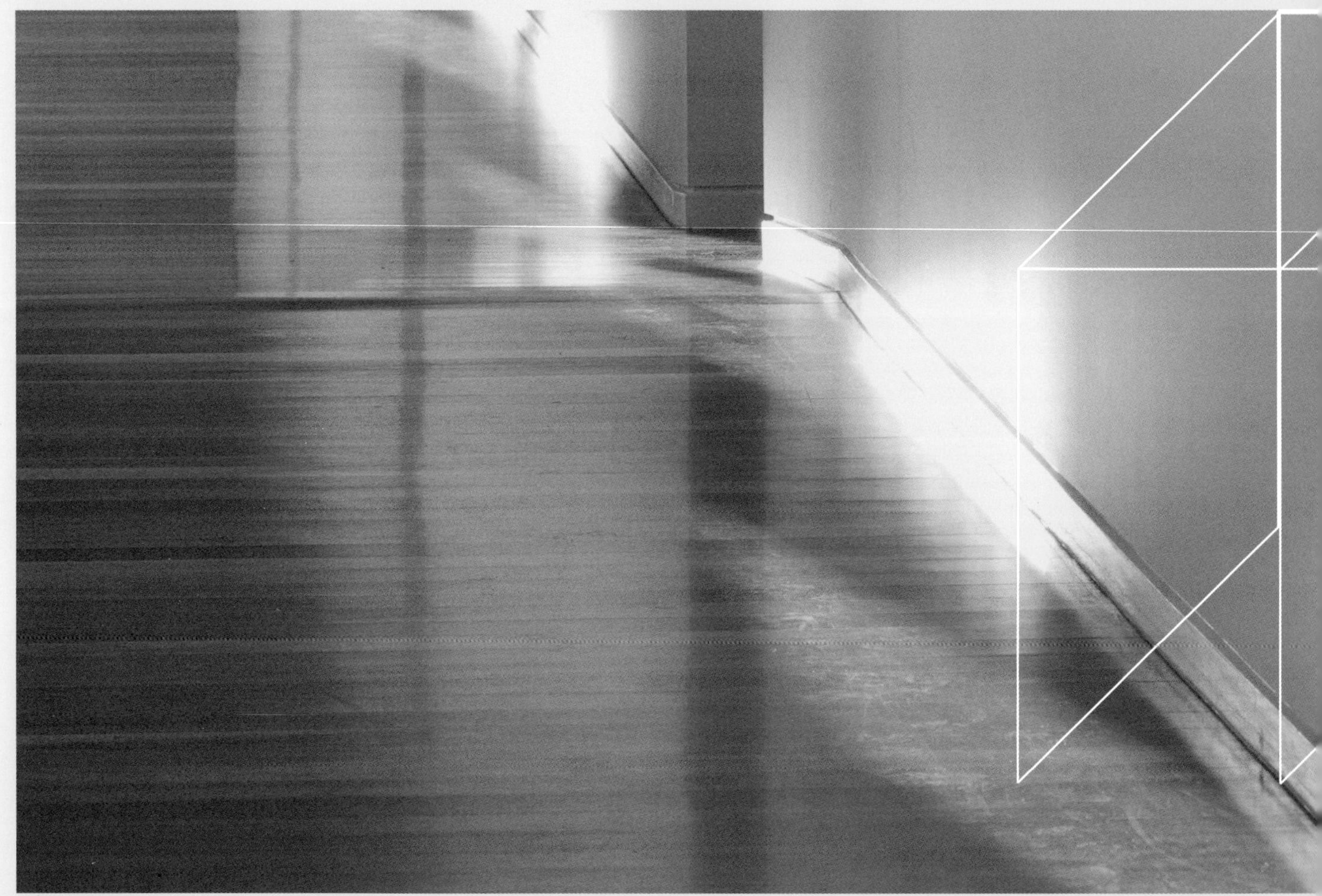

Max Pritchard Architect

Born 1947, Kangaroo Island, South Australia
Lives Adelaide, South Australia
Max Pritchard Architect, established 1986, Adelaide, South Australia

Recognised both nationally and internationally by his peers, Max Pritchard's architectural practice is focused on producing residential and tourism architecture that causes minimal impact to its surroundings, and which 'touches the earth lightly'. After studying at the University of Adelaide in the 1960s, Pritchard travelled extensively throughout South East Asia, India, Nepal, Afghanistan, Iran and South America.

During this time Pritchard was exposed to many new forms of housing and construction methods used by local Indigenous people. Interrogating these buildings for their relationship and response to the physical environment and climatic conditions, Pritchard has assimilated the key ideas of sustainability and suitability into his contemporary designs. This respect for the land can also be traced to Pritchard's childhood growing up on Kangaroo Island, a wild and beautiful terrain, where he would later have the great fortune to design the sophisticated Southern Ocean Lodge, in 2009.

Pritchard's long apprenticeship spent on building sites in various trades and then in a small architectural office, led to him establishing his architectural practice in 1986. Accolades for his designs came early — the first home he designed received an Award of Merit. After 15 years as a sole practitioner the demands of his business saw Pritchard expand the practice, establishing Max Pritchard Architect in 2001, a team of four architects, currently based in Glenelg, South Australia.

The award-winning Barossa House, 2012, is the third in what Pritchard describes as a series of glass houses — the first being his own house built in 1989 at Kingston Park, a beachside suburb south of Adelaide. Using the principles employed in cable stay bridges, Pritchard produced a house that could be structurally minimal while limiting the disruption of the land around it. Cantilevered from the hillside, the Pritchard House is raised on four bridge-like pylons. With a floor level up to eight metres above the ground, the house seems to be perched amongst the tree tops. Thirty metres in length, the house is ribboned on both sides by floor-to-ceiling windows and glass sliding doors. North-facing, the house affords uninterrupted views along the coast, while the southern widows look back into the wooded hill. Not only providing stunning views, the large windows and doors allow great cross ventilation, a must in the hot summers of Adelaide.

Making the most of a site is one of the hallmarks of Pritchard's practice. Presented with a beautiful ten-acre woodland block an hour south of Adelaide, where a winter creek creates a billabong bounded by high rocky banks, Pritchard was challenged to produce a modest house that would not only complement the natural beauty of the site, but also achieve the best possible solar orientation, within a tight budget. Pritchard's solution was to design a house as a bridge over the creek bed. Touching the land at four relatively small concrete pads embedded in the rock, Bridge House, 2008, is a modest 110m² steel-framed dwelling that includes many of the design principles — such as light, glass and ventilation — employed in the Pritchard House.

The most recent of the glass houses is the Barossa House. Perched high on the top of the hill, outside Lyndoch on the Southern Ridge of the Barossa Valley, Pritchard has orientated the house so it looks north, taking in the sweeping panoramic views of the valley. Like the Bridge House, which brings trees and birds to eye level, the most majestic view from the house is captured from a sunken lounge, where the sky and landscape fill the impressive glass windows.

Margaret Hancock Davis

Previous page
Barossa House, 2012
Lyndoch, South Australia
Photos: Sam Noonan

▸ ▸▸
Pritchard House, 1989
Kingston Park, South Australia
Photo: Trevor Fox

▸ ▸▸
Bridge House, 2008
Ashbourne, South Australia
Photos: Sam Noonan

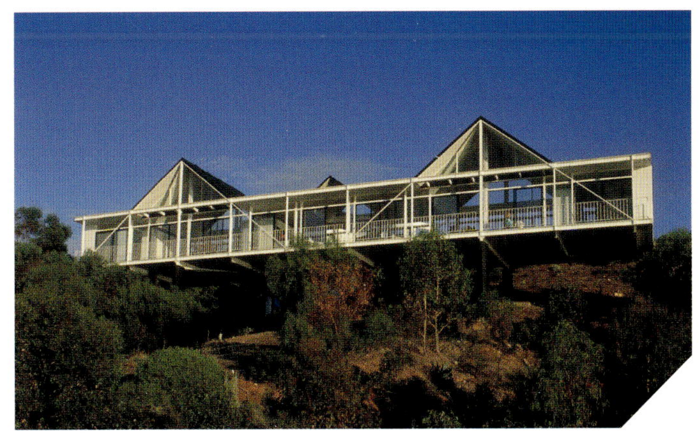

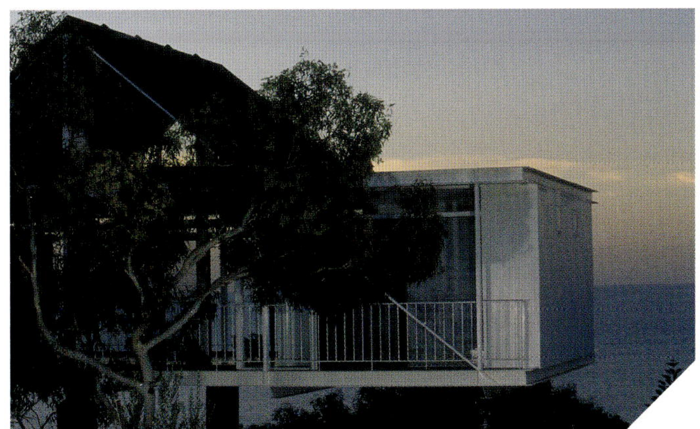

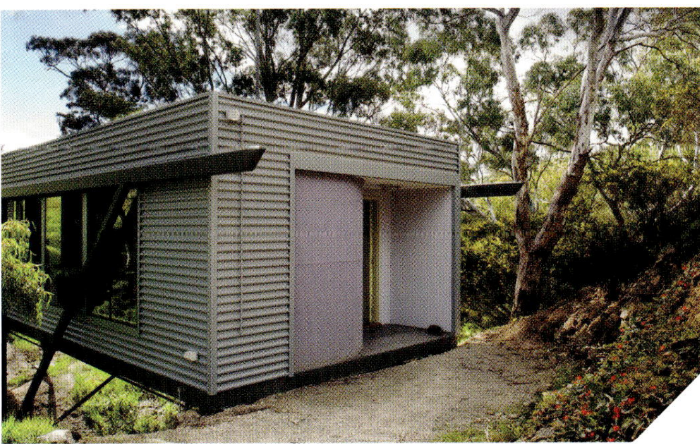

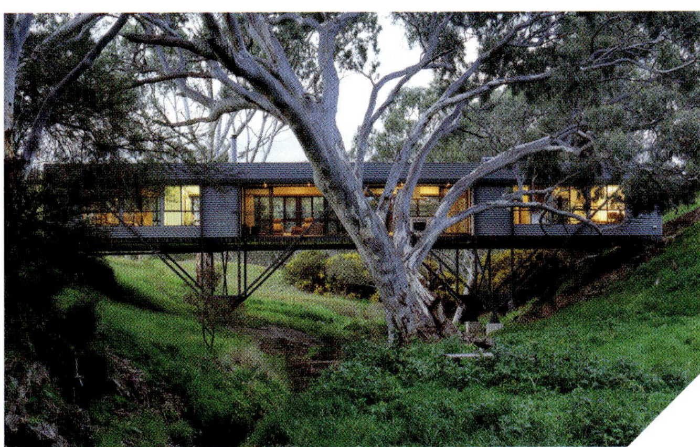

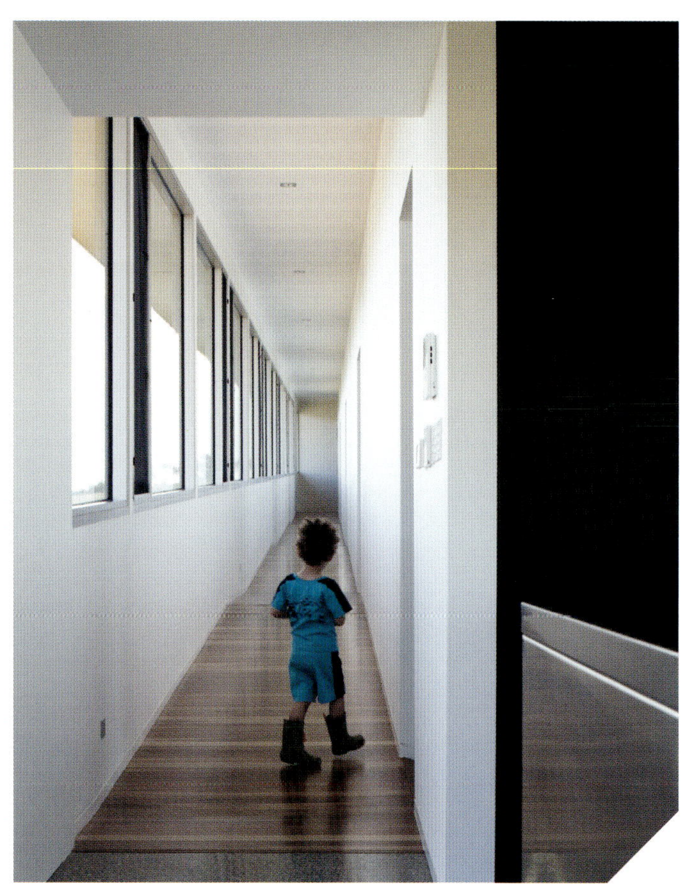

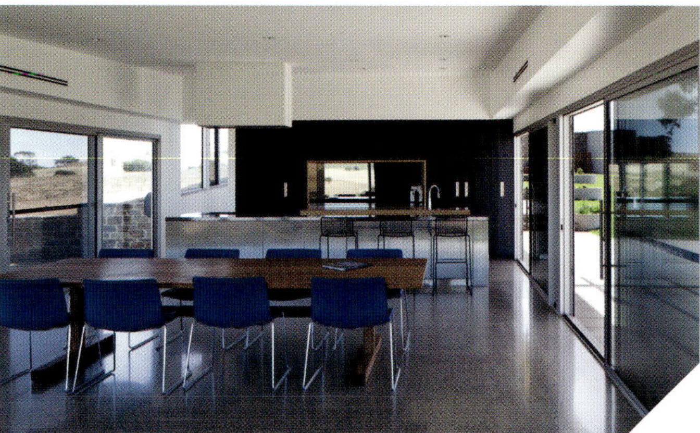

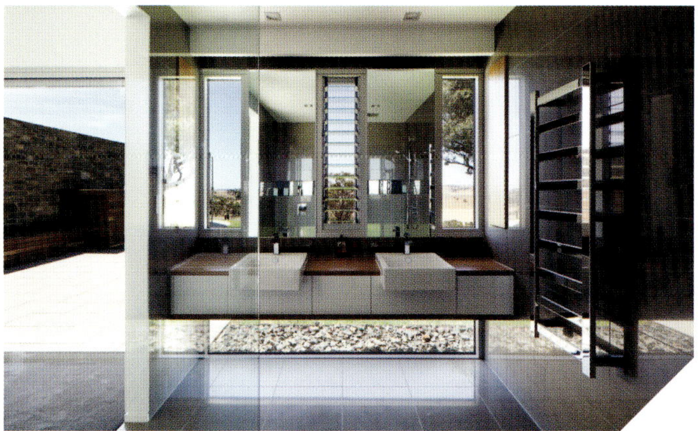

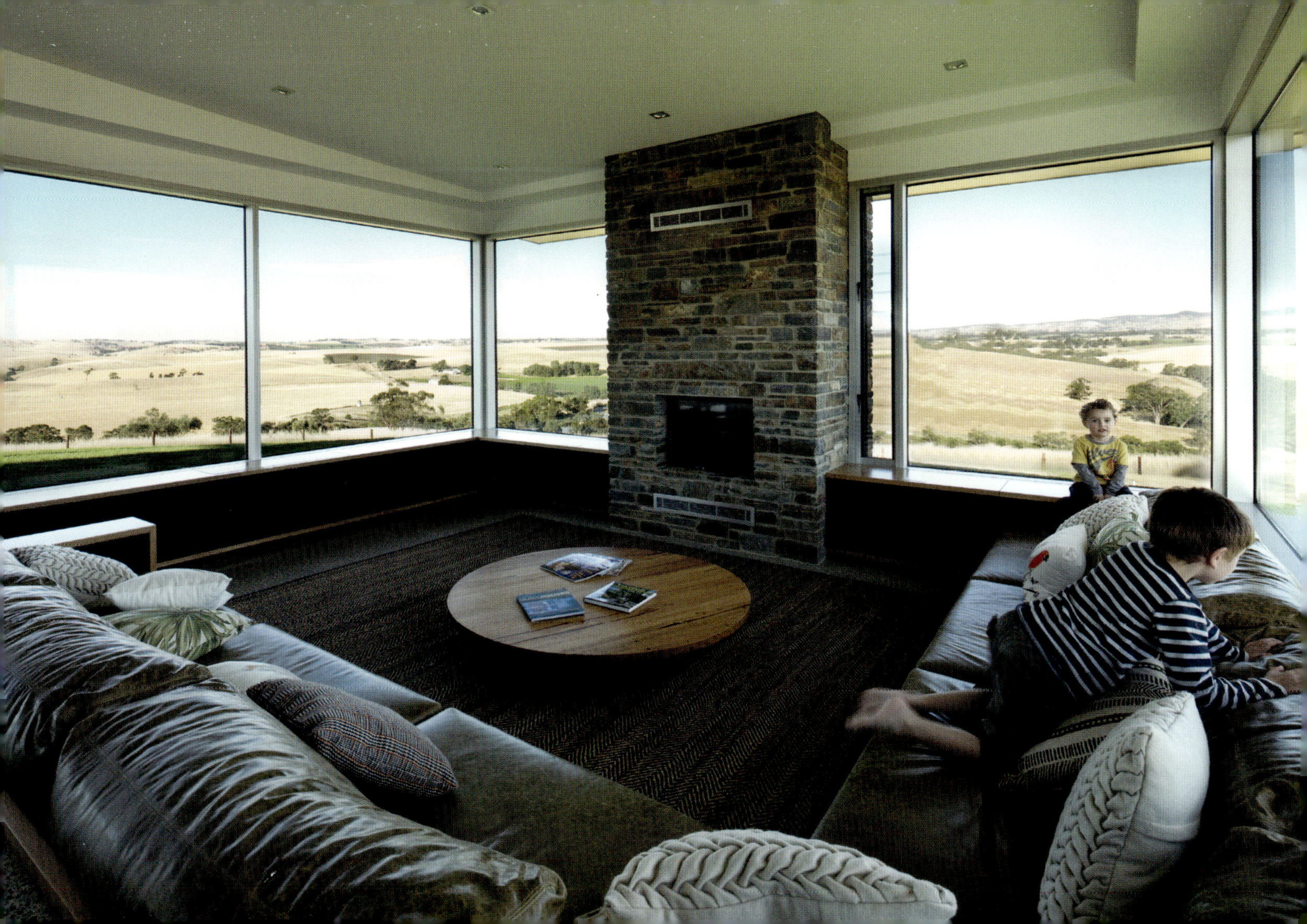

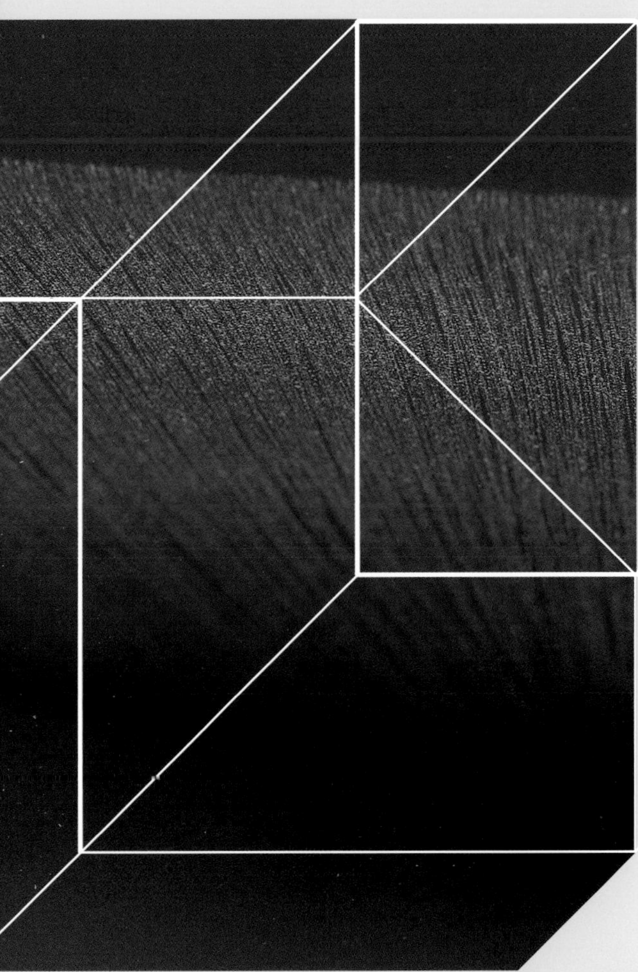

Mel Douglas

Born 1978, Burnie, Tasmania
Lives Canberra, Australian Capital Territory

Mel Douglas's reductively meditative works embody an unnerving quiet beauty. Suggesting light, space and time, her restrained colour palette and minimalist line enables her to reveal the elemental nature of glass. Sustaining her practice for over 15 years, her rigorous investigation of line, form, proportion and negative space has seen her produce a rich and considered body of work. She is recognised nationally and internationally as a leading contemporary glass artist.

A graduate of the Canberra School of Art at the Australian National University, Douglas began her arts training in the ceramics department. Here she was introduced to work by potters such as Hans Coper (1918–1980) and Gwyn Hanssen Pigott (1935–2013), both of whom have influenced her work.

Hans Coper's works seem to hover and float in space and, through close examination of these objects, Douglas has become keenly aware of how the specific relationship between the inside and outside of an object, and its proportions, can influence the way we see it grounded on a surface. Highlighting or exaggerating some parts of the form and playing with the subtlety of outside textures, Douglas's works seemingly come to a rest at a precarious angle, creating an innate tension as they appear to teeter on the edge of falling.

The carefully orchestrated still-life arrangements of Australian potter Hanssen Pigott encouraged Douglas to investigate the subtleties and nuances of the vessel. Considering the importance of subtle changes in shape and form, and looking closely at the relationship of objects with the space they inhabit, Pigott's still lifes have revealed to Douglas the power that negative space has to create stillness with the use of pauses and intervals. This knowledge has become an integral part of the display and presentation of her work.

Both glass blowing and ceramics are processes in which a liquid or viscous form of the material is manipulated before it bonds and hardens into its final form. Hardening occurs in ceramics with the introduction of heat, whilst glass hardens when cooled . Being molten, glass cannot be handled directly during the forming process; rather, contact is mitigated with range of tools that become an extension of the maker's hand.

Once the glass has cooled the surface can be held and worked directly. Through grinding, hand sanding and engraving, artists are able to create contrasts between high-gloss polished and reflective surfaces and matte finishes that add warmth.

After refining her forms with grinding and sanding, Douglas works the surfaces of her blown glass with a hand-held engraver. Meticulously, she slowly builds layers of finely calibrated lines on the surface. The austerity of her minimalist line can be traced to the influence of artists she greatly admires: Sol LeWitt (1928–2007) and Ellsworth Kelly (1923–).

Douglas's line work traces, or acts counter to the form, exaggerating its proportions and increasing the tension within the work. Transforming the high-gloss black into a grey scale, her forms challenge our perceptions about its materiality. Though these lines could be produced using more mechanical processes, the layering of slight imperfections is important feature to Douglas, as they evidence the artist's hand.

Douglas's works are not only the product of hours of precise hand-engraving, they are also the final distillation of many months of preparatory drawings and maquette making. She obsessively produces journals full of drawings, ideas and inspirational images, which allow Douglas to explore form, scale, line and proportion. She often draws something over and over, to review the many possible configurations of angle and line

Previous page
Ballast (detail), 2013
blown, coldworked and engraved glass
200 x 520 dia.
Photo: Stuart Hay

▸

Mel Douglas obsessively keeps artist journals testing ideas through preliminary drawings and black foam models.
Photo: Courtesy of artist

▸▸

Mel Douglas working in her studio.
Photo: Charles Higgins

▾

Point.line.plane exhibition, 2013
Installation view,
Sabbia Gallery, Sydney
Photo: Mel Douglas

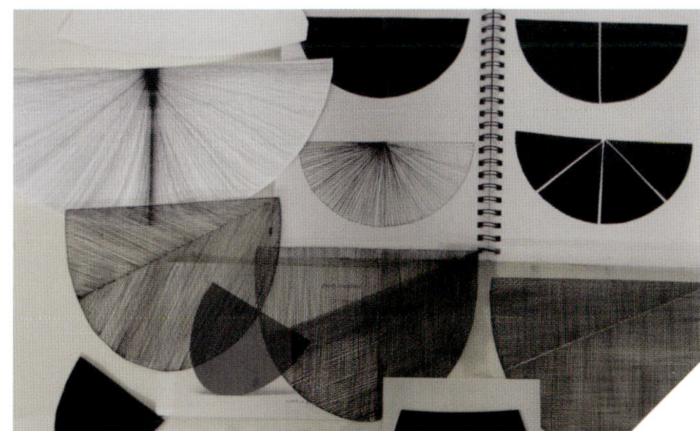

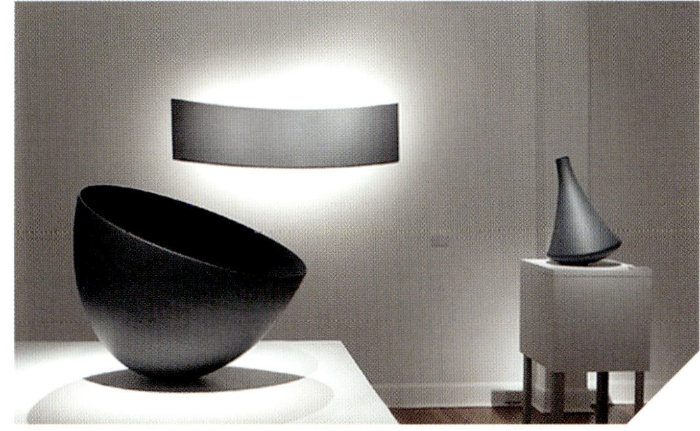

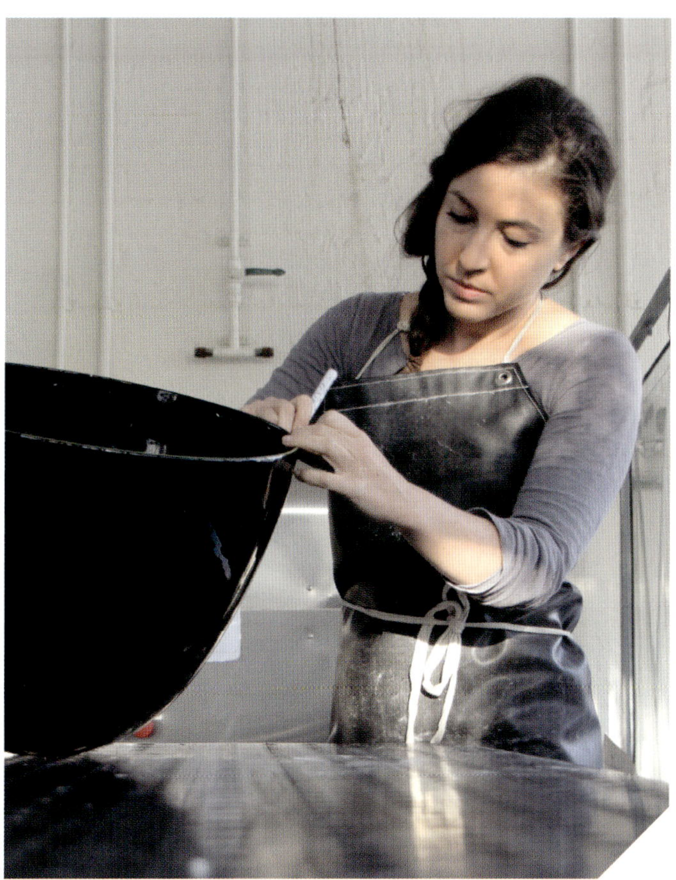

coverage. The varying suggestions dramatically impact the sense of calm or stillness in a piece.

In 2002, Douglas won the prestigious Ranamok Glass Prize, in 2007 the LinoTagliapietra Prize of Young Glass at the Glasmuseet Ebeltoft in Denmark, and in 2014 she won the Art Gallery of Western Australia's Tom Malone Prize. Her work is found in many significant collections, including the National Gallery of Australia, the National Art Glass Collection at Wagga Wagga Art Gallery, the Corning Museum of Glass and the Cincinnati Art Museum (both USA).

Margaret Hancock Davis

Overleaf left
High Tide (detail), 2012
blown, cold worked
and engraved glass
230 x 510 x 510
Photo: Stuart Hay

Overleaf right
Sway, 2013
kiln formed, cold worked
and engraved glass
500 x 600 x 45
Photo: Stuart Hay

▸
Turning tide #2,
Gradient, and *Linear*, 2014
blown, cold worked
and engraved glass
210 x 220 dia.
210 x 220 dia.
230 x 240 dia.
Photo: Stuart Hay

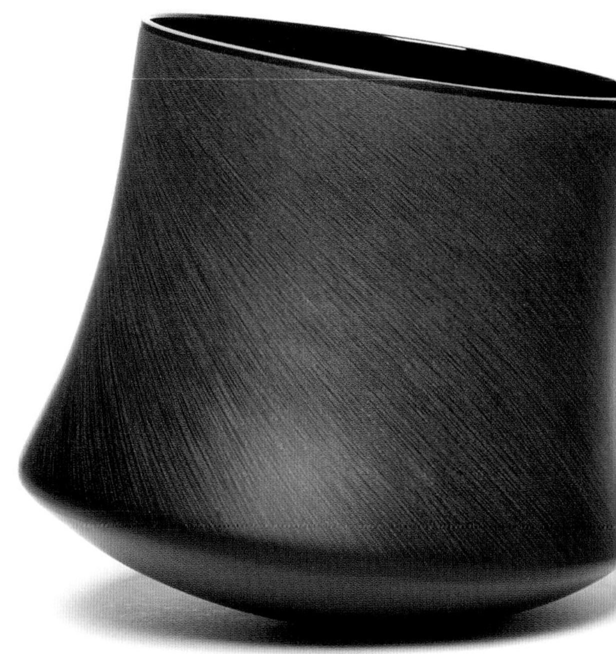

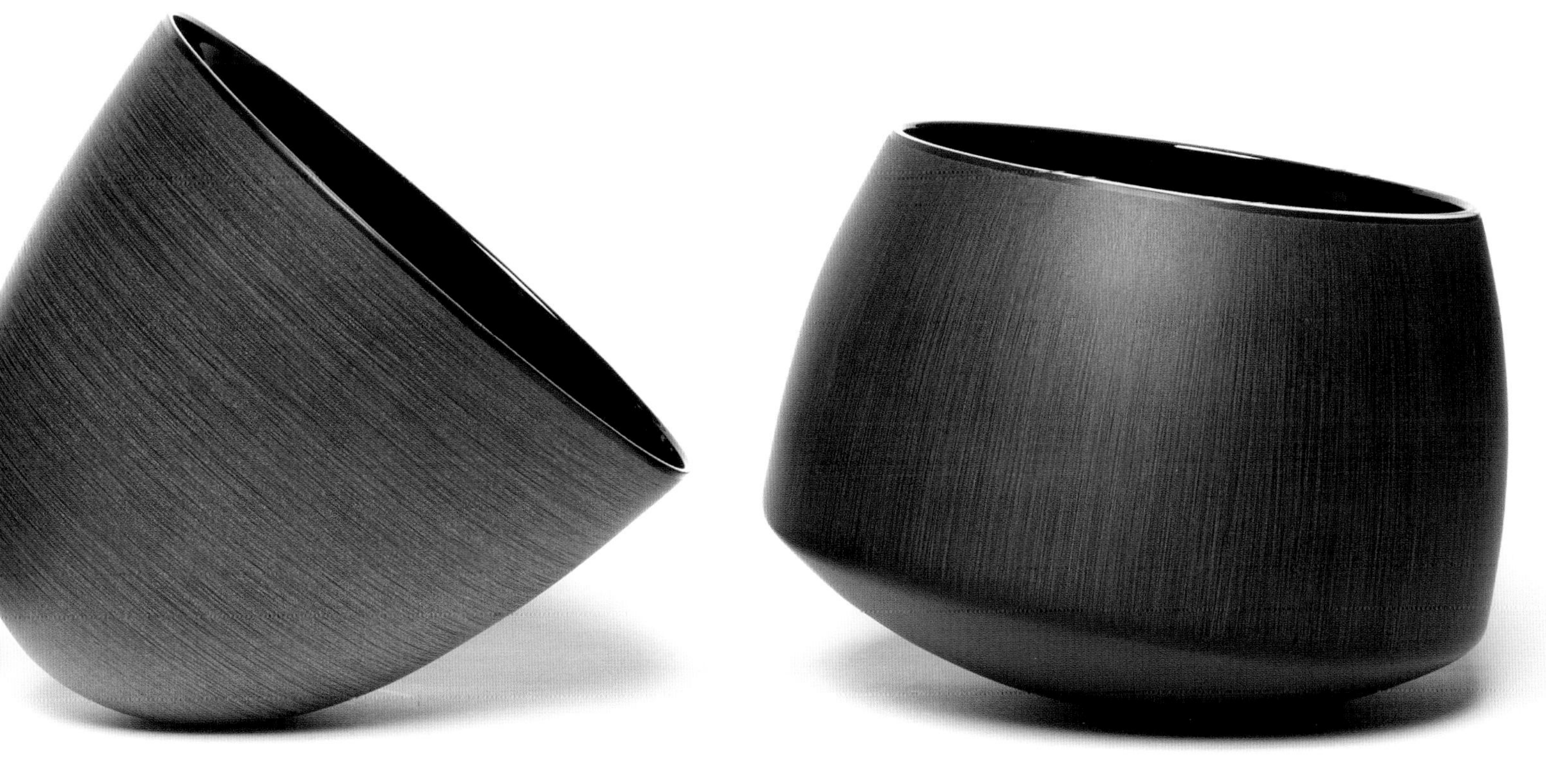

'The simplicity of my work suggests stillness and silence, a meditation on the elements and concepts of light, space and time. That sense of reduction and finding the simplest way to realise my ideas is something I strive for, reducing elements to their simplest components: form and space.

I am interested in the space that surrounds an object, space that is able to hold and suspend. Exploring how objects balance and sit in space, holding on to that last moment of stillness before they spill over. The engraved lines of light add to this tension, tilting the objects off centre. This sense of anticipation generates between the object and the surrounding space.

I aim to concentrate the viewer's attention on the proportion and linear relationships of the work. Each line is a unique mark influenced by the object's physical shape and surface; it is a contour, a stroke and an outline.

I see my works as three-dimensional drawings, lines tracing, outlining and building form. Linear marks that highlight or exaggerate proportion. Building surfaces through repetitive cross-hatching, giving flat planes life and depth.'

Mel Douglas

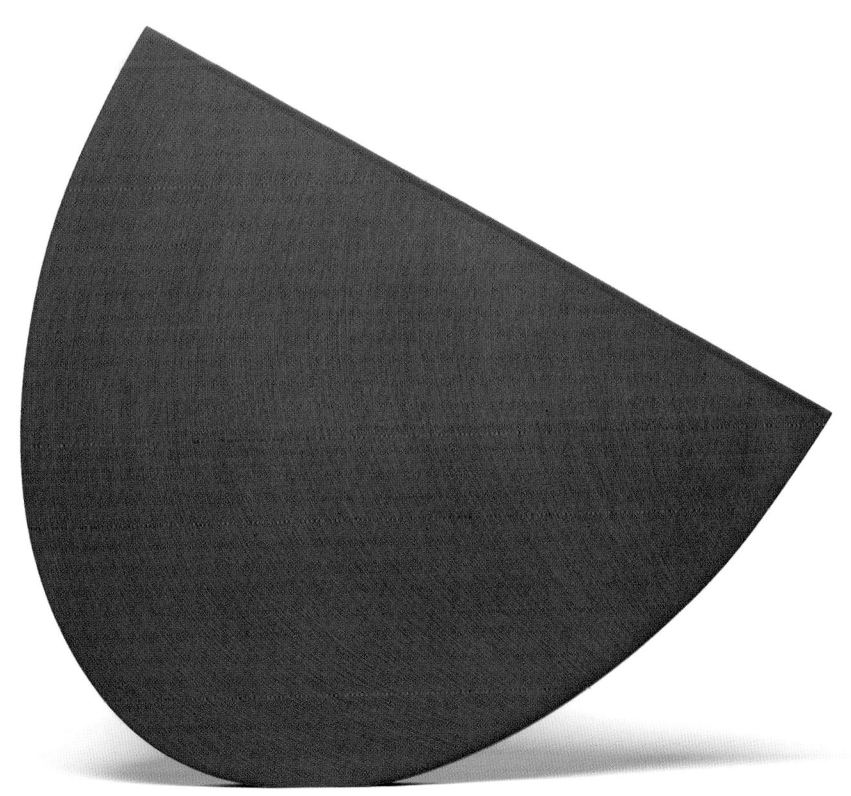

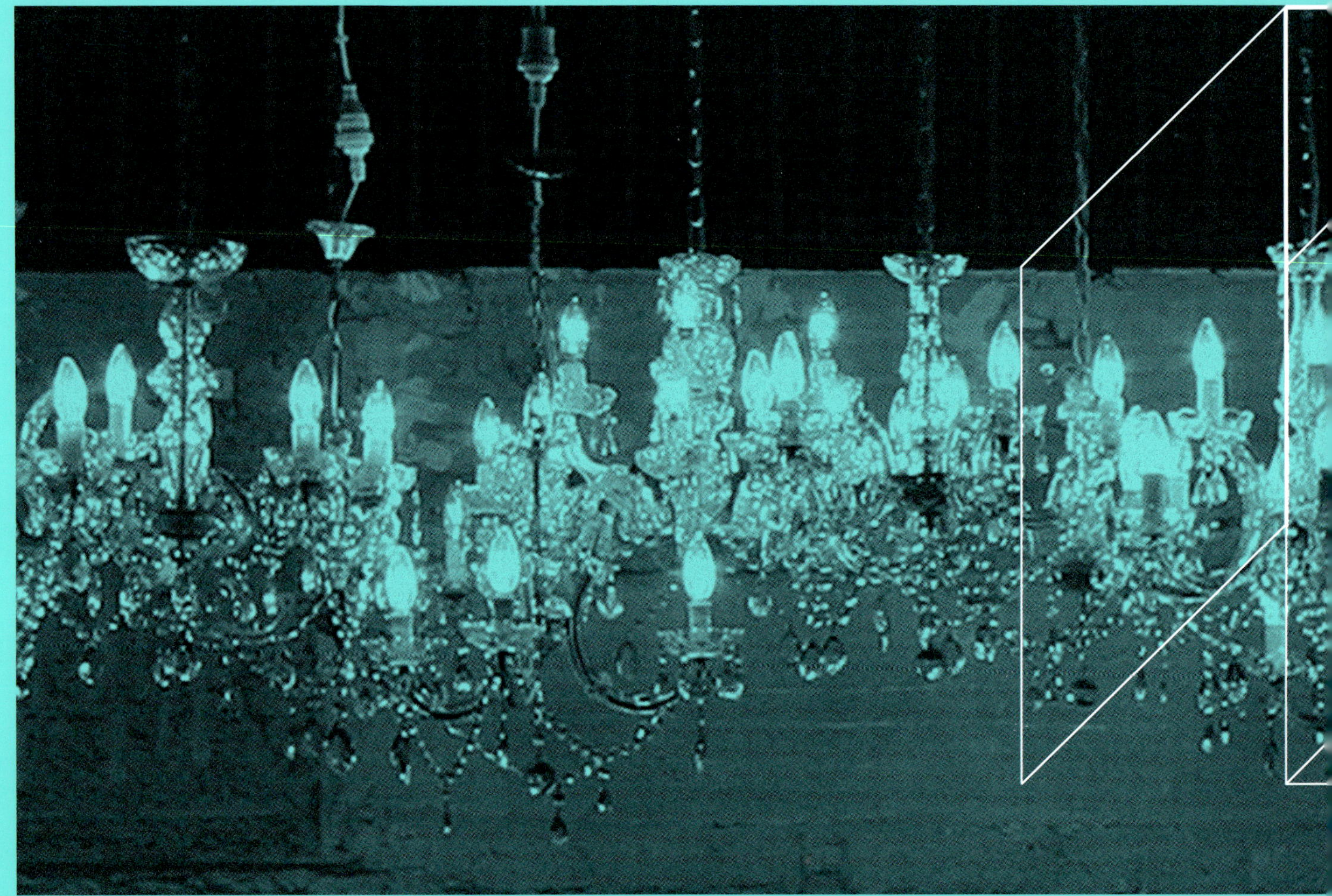

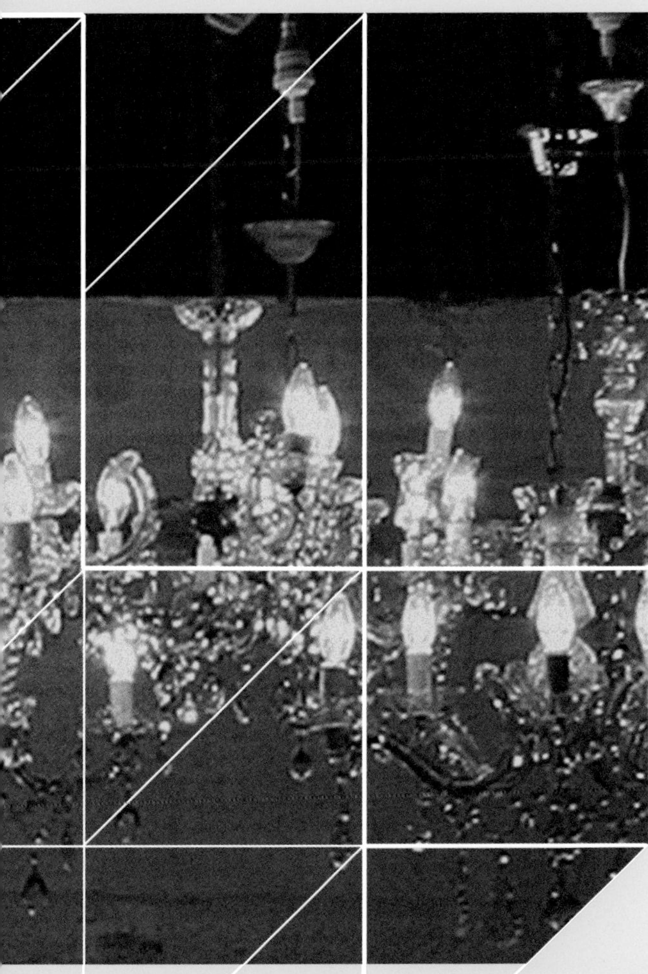

Nicholas Folland

Born 1967, Adelaide, South Australia
Lives Adelaide, South Australia

Nicholas Folland is an artist primarily producing sculptural works and installations. Before studying visual arts at the University of South Australia he originally enrolled in Human Environments (now known as Interior Architecture), following a specific interest in theatre design. Influences of these early interests remain present in his work today, and he describes his larger installations as 'theatre without actors'.

Folland is interested in spatial practices and increasingly engaged in creating site-specific works for residential and commercial spaces. Most of these have been based to some extent on previous exhibition works, and on several projects he has worked collaboratively with his architect brother Mark Folland, operating within predetermined design parameters and a specific client brief.

Glass has been an important recurring material in Folland's work, in which he re-interprets the ordinary and banal to create poetic statements alluding to personal and shared identities. The majority of the glass used in his work is ready-made and sourced from op-shops and flea markets. With the inkling of an idea in mind, he searches for specific items, having identified particular materials or objects that contain a history or familiarity that he can manipulate. He says of the glassware he currently collects:

> it must reflect faceted crystal, even if it's pressed glass. It can't contain pictorial elements, such as flowers, as these signs refer outside of the object itself ... Shape, size and colour are also specifically defined.

In 2009 Folland created *Floe*, 2009, for the exhibition *Colliding Worlds* at the Samstag Museum, in which approximately 2000 glass crystal items, including drinking glasses, bowls and vases, were individually suspended to form a floating island landscape. A similar work was commissioned for *Parallel Collisions: 2012 Adelaide Biennial of Australian Art*, at the Art Gallery of South Australia.

Following a series of conversations in 2007 with multi-disciplinary artist and designer Deb Jones, who was at the time lead designer at JamFactory's Glass Studio, Folland had the opportunity to work with JamFactory's Glass Studio to develop a body of work based on an idea about laboratory glass forms with surfaces like faceted crystal-ware. He worked closely with the studio staff to find ways to realise the idea and resolve his material concerns.

Folland has also undertaken a residency at the Canberra Glassworks, where the facilities and support enabled him to produce a number of cast works including *Fetch*, 2012. He notes that his working methodology was very different to those who normally work with glass there:

> I don't work in the same way as craftspeople. It's not through a physical process of exploring materials that my ideas come about. I spent the first few weeks of the residency developing ideas, making nothing, while all the others were very hands-on with the material.

Following his graduation from the University of South Australia in 1999, Folland was awarded a prestigious Samstag Scholarship, which enabled him to study in Rotterdam and Barcelona. He completed a Masters degree at the University of Sydney in 2009, and is currently Head of Contemporary Studies at Adelaide Central School of Art. His work is held in several major public collections in Australia, including the National Gallery of Victoria, Melbourne, the Art Gallery of South Australia, Adelaide and the Museum of Contemporary Art, Sydney.

Brian Parkes

Previous page
Or or u, 2010
chandeliers
dimensions variable
Installation view, *CACSA Contemporary 2010 |The New New*, Contemporary Art Centre of South Australia, The Gallerie on North Terrace, 2010
Photo: Courtesy of the artist

▸

Nicholas Folland installing
Untitled (Jump-up), 2011–12
commissioned for
Parallel Collisions: 2012 Adelaide Biennial of Australian Art,
Art Gallery of South Australia.
Photo: Saul Steed

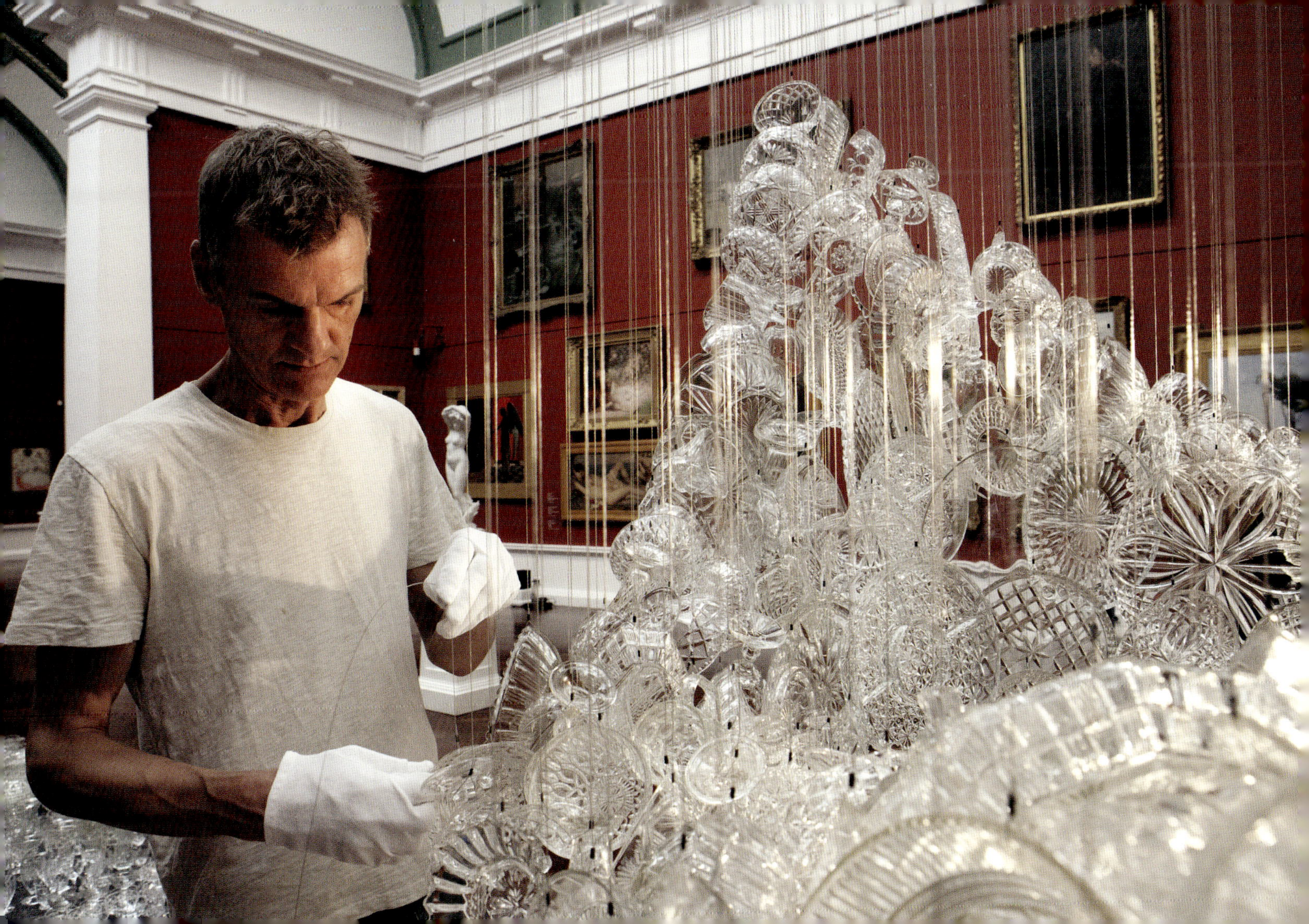

▸

I hang out here all the time, 2008
chandelier, refrigeration unit, 12v lighting, dimensions variable, permanent installation, Colonist Tavern, Norwood, South Australia
Photo: Courtesy of the artist

▸▸

Fetch, 2012
recast antique crystal water jug
480 x 250 x 50
Photo: Courtesy of the artist

▸▸▸

Untitled (Jump-up), 2011–12
crystal and glassware, nylon coated stainless steel wire
2300 x 5000 x 4600
Installation view,
for *Parallel Collisions: 2012 Adelaide Biennial of Australian Art*, Art Gallery of South Australia.
Photo: Saul Steed

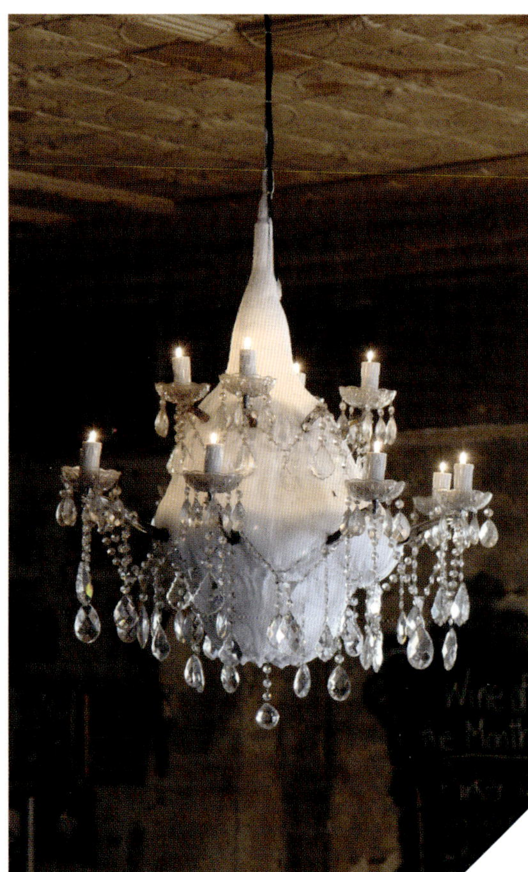

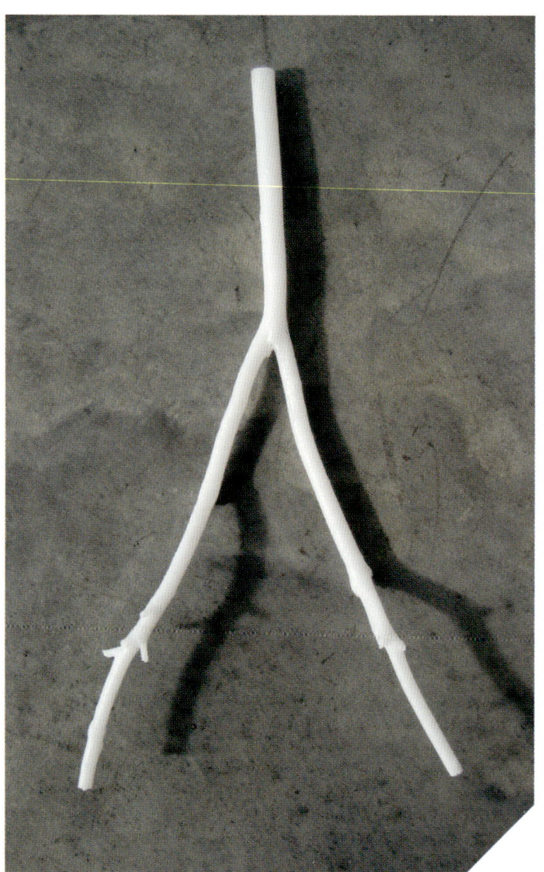

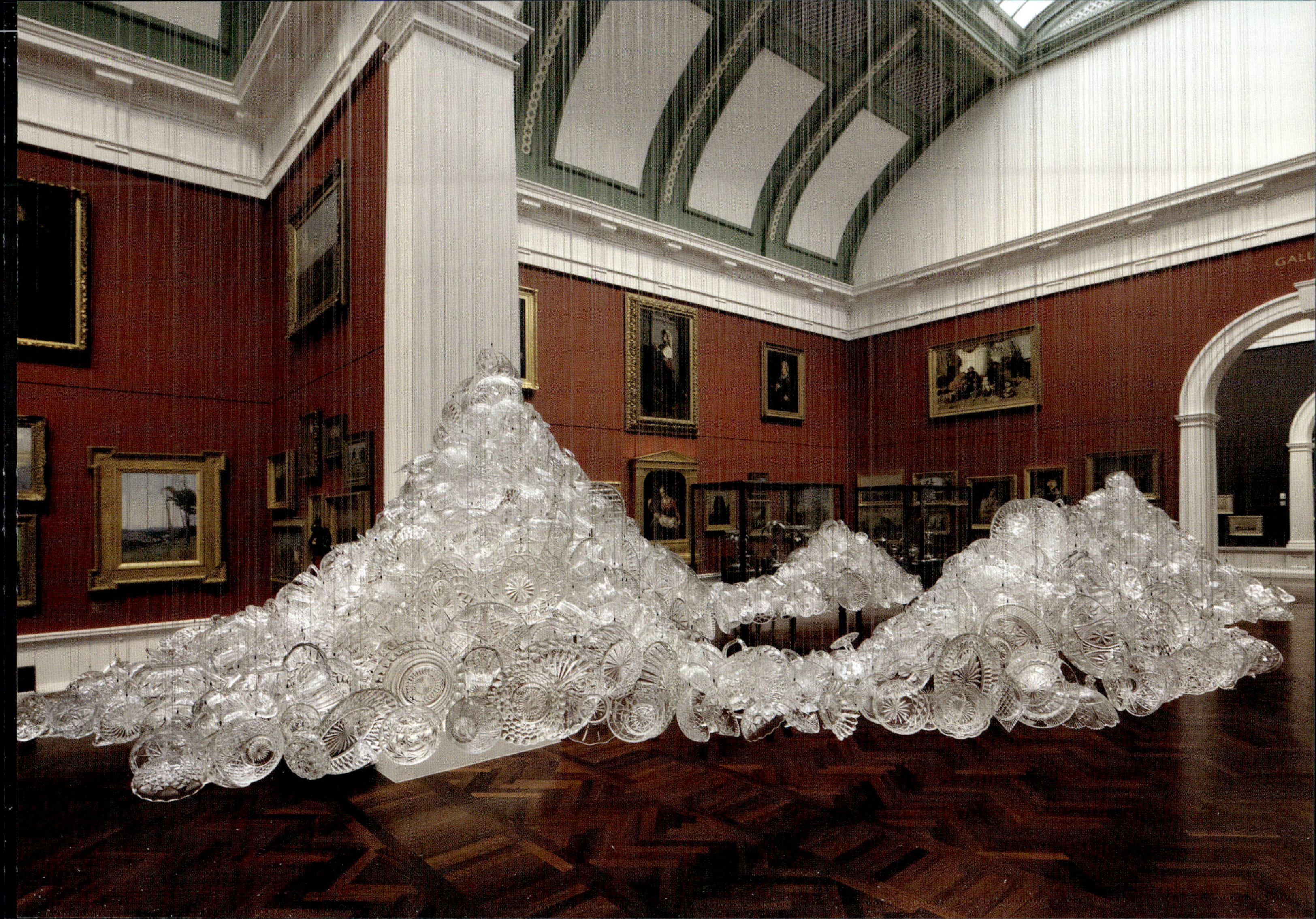

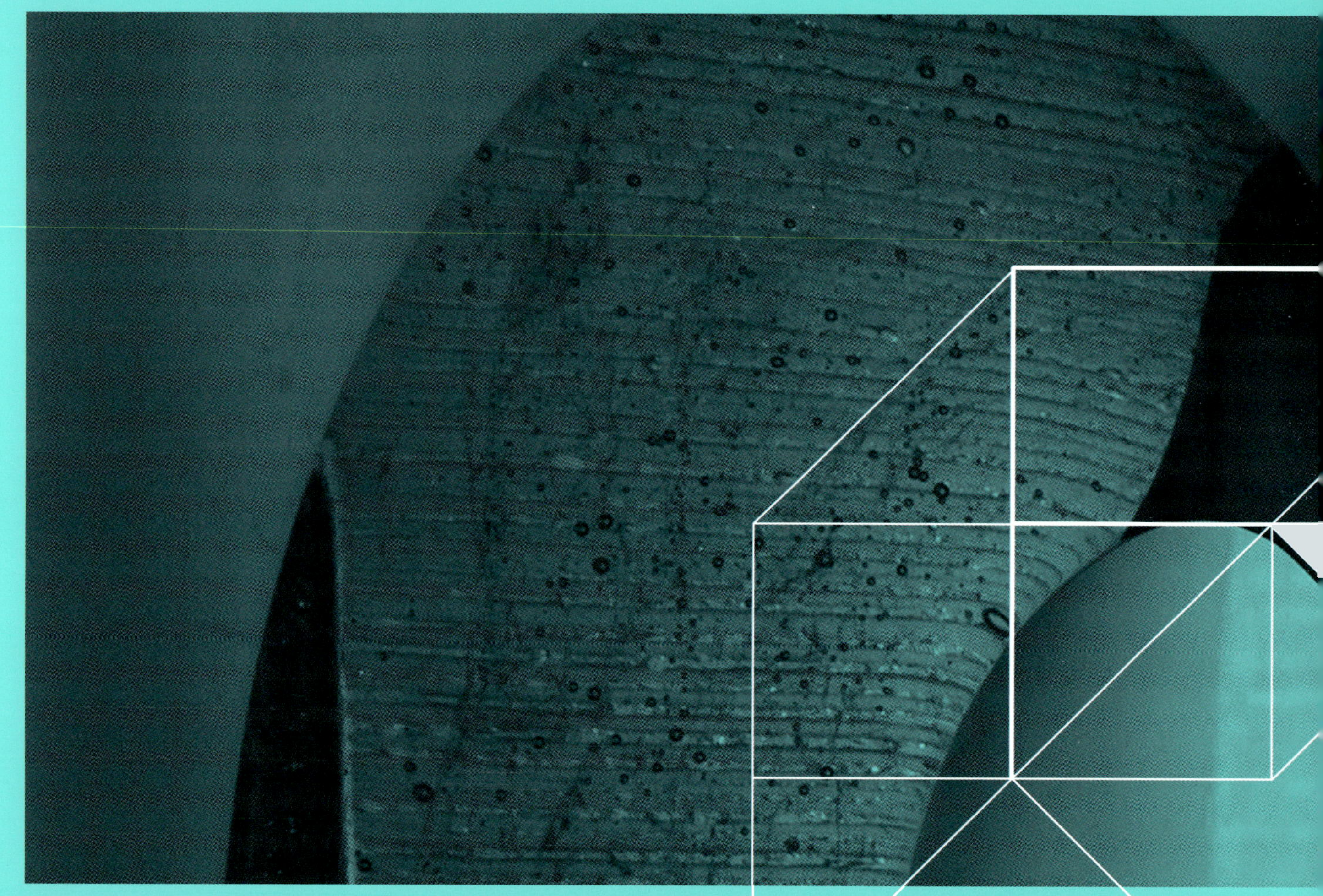

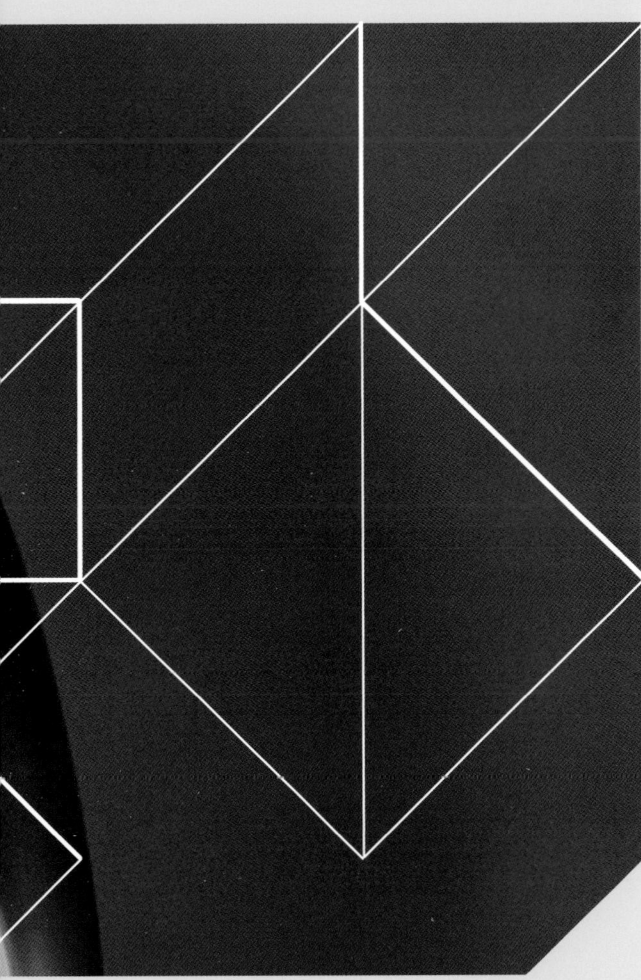

Richard Whiteley

Born 1963, East Dean, England
Lives Queanbeyan, New South Wales

The many biographical entries written about Richard Whiteley in books, catalogues and journals usually start with the fact that he became an apprentice in stained glass at the age of 16. It is a significant fact that speaks poignantly to a life-long engagement with the material. Today Whiteley is considered one of the most influential figures in Australian art glass, as both an artist and an educator.

Since 2002, he has been Associate Professor and Head of the Glass Workshop at the Canberra School of Art, Australian National University — considered widely as one of the leading study programs for artists working in glass anywhere in the world. Prior to this, he was a lecturer in Glass at Sydney College of the Arts at the University of Sydney, and has been a guest lecturer or instructor at various institutions in Australia, New Zealand, China, Japan, the United States and the United Kingdom.

Following his apprenticeship at Spectrum Studios in Victoria, Whiteley completed an undergraduate degree at the Canberra School of Art, Australian National

University in 1987, making him part of the early crop of students to emerge from the program established there by Klaus Moje in 1982. The academic foundation laid by Moje — which combined rigorous skills-based training in the techniques of working with glass with a highly conceptual framework — has been a hallmark of Whiteley's own practice, and continues to inform the dynamic program he now runs in Canberra.

While in the final year of his degree, Whiteley received funding from the Australia Council to attend the annual Pilchuck Glass School — an international centre for glass art education in Seattle — to undertake a cast-glass workshop with Czech masters Stanislav Libenský and Jaroslava Brychtová. Whiteley has returned to Pilchuck several times, initially as an assistant to Moje and then as an instructor each time since.

Having additionally completed a Master of Fine Arts in Sculpture at the University of Illinois in 1992, Whiteley maintains many strong links to the United States (where the art glass movement is so well supported), particularly through the Pilchuck School, the Corning Museum of Glass and the Bullseye Glass Company.

Whiteley's work focuses primarily on cast glass and his works explore voids within glass as the primary constructive agent. Drawing and model making are where the work starts. Once models for works are realised, there are several forming stages to prepare a mould so it is ready for casting the glass. The casting moulds are made with refractory materials, and these are loaded into kilns with glass ingots. The time each casting spends in the kiln is usually between three to seven weeks. For most of this time the glass is cooling, very slowly, because of the annealing needs of the thick and unusual shapes in glass.

Once the casting is out of the kiln, the sculpture is still very raw and needs to be carved and cold worked (cut, ground, polished). Whiteley considers these raw cast forms as rough blanks, and the process of carving and shaping them is important for him to build the right translucency and softness in the sculpture. He mainly uses stone carving tools that have been adapted to work with glass for these processes. A single work can take several weeks or even months to complete.

Brian Parkes

Previous page
Oscillate (detail), 2013
cast glass
350 x 255 x 116
Photo: Greg Piper

▸
Ocularis, 2010
cast glass,
380 x 760 x 130
Photo: Greg Piper

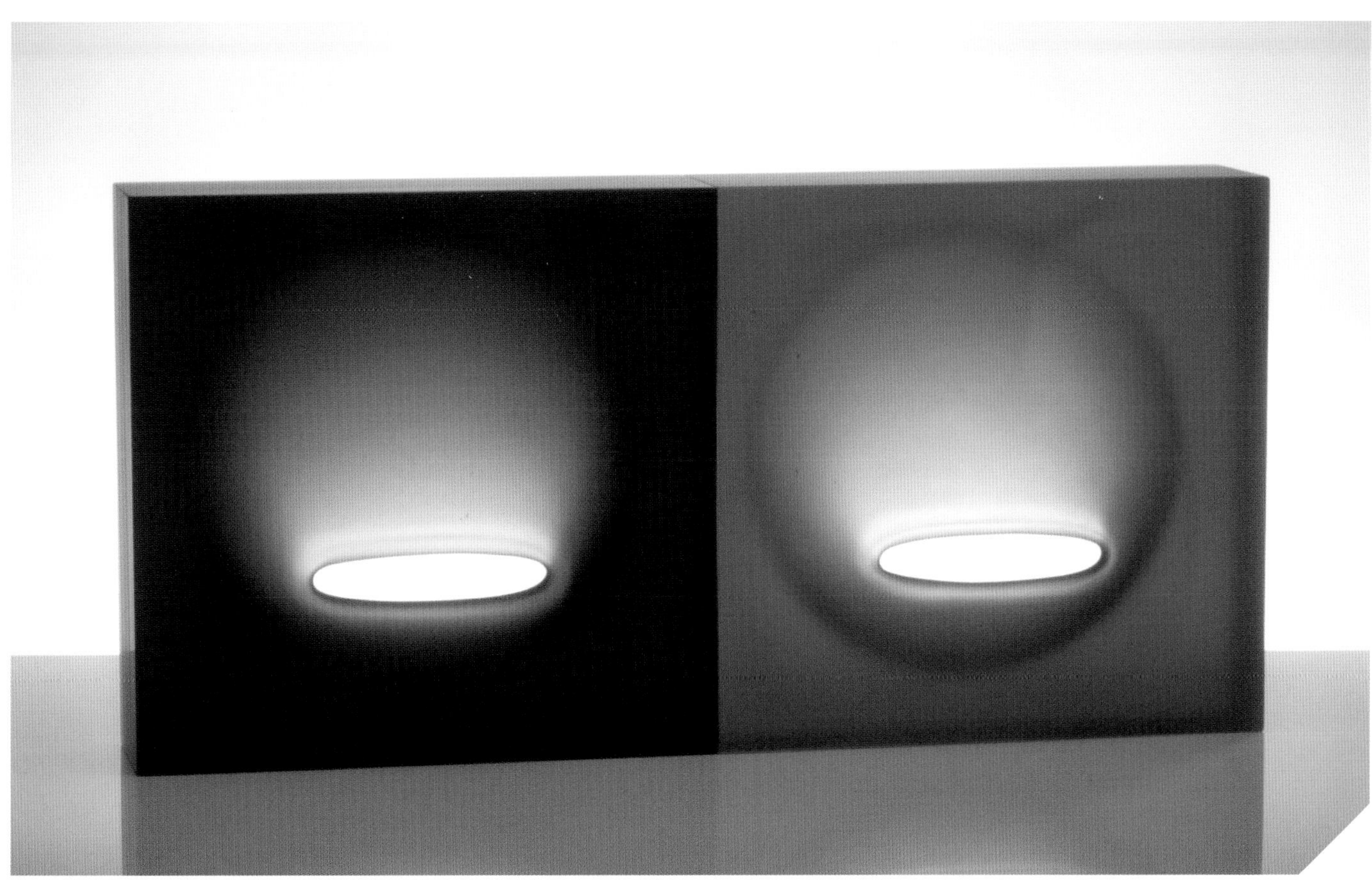

▸
Richard Whiteley working.
Photo: Courtesy of the artist

▸▸
Lung, 2013
cast glass
384 x 285 x 135
Photo: Greg Piper

▸▸▸
Oscillate, 2013
cast glass
350 x 255 x 116
Photo: Greg Piper

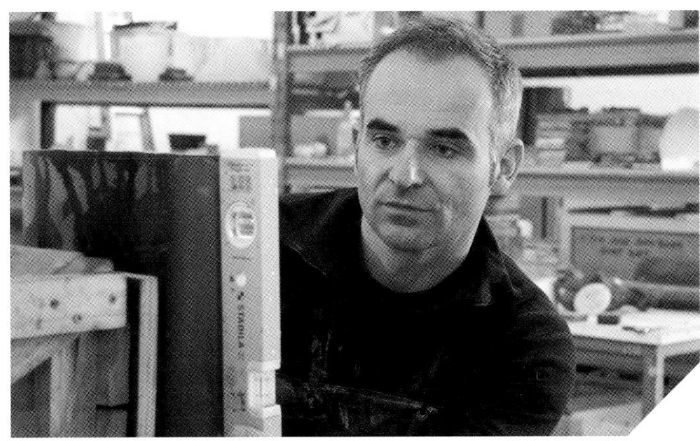

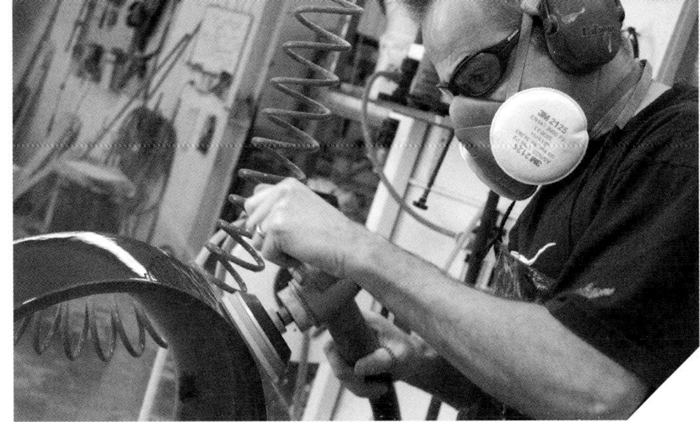

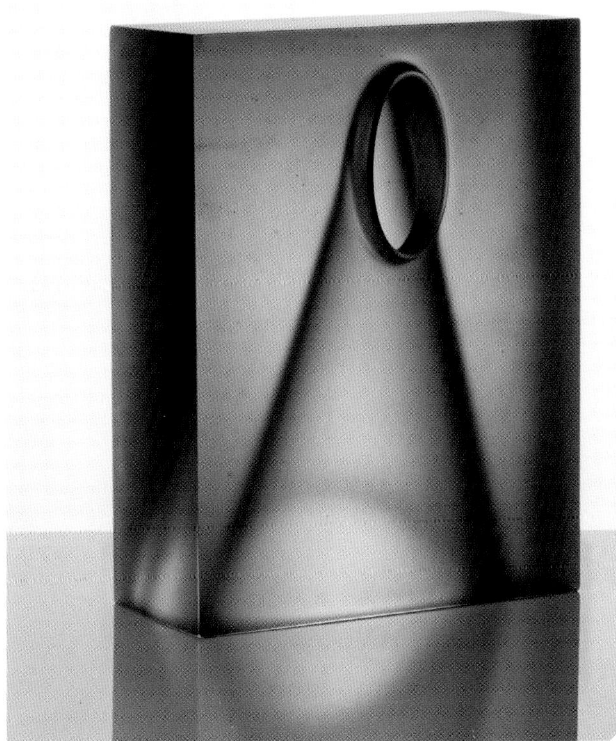

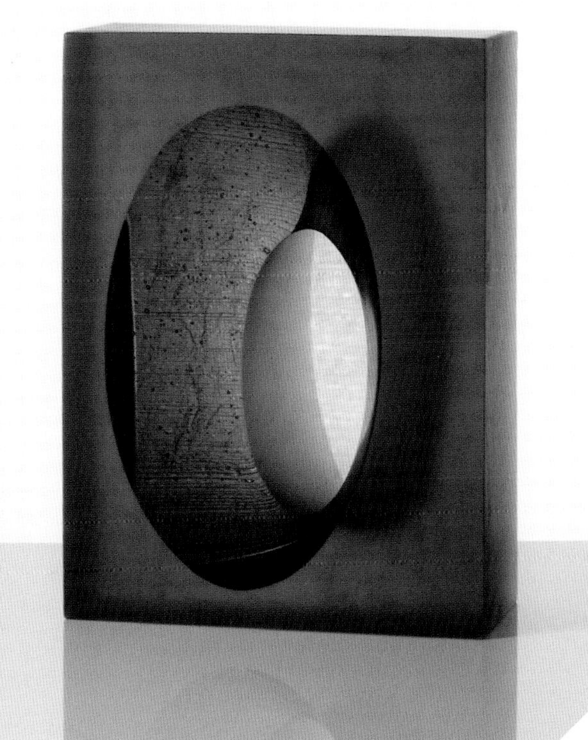

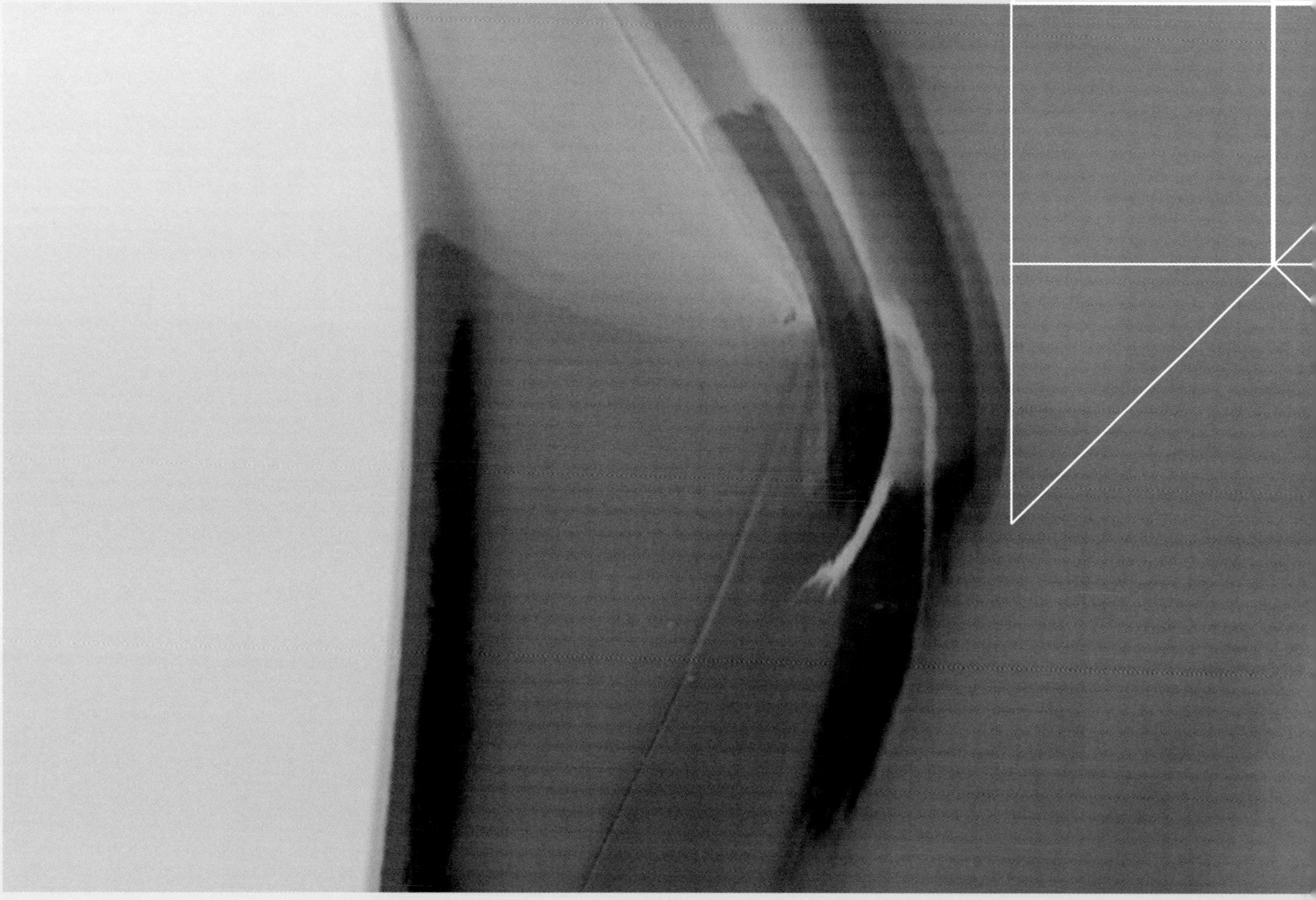

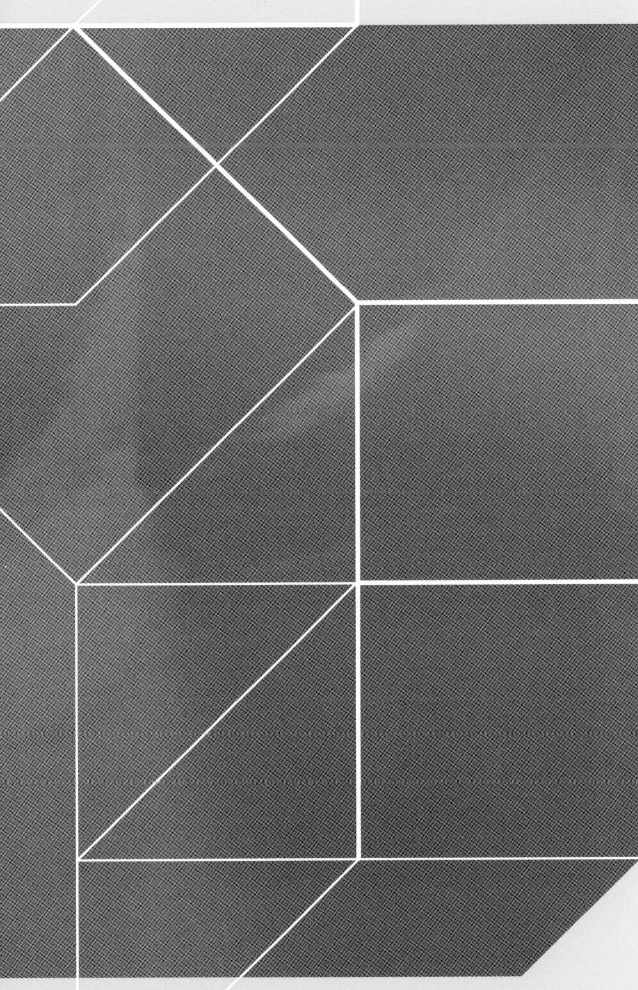

Ruth Allen

Born 1983, Auckland, New Zealand
Lives in Melbourne, Victoria

With sustainability and a concern for the environment at the core of her practice, glass artist Ruth Allen was interested in finding a way to reduce the ecological footprint of her business. Her solution is a simple action that contributes to a greater shift — to upcycle. Running a glass studio in Coburg North, Melbourne, she collects old, used glass bottles and transforms them into trendy vessels, tumblers, vases and, more recently, into pendant lights. She says:

> There is such a wealth in recycling, reusing and reclaiming. I know that I feel great when drinking from a recycled stubby. It's not just a glass; it is a concept. A concept that I believe contributes to transforming the culture and conversation of our time.[1]

Since studying at the Canberra School of Art, Australian National University, Allen's glass practice has taken on many forms, including running a hot-glass studio in Auckland and undertaking a Masters degree at Monash University. Within her artistic practice she is known for creating large-scale glass installations, which often incorporate light, sound and movement. After finishing her Masters, Allen and her partner purchased a warehouse that they transformed into a glass studio. Here, Allen sought to find a commercially viable product that could help support her artistic practice and be a profitable outlet for her craft skills. From this she developed Sustainable Stubbies, a project that upcycles used glass bottles, combining her skills as a maker with her desire to create a sustainable practice.

Working with recycled glass means that Allen works with a fairly limited range of equipment in the studio. Using a kiln to bring the glass bottles up to a working temperature, she has no need for a furnace. She has developed custom equipment for the upcycling process, including an old bathtub with burners underneath where bottles are simmered and scrubbed to remove the label and adhesives. Allen works with a small team, which grows and shrinks depending on demand and the time of year. It is a laborious process, but Allen says she enjoys the challenge that each bottle brings.

In deciding on a design for each stubby, Allen's process has become intuitive, based on her experience working with many different bottles. Each bottle is worked by hand, responding to characteristics including the shape of the bottle, or the thickness of the glass. Some of it is about practicality: a square gin bottle doesn't lend itself to becoming a carafe, but can make a wonderful vase. Her *In the spirit set*, 2012, is a great example, with the tall Sambuca bottle transforming into a carafe, and a set of four low cut tumblers all with the familiar faceted base design of the Sambuca bottle. The set was a finalist for Launch Pad 2012 and the winner of the 2012 Melbourne Design Awards in the Product Design — Homewares division.

One of the admirable aspects of Allen's business is the community that has developed around the collection of used bottles. When she began selling at markets, a number of customers would give her feedback and ideas. Friendships would develop and these customers would turn into repeat buyers and deliverers of empty bottles. Today, Allen has cafes and restaurants that share in the community of collecting used bottles. It links back to Allen's original premise for the Sustainable Stubbies — a business that contributes to a cultural shift towards re-use and environmental consciousness within the wider community.

Adele Sliuzas

1. Ruth Allen, in an interview with Jane Riley, for the design blog *Who'd have thought*, March 2014, viewed 22 August 2014, http://blog.whodhavethought.com/2014/03/19/ruth-allen-glass-sculptor/

Previous page
Dimple green tumbler (detail), 2014
reclaimed and hot-worked glass Stella Artois bottle
150 x 60 dia.
Photo: Joshua Rowell

▸
Ruth Allen at work in her Coburg North studio.
Photo: Courtesy of the artist

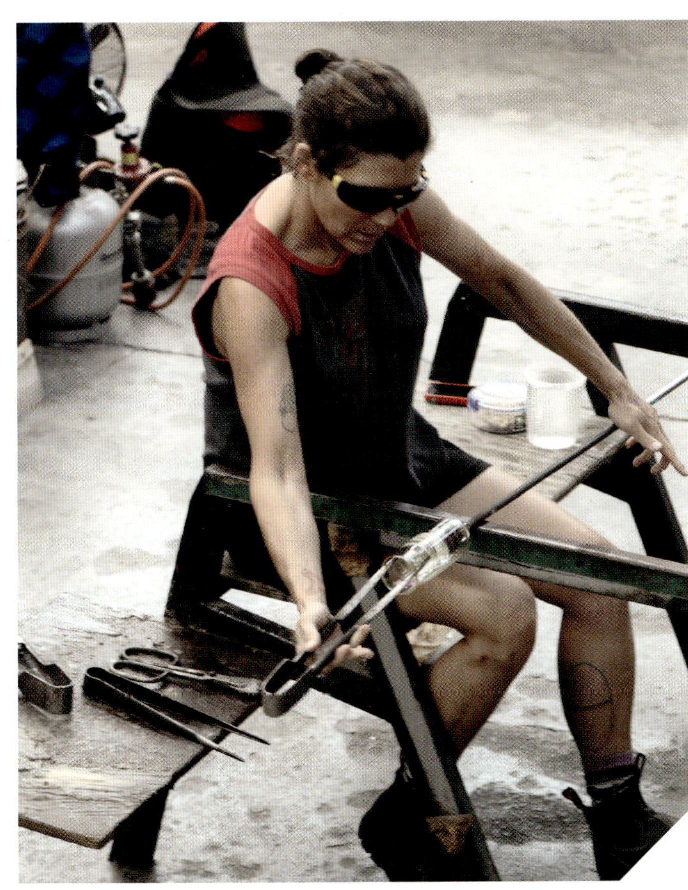

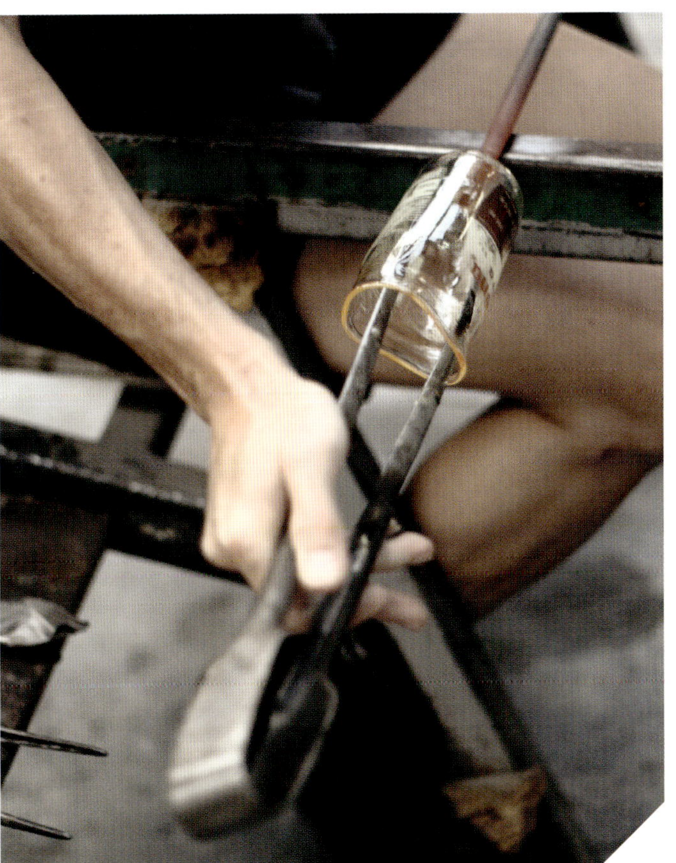

Sustainable Stubbies

The unique characteristics of each glass bottle influence the design of Allen's *Sustainable Stubbies*. The set has been upcycled from Coopers beer bottles, and includes a carafe made from a long neck and a set of tumblers cut from Coopers stubbies. The re-purposed bottes are hot manipulated in Allen's Melbourne studio, and are transformed from waste product into something you might use every day. Allen highlights the adequacy of items that could otherwise become landfill and, at the same time, has built a profitable business that utilises her skills as a craftsperson.

▸

Coopers tumbler, 2014
reclaimed and hot worked glass Coopers bottle
150 x 60 dia.
Photo: Joshua Rowell

▸▸

Dimple green tumbler, 2014
Photo: Joshua Rowell

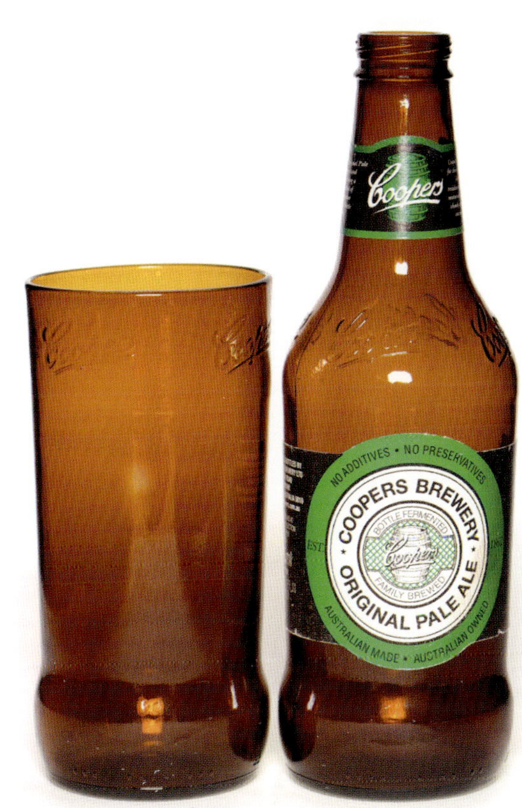
Coopers
NO ADDITIVES • NO PRESERVATIVES
COOPERS BREWERY
BOTTLE FERMENTED
FAMILY BREWED
ORIGINAL PALE ALE
AUSTRALIAN MADE • AUSTRALIAN OWNED

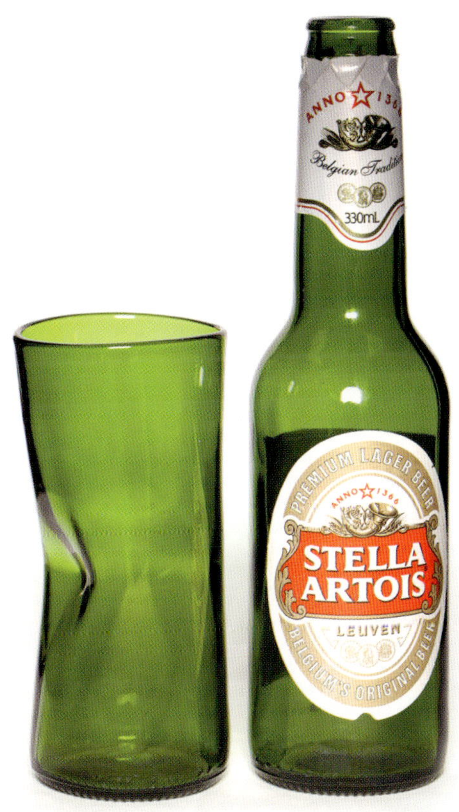
330mL
PREMIUM LAGER BEER
ANNO 1366
STELLA ARTOIS
LEUVEN
BELGIUM'S ORIGINAL BEER

Ruth Allen

▸

In The Spirit set, 2012
reclaimed, hot worked
glass Galliano bottles
decanter 380 x 80 dia.
glass 95 x 85 dia. each
Photo: Zosia Fabijanska

▸▸ ▸▸▸

In The Spirit vase, 2012
reclaimed, hot worked
glass Galliano bottle
380 x 80 dia.
Photo: Zosia Fabijanska

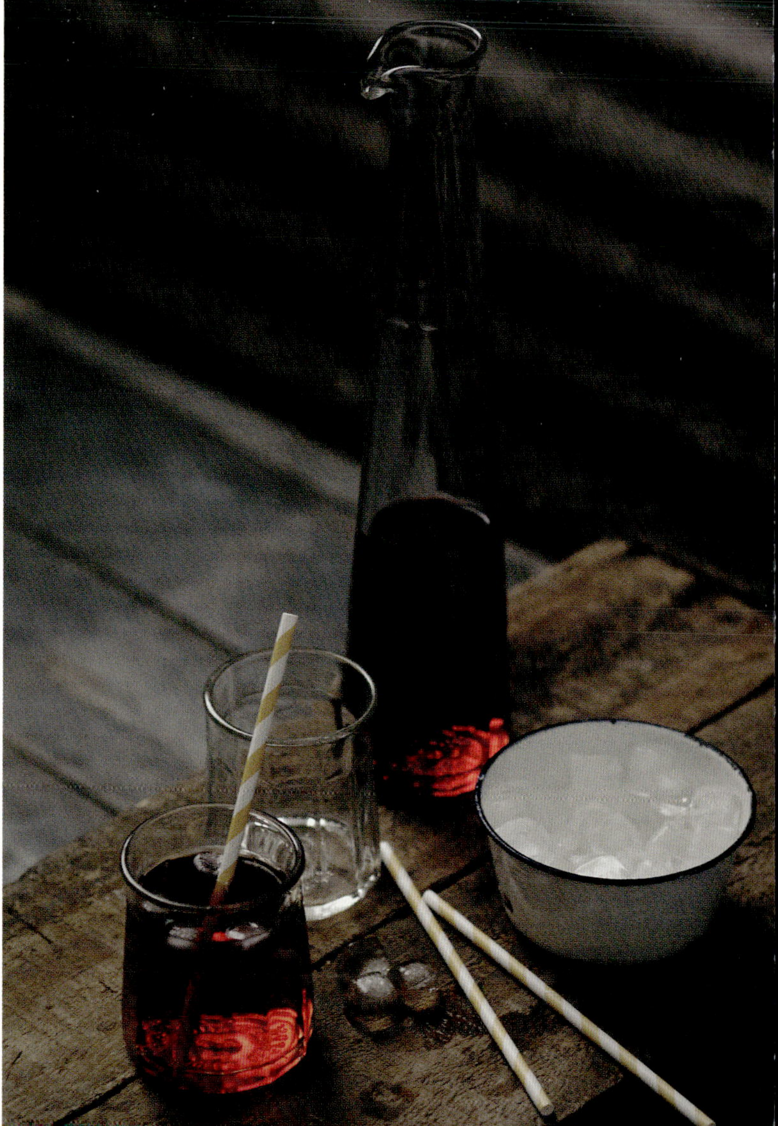

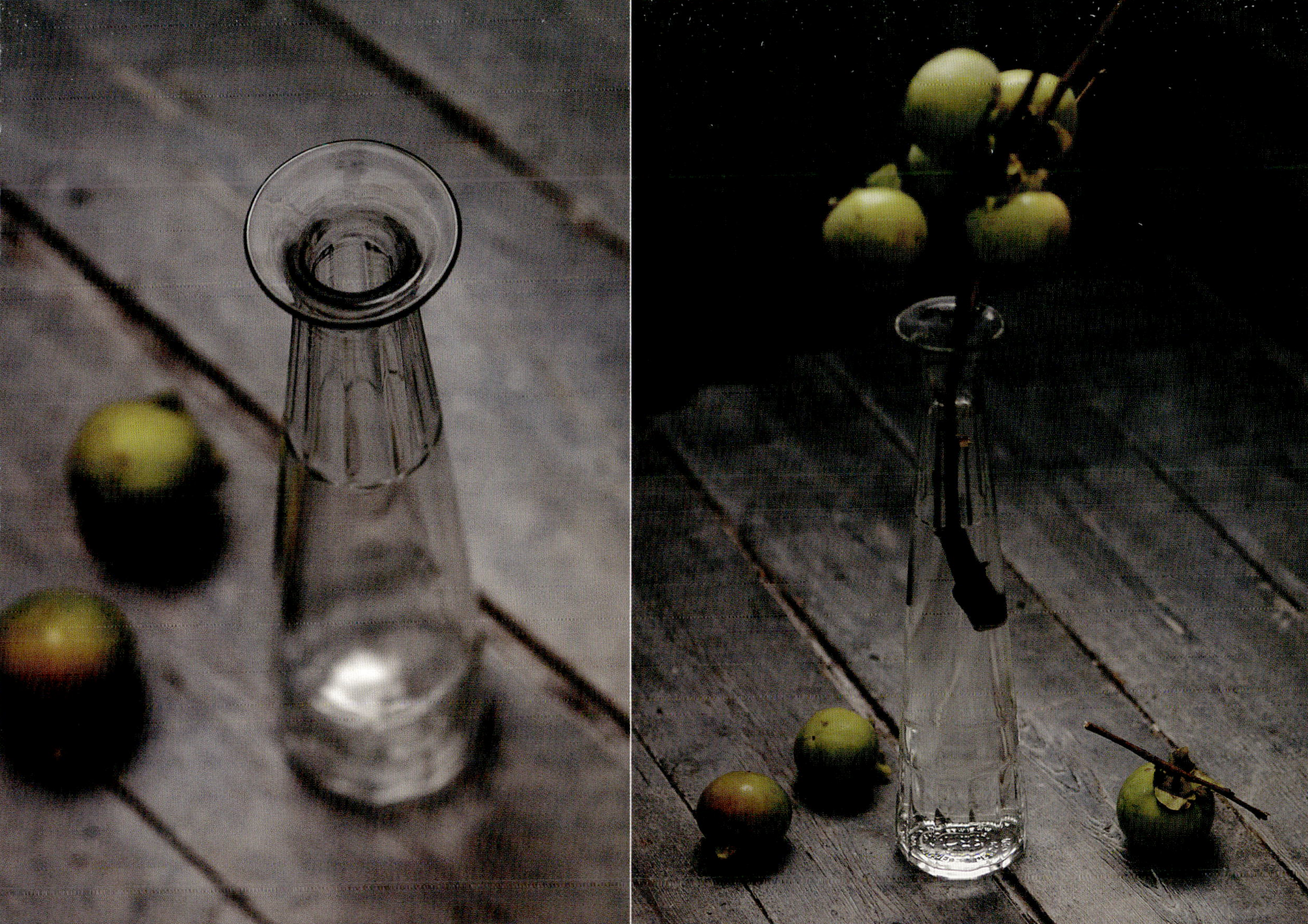

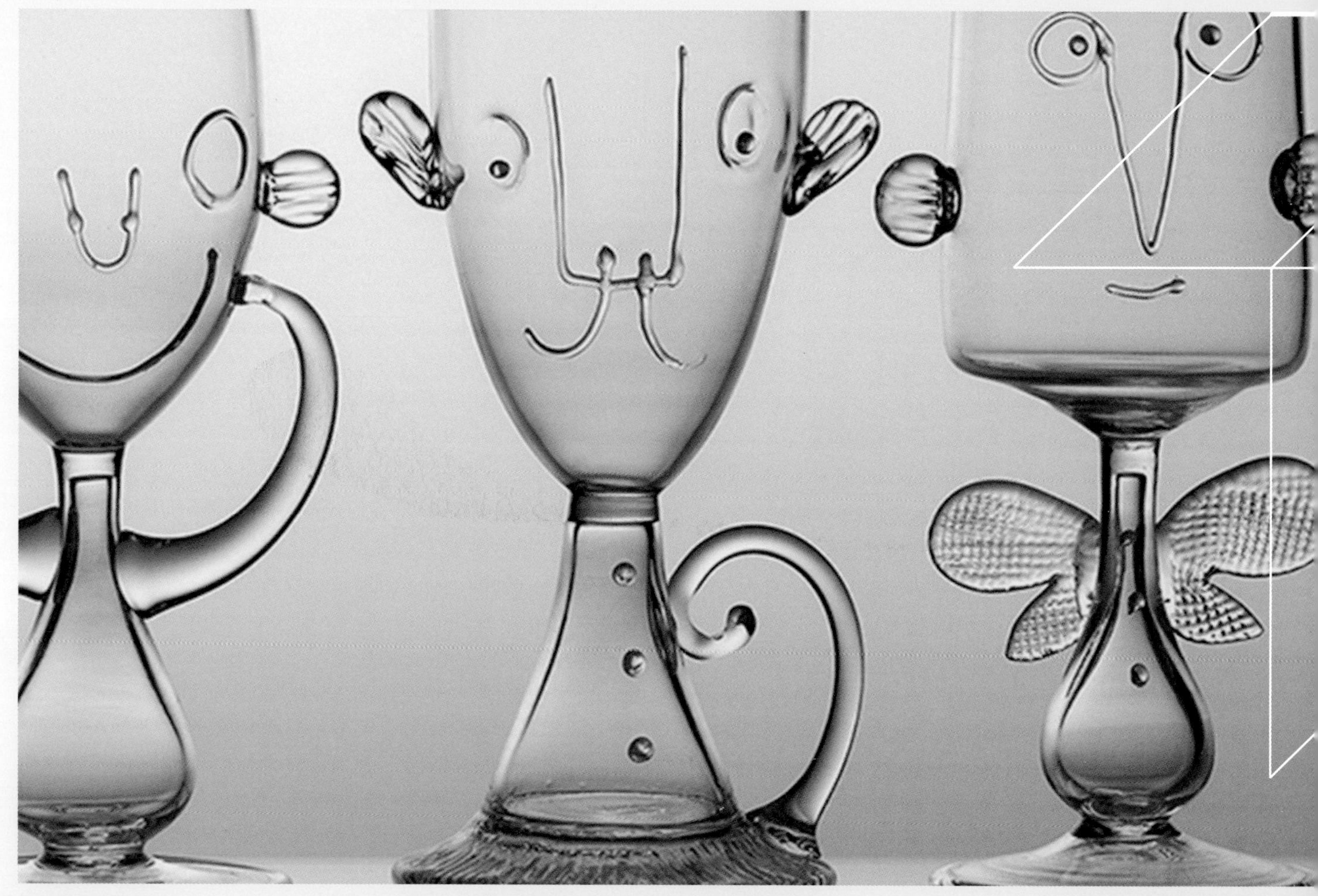

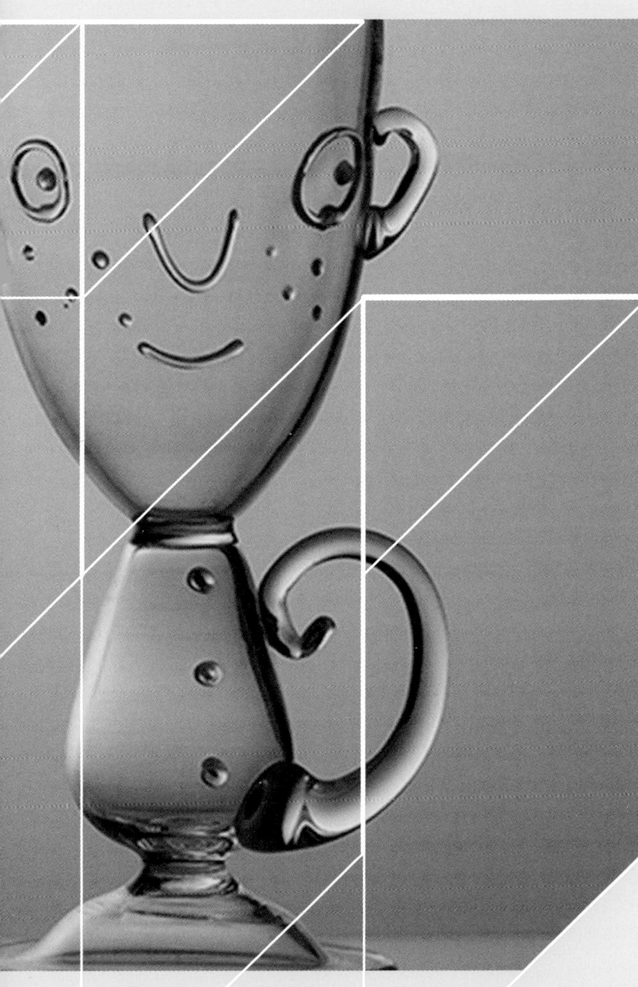

Tom Moore

Born 1971, Canberra, Australian Capital Territory
Lives Adelaide, South Australia

Well known for his maximalist style, Tom Moore is one of Australia's most respected glass artists. Originally from Canberra, he began his career in glass at the Canberra School of Art, Australian National University, and went on to undertake an Associateship at JamFactory in 1995 under the mentorship of Nick Mount. Working with blown and hot-sculpted glass, he is a creator of fantastical worlds inhabited by unusual and hybrid creatures. Part animal, part plant and part machine, his characters are exhibited within elaborate constructed environments, in which they act out surreal narratives. Underpinning his work is a concern for the physical world, translated through stories of the triumph of nature over industry and the recurring motif of sprouting green fronds.

Moore is a technically rigorous glass maker, both as a production glass blower and within his sculptural practice. Drawn to the seemingly impossible intricacy of Venetian glass techniques, he creates patterns in twisted glass cane. The changeable nature of glass is key to how he creates his complex patterns: the coloured glass is heated, applied and fused to the liquid clear glass, then twisted, stretched, cut and re-joined, before becoming part of a sculpture. Challenging himself as a craftsperson, Moore has become a specialist in the field of ancient and obscure Venetian techniques.

Decades of experience as a production glass blower add another layer to Moore's practice. As JamFactory's Glass Studio Production Manager for the past 15 years, he has led the team of Associates to create trophies, commissions and JamFactory product. Often working on large runs, he enjoys the process of making the same shape over and over again. As a technically ambitious maker, repetition has strengthened his abilities with the material. Moore is hopeful that one day he will be awarded one of the thousands of trophies he has made.

Commenting on contemporary issues of science and the natural environment, Moore plays with the themes of preservation and generation of life in his work. In his recent solo exhibition, *Life Preserver*, at Helen Gory Galerie in 2014 and within his Ranamok Prize-winning work *Massive Microscopic Bud*, 2013, bell jars showcased his creatures as specimens of scientific curiosity. Unlike stagnant and dusty museum displays, in these works life is generative and the bell jars themselves are sprouting. These life-giving properties are echoed in the eyes that appear in unusual places all over the works. The eye is a powerful motif for Moore, and he uses it to create a level of sentience. There is an emotional impact achieved from placing eyes on an inanimate object — a lumpy beige blob is suddenly imbued with agency, emotion and the power to look back at the viewer.

Moore was the 2013 winner of the illustrious Tom Malone Prize for contemporary glass artists from the Art Gallery of Western Australia. Celebrated for his craftsmanship and his playful take on traditional techniques, Moore's works have been collected by major cultural institutions around Australia and the USA. He has held solo exhibitions at Helen Gory Galerie, the Hughes Gallery and JamFactory, and his work was included in *Making it New: Focus on Contemporary Australian Art* at the Museum of Contemporary Art, Sydney in 2009.

Adele Sliuzas

Previous page
Mixed Dozen (detail), 2012
hot joined blown and solid glass
220 x 130 x 90 each
Photography: Grant Hancock

▸

Vanished Vim drawing, 2010
charcoal and
water colour on paper
297 x 420
Photo: Grant Hancock

▸▸

Tom Moore working in the studio, adding handle to large blown glass form at the Museum of Glass, Tacoma, USA, 2013.
Photo: Greg Owen

▾

Vanished Vim, 2010
hot joined blown and solid glass
220 x 400 x 120
Photo: Grant Hancock

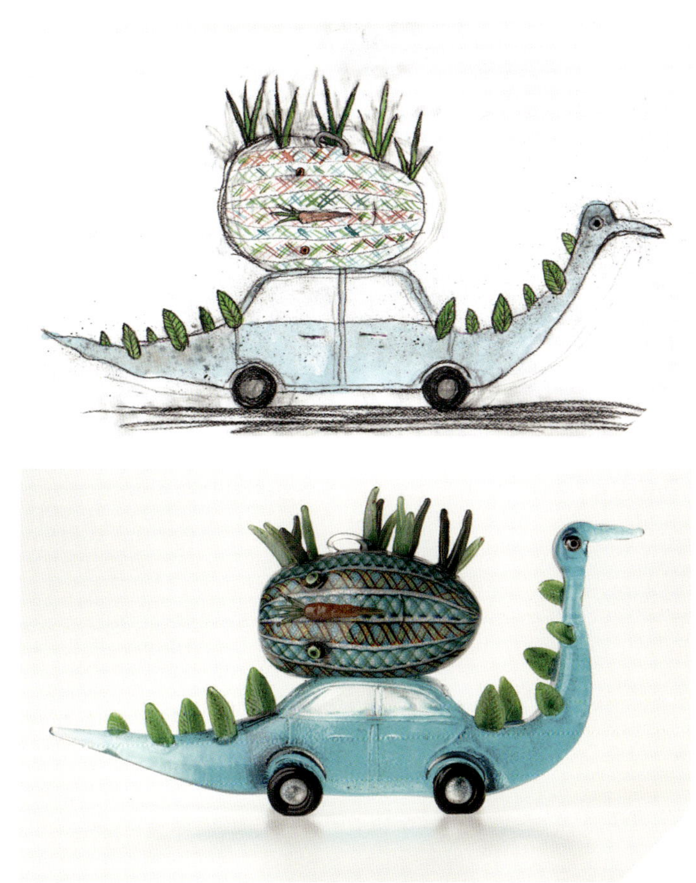

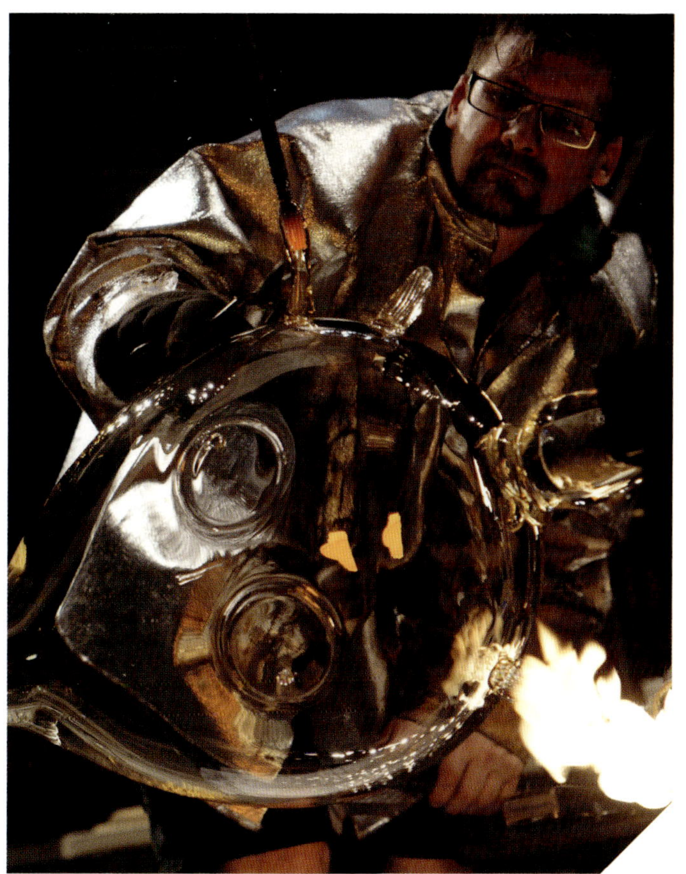

▸

Tom Moore, *Moore is More*, 2009
four ponds with glass objects, painted walls, cardboard scenery, dirt and fountain
dimensions variable
Installation view, *Making it New: Focus on Contemporary Australian Art* at the Museum of Contemporary Art, Sydney
Photo: Jenni Carter

▸▸

Confederacy of Amalgamated Figments, 2013
hot joined blown and solid glass
dimensions variable
Photo: Grant Hancock

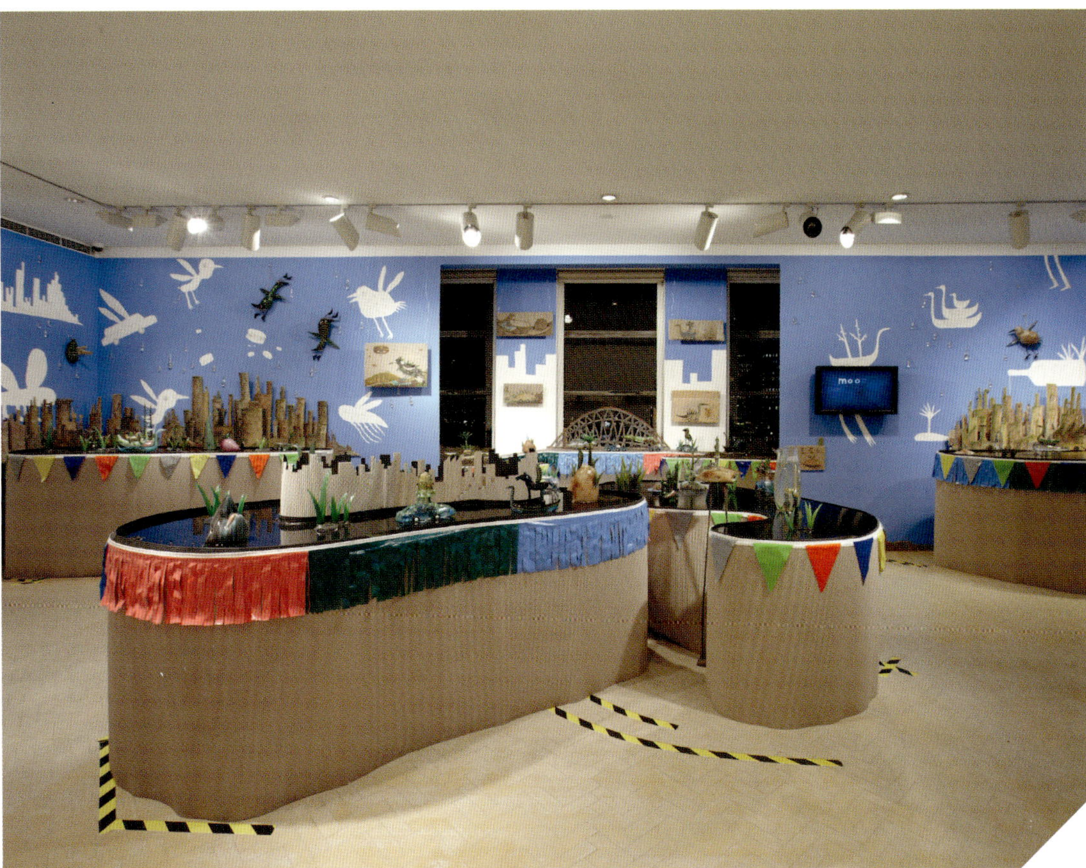

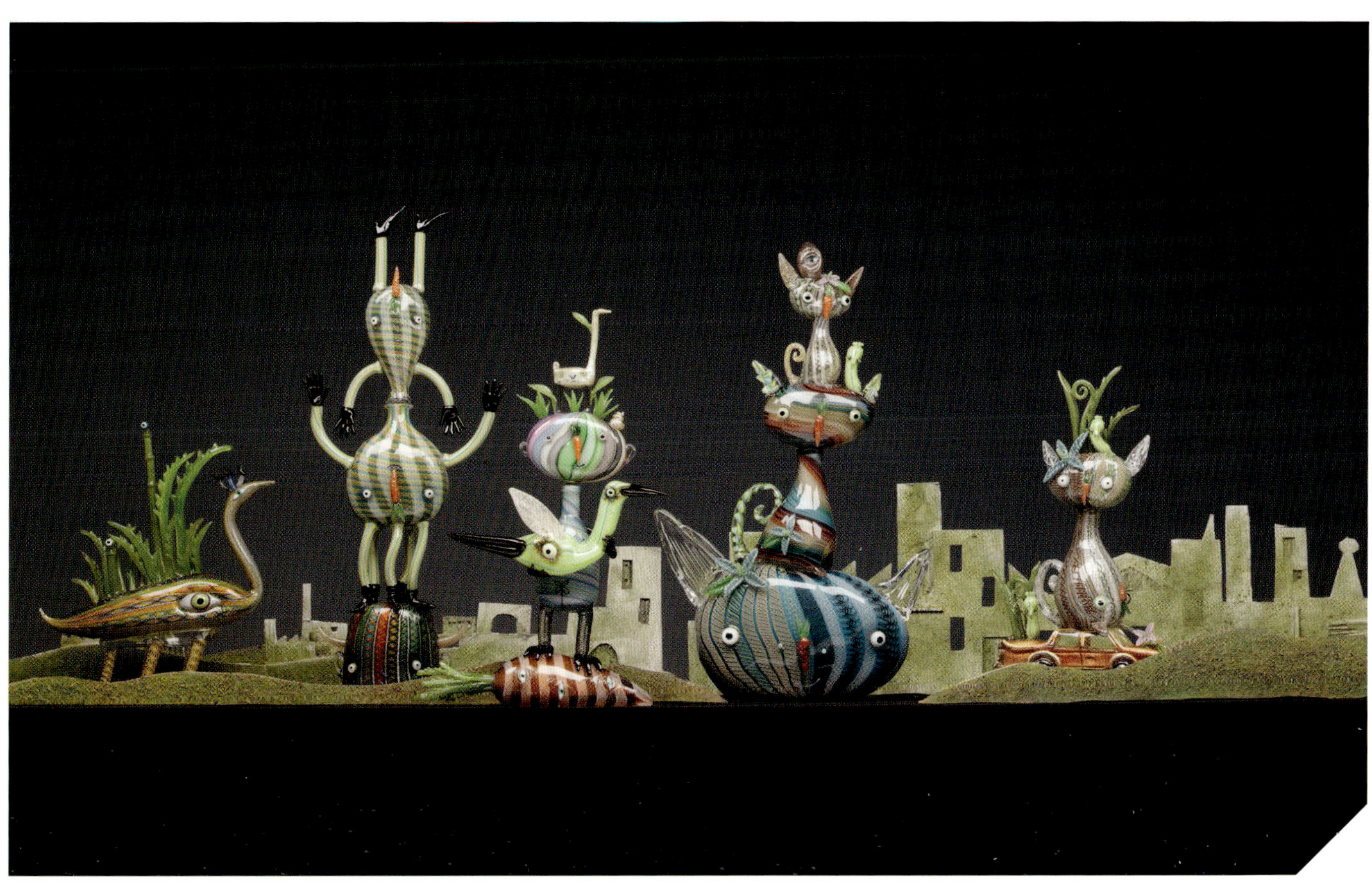

Jacob's ladder

Jacob's ladder, 2014, is a fantastical and strange world within a world. The work features a sprouting potato, which slyly gazes back at the viewer from human-like eyes. The bell jar itself — which covers and protects the potato — has eyes and ears (which double as handles). Surprisingly, the green fronds sprouting from the potato's crown have formed into a tall green ladder, reminiscent of Jack and the beanstalk, or the biblical tale of the stairway to heaven, from which the work takes its name. Rakishly perched above the bell jar, brightly patterned ribbons of colour run through the body of a fish, which functions as a slimy and surreal party hat.

▸
Jacob's Ladder with city, 2014
hot joined blown and solid glass, wooden base, cardboard city,
840 x 340 x 270
Photo: Grant Hancock

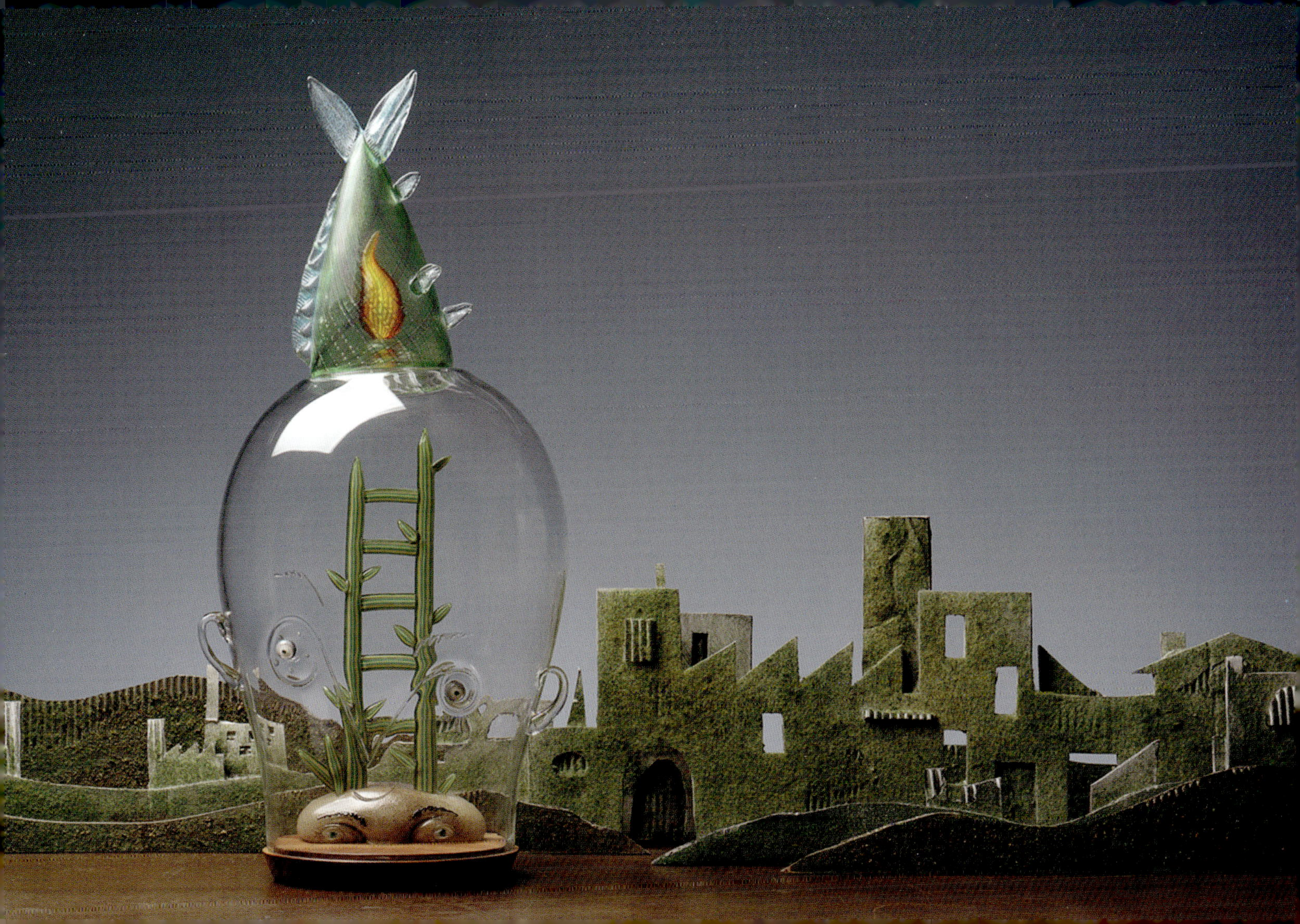

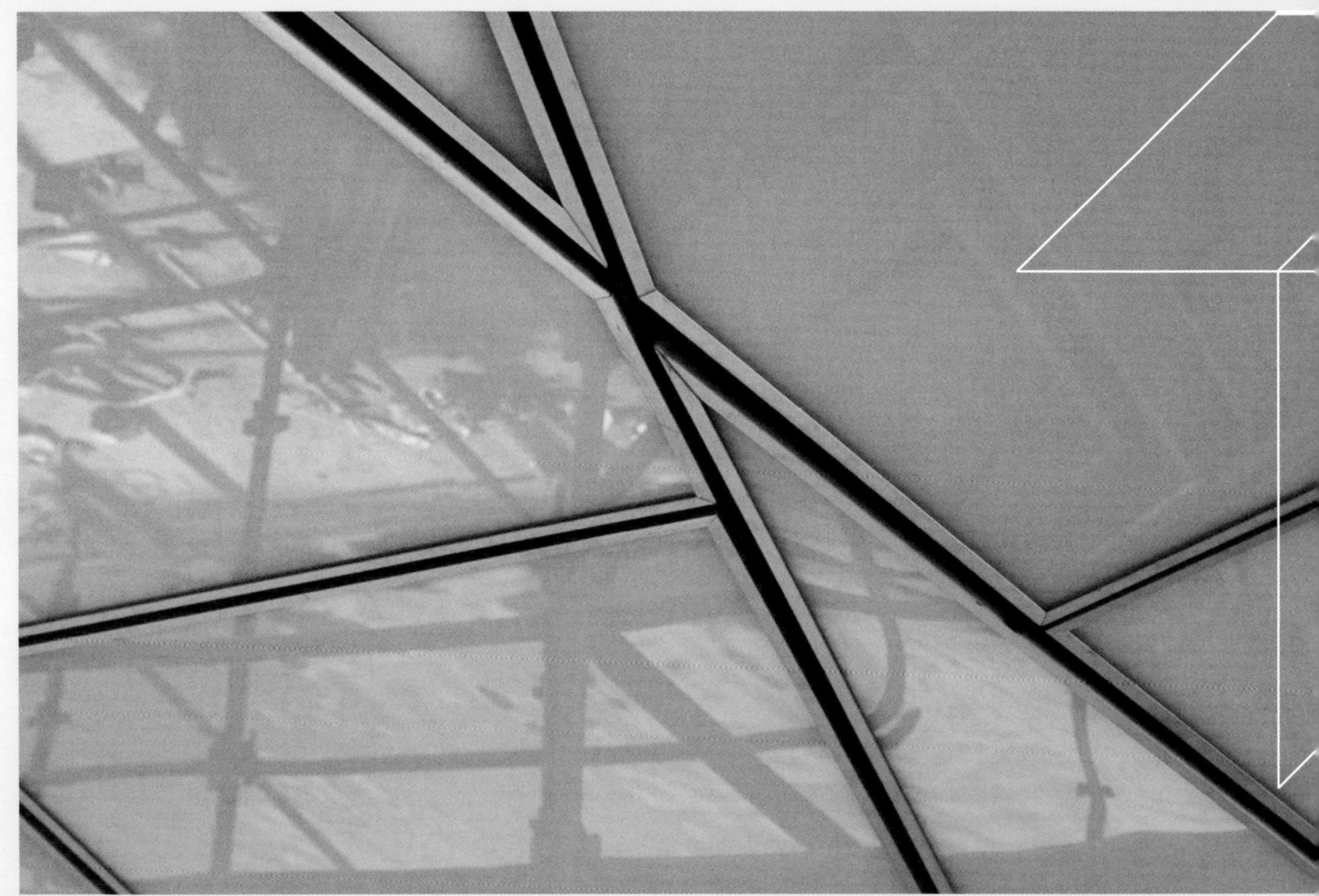

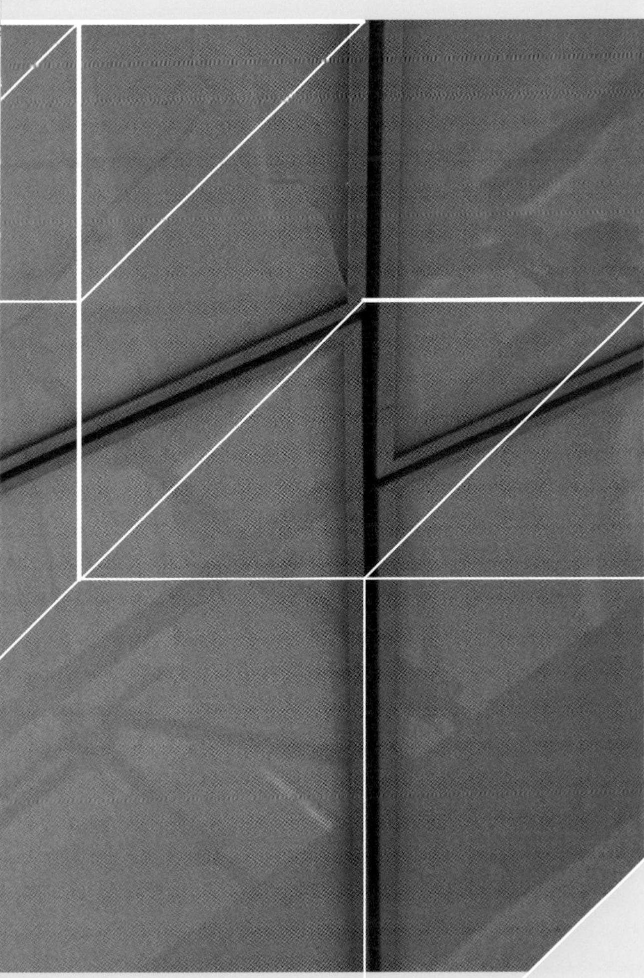

Tonkin Zulaikha Greer / Taylor Cullity Lethlean / Aurecon

TZG established 1987, Sydney, New South Wales
TCL established 1989, Adelaide, South Australia
Aurecon established 2009 after the merger of three international engineering consultancies

River Torrens Riverbank Precinct Pedestrian Bridge, 2012–14, is a major new work of urban infrastructure developed by Tonkin Zulaikha Greer architects in collaboration with engineers and urban designers Aurecon and landscape architects Taylor Cullity Lethlean.

Project architects Tonkin Zulaikha Greer (TZG) have a special interest in public spaces, public buildings and 'edge' architecture, and often provide buildings with roles and uses outside their traditional functions. For TZG, the civic nature of architecture is explored in buildings with a significant public use, or with a positive relationship to the public domain of the city.

The new $40 million Riverbank Bridge Adelaide provides a new pedestrian connection between the city's highly-visited Festival Centre, railway station and the recently redeveloped Adelaide Oval. The bridge arc has been designed to mirror the River Torrens and pivots to connect two key destination points on the north and south banks. This arc creates a strong

River Torrens Riverbank Precinct Pedestrian Bridge

The Riverbank Bridge Adelaide provides a new pedestrian connection between the city's highly-visited Festival Centre, railway station and the recently redeveloped Adelaide Oval. The bridge arc has been designed to mirror the River Torrens, cantilevering out over the river to culminate in a dramatic artificial waterfall. Glass is integral to the design, cladding almost all of the external surfaces. Sweeping through the Riverbank precinct, the energetic curve of the bridge, has a lightness despite its considerable structure, due to the use of the cladding to reflect both the surrounding water and greenery. This curvaceous glass bridge and surrounds successfully deliver a generous new urban space to Adelaide. The design embraces both site and context to create a resilient platform embedded with thoughtful consideration for culture, community and environment.

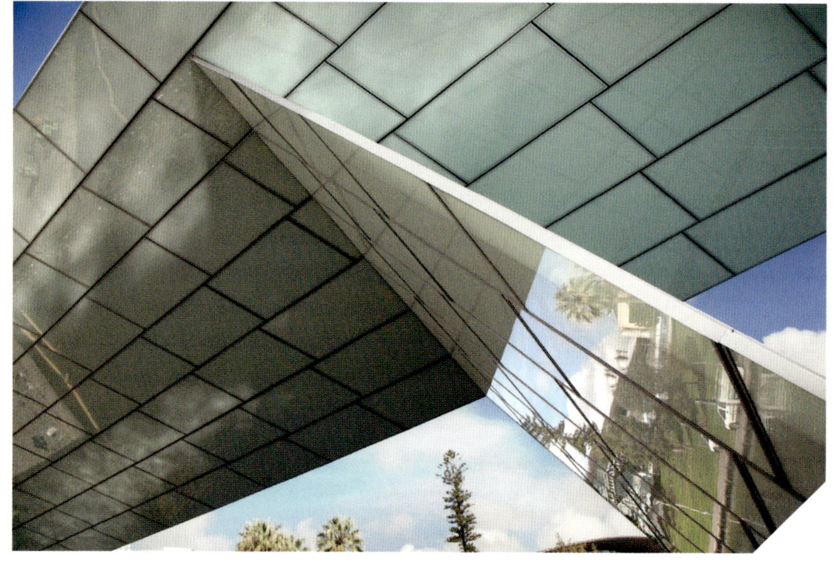

Overleaf left
At its northern end, the bridge cantilevers out over the river to culminate in a dramatic artificial waterfall aerating the water below.
Photo: John Gollings

Overleaf right
The elegant curve of the bridge sweeps from two iconic Adelaide landmarks, the Adelaide Festival Centre on the south bank and Adelaide Oval to the north.
Photo: John Gollings

▲
The glass panelling of the bridge provides a reflective surface mirroring the surrounding landscape and water.
Photo: John Gollings

▶
Riverbank Bridge Adelaide, 2012–14
Photo: John Gollings

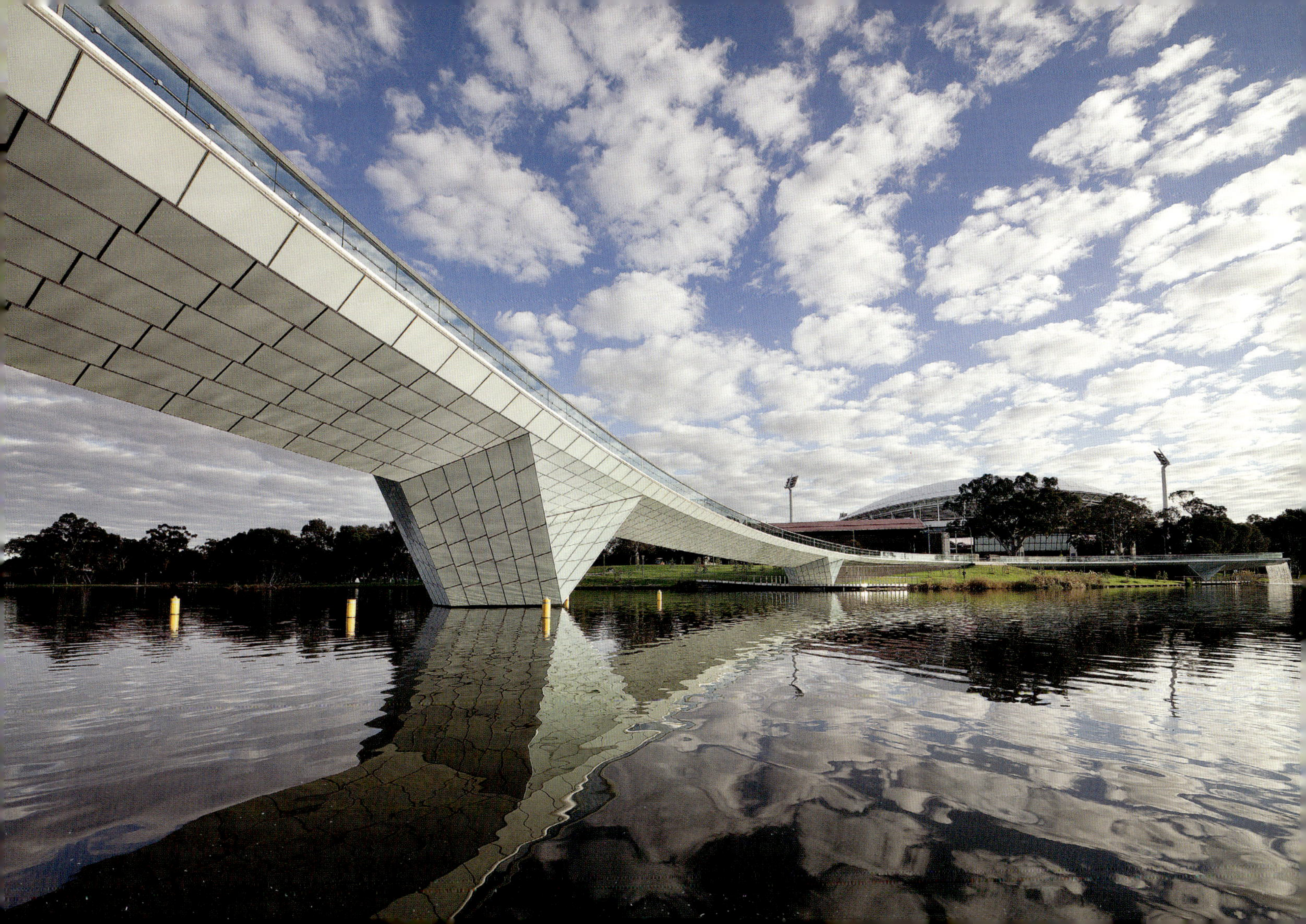

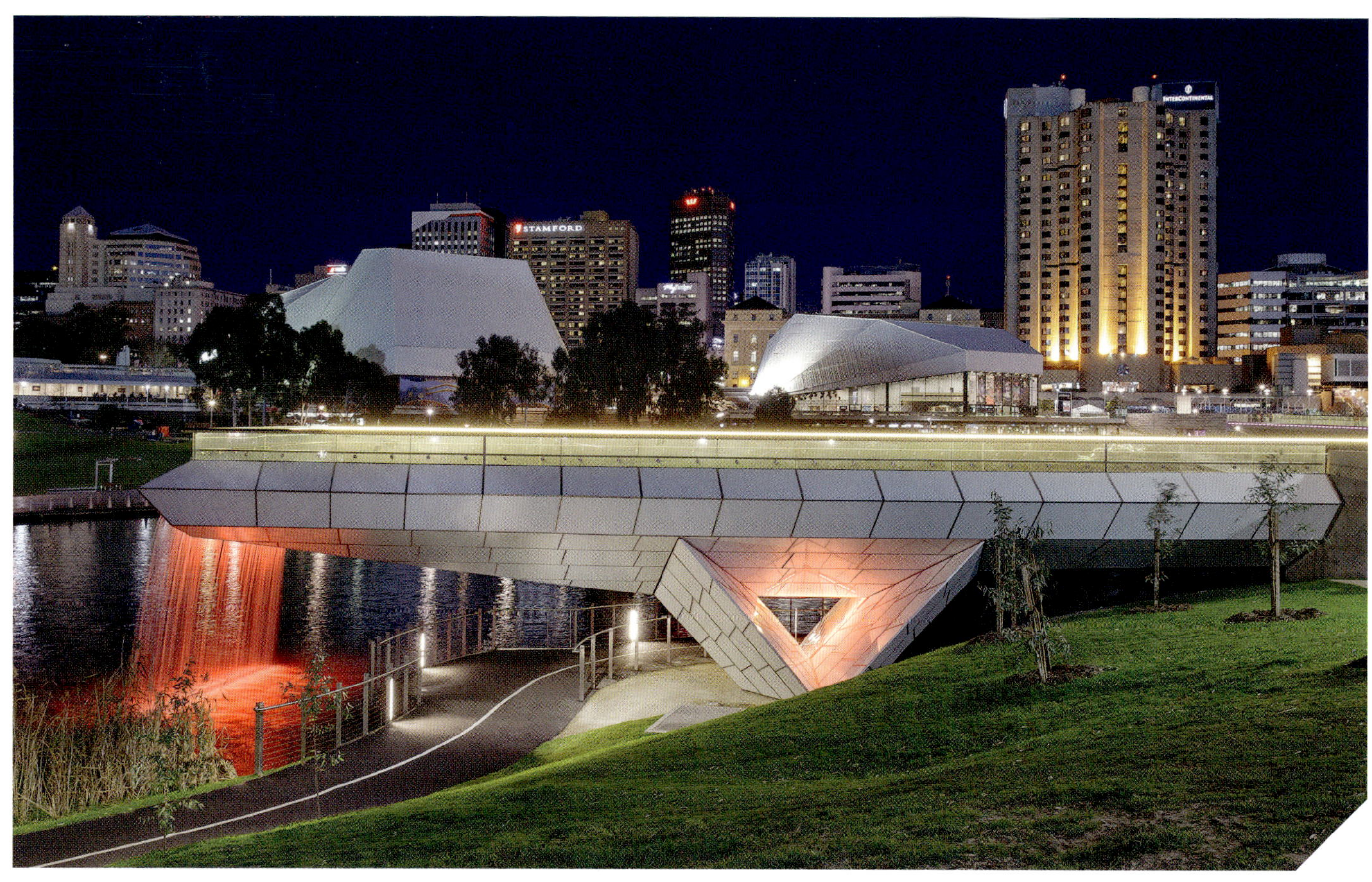
STAMFORD
INTERCONTINENTAL

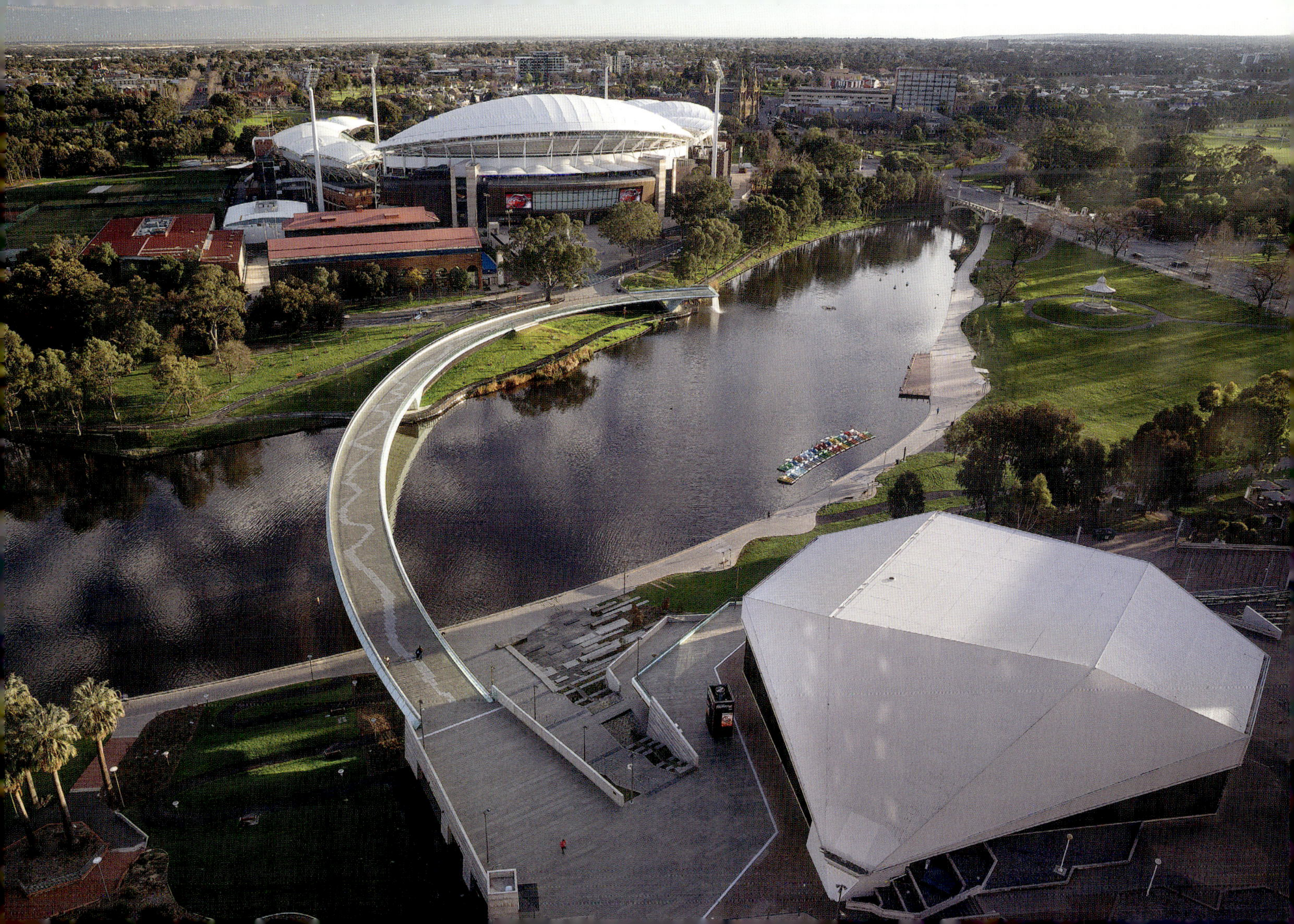

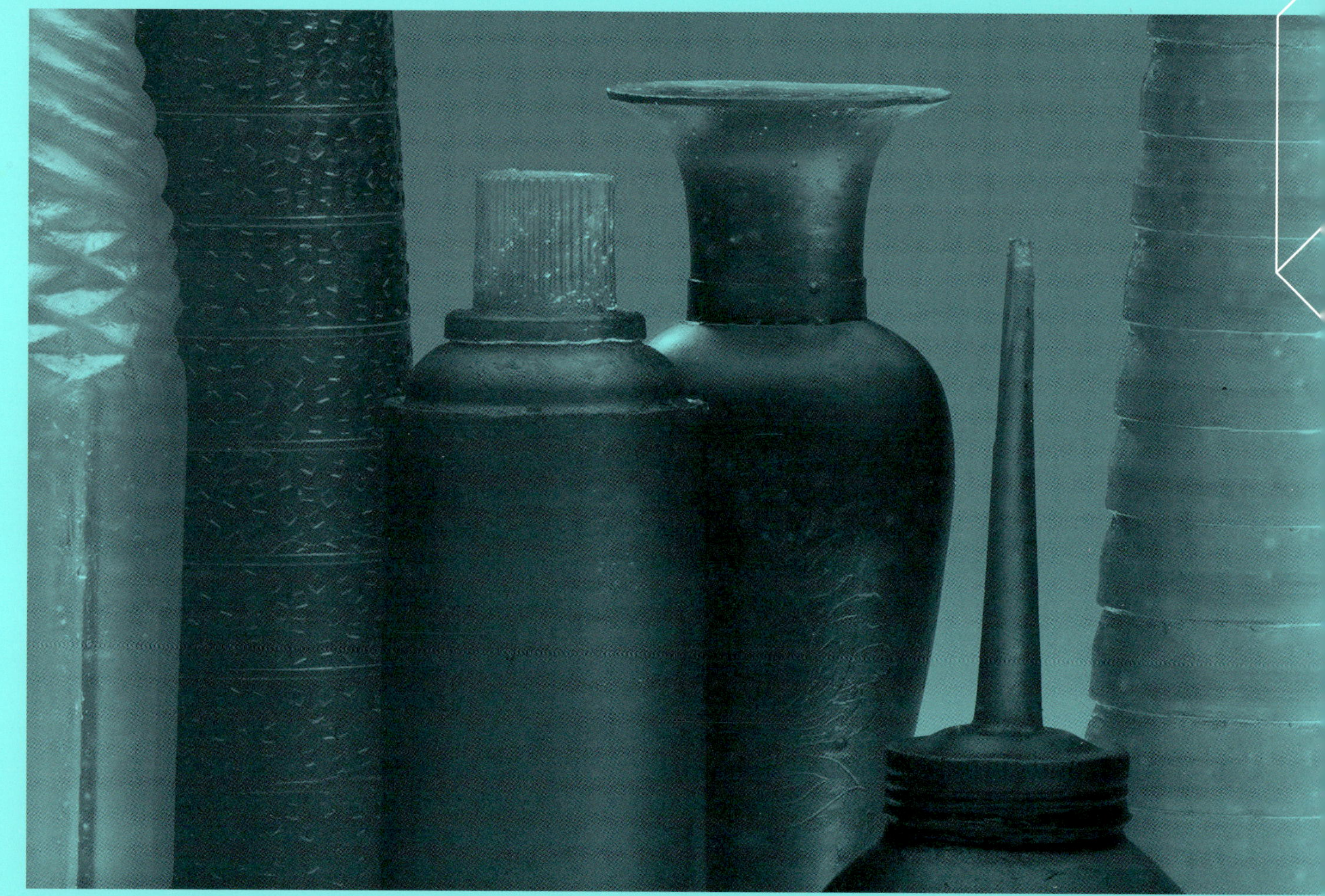

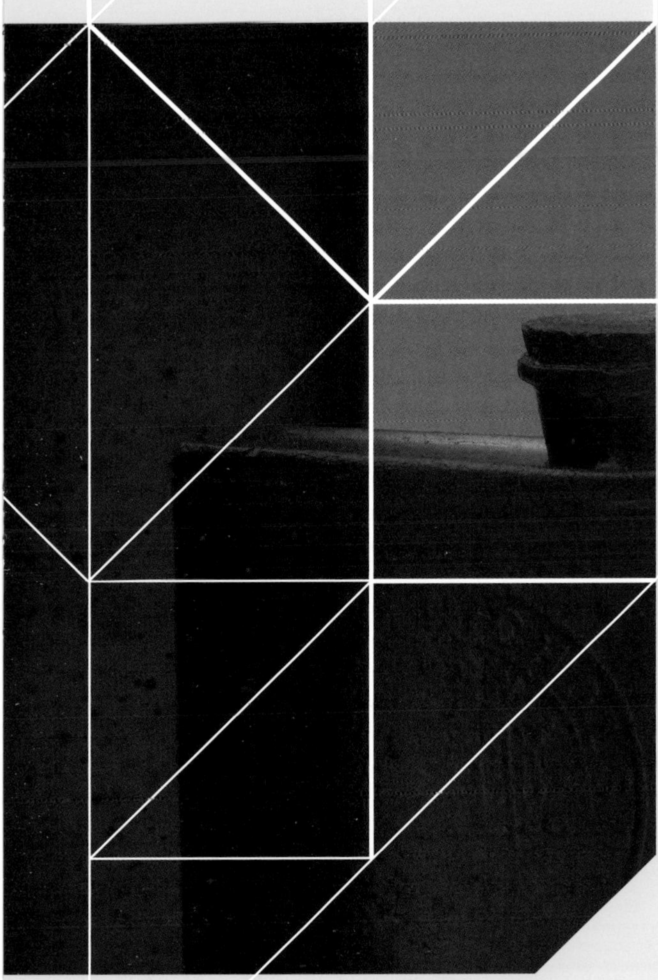

Wendy Fairclough

Born 1958, Wanganui, New Zealand
Lives Adelaide, South Australia

Known for her beautiful lead crystal and blown-glass still lifes, Fairclough's artistic career began as a printmaking and sculpture major at the South Australian School of Art, University of South Australia. While studying for a graduate diploma in Education and Training of Adults in 1998, she became entranced by glass during a weekend workshop with leading glass artist Nick Mount. Once hooked, Fairclough furthered her studies with a Bachelor of Applied Art majoring in glass, which she completed in 2000.

As with the change in media, Fairclough can pinpoint a major turning point in her conceptual approach to art making, during the 2000 Adelaide Festival of the Arts.[1] Born in New Zealand in the shadow of Mount Ruapehu on the Whanganui River — a dramatic landscape of lush greens and heavy oppressive skies, and so vastly different to the parched flat surrounds of the Adelaide Plains — Fairclough often keenly feels a *'le mal du pays'* for New Zealand. The exhibition, *From Appropriation to Appreciation: Indigenous influences and images in Australian visual art* challenged her,

Compose.1

Making cast lead crystal glass is a process of positive and negative reversal. Casting from real-life objects, Fairclough's first step is to make the original item hard, solid and waterproof. Once prepared, she makes the first of several mould impressions, using silicon rubber at first, as it picks up the minute details of the object. Once created, the silicon rubber mould is supported in a plaster dam before liquefied wax is poured into it. When the wax cast is set, Fairclough removes any imperfections before it is placed within the final refractory mould in which the wax is steamed out, leaving the impression for the molten-lead crystal glass. The glass is fired in the kiln and, depending on scale, this process can take between five to ten days. Once the glass cast is cooled, Fairclough must remove the refractory mould, then clean up, grind or polish the final surface.

▸
Compose.1, 2012
cast lead crystal
220 x 245 x 130
Photo: Grant Hancock

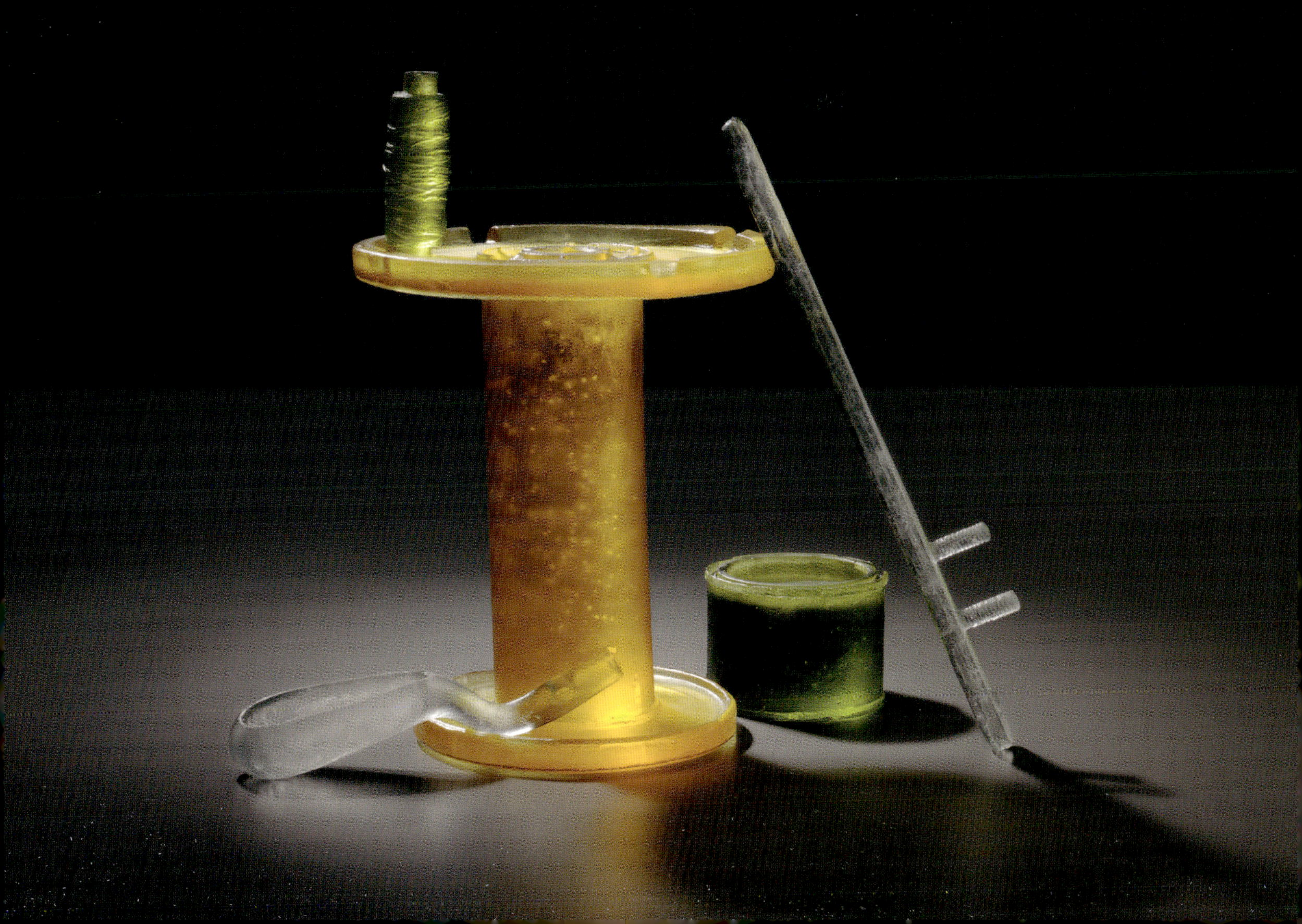

▸
Tribute, 2014
cast lead crystal,
wooden ironing board
1040 x 1220 x 300
Photo: Grant Hancock

▸▸
Tribute (detail), 2014

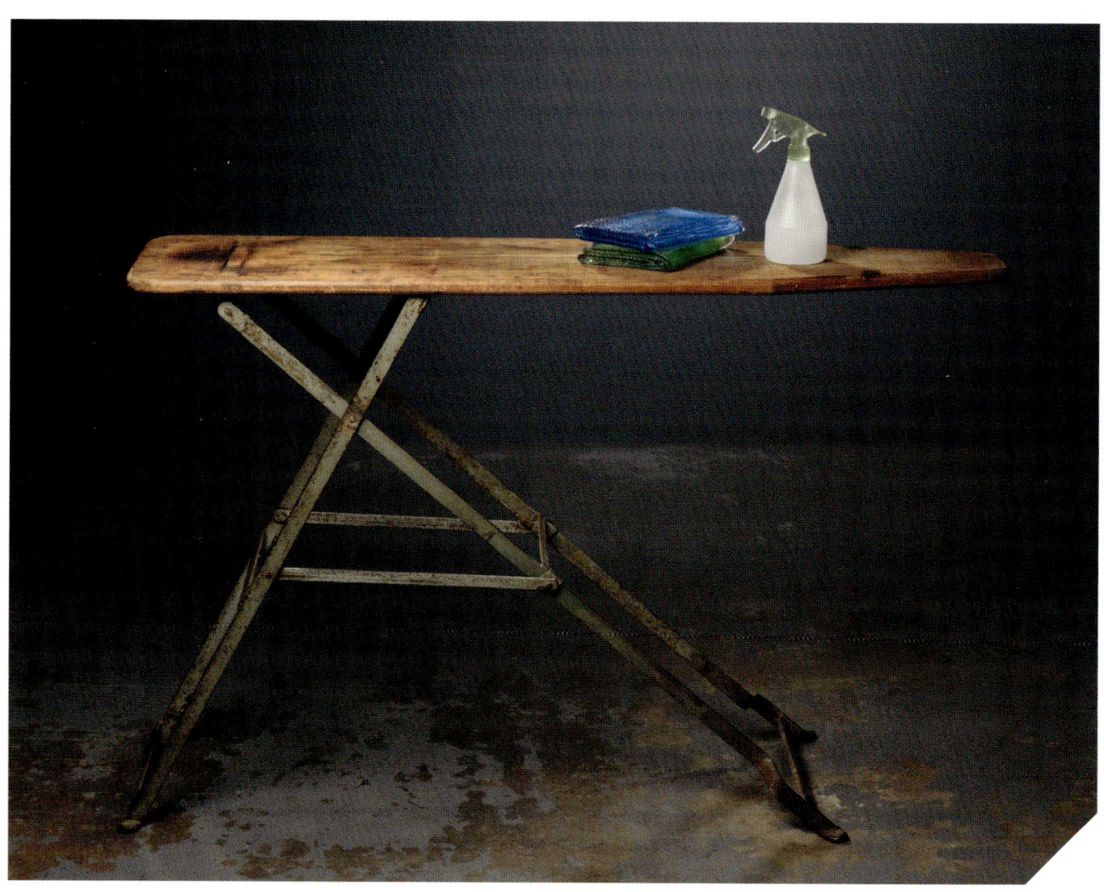

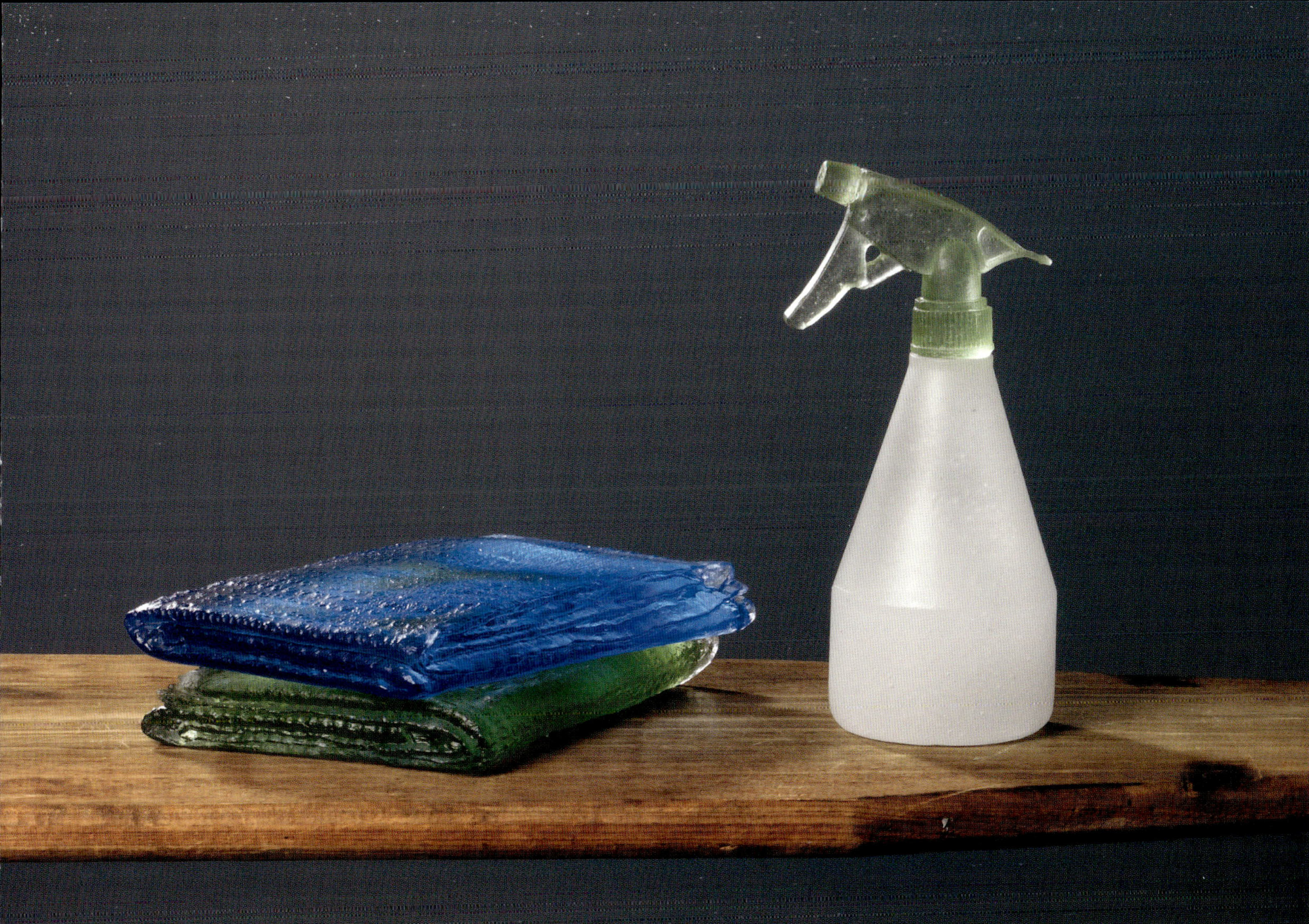

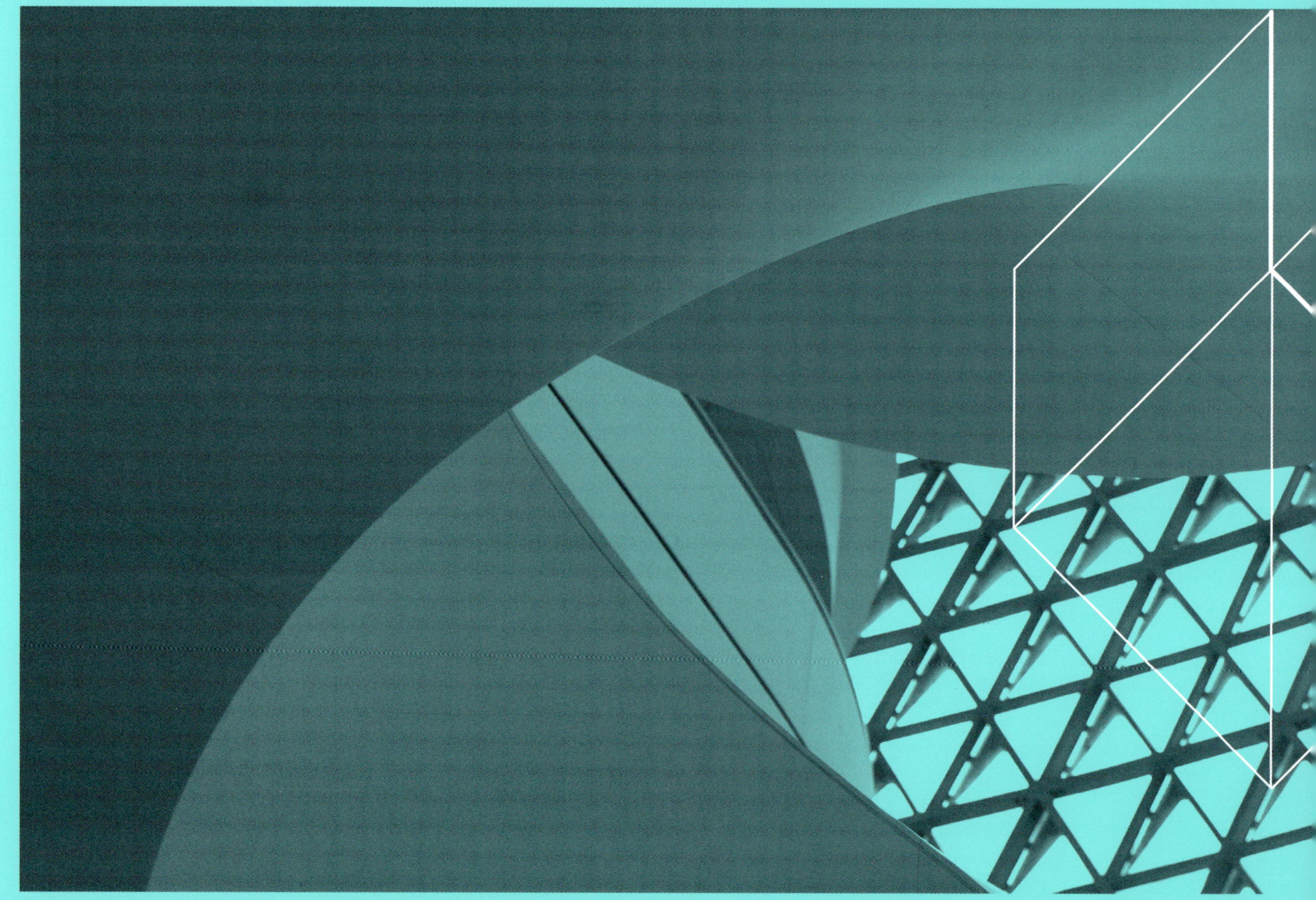

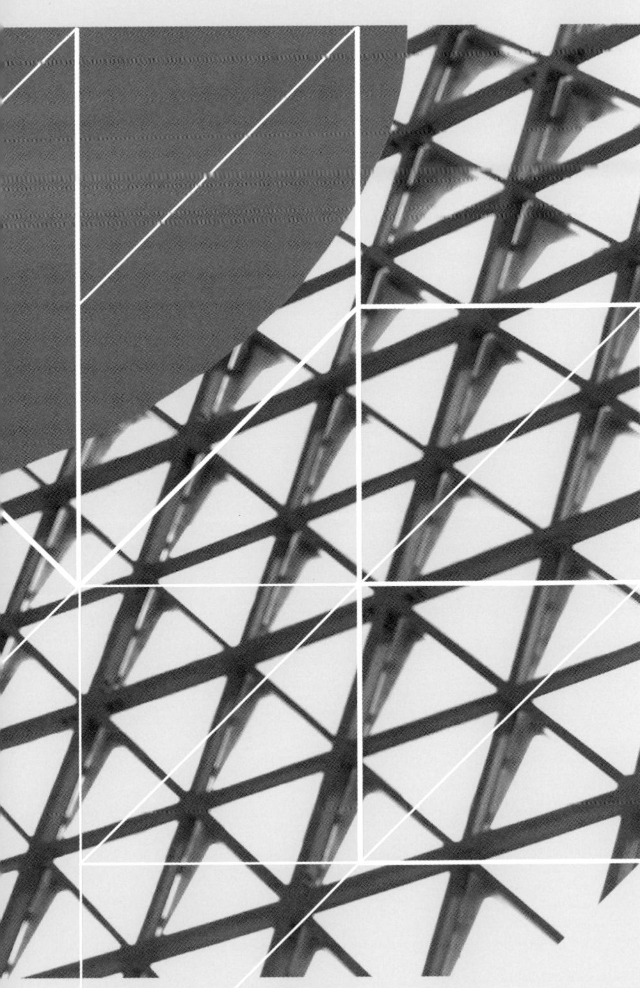

Woods Bagot

Established 1869, Adelaide, South Australia

Woods Bagot is a global design and consulting firm, with more than 850 staff working across studios in Australia, Asia, the Middle East, Europe and North America. In 2014 it was ranked as the seventh largest architecture firm in the world, with expertise spanning architecture, interior design, master planning and urban design.

Woods Bagot is one of a number of major international architecture practices that began in South Australia, and the firm has contributed many great buildings to that state's capital city, Adelaide, over the past 140 years. Its most recent completed project in that city — the South Australian Health and Medical Research Institute (SAHMRI), 2013 — is perhaps its most iconic.

The SAHMRI is a $200 million Commonwealth-funded research facility providing a 25,000 m^2 flagship for world-class health and medical research. The architecture and interiors, both by Woods Bagot, aim to inspire and promote the building's function. The central proposition for the design was to create a new and liberating lab typology that would promote collaboration and medical discovery, and attract the best researchers from around the world.

SAHMRI builds upon the quality of the North Terrace Boulevard and is a catalyst for the urban regeneration of a new medical and health precinct to the west side of the city. The built form arrangement of SAHMRI acknowledges its sense of place within the green belt of the Adelaide parklands. The lifting of the building allows the parklands to extend below and create a notion of a 'building in the parkland'. The open ground plane and integrated landscape allow greater activation and porosity through the site.

The building's unique triangulated dia-grid facade responds to its environment like a living organism, acting as an articulated sunshade that deals with sunlight, heat load, glare, and wind deflection, while maintaining views and daylight.

Following intensive environmental analysis with consultants Atelier Ten, Woods Bagot used parametric modelling tools to integrate environmental, programmatic and formal requirements into the facade. The complex exterior was developed in collaboration with structural/facade engineers Aurecon, and combines a structural steel sub-frame with an external aluminium suite and custom glazing.

The glass skin incorporates 6290 double-glazed triangular glass panels with sunshades that have been designed and oriented for optimum thermal and light efficiency. As a result, the size of the chevron-shaped shades varies across the surface of the building. Fabrication of the facade system took five months and the erection occurred over six months.

One of the key drivers for the design of the interiors was to encourage and enhance collaboration between the 600 or so researchers expected to work in the building's laboratories. The interior scheme enhances visual and physical connection between spaces and levels, with the inclusion of two large atria, a series of bridges, an interconnecting spiral staircase and extensive use of internal glazing. The architects wanted the activity within to be transparent, so that the occupants would not feel confined and would have constant visual contact with the outside world, including some wonderful views over the Adelaide parklands.

As with any complex contemporary architectural project, there was a multitude of contributing collaborators responsible for the design of the SAHMRI. However, the 'global studio' model employed by Woods Bagot, which supports collective authorship, allowed the input of staff from its Adelaide, Melbourne and New York studios.

Brian Parkes

Previous page
South Australian Health and Medical Research Institute (SAHMRI), 2013
North Terrace, Adelaide, South Australia
Spiral stair and glass facade detail of north eastern atrium.
Photo: John Gollings

▸

Facade view into spiral stair and Northeastern atrium.
Photo: John Gollings

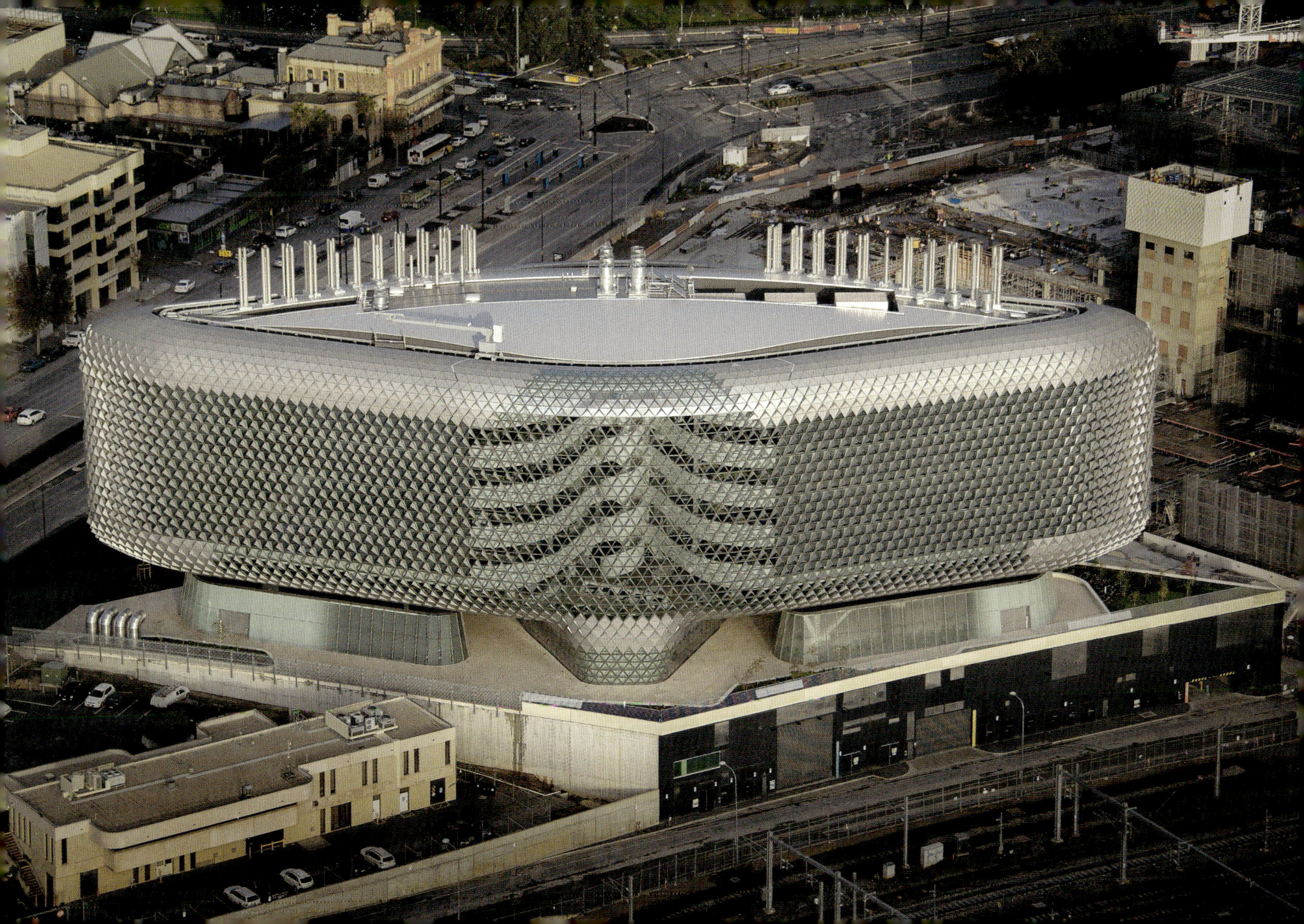

South Australian Health and Medical Research Institute

Glass has been used extensively within the interior and exterior of the SAHMRI building, 2013, to achieve a number of sustainability and amenity objectives. Together with the passive design form, the unique triangulated facade and sunshade is designed to improve the building's performance and to create a healthier internal environment. High performance double-glazed panels, with metallic 'E' coat on the back face of the external sheet, have been used to minimise radiant heat while maximising natural light and external views. The transparency created also allows views from outside into the internal workings of the building, promoting the importance of the activities within.

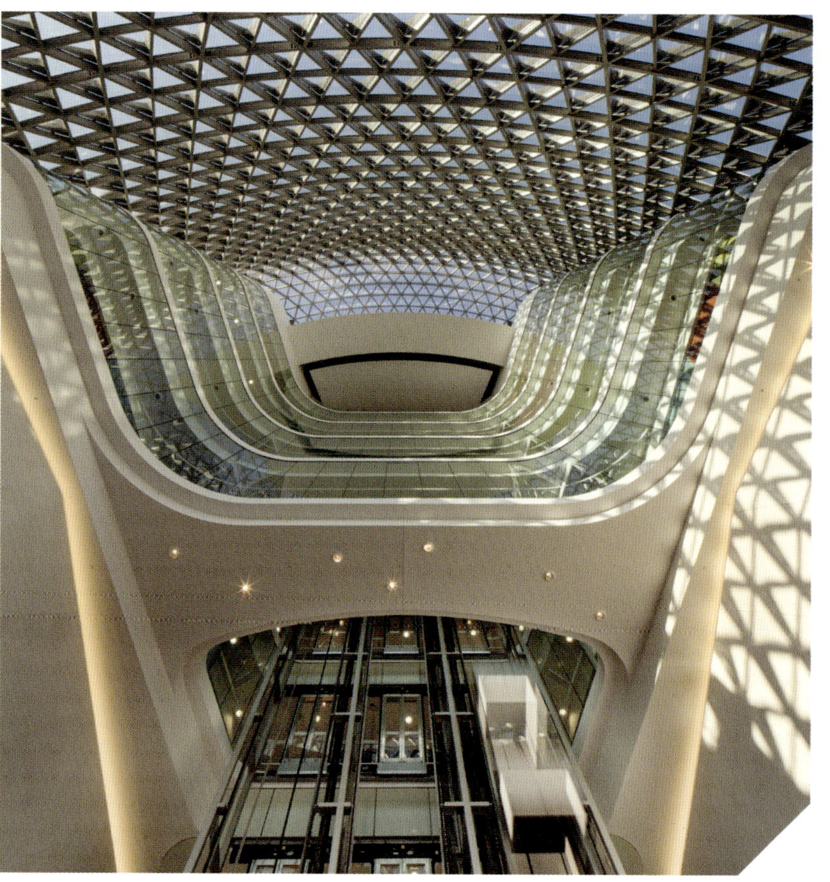

▸

View looking up at public entry atrium showing glazed lifts and internal bridges.
Photo: Trevor Mein

▸▸

View of south western facade.
Photo: Trevor Mein

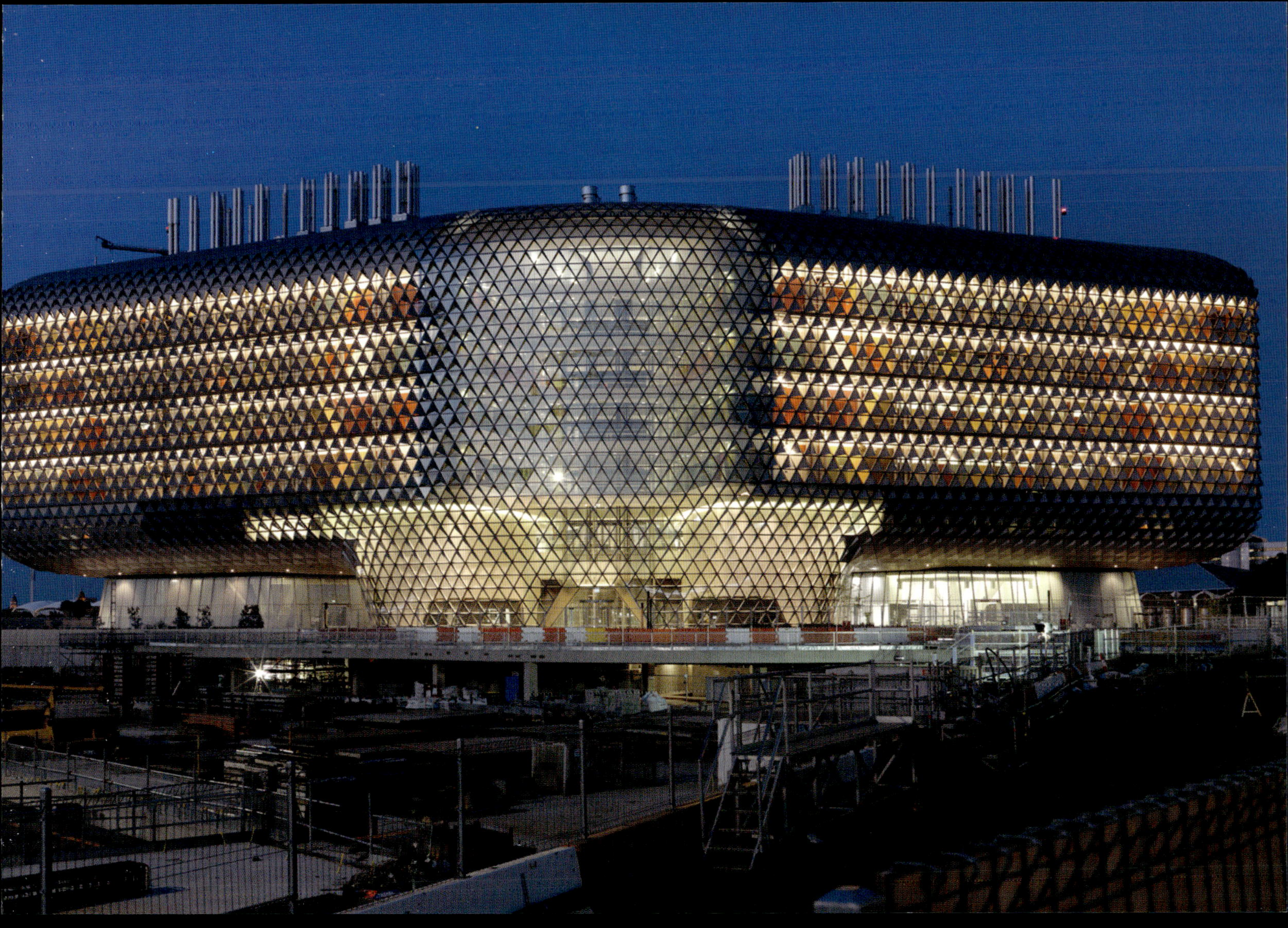

▸ ▸▸
Wishing to foster collaboration within labs, the interior scheme has been designed to create both visual and physical connections between spaces.
Photo left: Trevor Mein
Photo right: Peter Clarke

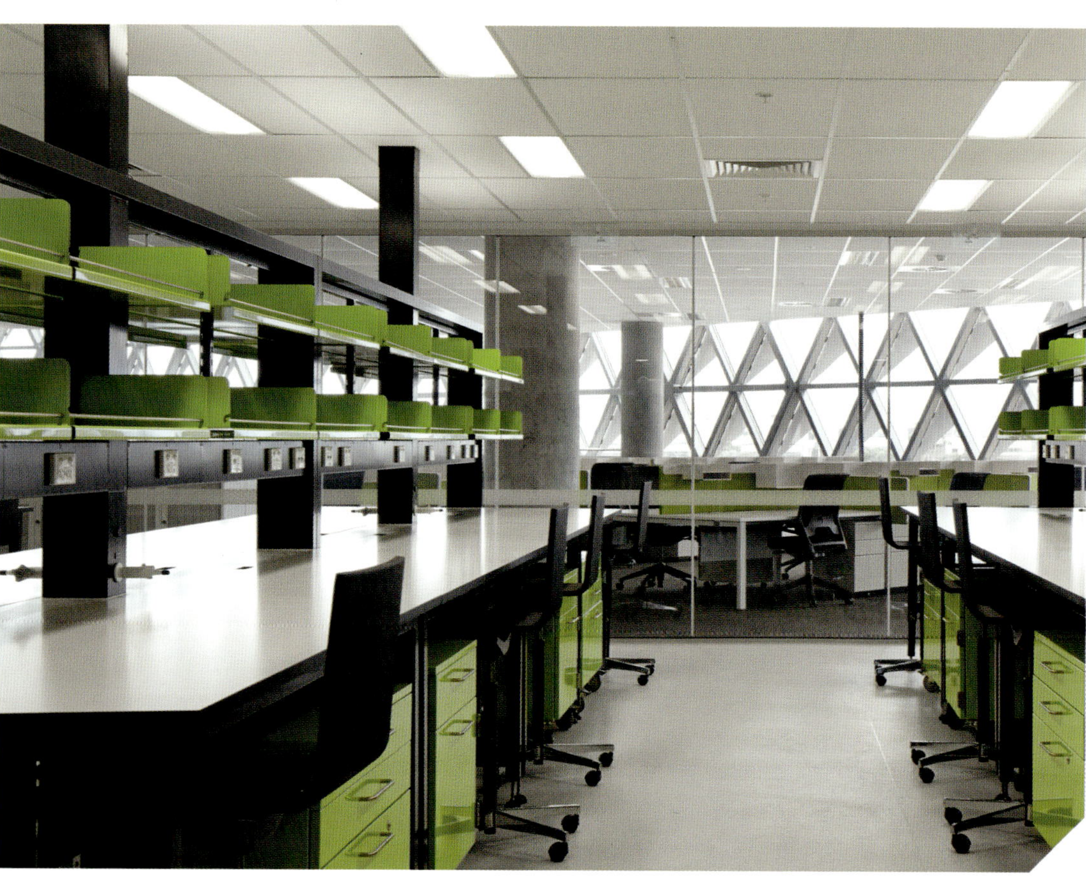

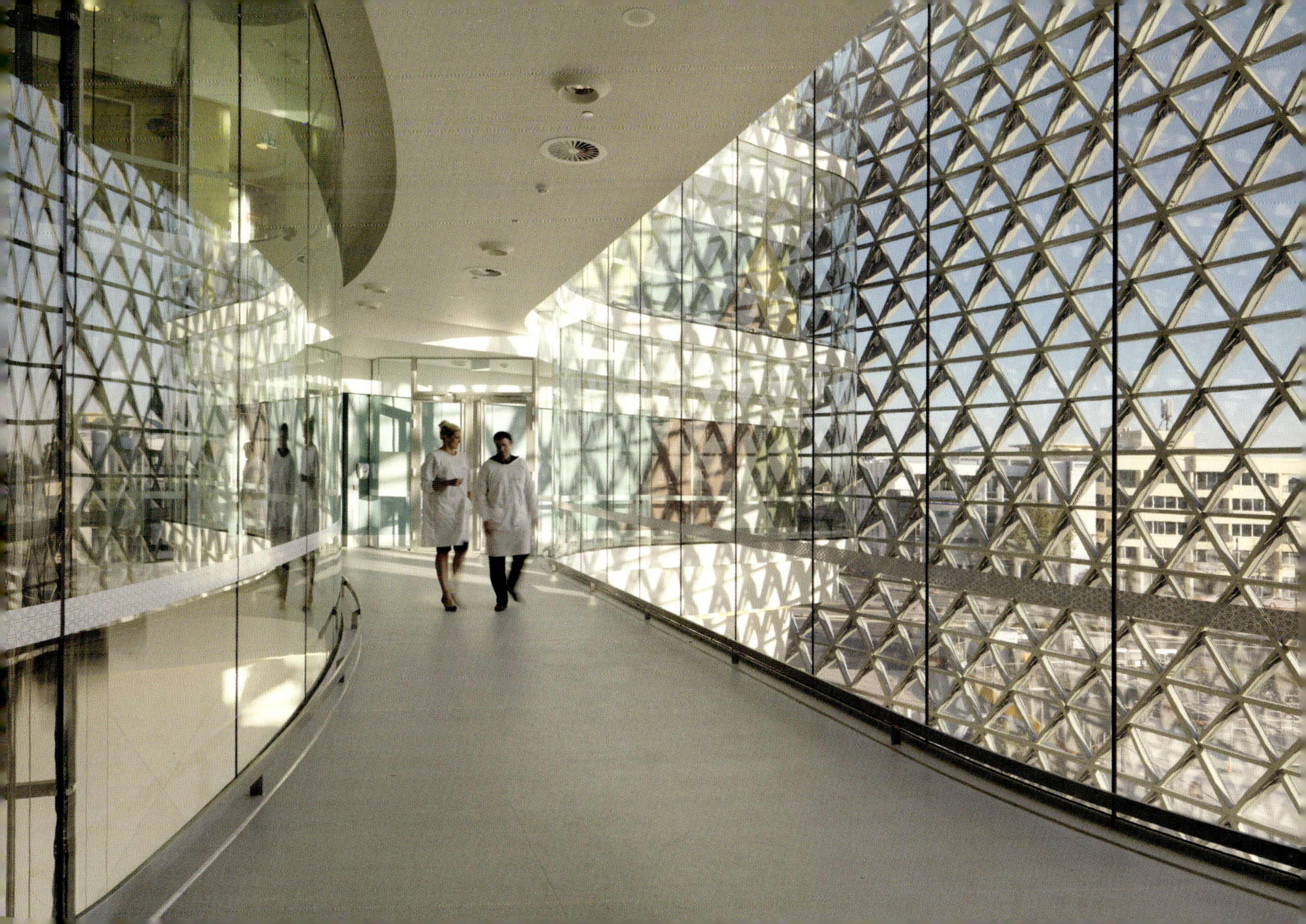

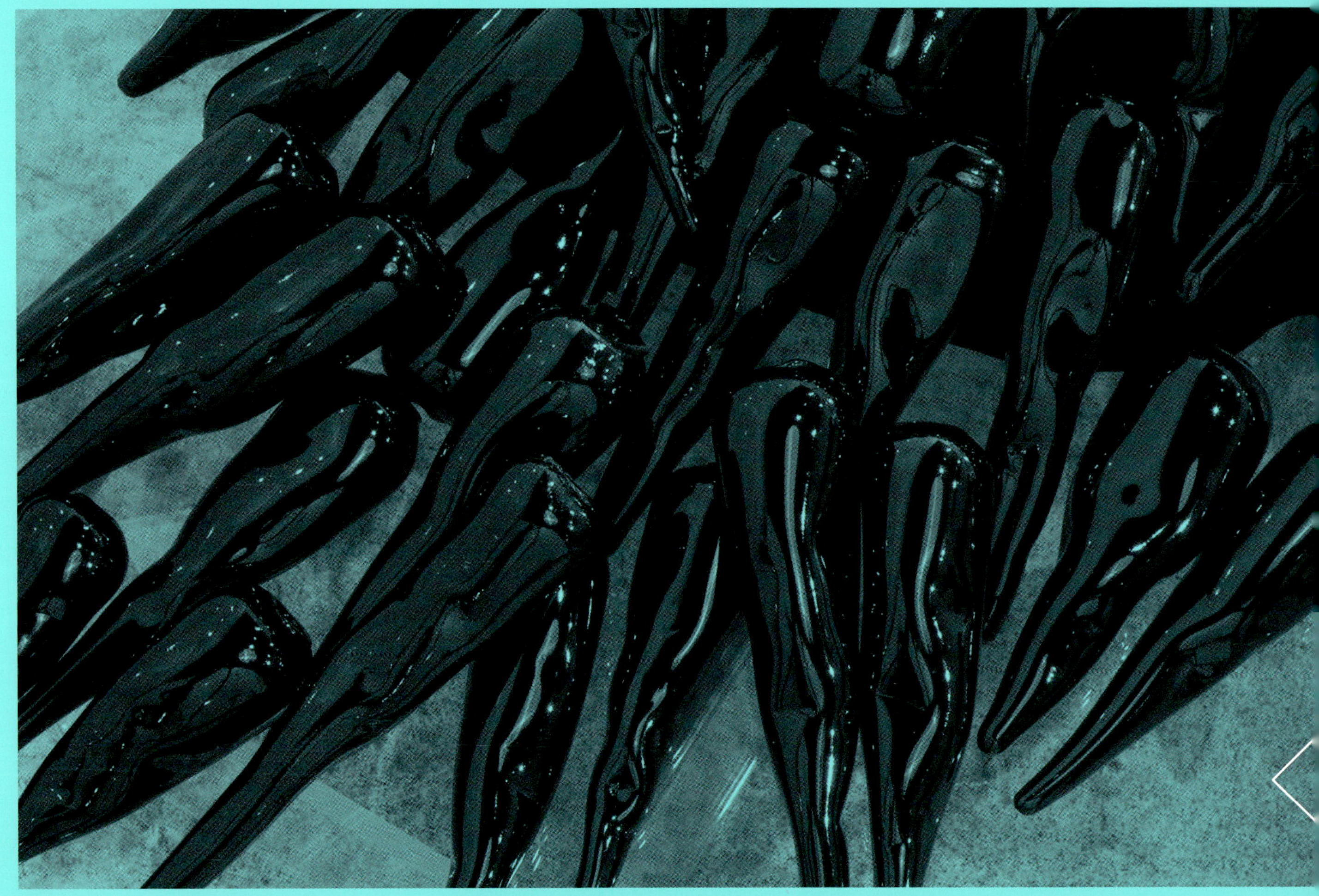

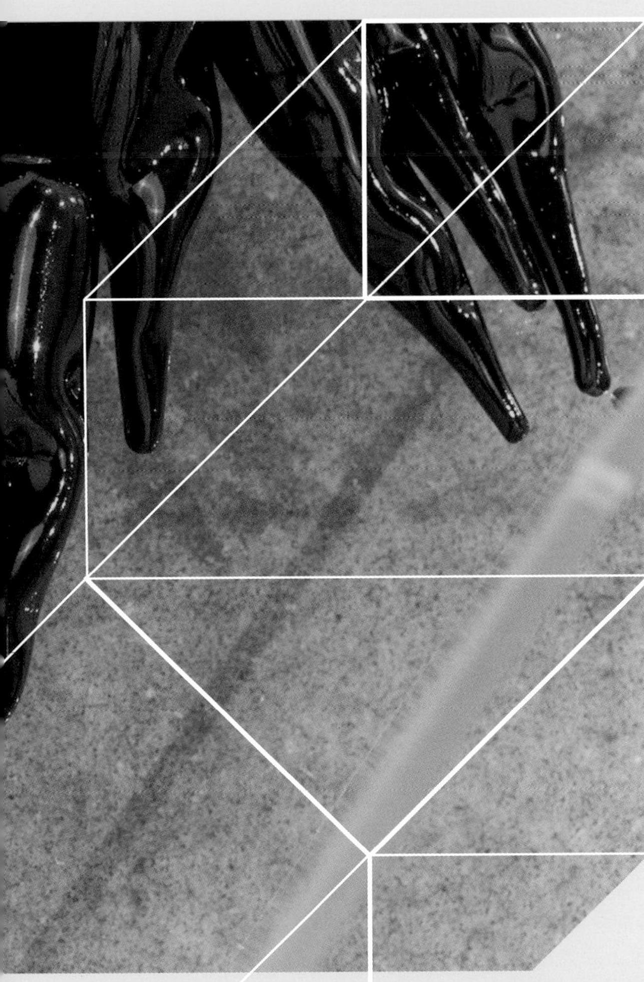

Yhonnie Scarce

Born 1972, Woomera, South Australia
Lives Melbourne, Victoria

Bringing light to the uncomfortable truth of Australia's settlement, and its ongoing race relations, Yhonnie Scarce is one of the first contemporary Australian artists to explore the political and aesthetic power of glass. A Kokatha, Nukunu and Mirning woman, Scarce's homelands are the desert country of the vast Nullarbor Plain and Great Australian Bight, and it is therefore not a chance occurrence that the transmutation of sand through heat into glass is a material rich with analogy.

As a material, glass can be both incredibly strong and intensely fragile, and for Scarce this is a perfect metaphor for the effects of colonisation on Aboriginal culture — having been brought to its breaking point, it has managed to sustain itself. As Scarce states, 'if glass breaks, it's always going to leave something behind'.

Drawing upon her family's history, the effects of assimilation, missionaries and the manipulative role of anthropologists, the trace of glass left behind becomes quite literal at the Koonibba Aboriginal community cemetery. Located 40 kilometres north-west of Tjutjuna (Ceduna) on the Eyre Peninsula, Scarce's ancestors, including her grandfather and uncle, are buried in weathered glass-bejewelled burial mounds. *Oppression, repression (family portrait)*, 2004, speaks of the effects of Lutheran mission life on Scarce's family. In this work pickling jars, embossed with the words 'new and improved', are used to contain and constrict. On top of the jars there are frosted blown-glass bush foods, all endemic to the area of the Koonibba mission; while inside, there are sealed photographs of Scarce's grandfather, mother and siblings, the jar a way of isolating her family from the nourishment of their culture and homelands.

Alongside works that directly reference her family's history, Scarce is keenly aware of the need to create larger-scale works that commemorate Aboriginal lives lost through colonisation. In 2008, she was the recipient of the inaugural Qantas Foundation Encouragement of Australian Contemporary Art Award, which enabled her to travel to Europe to research memorials. In Berlin, Scarce was struck by the powerful *Holocaust Memorial* (*Memorial to the murdered Jews of Europe*), designed by architect Peter Eisenman and engineer Buro Happold, and she questioned why such memorials do not exist in Australia for Aboriginal people. The Holocaust Memorial gave her a means and a language to investigate the scale and extent of the murders in Australia.

Exhibited in *Personal structures, time space existence* — an official satellite event of the 55th Venice Biennale in 2013 — *Blood on the wattle*, 2013 contains nearly 300 blown-glass long yams sealed inside a Perspex coffin, representing Aboriginal deaths since the arrival of the First Fleet. It has been estimated that following colonisation around 300,000 to one million Aboriginal people have lost their lives due to the aggressive incursions into Aboriginal land and the introduction of crippling diseases in communities of Aboriginal people who had little or no resistance to them. The title of this work refers to the 1988 book by Bruce Elder, in which Elder discusses Australia's hidden history of atrocities and massacres.[1] Scarce created a 'sister' of this work for *Melbourne now — Blood on the wattle (Elliston South Australia 1849)*, 2013.

Scarce graduated from the South Australian School of Art, University of South Australia in 2004, and completed a Masters at Monash University in 2010. She regularly travels between Melbourne and Adelaide for exhibitions and to produce works. Scarce's work is held in the Art Gallery of South Australia, the National Gallery of Victoria, the National Gallery of Australia, Flinders University Art Museum, the Museums and Art Galleries of the Northern Territory, the Owen and Wagner Collection at the Hood Museum of Art, USA and numerous private collections.

Margaret Hancock Davis

1. Elder, B. *Blood on the Wattle: Massacres and Maltreatment of Australian Aborigines Since 1788*, New Holland Publishers, 1999.

Previous page
Blood on the Wattle (detail), 2013
292 pieces blown glass, perspex, steel, aluminium and fabric
600 x 2100 x 700
Photo: Janelle Low

▸

Yhonnie Scarce working in the studio.
Photo: James Grose

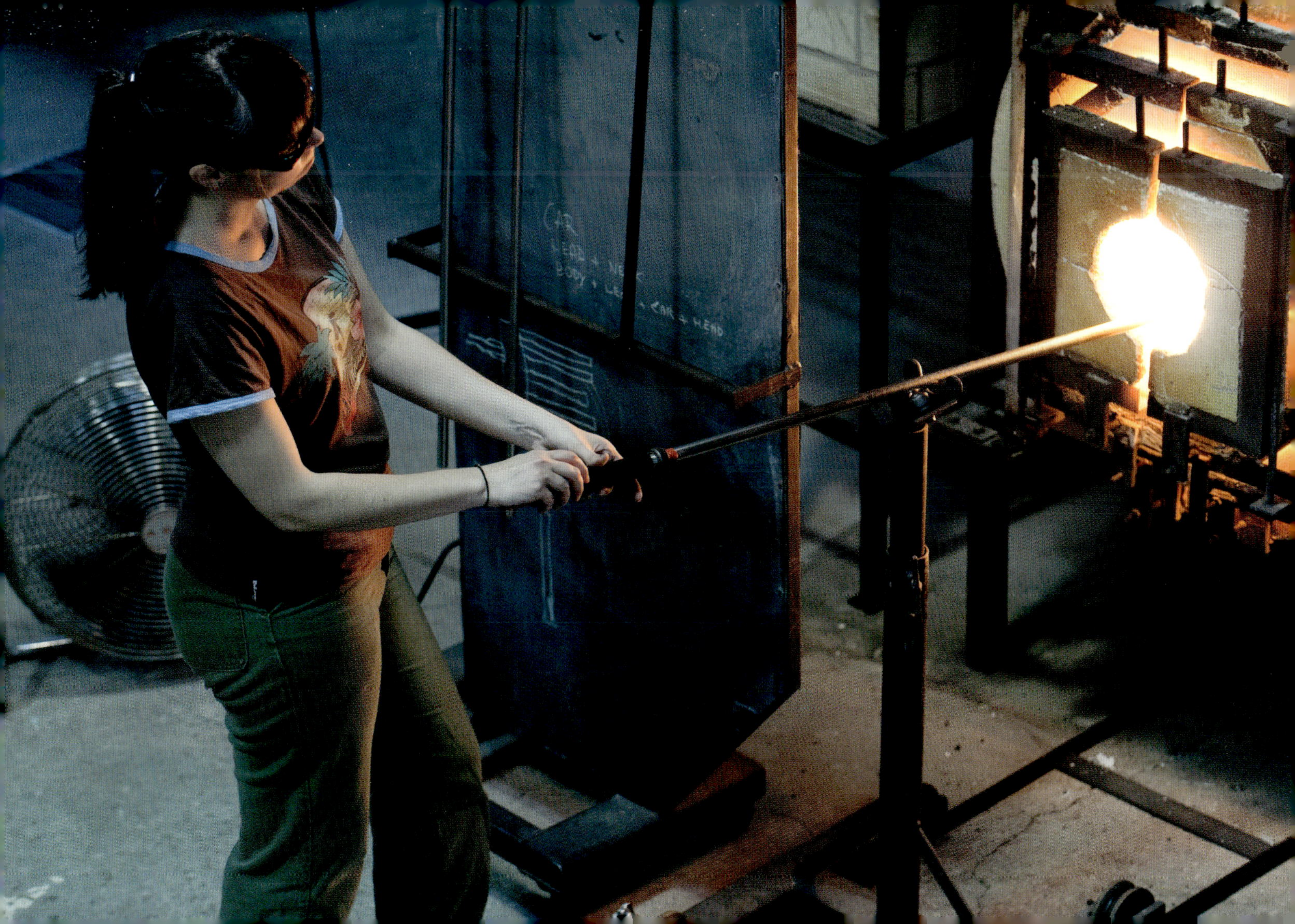

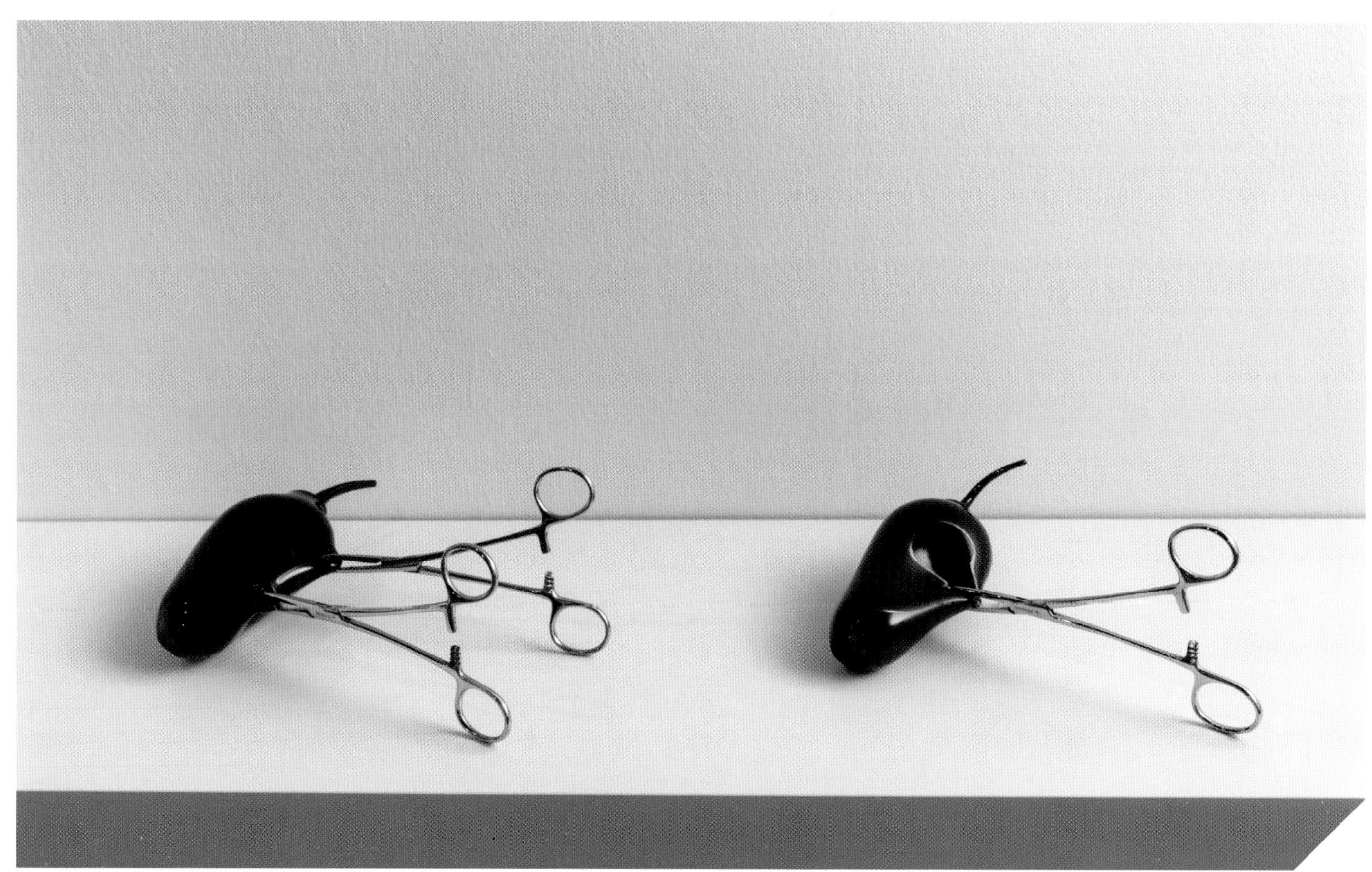

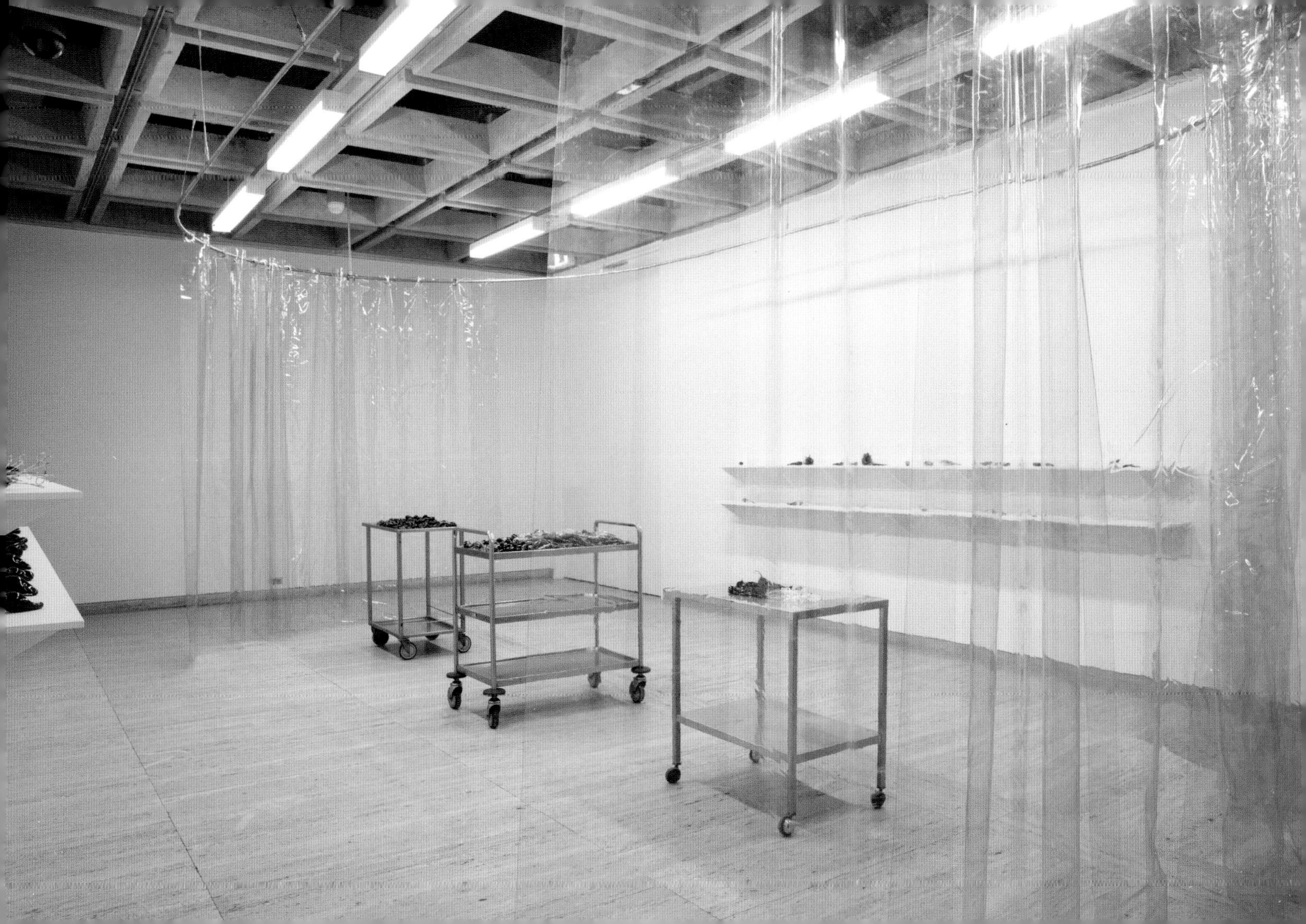

Previous page left
Weak in Colour But Strong in Blood (detail), 2014
blown glass and found components
dimensions variable
installation for the *You Imagine What You Desire: 19th Biennale of Sydney*, 2014 at the Art Gallery of New South Wales
Photo: Janelle Low

Previous page right
Weak in Colour But Strong in Blood, 2014

▸
Oppression, repression (family portrait), 2004
glass, tin, colour inkjet prints
dimensions variable
National Gallery of Victoria, Melbourne, purchased with funds donated by Judith and Leon Gorr, 2010
Photo: National Gallery of Victoria

▸▸
Blood on the Wattle, 2013
292 pieces blown glass, Perspex, steel, aluminium and fabric
600 x 2100 x 700
Shown at Palazzo Bembo, *Personal Structures*, a satellite project of the *55th Venice Biennale*
Photo: Janelle Low

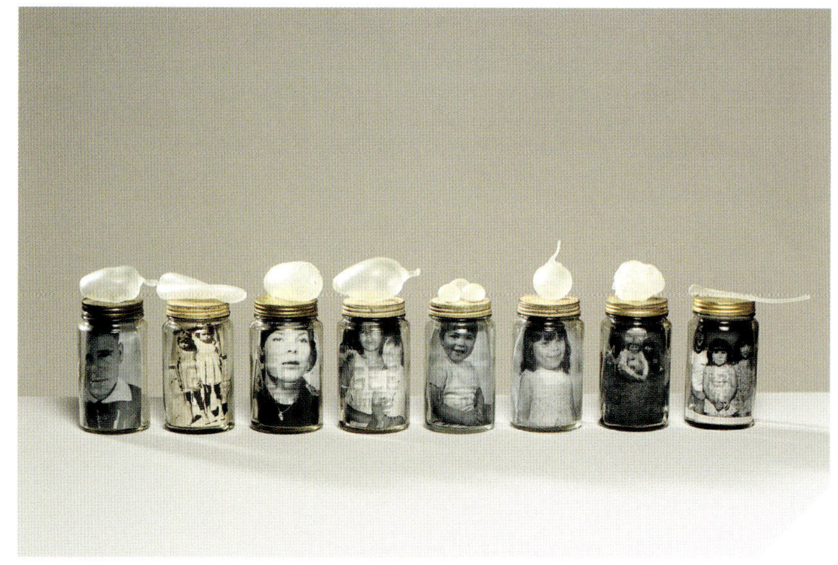

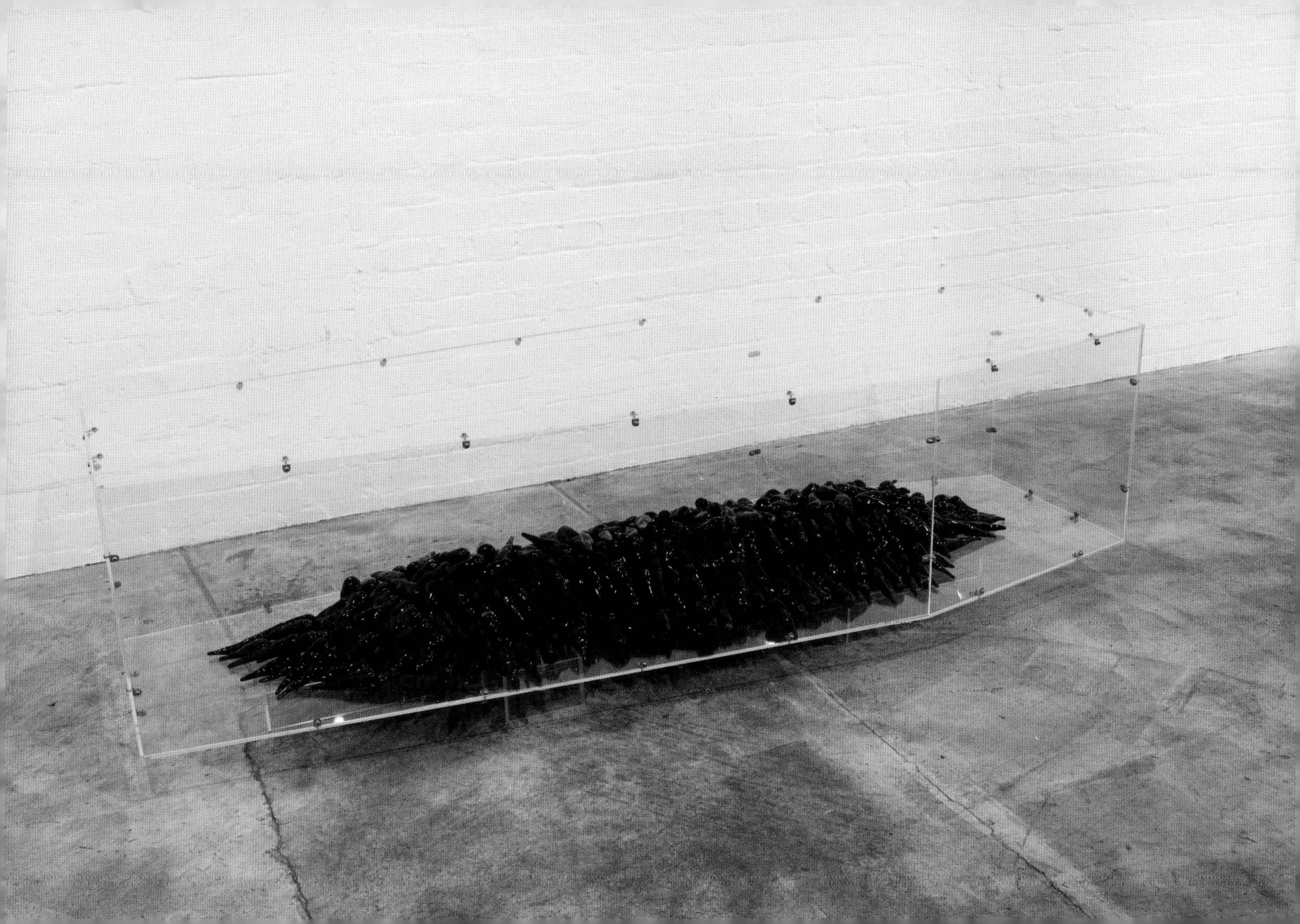

Not willing to suffocate

Squeezed to near breaking point, the glass bush bananas of *Not willing to Suffocate,* 2012, are held tight by the metaphorical grip of colonisation. They reference the highly controversial studies carried out on Aboriginal people — including members of Scarce's own family — by researchers and ethnographers such as Norman Tindale throughout the 1920s and '30s. The black-lustre bruising on the fruit reflects the constant sense of suffocation and experimentation experienced by Aboriginal Australians, due to the government and missionary policies that controlled their ability to express their culture. This work was a finalist in the Cicely and Colin Rigg Contemporary Design Award 2012 at the National Gallery of Victoria.

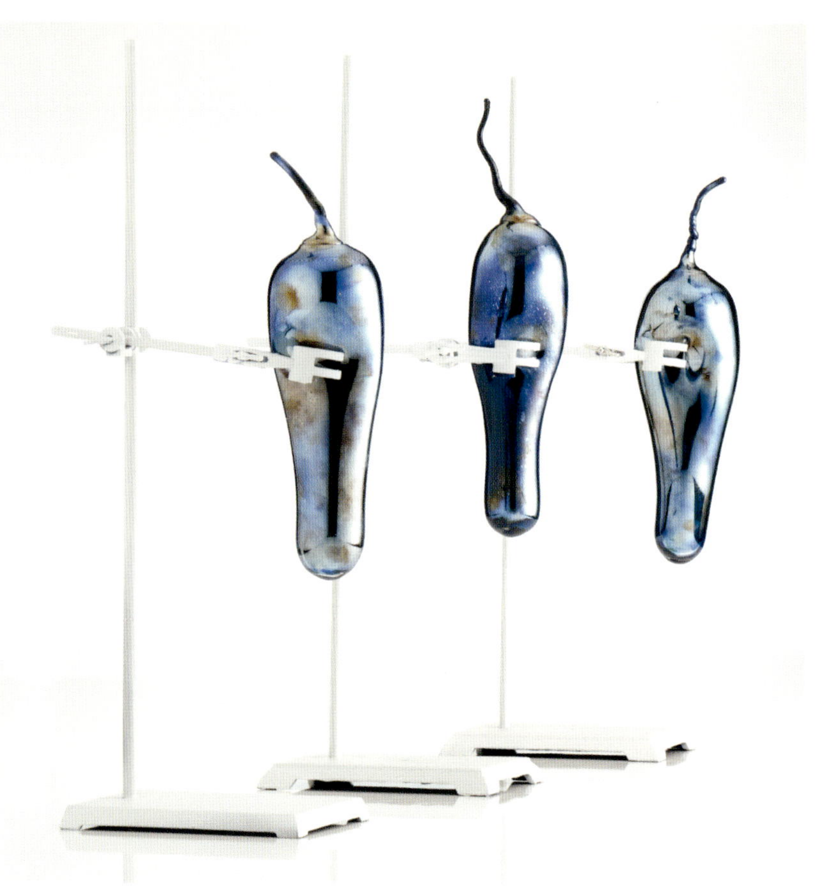

▸

Not Willing to Suffocate, 2012
blown glass, painted metal
650 x 150 x 200 each
Photo: Janelle Low

▸▸

Not Willing to Suffocate
(detail), 2012
Photo: Janelle Low

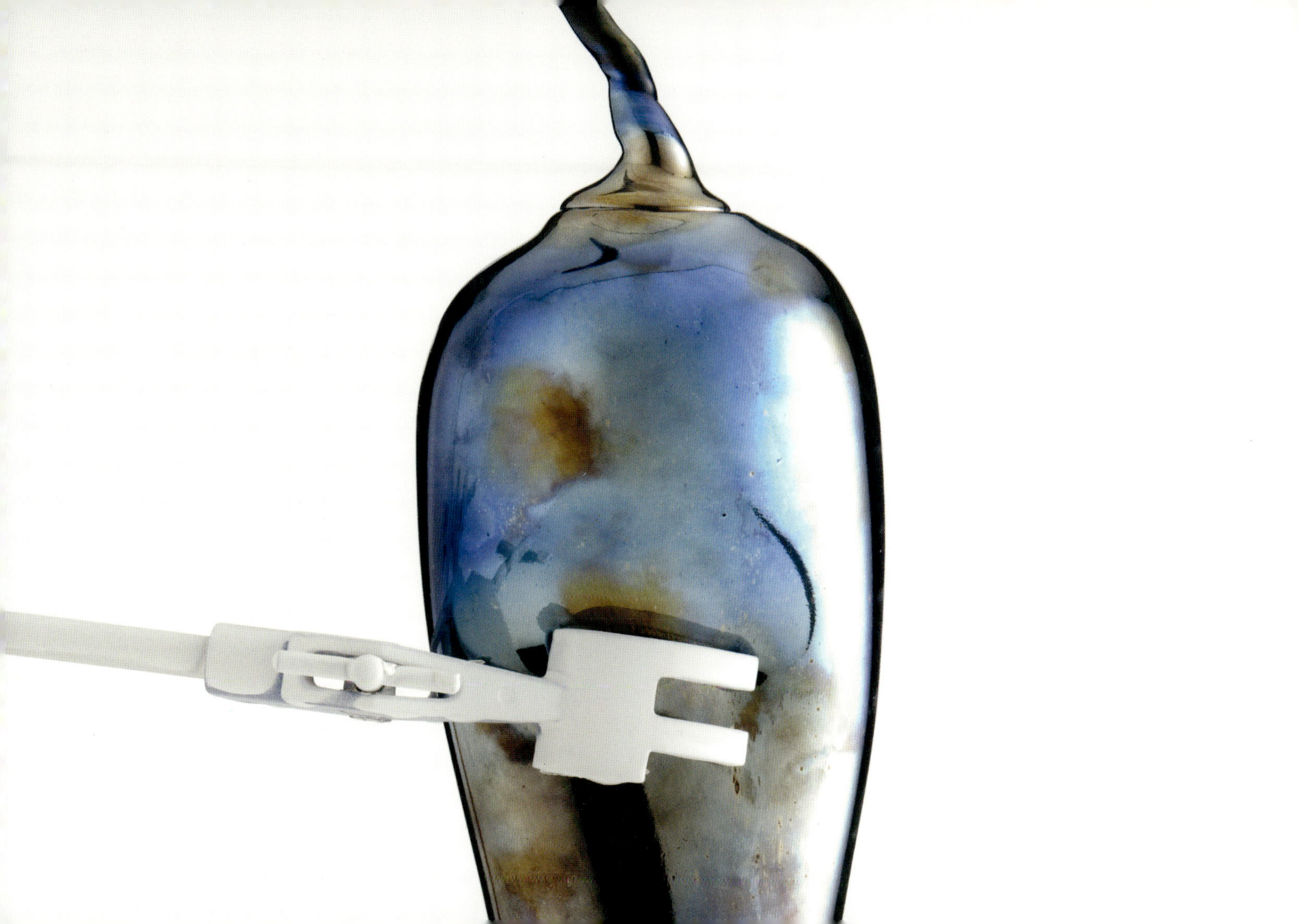

Contributors

Margaret Hancock Davis (co-curator) is Senior Curator at JamFactory. Her curatorial projects include *From the Earth: Contemporary Indigenous Ceramics* (2008) and *Prototyping: Making Ideas* (2011), the international exhibition *Southern Stars: Northern Lights* (2009) for Blue Coat Liverpool, as well as the Visions of Australia-funded exhibitions *Stephen Bowers: Beyond Bravura* (2013), and *Designing Craft/Crafting Design: 40 years of JamFactory* (2013), which she co-curated. Prior to her role as curator at JamFactory, she was Project Coordinator of the International Craft Initiative, which presented Australian craft at key international events including SOFA (Chicago), Collect (London) and Talente (Munich), as well as working as the gallery assistant. Margaret has written texts for a number of exhibition catalogues and magazines.

Brian Parkes (co-curator) is Chief Executive Officer and Artistic Director at JamFactory. For ten years prior to this he was Associate Director and Senior Curator at Object Gallery in Sydney and has curated numerous exhibitions, including the landmark survey of contemporary Australian design, *Freestyle: New Australian Design for Living* (2006–08), and he was co-curator of the acclaimed touring exhibition *Menagerie: Contemporary Indigenous Sculpture* (2009–12). In 2007 Parkes was one of ten curators invited by Phaidon Press, London to contribute to *&Fork*, a book profiling 100 emerging product designers from around the world, and in 2008 he was an Adjunct Curator for the Museum of Arts and Design, New York. In 2013 he co-curated the inaugural exhibition in this series *WOOD: art, design, architecture*.

Contributors

Stephen Goddard (catalogue and exhibition designer) is a multi-award-winning exhibition and visual communications designer, and Creative Director of Project Two. Recent achievements have included his role as co-curator and designer for *I Spy: Windows and doors in art*, 2013, for Lake Macquarie City Art Gallery, exhibition designer for *Acropolis*, 2013, *True to Form*, 2013, and *Points of Focus*, 2014, for the Nicholson and Macleay Museums, exhibition graphics for *Resolved: Journeys in Australian design*, 2014, and publication and exhibition design for the major touring exhibition *Lola Greeno: Cultural Jewels*, 2014, for Object: Australian Design Centre. He has recently designed a series of external posters for the Australian Embassy in Tokyo and been named a finalist in the 2014 Australian Graphic Design Association awards for the exhibition designs for both *WOOD: art design architecture*, 2013, for JamFactory and *Lola Greeno: Cultural Jewels* for Object.

Robert Cook (essay writer) is Curator of Contemporary International Art at the Art Gallery of Western Australia. Prior to working at the AGWA, Cook was Curator of Western Australian Art at the Lawrence Wilson Art Gallery, University of Western Australia. In 2013 he was the guest curator of *Primavera*, the Museum of Contemporary Art's annual exhibition for young artists. Cook's art writing has been featured in art publications in Australia and internationally. As well as art writing, he has written fiction and personal essays for *WON Magazine*, *Un magazine* and *isnotmagazine*. He has also edited issues of *Craftwest*, *Photofile* and *Object* magazines and is currently a co-editor, with artist Benjamin Forster, of *Un magazine*.

Penny Craswell (essay writer) is Communications Manager (Australia) at Woods Bagot and founder of *The design writer* blog. A former editor of *Artichoke* magazine, Craswell has also worked as an editor at *Indesign* magazine and Amsterdam-based *Frame* magazine, with a total of 12 years experience as an editor and writer in the fields of design, architecture and art. She is currently working on a Masters of Design at the University of New South Wales Art & Design.

Stephen Forbes (essay writer) has been Director of the Botanic Gardens of Adelaide since 2001. He began his career working on botanical surveys in south-eastern Australia and later in the Kimberley region of Western Australia. He has worked at the Royal Botanic Gardens in Melbourne, Kings Park and Botanic Gardens in Perth and the Royal Botanic Gardens in Sydney, where he was responsible for significant upgrading of programs and infrastructure in the lead-up to the Sydney 2000 Olympic Games. Forbes has published widely on plant systematics, floristic survey, landscape management and urban nature conservation.

Thomas Mical (essay writer) is Associate Professor of Architecture at the School of Architecture, Art and Design, University of South Australia. He has practised architecture in Chicago and Tokyo, and wrote his PhD at Georgia Tech on metaphysical urbanism. He edited *Surrealism and architecture* (Routledge, 2004) and has helped develop a PhD program in spatial alterity at Carleton University. He recently participated in the US National Endowment for the Humanities Summer Institute on Modernity in India, and is interested in the unfulfilled promises of globalisation theory for speculative urban architecture.

Ewan McEoin (profile writer) is Director of Studio Propeller and Design Consultant National Gallery of Victoria. He was Creative Director of *Unlimited: Designing for the Asia Pacific*, which is the Queensland Government's international design triennial launched in 2010, and Creative Director of the Victorian Government's *State of Design Festival* from 2008 to 2012. Prior to founding Propeller, McEoin was the longstanding Editor of *(inside) Australian Design Review*.

Adele Sliuzas (profile writer) is Assistant Curator at JamFactory. Her curatorial projects include *Be Consumed: Creative collaborations from the Barossa* (2014), *Bloom space* (2012) at the Australian Experimental Art Foundation, and *Take care* (2012), as part of the Arts SA Emerging Curators Program. She has written for a number of publications and runs a Critical Reading Group, forming a dialogue about contemporary art, research and theory.

Acknowledgements

A project of this scale requires many heads and many hands and the co-curators would like to sincerely thank everyone involved. First and foremost we thank the 23 exhibitors for their enthusiasm and commitment towards this project, and in many cases, their staff, assistants or partners for assisting us in our requests for information and images. We also acknowledge the commercial galleries who represent some of the artists featured in the exhibition: Arc1, Melbourne; Bullseye Gallery, Portland, USA; Dianne Tanzer gallery + projects, Melbourne; Dominik Mersch Gallery Sydney; Fine Art Society, London, UK; Foster White Gallery, Seattle, USA; Gaffer Studio Glass, Hong Kong; Gallery Funaki, Melbourne; Greenaway Art Gallery, Adelaide; Hugo Michell, Adelaide; Narek Galleries, Tanja; Ryan Renshaw, Brisbane; Sabbia Gallery, Sydney; This is no fantasy, Melbourne.

We would also like to thank the Directors and the relevant staff at each of the confirmed tour venues who will be hosting the exhibition as it tours around Australia from 2015 through to 2018: Murray Bridge Regional Gallery; Signal Point Gallery, Goolwa; Wagga Wagga Art Gallery; School of Art Gallery, Australian National University, Canberra; Bathurst Regional Art Gallery; Western Plains Cultural Centre, Dubbo; Lake Macquarie City Art Gallery; QUT Art Museum, Brisbane; Cairns Regional Art Gallery; Caboolture Regional Gallery; UTS ART Gallery, University of Technology, Sydney; Design Centre Tasmania, Launceston; Mornington Peninsula Regional Art Gallery, Mornington.

The design of this exhibition involved a dynamic collaboration between experienced lead designer Stephen Goddard and a team from JamFactory's studios including Creative Director Metal Design Studio Christian Hall and Associates Angela Giuliani and Stephen Soeffky. We also must acknowledge the great work of JamFactory's installation team members Peter Carroll and Daniel Guest.

We are very proud of this catalogue and we must offer our final thanks to the writers and photographers, printing coordinator Kirsty Wright from Imago, copy editor Theresa Willsteed and lastly, designer Stephen Goddard for bringing all of the elements together so elegantly in this wonderful publication.

Margaret Hancock Davis and Brian Parkes